YOUR
ASTROLOGY
GUIDE
2008

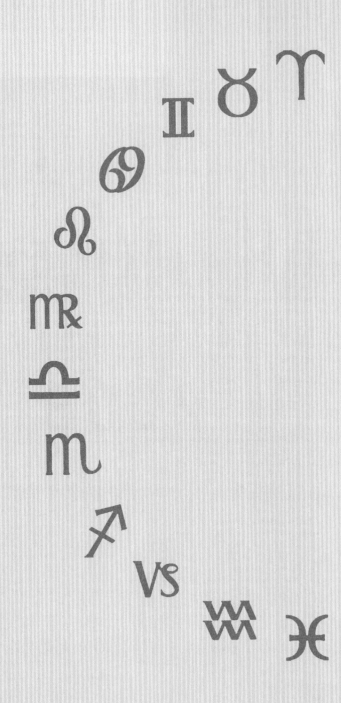

YOUR ASTROLOGY GUIDE

2008

RICK LEVINE & **JEFF** JAWER

STERLING

New York / London
www.sterlingpublishing.com

STERLING and the distinctive Sterling logo are registered trademarks of
Sterling Publishing Co., Inc.

Library of Congress Cataloging-in-Publication Data Available

10 9 8 7 6 5 4 3 2 1

Published by Sterling Publishing Co., Inc.
387 Park Avenue South, New York, NY 10016
© 2007 by Sterling Publishing Co., Inc.
Text © 2007 Rick Levine and Jeff Jawer

Distributed in Canada by Sterling Publishing
c/o Canadian Manda Group, 165 Dufferin Street
Toronto, Ontario, Canada M6K 3H6
Distributed in the United Kingdom by GMC Distribution Services
Castle Place, 166 High Street, Lewes, East Sussex, England BN7 1XU
Distributed in Australia by Capricorn Link (Australia) Pty. Ltd.
P.O. Box 704, Windsor, NSW 2756, Australia

Original Book design: 3+Co., New York

Sterling ISBN-13: 978-1-4027-4841-7
         ISBN-10: 1-4027-4841-8

For information about custom editions, special sales, premium and
corporate purchases, please contact Sterling Special Sales
Department at 800-805-5489 or specialsales@sterlingpub.com.

TABLE OF CONTENTS

Acknowledgments   7

Introduction   8

PART 1: ASTROLOGY & YOU   17
How to Use This Book—Astrology Basics   19
The Planets, The Houses, and Aspects   27
Astrology World Report 2008   39

PART 2: 2008 ASTROLOGICAL FORECASTS   55
ARIES   (March 21–April 19)   57
TAURUS   (April 20–May 20)   87
GEMINI   (May 21–June 20)   117
CANCER   (June 21–July 22)   147
LEO   (July 23–August 22)   177
VIRGO   (August 23–September 22)   207
LIBRA   (September 23–October 22)   237
SCORPIO   (October 23–November 21)   267
SAGITTARIUS   (November 22–December 21)   297
CAPRICORN   (December 22–January 19)   327
AQUARIUS   (January 20–February 18)   357
PISCES   (February 19–March 20)   387

ACKNOWLEDGMENTS

Many people have contributed to this annual book, both in conception and in production. First of all, our heartfelt thanks to Paul O'Brien, the creative genius behind Tarot.com, who led us to this project. Paul is our agent, our friend, and his vision opened the doors to make this book possible. On the production side, we are grateful for our editor, Gail Goldberg. Her ability to clarify concepts, untangle sentences, and sharpen our words is matched by her commitment to presenting astrology in an intelligent light. We appreciate her energetic Mars in efficient Virgo; her persistent attention to detail has challenged us to write a better book. Of course we are very grateful to Michael Fragnito, editorial director at Sterling Publishing, for his initial vision of what this book could be, his tireless support for the project, and his trust in our work. Barbara Berger, Sterling's supervising editor on this book, has shepherded the project with Taurean persistence and good humor under the ongoing pressures of very tight deadlines. We thank Laura Jorstad for her refinement of the text, and project editor Mary Hern for her careful guidance. We are thankful to Charles Nurnberg, Jeremy Nurnberg, Jason Prince, Karen Nelson, Elizabeth Mihaltse, Rebecca Maines, and Rachel Maloney at Sterling. Thanks go to Bob Wietrak and Jules Herbert at Barnes & Noble, and whoever said yes in the beginning. We appreciate 3+Co. and Asami Matsushima for the original design; and thanks for the art and ideas from Jessica Abel and the rest of the Tarot.com team. Thanks, as well, to Tara Gimmer and company for the cover photo.

Rick: Thank you, Jeff, for being such a great writing partner and friend. You are the methodical and reliable Taurus that I need to keep me on track. Your astrology wisdom, writing skills, and commitment to excellence continue to be an inspiration. And I would like to add my personal thanks to Gail Goldberg. She makes my job harder, for she not only changes my grammar, but also challenges my thinking. Thanks, Gail, for your unwavering vision of what this book can be, for participating with fiery compassion, and for knowing that we do make a difference.

Jeff: Thanks, Rick, for the care, creativity, and good humor that you bring to this book. Your astrological expertise, skillful writing, and friendship have turned an intense job into a joyful and inspiring one. Thanks to our super editor, Gail Goldberg, for adding so much heart, mind, and soul to this project. Your levels of commitment and competence are extraordinary contributions. Danick, Laura, and Lyana—you are the people I love living with every day. Thanks for sharing the ride with me.

INTRODUCTION

YOU ARE THE STAR OF YOUR LIFE

The more you learn about yourself, the better able you are to wisely use the energies in your life. For more than 3,000 years, astrology has been the sharpest tool in the box for describing the human condition. Used by virtually every culture on the planet, astrology continues to illuminate the link between individual lives and planetary energies and cycles.

The purpose of this book is to help you take a more active role in creating your present and, by extension, your future by showing you how to apply astrology's ancient wisdom to today's world. Our aim is to facilitate your day-to-day journey by revealing the turns in the road of life and describing the best ways for you to navigate them.

Astrology's highest use is to enable you to gain knowledge of yourself and perspective of your surroundings. It is common to go through life feeling blown about by forces beyond your control. Astrology can help you see the changing tides within and outside you. By allowing you to recognize the shifting patterns of mood and circumstance at work in your life, it helps you to stay centered and empowered. As you follow along in this book, you will grow to better understand your own needs as well as the challenges and opportunities you encounter.

In *Your Astrology Guide: 2008*, we describe the patterns of your life as they are reflected in the great cycles of the sky above. We do not simply predict events, although we give examples of them throughout the book. Rather, we are reporting the planetary energies—the cosmic weather in which you are living—so that you understand these conditions and know how to use them effectively. The power, though, is not in the stars, of course, but in your mind, your heart, and the choices that you make every day. Regardless of how strongly you are buffeted by the winds of change or bored by stagnation, your mind has many ways to see any situation. Learning about the energies of the Sun, Moon, and planets will both sharpen and widen your perspective. Thousands of years of human experience have proven astrology's value; our purpose is to show you how to enrich your life with it.

The language of astrology gives the gift of awareness, not a rigid set of rules. It works best when blended with common sense, intuition, and self-trust. This is your life, and no one knows how to live it as well as you. Take what you need from this book and leave the rest. Think of the planets as setting the stage for the year ahead, but it is you who are the writer, director, and star of your life.

ABOUT US

We were practicing astrology independently when we joined forces in 1999 to launch StarIQ.com. Our shared interest in making intelligent astrology available to as wide an audience as possible led to StarIQ, as well as a relationship with Tarot.com and the creation of this book. While we have continued to work independently as well, our collaboration has been a success and a joy as we've made our shared goals a reality, and we plan for it to continue long into the future.

RICK LEVINE

I've always wanted to know the answers to unanswerable questions. As a youth, I studied science and mathematics because I believed that they offered concrete answers to complex questions. I learned about the amazing conceptual breakthroughs made by modern man due to the developing technologies that allowed us to peer into the deep reaches of outer space and also into the tiniest subatomic realms. But as I encountered imaginary numbers in higher mathematics, along with the uncertainty of quantum physics, I began to realize that our modern sciences, as advanced as they are, would never satisfy my longing to understand my own individual life or the world around me. I learned that our basic assumptions of time and space fall apart at both ends of the spectrum—the very big and the very small. I became obsessed with solving the puzzle of the cosmos and discovering its hidden secrets.

As a college student at the State University of New York at Stony Brook in the late sixties, I studied psychology and philosophy, and participated in those times as a student of the universe. I read voraciously and found myself more interested in the unexplainable than in what was already known. As a psychology student, I was less concerned with running rats through mazes than with understanding how the human mind worked. I naturally gravitated to the depth psychologies of Sigmund

Freud and Carl Jung. Additionally, the life-altering information coming from the humanistic psychology movement presented me with an academic framework with which to better understand how human potential could be further developed. I knew then and there that human consciousness was expanding and that I wanted to be a part of this evolutionary process. In this environment, I first encountered the writings of R. Buckminster Fuller. He appealed to my scientific mind-set, but blessed me with new ways to view my world. In the early 20th century, Albert Einstein had clearly demonstrated that energy is simply the transformation of light into mass and mass into light—but that was just an intellectual concept to me.

Bucky Fuller, however, went on to establish a scientific language to describe the relationships between mass and light, particles and waves. His incredible geodesic domes are merely representations of what he discovered. I began to understand that what we can see is but a faint shadow of the knowable universe. I learned that everything vibrates. There are no things out there, just different frequencies of vibration—many of which are so fast that they give us the illusion of a solid world. Even something as basic as the color green or red is merely a label for certain frequencies of light vibration.

This was my world when I first discovered that astrology was more than just a parlor game. Already acquainted with the signs of the zodiac, I knew that I was an impulsive Aries, a pioneer, and an independent thinker. I noticed how my friends and professors fit their sun signs. Then, I was astounded to learn that Jung's *Analytical Psychology of Four Types* was based upon the astrological elements of fire, earth, air, and water. And I was amazed to discover that a great scientist, such as Johannes Kepler—the Father of Modern Astronomy—was himself a renowned astrologer. The more I read, the more I realized that I had to become an astrologer myself. I needed to know more about astrology and how it works. Now, nearly 40 years later, I know more about astrology—a lot more—with still so much to learn.

Astronomers have their telescopes, enabling them to see things *tele*, or far away. Biologists have microscopes to see what is *micro*, or small. We astrologers have the horoscope, extending our view of the *horo*, or hour. For more than three decades, I have calculated horoscopes—first by hand, later with computer—and have observed the movement of time in its relationship to the heavenly bodies. I have watched the timing of the transitions in my own life and in the lives of my family, friends, and clients. I have been privileged to see, again and again, the unquestionable harmony between the planetary cycles and our individual lives.

I am proud to be a part of an astrological renaissance. Astrology has become increasingly popular because it fulfills our need to know that we are a part of the cosmos, even though modern culture has separated us from nature. It is not man versus nature. We are nature—and our survival as a species may depend on humanity relearning this concept. I take my role as an astrologer very seriously as I use what I have learned to help people expand their awareness, offer them choices, and educate them on how to cooperate with the cosmos instead of fight against it. I contributed to reestablishing astrology in academia as a founding trustee of the Kepler College of Astrological Arts and Science (Lynnwood, Washington). I maintain an active role in the international community of astrologers as a member of the International Society for Astrological Research (ISAR), the National Council for Geocosmic Research (NCGR), the Association for Astrological Networking (AFAN), and the Organization for Professional Astrology (OPA).

In 1999, I partnered with Jeff Jawer to create StarIQ.com, an innovative astrology Web site. Since then Jeff and I have been working together to raise the quality of astrology available to the public, first through StarIQ.com and, later, through our partnership with Tarot.com. It continues to be a real privilege and thrill to work with Jeff and to now offer the fruits of our labors to you.

JEFF JAWER

I've been a professional astrologer for more than 30 years. Astrology is my career, my art, and my passion. The excitement that I felt when I first began is still with me today. My first encounter with real astrology was in 1973 when I was going through a painful marriage breakup. All I knew about astrology at the time was that I was a Taurus, which didn't sound very exciting to me. "The reliable Bull is steadfast and consistent," I read. "Not given to risk taking or dramatic self-expression, Taurus prefers peace and comfort above all." Boring. Fortunately, I quickly discovered that there was more to astrology—much more.

An amateur astrologer read my chart for me on my 27th birthday, and I was hooked. I bought the biggest astrology book I could find, began intensive study, found a teacher, and started reading charts for people. Within a few months, I changed my major at the University of Massachusetts at Amherst from communications to astrology under the Bachelor's Degree with Individual Concentration program. There were no astrology classes at the university, but I was able to combine courses in astronomy, mythology, and psychology, with two special seminars on the history of astrology, to graduate in 1975 with a B.A. in the history and science of astrology. In 1976, I moved to Atlanta, Georgia, the only city in the United States with a mandatory examination for professional astrologers. I passed it, as well as the American Federation of Astrologers' professional exam, and served twice as president of the Metro Atlanta Astrological Society and as chairman of the City of Atlanta Board of Astrology Examiners.

For several years, I was the corporate astrologer for International Horizons, Inc., a company that sold courses on English as a second language in Japan. The owner had me research the founding dates of banks he was interested in acquiring so that I could advise him based on their charts. Later, he and I created Astro, the world's first electronic astrology calculator. In 1982, I was one of the founding members of the Association for Astrological Networking (AFAN), an organization that plays a major role in defending the legal rights of astrologers. AFAN joined with two other organizations, the International Society for Astrological Research (ISAR) and the National Council for Geocosmic Research (NCGR), to present the first United Astrology Congress (UAC) in 1986. UAC conferences were the largest astrology events in North America for more than a decade. I served on the UAC board for four years.

I began teaching at astrology conferences in the late 1970s, and there I met many of the world's leading astrologers, many of whom are my friends to this day. I have taught at dozens of conferences and local astrology groups around the United States. I have lectured at the World Astrology Congress in Switzerland four times, as well as in Holland, France, England, Belgium, Spain, Germany, Canada, Brazil, and Australia. However, the most important time for me personally was the two years I spent teaching for the Network of Humanistic Astrologers based in France. There I met my wife, Danick, in 1988. Her double-Pisces sensitivity has added to my work and my life immeasurably.

Counseling individual clients is the core of my professional life, as it is for most astrologers, but writing about astrology has always been important to me. I've written hundreds of articles for journals, magazines, books, Web sites, and newspapers ranging from the monthly calendar for *The Mountain Astrologer* to sun-sign forecasts for *CosmoGIRL!* magazine. Currently, I write "LoveScopes" (a weekly sun-sign romance horoscope), the "New Moon Report," and other specialized material for Tarot.com, AOL, and StarIQ.com. I've also been employed in the astrology industry as director of public relations for Matrix Software and vice president of Astro Communication Services, two of the field's oldest companies. Rick and I founded StarIQ in 1999, the beginning of our professional collaboration. We produce a daily audio forecast called *Planet Pulse*, and *StarTalkers*, a weekly radio broadcast. Early in my career, I contributed to pioneering the field of experiential astrology, also called astrodrama. It's been a great adventure to combine theater games, psychodrama, Gestalt techniques, visualization, movement, art, and sound to bring astrology to life in workshops around the world. To experience astrology through emotions and in the body, rather than by the intellect alone, can ground one's understanding of the planets and signs in a very useful way.

Think about Venus, for example. She's the goddess of love, the planet of beauty and attraction. What if you need more sweetness in your life? Imagine how Venus walks. Now, get up and do your own Venus walk to the kitchen. Feel in balance and graceful as your feet embrace the floor and as your hips sway. Be Venus; invite her presence to you. Glide, slide, and be suave; you're so beautiful. Remember this walk if you're feeling unloved and, the next thing you know, Venus will arrive. Each planet is different, of course, according to its unique character. You'll learn another dance from responsible Saturn—a slower march across the floor, head upright, shoulders back—steady and straight, but not too stiff. Try that one for self-discipline.

Astrology describes the energy of time, how the quality of Tuesday afternoon is different from Wednesday morning. Seeing when and where patterns arise in your life gives you clearer vision and a better understanding of the choices that are open to you. The rich language of astrology makes a cosmic connection that empowers you and rewards the rest of us as you fulfill more and more of your potential.

ASTROLOGY'S ORIGINS

Astrology is as old as time. It began when events in the sky were first observed to affect events here on Earth. The turning of day into night, the rising and falling of the tides with the Moon's cycles, and the changing seasons were watched by humanity long before written history, even at the very dawn of human civilization. Ancient Egyptians tracked the star Sirius to predict the flooding of the Nile River, which was essential to their agriculture. Babylonians, Mayans, Hindus, Chinese, and virtually every other group of people on the planet have practiced a form of astrology. Part science, part religion, calendar, mythology, and almanac, astrology remains the most comprehensive and coherent system for understanding life on this planet.

In the 2nd century AD, Claudius Ptolemy codified astrology, based on its origins in Mesopotamia and development in classical Greece. Astrology was an essential part of the scientific and philosophical evolution that gave birth to Western civilization. Another major path of development occurred in India, where Vedic astrology remains an integral part of the culture. Astrology was originally used to address collective concerns such as climate and warfare. It was rarely applied to the lives of individuals, except for rulers whose fates were considered tied to those of the nation. Astrology is still applied to public concerns, especially in the burgeoning field of financial astrology, which is used for stock-market forecasting. Today, however, the vast majority of astrology is applied to the lives of individuals through personal consultations, computer-generated reports, horoscope columns, books, and the Internet.

The importance of astrology has risen, fallen, and risen again in the Western world. Through the Renaissance and the Elizabethan period, astrology was part and parcel of daily life. Shakespeare's numerous references to it are just one indicator of its wide acceptance and popularity in his time. However, the rationalism of René Descartes and his followers took hold in philosophical circles and demanded that modern science exclude anything that cannot be proven according to its methods. Astrology was banished from academia in 1666, and it remained outside the intellectual mainstream for almost 300 years. Modern astrology began its rebirth in the early part of the 20th century largely due to the work of Alan Leo, the father of sun-sign astrology. A second, and larger, wave of interest grew out of the counterculture movement of the 1960s when interest in metaphysics and Eastern religions also gained momentum. The brilliant works of the Swiss psychologist Carl Jung and French-American astrologer Dane Rudhyar inspired a new generation of astrologers, including the authors of this book.

ASTROLOGY TODAY: EMPOWERMENT

Thanks to Jung, Rudhyar, and many other brilliant minds, modern astrology has largely separated itself from the fatalism of the past when, for example, the sighting of an approaching comet meant the king would die and nothing more. Today's astrology is, as Rudhyar wrote, "person-centered," with the focus on individual choice and personal growth rather than the simple prediction of events. In fact, while we do write about events in this book, we spend more time describing energy patterns and emotions for several reasons.

First, you're a unique individual. You may share characteristics and tendencies with fellow members of your sun sign, but you will experience them in your own way. In addition, you have a personal birth chart in which the positions of the Moon, planets, and other factors distinguish you from the other members of your sun-sign clan. Analyzing how all the planets and signs interact in a person's chart is the foundation of a personal consultation with a professional astrologer or a detailed custom report like those available at http://www.tarot.com/astrology/astroprofile.

ENERGY, EVENTS, AND EMOTION

At its essence, astrology describes energy. Energy can take many forms; it can be an event, emotion, or attitude. We suggest the possible outcomes of astrological events in this book, but they are examples or models of how the planetary energies might be expressed. Each person is going to experience these patterns in his or her own unique way. We have learned that it is more helpful to understand the underlying energy patterns of events than it is to describe them. You may not be able to change the world outside you, but you have an enormous range of choice when it comes to your thoughts and attitudes.

We are here to assist you with ideas and information rooted in history and woven into the cloth of our culture. We recognize and honor you as the center of your life. This book is not a collection of ideas that are foreign to your nature, but a recollection of human experiences that exist within all of us. Whether you know their meanings or not, all the signs and planets live within you. They are part of your human heritage, a gift of awareness, a language not meant to label you and stick you in a box, but a treasure map to yourself and the cosmos beyond. It is a glorious journey we all share. May your way be filled with light this year and in the years to come.

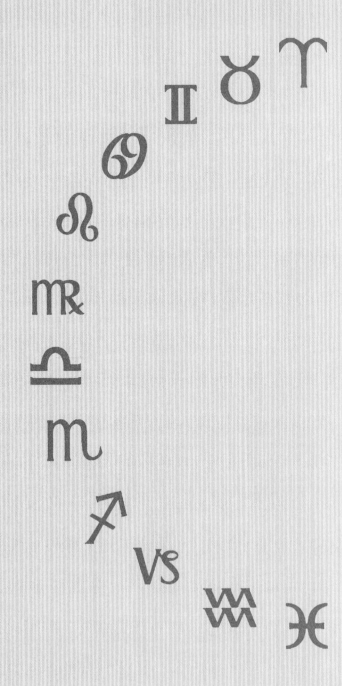

2008

PART 1
ASTROLOGY & YOU

HOW TO USE THIS BOOK

ASTROLOGY BASICS

WHAT'S YOUR SIGN?

In this book, we present a view of the year ahead for each sun sign. Your sign is based on the Sun's position at the moment of your birth. As most people know, the Sun travels through the twelve signs of the zodiac over the course of a year. However, the Sun doesn't change signs at the exact moment on the same date every year. If you were born within two days of the cusp (the end or beginning) of a sign, a more exact calculation may be required to determine your sun sign. So, if you are uncertain about your sign, consult an astrologer or get a free copy of your birth chart from http://www.tarot.com/astrology/astroprofile to determine the correct one. In addition to giving you the exact position of the Sun at the moment of your birth, an individual birth or natal chart includes the positions of the Moon and planets as well, which provides a much more detailed astrological view of your life. This information is used in private consultations and computer-generated astrology reports. The sun sign does not tell your entire astrological story. But it is powerful enough to light up your consciousness with ideas that can change your life.

For those of you who have your astrology chart, in addition to reading the chapter in this book on your sun sign, you will also want to read about your moon and rising signs as well. Your intuition will guide you as you integrate the information.

TRANSITS

The information presented in this book is based on the relationship of the planets, including the Sun and the Moon, to the twelve signs of the zodiac in 2008. The movement of the planets in their cycles and their geometric relationship to one another as they interact are called **transits**; they are the primary forecasting tool for astrologers.

As planets enter into specific relationships with one another, astrologers consider the astrological events that occur. For example, when the Sun and the Moon align in a certain way, an event called an **eclipse** occurs. As you read this book, many of you will study more than one sign, whether you are checking up on someone you know or on your own moon or rising sign. You will notice that certain dates are often mentioned repeatedly from sign to sign. This is because major planetary events affect everyone, but some more than others, and in different ways.

For example, in 2008, there is a New Moon Eclipse in Pisces on March 18. Everyone will feel the power of the eclipse, but their reactions will differ. It will be felt most immediately by Pisces and its opposite sign, Virgo. Since this particular eclipse is stressed by Pluto, it will also be challenging for Scorpios, the sign ruled by this planet. The cosmic weather rains on all of us; the water can be parted in twelve ways, each a door to a sign, a Self, another aspect of being human.

RULING OR KEY PLANETS

Every sign is associated with a key or ruling planet. There is an affinity between signs and their planetary rulers—a common purpose that connects them, like lungs with breathing or feet with walking. In astrology's early days, the Sun (Leo) and the Moon (Cancer) ruled one sign each, and the rest of the known planets—Mercury, Venus, Mars, Jupiter, and Saturn—ruled two. However, in the modern era, new planets have been discovered and astrology has evolved to reflect this. The discovery of Uranus in the late eighteenth century coincided with revolutions in the United States and France, triggered a technological revolution that's still going on today, and transformed astrology's traditional rulership system. Radical Uranus was assigned to rule inventive Aquarius, while its old ruler, Saturn, took a step back. Neptune, discovered with photography sixty-five years later, became the ruler of Pisces, nudging Jupiter into the background. And if Pluto hasn't purged Mars from Scorpio, it's certainly taken the dominant role in expressing this sign's energy.

We mention ruling planets quite a bit in the book as we track the cycles of a given sign. The sign Aries, named for the Greek god of war, is ruled by Mars, the Roman name for the same god. Transits of Mars, then, play a leading role in the forecasts for Aries. Venus is used in the same way in the forecasts for Taurus. For double-ruled Scorpio, Aquarius, and Pisces, we take the traditional and modern planetary rulers into account. The planets and the signs they rule are further discussed later in this section.

ELEMENTS

The four astrological elements are fire, earth, air, and water. The action-oriented fire signs—Aries, Leo, and Sagittarius—are warm and dynamic. The sense-oriented earth signs—Taurus, Virgo, and Capricorn—are practical and realistic. The thought-oriented air signs—Gemini, Libra, and Aquarius—are logical and sociable. The emotion-oriented water signs—Cancer, Scorpio, and Pisces—are intuitive and instinctual. Signs of the same element work harmoniously together. In addition, fire and air signs work well together, as do earth and water.

INGRESSES

An **ingress** is the entry of a planet into a new sign. The activities and concerns of the planet will be colored by that sign's energy. For example, when the communication planet Mercury enters Leo, the expressive qualities of that sign tend to make for more dramatic speech than in the previous sign, self-protective Cancer. When Mercury leaves Leo for detail-oriented Virgo, thoughts and words become more precise. Each planet has its own unique rhythm and cycle in terms of how long it takes that planet to move through all the signs. This determines how long it stays in one sign. The Moon, for example, flies through a sign in two and a half days, while Uranus takes seven years.

HOUSES

Your natal chart is divided into twelve astrological houses that correspond to different areas of your life. This book uses solar houses that place your sun sign in the 1st House. In this system, when a planet enters a new sign, it also enters a new house. Thus, the effect of a planet's ingress into a particular sign depends also on which house of the sign in question it's entering. For example, for a Gemini sun sign, Gemini is its own 1st House, followed by Cancer for the 2nd, Leo for the 3rd House, and so on. If you are a Taurus, your 4th House is Leo. As a Scorpio, your 8th House is Gemini. If this is confusing, don't worry about counting houses; we do it for you. The influence of an astrological event differs considerably based on which house of a sign it falls in.

You'll notice that there are many different, but related, terms used to describe each house, sign, and planet. For example, Mars is called feisty, assertive, impatient, or aggressive at different times throughout the book. Also, we use different house names depending on the emphasis we perceive. You'll find the 4th House described as the 4th House of Home and Family, the 4th House of Security, and the 4th House of Roots—all are valid. We change the descriptions to broaden your understanding, rather than repeat the same limited interpretation over and over. Later in this section is a brief description of all the houses.

ASPECTS

Aspects are geometrically significant angles between planets and a key feature of any astrological forecast. A fast-moving body like the Moon will form every possible aspect to every degree of the zodiac during its monthly orbit around the Earth. The Sun will do the same in a year, Mars in two years, Jupiter in twelve. The slower a planet moves, the less common its aspects, which makes them more significant because their effect is longer. A lunar aspect lasts only a few hours, and one from Mercury a day or two, but a transit like the Jupiter-Neptune square that occurs three times this year can last for a week or two or more.

The qualities of the two planets involved in an aspect are important to its meaning, but so is the angle between them. Soft aspects like **sextiles** and **trines** grease the cosmic wheels, while hard ones like **squares** and **oppositions** often reflect bumps in the road. **Conjunctions**, when two planets are conjoined, are arguably the most powerful aspect and can be easy or difficult according to the nature of the planets involved. To learn more about the nature of the aspects, turn to the next chapter.

The effect of an aspect on each sun sign is modified according to the houses of that sign where the planets fall. A Venus-Mars trine from Cancer to Scorpio is the harmonious expression of Venus's desire for security with Mars's instinct to protect. They are both in water signs, thus compatible. And if you are a Pisces, Venus in Cancer is in your 5th House and Mars in Scorpio is in your 9th, stirring romance and adventure. Alternatively, if you are a Gemini, Venus in Cancer is in your 2nd House and Mars in Scorpio is in the 6th. Applying the cozy relationship of a trine to Gemini's chart gives the interpretation that there will be a comfortable flow in the practical realms of money and work.

RETROGRADES

All true planets (i.e., excluding the Sun and Moon) turn **retrograde** from time to time. This means that the planet appears to go backward in the zodiac, revisiting recently traveled territory. As with other planetary phenomena, astrologers have observed specific effects from retrogrades. The days when planets turn from direct, or forward, motion to retrograde and back again are called **stations** (because the planet appears to be stationary). These are significant periods that emphasize the energy of the stationing planet.

A retrograde station, when backward motion begins, indicates the beginning of a relatively introspective cycle for that planet's energy. At a direct station, the energy that has been turned inward during the retrograde period begins to express itself more overtly in the outer world once again. Retrogrades can cause certain aspects to occur three times—first forward, then retrograde, then forward again. These triple events can be like a play that unfolds in three acts. The first aspect often raises an issue that's reconsidered or adjusted during the second transit and completed during the third.

LUNATIONS AND ECLIPSES

New Moons, Full Moons, and eclipses are important astrological events. These aspects involving the Moon are called **lunations**. Every month the Sun and Moon join together at the New Moon, seeding a fresh lunar cycle that affects us each in a personal way. The New Moon in the partnership sign of Libra sparks relationships, while the New Moon in the resource sign of Taurus brings attention to money. Two weeks later, the Moon opposes the Sun at the Full Moon. This is often an intense time due to the pull of the Moon in one direction and the Sun in another.

The Full Moon in Cancer, for example, pits the need (Moon) for inner security (Cancer) against the Sun in Capricorn's urge for worldly recognition. The Full Moon can be stressful, but it is also a time of illumination that can give rise to greater consciousness. At the Full Moon, instead of seeing yourself pulled apart by opposing forces, it helps to imagine that you're the meeting point where the opposition is resolved by a breakthrough in awareness.

Planets that form significant aspects with the New or Full Moon play a key role in shaping their character. A New Moon square Jupiter is challenged by a tendency to be overexpansive, a negative quality of that planet. A Full Moon conjunct Saturn is bound in seriousness, duty, or doubt symbolized by this planet of necessity.

Eclipses are a special class of New and Full Moons where the Sun and Moon are so close to their line of intersection with the Earth that the light of one of them is darkened. The shadow of the Moon on the Sun at a Solar Eclipse (New Moon) or of the Earth on the Moon at a Lunar Eclipse (Full Moon) makes them memorable. They work, in effect, like super New or Full Moons, extending the normal two- to four-week period of these lunations to an influence up to six months before or after the eclipse. An eclipse will affect each person differently, depending on where it falls in a chart. But they can be unsettling because they usually mark the ends of chapters in one's life.

HOW THIS BOOK IS ORGANIZED

In this book, we take a look at what 2008 holds in store for each of the twelve signs. We evaluate each sign according to the transits to it, its ruler, and its solar houses. The chapter on each sign begins with an overview of the year for the sign. Here we suggest some of the key themes that the sign will encounter in 2008 in general as well as in specific areas of life: love, career, money, health, home, travel, and spirituality. Each of these areas is identified with an icon, as shown at the top of the next page, for easy reference.

The overview is followed by a month-by-month analysis of all of the most important astrological events for that sign. This will enable you to look at where you are as well as what may be coming up for you, so that you can best make choices about how you'd like to deal with the planetary energies at work.

KEY TO ICONS IN OVERVIEW SECTIONS FOR EACH SIGN

 LOVE AND RELATIONSHIPS

 CAREER AND PUBLIC LIFE

 MONEY AND FINANCES

 HEALTH AND VITALITY

 HOME AND FAMILY

 TRAVEL AND HIGHER EDUCATION

 SPIRITUALITY AND PERSONAL GROWTH

TIMING, KEY DATES, AND SUPER NOVA DAYS

The monthly forecast for each sign includes a description of several Key Dates that month. (Eastern time is used throughout the book.) We provide some likely scenarios of what may happen or how someone born under the sign might experience the planetary effects at the time of the Key Dates. It is wise to pay closer attention to your own thoughts, feelings, and actions during these times. Certain Key Dates are called Super Nova Days because they are the most intense energetic periods, positive or negative, of the month.

Note that the exact timing of events, and your awareness of their effects, can vary from person to person, sometimes coming a day or two earlier or arriving a day or two later than the Key Dates given.

The period of influence of a transit from the Sun, Mercury, or Venus is a day before and a day after the exact aspect. A transit of Mars is in effect for about two days coming and going; Jupiter and Saturn lasts for a week or more; and Uranus, Neptune, and Pluto can be two weeks.

Although the Key Dates are the days when a particular alignment is exact, some people are so ready for an event that they'll act on a transit a day or two before. And some of us are so entrenched in the status quo or unwilling to change that it may take a day or two for the effect to manifest. Give yourself an extra day around each Key Date to utilize the energy, maximize the potential, and feel the impact of the event. If you find astrological events consistently unfold in your life earlier or later than predicted, adjust the dates accordingly.

Our goal is to help you understand what is operating within you, below the surface, rather than simply to tell you what's going to happen. This is where you have control so that, to a large degree, what happens is up to you. We describe which buttons are being pushed so that you can see your own patterns and have greater power to change them if you want. Every astrological event has a potential for gain or loss. Fat, juicy, easy ones can make us lazy, while tough ones can temper the will and make us stronger. It usually takes time and hindsight to measure the true value of an experience.

THE PLANETS, THE HOUSES,
AND ASPECTS

THE PLANETS

The planets are the basic building blocks of astrology. As our ancestors observed the cycles of these wandering stars, they attributed characteristics to them. Each of these richly symbolic archetypes represents a particular spectrum of meaning. Their intimate relationship to the Greek and Roman myths helps us tell stories about them that are still relevant to our lives today. No matter what your sun sign is, every planet impacts your life according to its symbolism and its placement.

THE SUN

Rules Leo

Keywords: *Consciousness, Will, Vitality*

The Sun is our home star, the glowing filament in the center of our local system, and is associated with the sign Leo. Our ancestors equated it with God, for it is the source of energy and is what animates us. In fact, we base our entire calendar system on the Earth's relationship to the Sun. It represents the core of individual identity and consciousness. The masculine Sun has dignity, courage, and willpower. We feel the Sun's role as our main purpose in life; it fuels our furnace to fulfill our mission. We recognize its brightness in anyone who has a "sunny" personality. It is charismatic, creative, and generous of heart. But it can also be proud, have too much pride, and turn arrogant or self-centered. When the Sun is shining, we can see the world around us; it gives us a world of "things" that we can name and describe. It could be said that the Sun symbolizes objective reality.

THE MOON

Rules Cancer

Keywords: *Subconscious, Emotions, Habits*

We've all seen how the Moon goes through its phases, reflecting the light of the Sun, and have felt the power of the Full Moon. Lunations are important astrological markers. The Moon changes signs every two and a half days and reflects the mood of the public in general. Although our year calendar is based upon the Sun, each month (comes from "moon"—*moonth*) closely approximates the cycle of the Moon. The Moon is closer to Earth than anything else in the heavens. Astrologically, it represents how we reflect the world around us through our feelings. The Moon symbolizes emotions, instincts, habits, and routine. It describes how we nurture others and need to be cared for ourselves. The feminine power of the Moon is also connected with the fertility cycle of women. Because it is the source of security and familial intimacy, our Moon sign is where we feel at home. The Moon is associated with the sign Cancer and with concerns about our home and family.

 MERCURY

Rules Gemini and Virgo

Keywords: *Communication, Thoughts, Transportation*

Mercury, the Heavenly Messenger, races around the Sun four times each year. Its nearly ninety-day cycle corresponds with the seasons of the calendar. Mercury, our intellectual antenna, is the planet of perception, communication, rational thought, mobility, and commerce. It is the mental traveler, able to move effortlessly through the realms of thought and imagination. Mercury organizes language, allows us to grasp ideas, enables us to analyze and integrate data, and assists us in all forms of communication. Cars, bicycles, telephones, delivery services, paperwork, and the mind itself are all manifestations of quicksilver Mercury, the fastest of the true planets. However, Mercury also has a trickster side and can cleverly con us into believing something that just isn't true. Mercury is associated with curious Gemini in its information-gathering mode, and with discerning Virgo when it is analytically sorting through the data.

VENUS

Rules Taurus and Libra

Keywords: *Desire, Love, Money, Values*

Venus is the goddess of love, our relationship antenna, associated with the spectrum of how we experience what is beautiful and pleasurable to us. With Venus, we attach desire to our perceptions. On one end, Venus can indicate romantic and sensual love. On the other end, Venus is about money and all things of value—financial and emotional. This manifests as our attraction to art, music, and even good food. Every beautiful flower and every act of love contains the essence of sweet Venus. We look to Venus to describe what we like—an important key to understanding partnerships, particularly personal ones. To a certain extent, our chemistry with other people is affected by Venus. Although Venus is traditionally associated with femininity, both women and men are impacted by its rhythms. A morning star, Venus rules Taurus and is associated with the simple and sensual side of physical reality. As an evening star, it rules Libra, where it represents the more intellectual side of love and harmony.

 MARS

Rules Aries, co-rules Scorpio

Keywords: *Action, Physical Energy, Drive*

Mars, the god of war, is the planet of action, physical energy, initiative, and aggression. It is the first planet beyond Earth's orbit, and its role is to take what we have and extend it to the outer world. Mars represents the masculine force of individuality that helps define the ego and our sense of unique identity. It represents how we move forward in life and propels us toward new experiences and into the future. Mars drives us to assert ourselves in healthy ways, but the angry red planet can also be impatient and insensitive, engendering violence and destruction. When insecure, it turns offensive and can attack others. Mars can also express erotic passion, the male counterpart of the female Venus; together they are the cosmic lovers. As the pioneering risk taker, Mars rules fiery Aries. As a volcanic force of power, it is the traditional ruler of Scorpio.

JUPITER

Rules Sagittarius, co-rules Pisces

Keywords: *Expansion, Growth, Optimism*

Jupiter is the largest of the true planets. It represents expansion, growth, and optimism. It was called the Greater Benefic by ancient astrologers due to its association with good fortune. Today, modern astrologers understand that too much of a good thing is not necessarily beneficial. Jupiter rules the excesses of life; undoubtedly, it's the planet of bigger, better, and more. Wherever there's too much, you're apt to find Jupiter. Often called the lucky planet, Jupiter symbolizes where opportunity knocks. Yet it is still up to us to open the door and walk through. Jupiterian people are jovial, but this gassy giant is also associated with humor, philosophy, enthusiasm, and enterprise. In its adventurous mode, Jupiter rules globetrotting Sagittarius, but as the planet of religion and belief systems, it has a traditional connection to Pisces.

♄ SATURN

Rules Capricorn, co-rules Aquarius

Keywords: *Contraction, Maturity, Responsibility*

Saturn is the outermost planet visible to the naked eye, and as such represented the end of the road for our sky-watching ancestors. In premodern times, Saturn was the limit of our human awareness; beyond it were only the fixed stars. Now, even with our telescopic capability to peer farther into the vastness of space and time, Saturn still symbolizes the limits of perception. It is about structure, order, necessity, commitment, and hard-earned accomplishments. It's the stabilizing voice of reality and governs rules, regulations, discipline, and patience. Saturn is Father Time, and represents the ultimate judgment that you get what you deserve. But Saturn isn't only stern or rigid; it is also the teacher and the wise old sage. When we embrace Saturn's discipline, we mature and learn from our experiences. As the serious taskmaster, Saturn is the ruler of ambitious Capricorn. As the co-ruler of Aquarius, Saturn reminds us that rigid rules may need to be broken in order to express our individuality.

CHIRON

(Does not rule a sign)
Keywords: *Healing, Pain, Subversion*

Chiron is the mythological Wounded Healer, and although not a true planet in the traditional sense, it has become a useful tool for modern astrologers. Chiron is a relative newcomer to the planetary lineup and was discovered in 1977 between the orbits of Saturn and Uranus. It describes where we can turn our wounds into wisdom to assist others. It is associated with the story of the wounded Fisher King, who, in medieval tales about the Holy Grail, fished (for souls) in order to salve his incurable suffering. Chiron not only symbolizes where and how we hurt, but also how our words and actions can soothe the pain of others. It doesn't, however, always play by the rules and can work against the status quo. Its rhythms can stir up old memories of emotional discomfort that can lead to increased understanding, vulnerability, and the transformation of heartache and grief into the gifts of love and forgiveness.

 URANUS

Rules Aquarius
Keywords: *Awakening, Unpredictable, Inventive*

Uranus is the first planet discovered with technology (the telescope). Its discovery broke through the limitations imposed by our five senses. It symbolizes innovation, originality, revolution, and delighting in unexpected surprises. Uranus operates suddenly, often to release tensions, no matter how hidden. Its action is like lightning—instantaneous and exciting, upsetting and exhilarating. Uranus provokes and instigates change; its restless and rebellious energy hungers for freedom. Its high frequency and electrical nature stimulate the nervous system. This highly original planet abhors the status quo and is known to turn normal things upside down and inside out. As the patron planet of the strange and unusual, it is the ruler of eccentric Aquarius.

NEPTUNE

Rules Pisces

Keywords: *Imagination, Intuition, Spirituality*

Neptune is god of the seas, from which all life arises and is eventually returned. Imaginative Neptune lures us into the foggy mists where reality becomes so hazy that we can lose our way. It is the planet of dreams, illusions, and spirituality. It dissolves boundaries and barriers, leading us into higher awareness, compassion, confusion, or escapism. Grasping the meaning of Neptune is like trying to hold water in our hands. No matter how hard we try, it slips through our fingers—for Neptune is ultimately elusive and unknowable. It rules all things related to fantasy and delusion. A highly spiritual energy, the magic of Neptune encourages artistic vision, intuitive insight, compassion, and the tendency to idealize. Neptune governs the mystic's urge to merge with the divine and is associated with the spiritual sign Pisces.

PLUTO

Rules Scorpio

Keywords: *Passion, Intensity, Regeneration*

Pluto, lord of the underworld, is the planet of death, rebirth, and transformation. As the most distant of the planets, Pluto moves us inexorably toward a deeper understanding of life's cycles. Under Pluto's influence, it often seems as though the apparently solid ground has disintegrated, forcing us to morph in ways we cannot intellectually understand. Pluto is the mythological phoenix, a magical bird that rises from the ashes of its own destruction by fire. It contains the shadow parts of ourselves that we would prefer to keep hidden, but healing and empowerment come from facing the unfathomable darkness and turning it into light. Manipulation and control are often issues with Pluto. A healthy relationship with Pluto adds psychological understanding and clarity about our motivations. As the ruler of magnetic Scorpio, it is associated with power and emotional intensity.

☊ ☋ NODES OF THE MOON

(Do not rule a sign)
Keywords: *Karma, Soul, Past Lives*
The Nodes of the Moon are opposing points where the Moon's orbit around the Earth intersects the Earth's orbit around the Sun. Although not real planets, these powerful points have an astrological influence in that they describe the ways we connect with others. They are useful in understanding the challenges and opportunities we face in our soul's journey through its lifetime here on Earth. For many astrologers, the Lunar Nodes are symbolic of past lives and future existences. The South Node, at one end of the nodal axis, represents the past—the unconscious patterns of our ancestral heritage or those brought into this life from previous incarnations. These are often talents that can easily be overused and become a no-growth path of least resistance. At the other end, the North Node represents the future—a new direction for growth, development, and integration.

THE HOUSES

Every astrology chart is divided into twelve houses, each ruling different areas of life and colored by a different sign. Just as planets move through the zodiac signs, they also move through the houses in an individual chart. The twelve houses have a correspondence to the twelve signs, but in an individualized chart, the signs in each house will vary based on the sign on the cusp of the 1st House, called a rising sign or ascendant. The rising sign is determined by the exact time of your birth. We use solar houses, which place the sun sign as your 1st House, or rising sign.

1ST HOUSE

Corresponding Sign: Aries
Keywords: *Self, Appearance, Personality*
A primary point of self-identification: When planets move through this sector, the emphasis is on your individuality and surface appearances. It is often associated with how we interact with others when we first meet them. Planets here tend to take on great importance and become more integrated into your personality.

2ND HOUSE

Corresponding Sign: Taurus

Keywords: *Possessions, Values, Self-Worth*

Associated with values, resources, income, and self-esteem: When planets move through the 2nd House, they can modify your attitudes about money and earning. This is a concrete and practical area of the chart, and although it is linked to possessions, the 2nd House typically does not include things you cannot easily move, such as real estate or what you share with someone else.

3RD HOUSE

Corresponding Sign: Gemini

Keywords: *Communication, Siblings, Short Trips*

Relates to how you gather information from your immediate environment: It's associated with the day-to-day comings and goings of your life. **Siblings** can be found here, for this is where we first learn to build intimacy when we're young. Planets moving through this house can affect the pace and quality of your day and how you communicate with those around you.

4TH HOUSE

Corresponding Sign: Cancer

Keywords: *Home, Family, Roots*

Associated with the earliest imprints of childhood, your family roots, and how you're connected to your own feelings: This is your emotional foundation and describes what you need to feel at home. This is where you are nurtured, so when planets travel through this sector, they stir up issues of security and safety. As the deepest place in your chart, it is sometimes only you who knows about it.

5TH HOUSE

Corresponding Sign: Leo

Keywords: *Love, Romance, Children, Play*

Associated with fun, but also represents self-expression, creativity, love affairs, and children: The 5th House is about the discovery of self through play, and includes sports, games, and gambling. When planets move through your 5th House, they can excite you to take risks and connect with the innocence of your inner child.

6TH HOUSE

Corresponding Sign: Virgo
Keywords: *Work, Health, Daily Routines*
Related to service and working conditions: Like the 3rd House, it describes your daily life, but the consistency of it rather than the noisy distractions—it's where you strive for efficiency and effectiveness. Planets here modify your habits, diet, and exercise. Although considered the house of health and hygiene, transits here don't always indicate illness; they can also increase our concern for healthier lifestyles.

7TH HOUSE

Corresponding Sign: Libra
Keywords: *Marriage, Relationships, Business Partners*
Encompasses one-to-one relationships: Its cusp is called the descendant and is the western end of the horizon. It's where and how we meet other people, both personally and professionally. In a larger sense, this is how you project who you are onto others. Planets moving through here can stimulate intimate relationships, but can also increase the intensity of all of your interactions with the outside world.

8TH HOUSE

Corresponding Sign: Scorpio
Keywords: *Intimacy, Transformation, Shared Resources*
A mysterious and powerful place, associated with shared experiences, including the most intimate: Traditionally the house of sex, death, and taxes, it's the place where you gain the deepest levels of relationships, personally and professionally. When planets move through your 8th House, perspectives can intensify, intimacy issues are stimulated, and compelling transformations are undertaken.

9TH HOUSE

Corresponding Sign: Sagittarius
Keywords: *Travel, Higher Education, Philosophy*
Associated with philosophy, religion, higher education of all kinds, and long-distance travel: It's where you seek knowledge and truth—both within and without. Planets moving through this house open portals to inner journeys and outer adventures, stretching your mind in ways that expand your perspectives about the world.

10TH HOUSE

Corresponding Sign: Capricorn
Keywords: *Career, Community, Ambition*
The most elevated sector of your chart; its cusp is called the midheaven: This is the career house, opposite to the home-based 4th House. When planets move through your 10th House, they activate your ambition, drive you to achieve professional excellence, and push you up the ladder of success. This is where your public reputation is important and hard work is acknowledged.

11TH HOUSE

Corresponding Sign: Aquarius
Keywords: *Friends, Groups, Associations, Social Ideals*
Traditionally called the house of friends, hopes, and wishes: It's where you go to be with like-minded people. The 11th House draws you out of your individual career aspirations and into the ideals of humanity. Planets traveling here can activate dreams of the future, so spending time with friends is a natural theme.

12TH HOUSE

Corresponding Sign: Pisces
Keywords: *Imagination, Spirituality, Secret Activities*
Complex, representing the ending of one cycle and the beginning of the next: It is connected with mysteries and places outside ordinary reality. When planets move through this house, they stimulate your deepest subconscious feelings and activate fantasies. It's a private space that can seem like a prison or a sanctuary.

ASPECTS

As the planets move through the sky in their various cycles, they form ever-changing angles with one another. Certain angles create significant geometric shapes. For example, when two planets are 90 degrees apart, they conform to a square. A sextile, or 60 degrees of separation, conforms to a six-pointed star. Planets create aspects to one another when they are at these special angles. All aspects are divisions of the 360-degree circle. Aspects explain how the individual symbolism of a pair of planets combines into an energetic pattern.

CONJUNCTION

0 degrees ★ **Keywords:** *Compression, Blending, Focus*
A conjunction is a blending of the separate planetary energies involved. When two planets conjoin, your job is to integrate the different influences—which in some cases is easier than others. For example, a conjunction of the Moon and Venus is likely to be a smooth blending of energy because of the similarity of the planets. But a conjunction between the Moon and Uranus is likely to be challenging because the Moon needs security, while Uranus prefers risk.

SEMISQUARE AND SESQUISQUARE

45 and 135 degrees ★ **Keywords:** *Annoyance, Mild Resistance*
Semisquares and sesquisquares are minor aspects that act like milder squares. They're one-eighth and three-eighths of a circle, respectively. Like the other hard aspects (conjunctions, oppositions, and squares) they can create dynamic situations that require immediate attention and resolution. Although they are not usually as severe as the other hard aspects, they remind us that healthy stress is important for the process of growth.

SEXTILE

60 degrees ★ **Keywords:** *Supportive, Intelligent, Activating*
Sextiles are supportive and intelligent, combining complementary signs—fire and air, earth and water. There's an even energetic distribution between the planets involved. Sextiles often indicate opportunities based on our willingness to take action in smart ways. Like trines, sextiles are considered easy: The good fortune they offer can pass unless you consciously take an active interest in making something positive happen.

QUINTILE

72 and 144 degrees ★ **Keywords:** *Creativity, Metaphysics, Magic*
Quintiles are powerful nontraditional aspects based on dividing the zodiac circle into five, resulting in a five-pointed star. Related to ancient goddess-based religious traditions, quintiles activate the imagination, intuition, and latent artistic talents. They're clever, intelligent, and even brilliant as they stimulate humor to relieve repressed tensions.

SQUARE

90 degrees ★ **Keywords:** *Resistance, Stress, Dynamic Conflict*

A square is an aspect of resistance, signifying energies at odds. Traditionally, they were considered negative, but their dynamic instability demands attention, so they're often catalysts for change. When differences in two planetary perspectives are integrated, squares can build enduring structures. Harnessing a square's power by managing contradictions creates opportunities for personal growth.

TRINE

120 degrees ★ **Keywords:** *Harmony, Free-Flowing, Ease*

A trine is the most harmonious of aspects because it connects signs of the same element. In the past, trines were considered positive, but modern astrologers realize they are so easy that they can create a rut that is difficult to break out of. When two planets are one-third of a circle apart, they won't necessarily stimulate change, but they can often help build on the status quo. With trines, you must stay alert, for complacency can weaken your chances for success.

QUINCUNX

150 degrees ★ **Keywords:** *Irritation, Adjustment*

A quincunx is almost like a nonaspect, for the two planets involved have a difficult time staying aware of each other. As such, this aspect often acts as an irritant, requiring that you make constant adjustments without actually resolving the underlying problem. This is a challenging aspect because it can be more annoying than a full-fledged crisis. Quincunxes are a bit like oil and water—the planets are not in direct conflict, but they have difficulty mixing with each another.

OPPOSITION

180 degrees ★ **Keywords:** *Tension, Awareness, Balance*

When two planets are in opposition, they are like two forces pulling at either end of a rope. The tension is irresolvable, unless you are willing to hold both divergent perspectives without suppressing one or the other. More often than not, we favor one side of the opposition over the other and, in doing so, project the unexpressed side onto others or situations. For this reason, oppositions usually manifest as relationship issues.

ASTROLOGY

WORLD REPORT 2008

Astrology works for individuals, groups, and even humanity as a whole. You will have your own story in 2008, but it will unfold among 6.7 billion other tales of human experience in the year ahead. We are each unique, yet our lives touch one another; our destinies are woven together by weather and war, by economy, science, politics, religion, and all the other threads of life on this planet. We make personal choices every day, yet there are great events beyond the control of any one individual. When the power goes out in a neighborhood, it affects everyone, yet individual astrology patterns will describe the personal response of each person. Our existence is both an individual and collective experience.

We are living at a time when the tools of self-awareness fill bookshelves, Web sites, and broadcasts, and we benefit greatly from them. Yet despite all this wisdom, conflicts among groups cause enormous suffering every day. Understanding personal issues is a powerful means for increasing happiness, but knowledge of our collective issues is equally important for our safety, sanity, and well-being. This astrological look at the major trends and planetary patterns for 2008 provides a framework for understanding the potentials and challenges we face together, so that we can advance with tolerance and respect as a community and fulfill our potentials as individuals.

The astrological events used for this forecast are the transits of the outer planets, Chiron, and the Moon's Nodes, as well as the retrograde cycles of Mercury and eclipses of the Sun and the Moon.

MAJOR PLANETARY EVENTS

JUPITER IN CAPRICORN: MATERIALIZING SUCCESS

December 18, 2007–January 5, 2009

Optimistic Jupiter is ready to climb a mountain this year. Instead of simply heading off on an adventure, the planet of expansion's passage through industrious Capricorn is a time to set goals, plan a course of action, and reach the summit of success. Jolly Jupiter is usually happy exploring the world, seeking new experiences, and expanding the mind. But Saturn-ruled Capricorn puts the giant planet in a productive mood where the name of the game is getting results. Opportunities come for those who do their homework and demonstrate the patience and commitment to prove their worthiness. There's less room for sloppiness for those who want chance to turn in their favor. Good luck is earned only by solid effort this year.

Jupiter in Capricorn is a time to turn beliefs into reality. Idealistic philosophies lose their meaning unless practice brings them down to earth. The enormous planet loves the biggest ideas, but Capricorn's practicality will test them against the weight of experience. The dark side of Jupiter's presence here is materialism that values worldly achievement more than spiritual awakening. Instead of living up to standards that may be difficult to reach, it will be tempting to lower the standards or just do away with them entirely. The ambitious nature of Capricorn, with a tendency to divide the world into winners and losers, could crush idealism under the pressure to come out on top. However, those committed to a particular religion or belief system are likely to be more disciplined in the practice of their faith and will experience real progress toward achieving their goals without hurting others.

Hope for a balanced approach to ambition occurs with positive trines between Jupiter and Saturn in January, September, and November. These healthy alignments between the planets of expansion and contraction bring the wisdom of self-restraint and a willingness to earn one's rewards honestly. Those who play by the rules should get what they deserve, while those who cut corners are likely to slide right off the track and slip farther from their aspirations. The Jupiter-Saturn trine in earth signs adds conscientiousness and a capacity to put in the time necessary to attain one's goals. While incidents of impatience are unavoidable from time to time, the consistent background harmony between Jupiter and Saturn provides much-needed stability for individuals, institutions, and the Earth itself. Problems can be defined with clarity and a big-picture perspective that helps establish effective strategies. The potential to advance personal and collective agendas is great when resources are well managed and other practical issues are addressed.

Positive 60-degree sextiles between Jupiter and inventive Uranus in late March, May, and November supply a plethora of fresh ideas that help us avoid repeating old mistakes. The pragmatism of Jupiter and Saturn in earth signs has a conservative side that would normally resist untested concepts. But Uranus's aspects with Jupiter weave intuition into the year's fabric to brighten it with originality. Jupiter's friendly relationships with the planets of the old tried and true (Saturn) and new and untested (Uranus) combines the best of the past and the future. Solid experience supports experimentation that can make a better tomorrow. Technological advances improve the quality of day-to-day life, and personal goals should be met with a combination of ingenuity and hard work. There's no need to choose between old methods and new possibilities—the two work together in harmony.

SATURN IN VIRGO: MANAGING THE DETAILS

September 2, 2007–October 29, 2009

Saturn, the planet of boundaries and limitations, takes twenty-nine years to orbit the Sun and pass through all twelve signs of the zodiac. It demands serious responsibility, shows the work needed to overcome obstacles, and teaches us how to build new structures in our lives. Saturn thrives on patience and commitment, rewarding well-planned and persistent effort but punishing sloppiness with delay, disappointment, and failure.

Saturn's passage through detail-oriented Virgo is a time to perfect skills, cut waste, and develop healthier habits. Saturn and Virgo are both pragmatic, which makes them an excellent pair for improving the quality of material life. Organizational upgrades and maintenance projects increase efficiency for individuals and organizations. Education and training become more valuable due to the increasing demand for highly specialized skills. Carelessness grows more costly as minor errors can escalate into major problems. Systems break down easily, requiring closer attention than usual. Bodies can be more susceptible to illnesses caused by impure food or water, making this an ideal time to improve your diet. Environmental issues grow in importance as we approach a critical point in the relationship between humanity and planet Earth. Fortunately, Saturn in exacting Virgo is excellent for cleaning up unhealthy toxins produced by old technologies and in leading the way to develop new ecologically friendly systems for the future.

Virgo is the sign of the worker, putting labor issues and employee rights in the spotlight. This could mark a major turning point for unions by accelerating their rate of decline or finding new issues and alliances that restore their lost influence on political life. The globalization of the workforce has already changed the way companies do business, and we can expect this trend to continue, placing additional strains on the economy. And as corporations continue to grow beyond national boundaries, fears about internationalization can fuel the ongoing debate about the discrimination facing foreign workers. But Virgo is less interested in unrestrained consumerism than it is in acquiring useful things. This can open the door to a new era of relatively modest consumption and shift the economy away from purchases of more cars, bigger homes, and disposable goods. Do-it-yourself classes and products, personalized services, pets, and outdoor activities will continue to increase in popularity.

Saturn in Virgo highlights flaws and makes it easier to be critical of oneself and others. Yet its true purpose is to solve problems, not simply complain about them. Recognizing our weaknesses can sometimes be a source of despair, but the functional combination of Saturn's commitment and Virgo's analytical skills gives hope that effective change is well within our grasp. Small steps in a positive direction can slowly build up to a tidal wave of improvement wherever you place your attention this year.

URANUS IN PISCES: BREAK ON THROUGH TO THE OTHER SIDE

March 3, 2003–May 27, 2010

Uranus takes eighty-four years to orbit the Sun, spending about seven years in each sign. This longer transit's influence tends to be less obvious in daily life than those of faster-moving Saturn and Jupiter. Nevertheless, its eventual impact can be even greater. This planet of liberation in Pisces, the last sign of the zodiac, is about breaking down the barriers of faith, fantasy, and illusion that subtly shape our lives. The most powerful ones lie just beyond the border of consciousness, yet hold our minds in a universe of assumptions that are almost never questioned. Uranus's presence in Pisces, though, tears down these invisible walls and awakens us from sweet dreams and nightmares alike.

Pisces is a water sign and Uranus rules electricity, so this combination suggests we may see the development of new technologies that transform water into usable electric power. Also, because karmic Saturn opposes water-bound Uranus in November—a transit that lasts through September 2009—we can expect to suddenly encounter new realities concerning water as a natural resource, for both drinking and agriculture. Stories of severe water pollution, unavailable drinking water, or problems with the fishing industry may flood the mainstream media. However, this is shown not just by Uranus's presence in Neptune's sign Pisces, but also by Neptune's presence in Uranus's signs Aquarius. This exchange of ruling planets is called "mutual reception" and indicates closer connections among the planets and signs involved. Uranus is scientific, the first planet discovered by telescope. Neptune is spiritual, so we can expect continuing debate between academia and religion over evolution theory versus intelligent design, stem cell research, cloning, and the right to die.

Uranus is a planet of individuality, the unique and original singular force that steps outside the norm to revolutionize the world. Small radical groups or even one person can make powerful changes with influence that ripples around the globe. Expansive Jupiter's tense squares to Uranus on January 22, May 10, and October 9 multiply these radicalizing forces. They may arise as explosive social or political events, but the potential for breakthroughs in consciousness is just as dynamic. The challenge, both collectively and personally, is to maintain a calm center in the middle of the storm. The solid values of a person or nation applied in a flexible and up-to-date manner permits intelligent responses as opposed to dangerous knee-jerk reactions. Change is a natural process, even when it comes with unexpected ferocity. Survival depends upon managing evolution skillfully rather than resisting it blindly.

NEPTUNE IN AQUARIUS: SPIRIT INTO SCIENCE

January 28, 1998–April 4, 2011
Aquarius is a sign of intellect and Neptune is a planet of faith. This is an unusual combination that inspires minds when operating at its best, but can also make for fuzzy arguments. This can be disorienting, bringing about possible detachment from a more spiritual path. The oppositions to Neptune from solid Saturn on February 28 and June 25, though, demand accountability from this vaguest of planets. Its spiritual ideals and promises for a better tomorrow are boldly challenged by the urgency of our needs today. A tug of war between the compassionate

and the intolerant may have one side leaping into unprecedented acts of charity while the other's insistence on religious purity resists current realities.

Neptune is associated with oil, so Saturn's oppositions to it will continue to create conflicts based on limited supplies, high prices, and environmental damage. Military engagements continue, fueled by the fear of dwindling resources and increased demand. Oil spills and accidents involving chemicals may be more frequent—it's interesting to note that the 1989 Exxon *Valdez* oil spill happened when Saturn was conjunct Neptune. However, technological inventions, perhaps involving biological agents, may reduce their potentially devastating effects. As mentioned on the previous page, water, our most precious liquid, is slated to become a more newsworthy subject, with tainted supplies and privatization fueling headlines.

As noted earlier with respect to Uranus in Pisces, the mixing of faith and science is both a gift and curse of Neptune in Aquarius. Doubting the wisdom of organized religion continues to be prominent as intellect replaces faith and increasing numbers of people are disillusioned with overzealous religious leaders. Deception and a willful denial of logic are to be expected. But for the metaphysically oriented, Neptune in Aquarius is likely to continue the popularization of technology as a way to understand our spirituality. An increasing number of scientists will join the ranks of quantum-thinking gurus such as Deepak Chopra, Bruce Lipton, and Fred Alan Wolf.

On an individual level, Neptune in Aquarius is part of a process for connecting feelings with intellect by recognizing the close relationship between emotions and thoughts. The mind is not simply a mechanical system that operates separately from the rest of the body—2008 is another good year to use Neptune activities such as meditation, yoga, or t'ai chi to calm jangled nervous systems and to integrate mind, body, and spirit peacefully.

PLUTO IN SAGITTARIUS: PHILOSOPHICAL EXTREMES

January 17, 1995–January 25, 2008
June 13, 2008–November 26, 2008
The reclassification of Pluto from planet to dwarf planet by the vote of several hundred astronomers has not changed its role in astrological analysis. There is an ironic justice in calling the "Lord of the Underworld" an outcast—and it certainly has not lost any of its power with all the publicity. Pluto, the most recently discovered

and slowest moving of the planets used by astrologers, represents transformation, a process that often takes us from the depths to the heights before finding a new point of balance. This powerful planet's long transit through Sagittarius, the sign of organized religion, was expressed most painfully with the September 11 attacks in the United States. The symbolism was astonishingly accurate, and the events predicted to the day by two well-known astrologers. Pluto represents death; Sagittarius is not only religion, but also faraway places and long-distance travel, as in airplanes. Saturn, the planet of structure, was in Gemini, the Twins (as in Twin Towers), and opposed by Pluto that fateful day. As that transit recedes into history, and is succeeded by an easier Saturn-Pluto trine on August 6, this harmonious relationship presents the possibility of putting fear into a more rational container. Rather than allowing ourselves and our leaders to surrender reason in the name of security, we are likely to realize that reason *is* our security.

Pluto's penchant for intolerance in opinionated Sagittarius will be with us through-out the year, and 2008 continues to present opportunities to evolve past the cultural schisms of the past with pragmatic Saturn's help. Still, some true believers tend to go to extremes from the fear that if they don't dominate, they will be defeated. Armageddon consciousness arises when organizations and individuals do not see ways of adapting to change they cannot control. The imagined destruction of their world produces the panic of absolutism and the end of dialogue.

PLUTO IN CAPRICORN: UNAVOIDABLE CHANGE

January 25, 2008–June 13, 2008
November 26, 2008–March 23, 2023

Tiny but powerful Pluto entering no-nonsense Capricorn signals a turn toward major change in society. Capricorn is associated with important institutions such as government and business, so transformative Pluto's visit begins a process of altering the significant structures that support our culture. Because Capricorn is an earth sign, we can expect a growing urgency in the serious environmental crises in front of us. Global warming, for instance, could place unforeseeable pres-sures on corporations, governments, and individuals, forcing inevitable upheavals that could radically impact our modern way of life. The accumulated effects of dumping toxins into the air, water, and soil are likely to become more evident dur-ing Pluto's long transit of this sign. Obviously, this could overpower all other issues and require a degree of change not seen since Pluto last transited this sign, from

1762 to 1778. Democracy, like the magical phoenix bird, arose from the destructive American and French Revolutions that ended monarchy and gave birth to the individual freedoms we now are struggling to keep.

The good news is that events of this magnitude do not occur overnight. The corruption of existing institutions takes time, enough for those capable of adapting to begin the necessary process of reform. Since Capricorn has to do with rule from the top, Pluto's transit may well knock down those who pull the levers of power. However, regardless of where state, church, education, and industry go, there is constructive work we can each do as individuals at this time. Since both Pluto and Capricorn are associated with power, the application of personal will is a critical issue. Instead of relying on others to maintain and advance civilization, we each have the capacity to increase our own tangible contribution to the world. Step one is a reexamination of career ambitions and life goals. For some, this could grow out of dissatisfaction or a sense of impotence in their lives. This is not likely to be the result of a single event or limited to Pluto's transit this year. We're at the beginning of a long process in which we seek a more purposeful life. Of course, this can feel like an overwhelming challenge, since meeting the increasing responsibilities we now have can be a daunting task. It is best, then, to address small but important issues, where it's possible to see results more quickly and gain the confidence to continue moving forward. Changes in diet, exercise patterns, attitude, and behavior, for example, are manageable yet significant. Make a plan and commit to working on it for as long as it takes. Progress may be slow, and it's natural to encounter resistance. Habits don't necessarily give themselves up easily. But slowly and surely, a sense of mastery grows with each small step forward. As a result, humanity will become more empowered—able to consciously create the future rather than unconsciously repeat mistakes of the past.

CHIRON IN AQUARIUS: THE WOUNDED COMMUNITY

February 21, 2005–April 19, 2010

Chiron, discovered in 1977 between the orbits of Saturn and Uranus, was named after a mythological centaur known for its healing powers. Astrologers studying the new member of the solar system have found it to be a meaningful point, and most have added it to their charts. Chiron in Aquarius represents wounds in communities and the ideals that bind them together. But its transit through this sign can lead to a shift away from traditional group identification to allow new alignments less rooted in old national, regional, or racial differences.

THE MOON'S NODES

MOON'S NORTH NODE IN AQUARIUS, SOUTH NODE IN LEO: COMMUNITY NEEDS OVER PERSONAL DESIRES

December 15, 2007–August 18, 2009

The North and South Nodes are opposing points, the Dragon's Head and Tail that connect the orbits of the Moon around the Earth and the Earth around the Sun. Habit pulls us toward the South Node, but it is the North Node that points in a direction of growth and integration. The North Node in Aquarius marks a period when we must accept the technologies we have created, even if they seem too futuristic or inhuman. The South Node sign of Leo is concerned with issues of the human heart, which may need to be temporarily set aside to make tough decisions that could impact the survival of the human race. Nostalgic emotional attachments to the past can place individual needs ahead of the community, but we are required now to bravely face our collective destiny. There is little room for self-centered narcissistic behavior now, while the intellectually driven Aquarius North Node increases our awareness of the interrelatedness of all humanity. This is an opportunity to move past our personal neuroses and tackle the larger issues all we face together.

MERCURY RETROGRADES

All true planets appear to move retrograde from time to time as a result of viewing them from the moving platform of Earth. The most significant retrograde periods are those of Mercury, the communication planet. Occurring three times a year for roughly three weeks at a time, these are periods when difficulties with details, travel, information flow, and technical matters are likely.

Although Mercury's retrograde phase has received a fair amount of bad press, it isn't necessarily a negative cycle. Because personal and commercial interactions are emphasized, you can actually accomplish more than usual, especially if you stay focused on what needs to be done rather than initiating new projects. But you may feel as if you're treading water—or worse yet, carried backward in an under-tow of unfinished business. Worry less about making progress than about the quality of your work. Extra attention should be paid to all your communication exchanges. Avoiding misunderstandings and omissions is the ideal way to preemptively deal with unnecessary complications. Retrograde Mercury is best used to tie up loose ends as you review, redo, reconsider and, in general, revisit the past.

This year, the three retrogrades are in intellectual air signs (Aquarius, Gemini, and Libra), which can be very useful for analysis and remedial studies that help you reevaluate what you already know so you can take your learning to the next step. Mercury has a natural affinity for the air signs, so you are empowered by your mental prowess during these times. But however intelligent you feel, don't become so enamored with the workings of your mind that you forget about the practical aspects of your body and the emotional needs of your heart. Mercury aspects Chiron, the Wounded Healer, multiple times during each of its three retrograde periods. Remembering the pain of previous failures can trigger current fears that get in the way of success. An acute awareness of our limits is enough to prevent us from even trying. The key is recognizing the difference between what once happened and what's occurring in the present. Forgiving others or yourself can also be a source of healing. But you cannot always think or talk your way through a complex emotional situation. During these Mercury retrograde phases, develop your language skills while remaining sensitive to that which cannot be put into words.

JANUARY 28–FEBRUARY 18 IN AQUARIUS: RECLAIM YOUR BRILLIANCE

Mercury retrograde in fixed Aquarius can trick you into confusing what you already know with everything there is to know. Make no mistake: This is an intelligent time for Mercury as it moves through the technological and futuristic sign of Aquarius. This retrograde emphasizes mental Mercury's conjunction to intuitive Neptune on January 22, realigning with the God of the Seas again on February 2. The temptation comes from believing that cool analysis can solve even the stickiest of emotional dilemmas. Actually, the most effective solutions can appear out of thin air. Have the courage to trust what comes from the realms of imagination or you might find yourself running through the same old logical patterns again and again, only to arrive at an unsatisfactory answer. Remember, your real brilliance may be more associated with your dreams than your ability to recall facts. Although Mercury turns direct on February 18, it doesn't align with Neptune for the third and final time until March 9, when the truth emerges and you can finally move on.

MAY 26–JUNE 19 IN GEMINI: INFORMATION OVERLOAD

Mercury is at home in the sign of versatile Gemini, making this retrograde period particularly strong. On the one hand, there is a compulsive tendency to reconsider your previous plans, review the collected data, and reevaluate earlier decisions you may have made without enough details. The fallacy, however, lies in the belief that more information is always better than less. Unfortunately, it can be quite challenging these days to tell which information is useful and which should be discarded. On the other hand, Mercury's role as the Trickster can plague you with missed connections, lost e-mail, and misplaced objects. A simple misspelling gone unnoticed could change the meaning of an entire sentence. It's important to pay attention to all the details so they don't turn things upside down. You have a chance on June 7 to tell someone you love what you really want as retrograde Mercury conjuncts sweet Venus. Just keep in mind that too many words can spoil the message.

SEPTEMBER 23–OCTOBER 15 IN LIBRA: SHARE YOUR IDEAS

In the days proceeding Mercury's turn backward, it slows down enough that both Venus and Mars, the cosmic lovers, catch up and then slide past it. Since Mercury is normally faster than both Venus and Mars, this is quite an unusual event, suggesting that you may put the cart in front of the horse by taking action before thinking about the consequences. It's possible to let your desires get ahead of you so your thought process becomes a cleanup mechanism rather than one of planning. This is the most socially oriented retrograde phase this year, for Libra is the sign of partnership. You can rely on your strong interpersonal skills, but gracious words could come so easily to you now that others might doubt your sincerity. Don't overplay your cards, especially since retrograde Mercury dynamically squares exuberant Jupiter on October 6. It will be easy to say so much that you lose whatever ground you might have gained. Sharing your ideas can turn them into a viable plan, but reserve your best stuff until Mercury direct is well on its way and pushing into new territory by the end of October.

ECLIPSES

Solar and Lunar Eclipses are special New and Full Moons that indicate meaningful changes for individuals and groups. They are powerful markers of events with influences that can appear up to three months in advance and last up to six months afterward. Eclipses occur when the New or Full Moon is conjunct one of the Moon's Nodes, usually in pairs twice a year. Solar Eclipses occur at the New Moon and are visible in unique paths, but not everywhere that the Sun appears in the sky. Locations where the eclipse is visible are more strongly influenced by it. Lunar Eclipses occur during Full Moons and are visible wherever the Moon can be seen.

FEBRUARY 6, SOLAR ECLIPSE IN AQUARIUS: COMMUNITY CONCERNS

A revolutionary point of view can put an end to old fantasies and give birth to new dreams as mental Mercury and idealistic Neptune join the Sun and Moon during this eclipse. Aquarius allows a wide-spectrum view in which we can see our individual lives within the larger context of teams, groups, and community. Chiron, the Wounded Healer, also joins the eclipse point, which can increase compassion globally, give birth to new social organizations, and stir more interest in charitable activities. Charismatic leaders may emerge with fresh ideas for reinvigorating society. But it could be difficult to determine which are capable of bringing about real change and which are simply masters of illusion. Enchanting tales of possibility are likely to be told, but many are simply distractions, clever stories to turn our minds away from the real issues we face. Useful ideas may seem unrealistic at first since Aquarius often paints a picture of an unfamiliar future that requires intellectual adjustment to fully understand. Yet a good idea still has its own logic. The conceptual breakthroughs possible now will make sense to those with open minds and bring inspiration to those with open hearts.

FEBRUARY 20, LUNAR ECLIPSE IN VIRGO: FIX WHAT'S BROKEN

This total eclipse of the Moon in critical Virgo reveals flaws in current systems, regardless of how much effort was put into building them. Serious Saturn conjunct the Moon reflects the hard work invested in the physical and emotional structures that are starting to fail now. A Lunar Eclipse is about letting go of the past, but both the Moon and Saturn are resistant to change. The analytical abilities of Virgo permit us to justify these outmoded patterns with reason and practicality. But the

Pisces Sun in opposition shows that the creative path of faith and imagination will take us farther than roads of duty, obligation, and habit. When daily details drain the joy out of life, it's clear that change is necessary. Yet we may feel the need to choose between a reality that's not fully satisfying and a dream that we fear will never come true. Fortunately, evolutionary Pluto forms a creative 120-degree trine with the eclipse that eliminates nonessential tasks to free up time and energy for more meaningful activities. Instead of getting bogged down worrying about the small stuff, this eclipse is ideal for growing by learning where and how to let go. Leaving an unrewarding job or giving up some petty responsibilities to gain time for artistic or spiritual pursuits is advantageous, as is forgiving yourself and others for the imperfection of being human.

AUGUST 1, SOLAR ECLIPSE IN LEO: CREATIVITY SHINES

Eclipses of the Sun are often associated with the fall of leaders. This one in the Sun's own sign of Leo is visible throughout central Russia and China, where changes at the top are most likely to occur. On a personal level, Solar Eclipses are reminders to tame the ego, to balance will with humility, and to temper external ambition with internal self-care. At its best, Leo is a sign of creative expression and generosity, but at its worst it represents the petulant child demanding every-one's attention. Oppositions to this Sun-Moon conjunction from Neptune and Chiron
add vulnerability and engender the kind of insecurity that may provoke immature behavior. Expect drama, but don't allow it to take over. Instead of giving in to the demands of others or to your own fears, step back and permit the storm to pass. Feeding situations with too much concern about wounded feelings or pride will only prolong the performance. From a positive perspective, this eclipse can bring healing through self-acceptance and recognition that even the biggest stories are only chapters in the book of life. True greatness comes with humility and realizing that talent is borrowed and never owned. When we remember this, the sources of creativity open up and supply us with more than enough to meet our needs.

AUGUST 16, LUNAR ECLIPSE IN AQUARIUS: MAKE NEW FRIENDS

This partial Lunar Eclipse is joined with nebulous Neptune, which could bring floods, fraud, and fakery into the headlines. Otherwise honorable organizations may be touched by scandal or exposed as severely underfunded. Individually, this eclipse is excellent for letting go of beliefs that don't correspond with your current reality. Outdated ideals or dreams may need to be discarded, which can be painful, but awakening to today's truth brings a breath of fresh air that clears clutter from the mind to see the present in a new light. Cooperation is the key with Aquarius, so recognizing where friends and allies are more hindrance than help is important. Compassion for your old companions is admirable, but don't let loyalty keep you attached to someone who drains your energy. You're not required to save those who won't help themselves, especially if they're trying to drag you down with them.

THE BOTTOM LINE

Some years are exceptional because of an extraordinary number of aspects among the outer planets. This year, however, stands out by its lack of apparent activity among the slowest-moving planets. Saturn's tense opposition to Uranus is the only aspect of this type in 2008, and even that doesn't happen until November. But this doesn't indicate a year of peace and quiet. On the contrary, there is much work to be done integrating significant changes from the past few years, dealing with the results of accumulated events, and preparing for what's coming next.

Saturn is often considered to be the most significant marker in determining changes in the astrological climate. Its stabilizing trine to Jupiter, the planet of growth, is a strong indication of the steady gains that can be made this year. If we can keep our feet on the ground while expanding our horizons, then the breakthroughs toward the end of the year can be thoroughly exciting. But the world can be rather unforgiving if we don't maintain a disciplined approach to what's most important, for the Saturn-Uranus opposition on November 4 can be a wake-up call that cannot be ignored.

The best time to prepare for a storm is during a time of calm. On the other hand, it's nearly impossible to begin necessary maintenance while battling with intense waves of change. For this reason, you must pay attention to the most practical aspects of your life and take initiative to make improvements wherever you can. Instead of coasting on your past achievements or just treading water, consider that your efforts this year will pay off in ways you do not yet understand, and it may take a couple of years for you to see the fruits of your current labors.

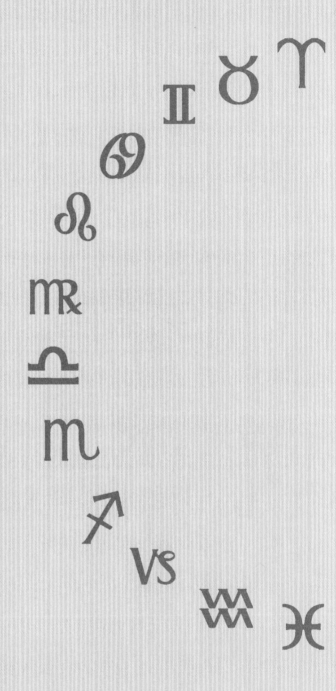

2008

PART 2

ASTROLOGICAL

FORECASTS

ARIES

MARCH 21–APRIL 19

ARIES OVERVIEW

Responsibility is your key word this year, Aries, especially at work. You won't lose your taste for fun and adventure, of course, but getting ahead in measurable ways may distract you from your usual playtime activities. In fact, work could become the new play for you, a form of competition with yourself to see how high you can climb on the ladder of success. **Set your own goals, though, rather than trying to meet those established by someone else.** Your natural independence may lead you to rebel if you feel you're being forced to respond to outside pressure. It's much healthier, and the likelihood of achievement is much higher, when you're motivated by your own desires. Saturn, the planet that makes things real, is in your 6th House of Daily Routines and Service this year. Upgrading your abilities with proper training and discipline is essential. **Developing competence increases confidence and is the best way to get out of a work-related rut.**

Give yourself a little time to get up to speed this year. Mars, your ruling planet, began moving retrograde in mid-November 2007. It stops in its tracks and resumes forward motion on January 30, but doesn't pass its shadow point (the degree where it originally turned retrograde) and regain its normal speed until early April. Patience is more than a virtue; it's a necessity. You're planning for the long term this year with Jupiter, the planet of opportunity and expansion, in ambitious but cautious Capricorn. Each step up should be taken carefully so that you assimilate your gains before pushing ahead to the next level. Demonstrating your ability to manage what you have on your plate earns respect from others and builds faith in yourself. **Although you love surprises and thrive on spontaneity, the challenge ahead of you is to practice self-discipline and pace yourself wisely.**

Powerful Pluto, the slowest-moving body used by astrologers, begins in late January a sixteen-year stay in Capricorn, where it will intensify experiences in your 10th House of Career and Community. Expansive Jupiter in the same area of your chart is bound to energize your desires for greater recognition this year, but Pluto's presence is a reminder that every gift has its price. Power struggles with those in positions of authority are very likely. Your willingness to take orders—which isn't your strong suit anyway—is likely to be reduced and can spur conflict with those who try to control you in any way. You might even encounter rebellion from subordinates who perceive you as a heavy-handed leader. The remedy for the first issue is to commit to changing your work life. A possible solution to the second is to adjust your management style. Either way, the point is to turn discontent into action. **Ignoring problems won't make them disappear, but using the friction they produce to intensify your feelings until you put yourself on a new path is sure to be rewarded.**

IT TAKES A VILLAGE

Your head counts as much as your heart when it comes to love this year. A Solar Eclipse in your 5th House of Romance on August 1 is the signal that simply following your feelings could lead you astray. A little intellectual distance won't kill the flames of desire—in fact, it can cool them just enough to ensure that they will endure. Impulsive emotional leaps can give you that wonderful airborne sensation that makes you feel you can fly, but the crash and burn that follows may not be worth the price. The ideal partner shares your beliefs, values, and a work style allowing you to build a relationship that supports the community as much as it does the two of you. A wide circle of like-minded friends and colleagues weaves a network of connections that will help you maintain a successful union.

CONTROLLED AMBITION

Think big with lucky Jupiter in your 10th House of Career. Ambition should be top priority, but it needs to be matched by careful planning. Set goals and then clearly define the steps you're going to take to reach them. Managing your time and energy is essential to turn a great opportunity into reality. This isn't about an impulsive attempt to change professions or try running a business of your own. It's the central point of a long-term campaign to raise your public profile. You are ready for more responsibility, whether it's in your current field or in a new one. Motivating yourself hasn't been an issue in the past, but the current challenge is to learn how to lead others in a constructive and professional manner.

PROFIT FROM PLAY

You should be able to turn a hobby into a source of income this year. It might not be enough to provide a full-time salary, but your creative talents have the potential to increase your revenues and your self-esteem. Investing in higher-quality equipment and further education in your field of interest is bound to pay off. The key is to do something because you love it rather than just pursuing the money. A small flow of funds that you're able to sustain over a long period of time will bring you much more personal satisfaction than a fast score that you're unlikely to repeat.

PREVENTIVE CARE

Serious Saturn in your 6th House of Health and Habits this year is a reminder to clean up your act. Cut down on the calories, colas, and carbs that clog your system, and load up on all the organic fruits and veggies you can find. Your body requires higher-quality fuel now, but there's no need to eliminate all the goodies you love. Drastic changes aren't likely to last, but a gradual upgrade from white bread to whole wheat is something you can stick to for the rest of your life. Check with a nutritionally oriented health practitioner to learn more about vitamins and minerals. Look for someone who asks plenty of questions instead of a person with a "one size fits all" approach to wellness. You're a unique individual who will be best served by a health care provider who takes the time to get to know you. Exercise is always smart, but there's no need to run marathons or climb Mount Rainier to stay in shape. The goal is to tune and tone yourself with gentler forms of physical activity like yoga or t'ai chi.

HOME IMPROVEMENT

Unfinished business left over from last year is ripe for action when Mars, your ruling planet, returns to your 4th House of Home and Family on March 4. It will remain in this area of your chart until May 9—prime time for making repairs and improvements, as well as dealing with emotional issues involving family members or roommates. Far-reaching Jupiter's opposition to this area of your chart throughout the year promotes family projects that gain public recognition. A well-equipped home office will support your professional ambitions.

FOLLOW YOUR PLAN

Strategic Jupiter, the ruler of your 9th House of Travel and Education, is in studious and ever-practical Capricorn, emphasizing business trips and classes to advance yourself professionally. Structured excursions are likely to work better now than free-flowing flights of fancy. Stick to a schedule, respect local customs, and follow the letter of the law wherever you go. You may be called upon to teach or to share your experiences with others. It's best to work from an outline or curriculum rather than delivering an extemporaneous presentation. If you're the student, pace yourself and complete your work on time—the results of last-minute cramming are likely to be disappointing. Practicing self-discipline this year will bring you more success.

INSIGHT PROMOTES GROWTH

Generous Jupiter forms favorable aspects with inventive Uranus in March, May, and October that can awaken your spiritual awareness with flashes of intuition. Unexpected gifts of insight allow you to recognize larger patterns from your past that give your life a greater sense of meaning. In November, structuring Saturn opposes Uranus to test these ideas against the limitations of your current environment. Frustration is possible when circumstances don't align with your new thinking, but this is the beginning of a process of learning how to apply your knowledge that may not finish until May 2009.

RICK & JEFF'S TIP FOR THE YEAR:
Acheivement Brings Freedom

Raising your public profile will add to the weight on your shoulders, so it's natural to unconsciously resist making yourself more visible. Yet the more you accomplish this year, the more support you will receive. Instead of sensing the burden of responsibility that success often brings, your inner strength will grow with an increasing sense of confidence. This builds your professional foundation, amplifies your power, and provides you with more options. Honest hard work won't slow you down or narrow your choices—it will reward you with greater freedom to create your optimum future.

JANUARY

BUILD FOR TOMORROW

There's unfinished business to complete as the year begins. Mars, your ruling planet, is still moving backward (retrograde) and won't shift into forward gear until **January 30**. Use this time to tie up loose ends and let go of unhealthy habits and unnecessary arrangements that are wearing you down. Issues could come to a head on **January 2** as an opposition between Mars and passionate Pluto pushes you as far as you can go. A tendency to either strike back or totally withdraw can make dialogue impossible. Intense feelings can be destructive or can help bring about transformation if you're able to talk about them without blame or self-recrimination. The ambitious New Moon in Capricorn on **January 8** landing in your 10th House of Career could trigger thoughts of changing your job or even starting your own business. Either of these could turn out to be a good idea—*if* you look and act carefully before you leap.

The first of three creative trines between Jupiter in Capricorn and Saturn in Virgo occurs on **January 21**. These slow-moving aspects in practical earth signs provide perspective and patience regarding work-related matters. The opportunistic vision of Jupiter and the planning skills of Saturn combine to frame out a realistic way to advance your ambitions. The second trine in September brings adjustments to your plan, and the last one in late November seals the deal. If you've done your homework, your future will be more secure. But you can't wait until September to act; the foundation is being laid right now. It's time to be a grown-up. Avoid distractions and set aside short-term desires if they take your attention away from long-term goals.

KEEP IN MIND THIS MONTH

You can't fuel a long journey without emotional nourishment. Despite all the work to be done, some pleasure is essential now if you're going to continue the ambitious pace.

KEY DATES

JANUARY 1-3 ★ *laser intensity*

Mars opposite Pluto on **January 2** starts the year with a growl. Tension strains relationships as power struggles and unresolved issues arouse an urge for fight or flight. Acting out can be volatile—but holding emotions in isn't healthy, either. Find an outlet for physical or mental aggressiveness to turn this turbine of temperament into productive activity. Clean the basement, throw out old papers, and eliminate extraneous activities that keep you from getting to the point. If you have a problem with someone, aim for a positive outcome rather than just venting. The fierceness of feelings can move mountains, but your intentions must be clear and your aim almost perfect to hit the target.

JANUARY 7–8 ★ *practical genius*
Mental Mercury flies into your 11th House of Groups on **January 7** to illuminate your understanding of community and teamwork. Your mind widens to include perspectives outside your own, which fosters cooperation with others. Bright ideas are sparked by friends, colleagues, and perhaps even strangers with offhand comments and unconventional observations. The New Moon in Capricorn on **January 8** is normally a serious affair—like the initiation into a secret society—but this one is spiced up with a brilliant sextile with inventive Uranus. The combination of the Sun and Moon meeting in goal-oriented Capricorn and a favorable alignment to the planet of originality helps you find a fertile place to plant your out-of-the-box ideas.

JANUARY 19–20 ★ *sparks fly*
A Venus-Mars opposition on **January 19** raises social tension, but it could be in a sexy way. The line between testing and teasing, though, can be hard to read, so unless you're on very solid ground with someone, don't be too aggressive. It's fine to take the initiative, but do it with finesse to keep the invitation from seeming like a challenge. The Sun enters intelligent Aquarius on **January 20** and joins Mercury in your 11th House of Friends. You gain status within a group as long as your desire to share is greater than your need to show off.

SUPER NOVA DAYS
JANUARY 28–30 ★ *switching gears*
Mercury the Messenger turns retrograde on **January 28** to begin three weeks of reflection and review. Double-check times and dates for meetings—information is readily lost or misunderstood during this period. Your planet Mars, though, turns direct on **January 30**, which allows you to gain more traction and start moving ahead again in your life. You're ready for a fresh start, as if this is your personal New Year. However, Mercury retrograde reminds you that all the facts aren't in yet, so don't try to make up for lost time by starting too fast.

FEBRUARY

NURTURE YOURSELF

You may still be in recovery mode this month with Mars passing through parts of Gemini previously visited during its recent retrograde cycle—**November 15, 2007–January 30**. Catching up on e-mail and phone calls is on the agenda, especially with Mercury the Communicator now in retrograde until **February 18**. Avoid downloading any more data into your already busy brain, if you can. Heavy activity in your 11th House of Groups and Friends can fill your social calendar and increase your workload. Think carefully before getting involved, no matter how much you want to serve the community, help a friend, or save the world. What begins as a voluntary task can pull you in so deeply that you have a hard time getting out of it. The New Moon in futuristic Aquarius on **February 6** is a Solar Eclipse conjunct imaginative Neptune. A new dream can grow where an old one dies, so don't hang on to a fading hope whose time has come and gone.

The Sun enters your 12th House of Privacy on **February 19**, beginning a month when you may prefer to be alone. Small gatherings are likely to be more comfortable than big ones. A need for more rest and recuperation shows up with a Lunar Eclipse in your 6th House of Health and Work on **February 20**. Demanding Saturn's conjunction to the Moon may reflect added pressures that could wear you down. Don't try to push through this by working harder and hoping fatigue will pass. The message is to lighten the load and pay more attention to your physical well-being. Improving your diet, making more time for exercise, and getting medical care if needed will make you more efficient in the long run.

> **KEEP IN MIND THIS MONTH**
>
> *You're better off skipping a party or two to catch up on sleep or take care of mundane tasks at home. You might be missed, but you won't be forgotten.*

KEY DATES

FEBRUARY 1 ★ *whistle while you work*

A juicy Venus-Jupiter conjunction in your 10th House of Career can earn you recognition and rewards. Your people skills shine because you're able to lead others in a way that makes work feel like play. This is a good time to reach for a job, promotion, or project that sparks your professional interest and increases personal satisfaction.

FEBRUARY 9 ★ *fated attraction*

A strange hookup between Venus and Mars, astrology's lovers, can attract some-one to you under unusual circumstances. You are nervous since you probably don't feel you're in control of the situation. If you can get past your discomfort, just flow with the energy and see where it leads. If you're still anxious, however, get out as quickly and quietly as you can.

SUPER NOVA DAYS
FEBRUARY 13-14 ★ *relationship u-turn*

Tense aspects from Mercury and Venus to your planet Mars make it difficult to feel connected with others on **February 13**. Different goals and values may produce conflict and heated conversation. Avoid pushing, though, because the situation can quickly resolve itself with a creative Sun-Mars trine on **February 14**. The rough edges are smoothed out as anger is transformed into constructive action. Maintain confidence in yourself and Valentine's Day could turn out to be much better than expected.

FEBRUARY 24-25 ★ *a little help from a friend*

February 24 can seem like a somber day with serious Saturn opposing the Sun. You may be worrying about details that you'd normally brush off, but it's hard to set aside your sense of responsibility and even self-doubt. You should be able to handle whatever is on your plate, but taking it on solo isn't much fun. However, a harmonious trine between Mars and the karmically connected Lunar North Node on **February 25** could come to the rescue in the form of a friend or ally who lends a helping hand. You don't even need to ask for support for someone to step in and share the load with you.

FEBRUARY 28 ★ *humor helps*

You have a gift for turning an awkward experience into one that puts people at ease today. A crunchy 135-degree sesquisquare between attractive Venus and active Mars tends to complicate relationships. Yet the Moon in fellow fire sign Sagittarius gives you a feeling of optimism that's suited for finding solutions rather than staying stuck with a problem. If your initial attempts to inject humor into the situation are not met with enthusiasm, don't give up. Your charm and creativity are flowing so well that you will come up with a way to turn frowns into smiles.

MARCH

TIME TO BE TENDER

Mars, your ruling planet, enters the sensitive, protective sign of Cancer on **March 4**. Attention tends to be drawn inward toward personal matters involving home and family. Enhancing your living space can make you feel more comfortable and secure. Create a place that nourishes and inspires your hopes and dreams. You tend to live in the present, Aries, but there are benefits to thinking about the past. Memories, both happy and sad, help you recognize patterns in your life that may have gone unnoticed. Understanding how you've come this far is a great asset for helping you go farther in the future. Now it's time to build a stable foundation by gathering information and networking to advance your career or launch a new business.

The New Moon in dreamy Pisces on **March 7** joins with inventive Uranus in your 12th House of Imagination and awakens original ideas that come out of the blue. Normally, this is just a passing lightning storm that excites the mind but doesn't produce lasting results. Generous Jupiter in enterprising Capricorn, however, supports this event with a practical vision to capture these flashes of insight and apply them strategically in your professional life. The sociable Libra Full Moon on **March 21** opposing the Sun in Aries highlights the contrast between independence and relationships. Intense Pluto and assertive Mars form 90-degree squares to this Sun-Moon opposition that are likely to provoke conflict. Frustration arises when others are too demanding or will not recognize your needs. These complications, though, can deepen a partnership if you're able to face your fears and do the hard work of creating a new balance between sharing and self-sufficiency.

> **KEEP IN MIND THIS MONTH**
>
> *Tune in to your tender spots, instead of pushing your emotions aside. Vulnerability is your strength because it reveals your true feelings.*

KEY DATES

MARCH 7-8 ★ *high intensity*

A potent opposition between Mars and Pluto could set off power struggles on **March 7**. However, it may also help you gain a focus that will allow you to overcome any obstacles. The Sun's union with unpredictable Uranus on **March 8** heightens the explosive mood and makes compromise more difficult. You're probably not inclined to meet others halfway, and might prefer to go it alone. If you need space, it's wiser to admit it rather than fighting to separate yourself from others.

MARCH 14–16 ★ *no sweat*
A healthy sextile between stable Saturn and active Mars on **March 14** is excellent for finding discipline without feeling stifled. There's an easy flow of energy that improves productivity without greater effort on your part. Impatience and anger are tempered by wisdom, allowing you to take on irritating issues with maturity. Sweet delights may come your way on **March 16** as lovely Venus makes a cuddly trine to Mars. This harmonious hookup enhances creativity and brings an easy touch to relationships.

SUPER NOVA DAYS
MARCH 18–21 ★ *speak your peace*
This busy period starts with smarts in action thanks to a positive Mercury-Mars trine on **March 18**. The Sun enters innovative Aries on **March 20**, beginning a new astrological year and reviving your natural enthusiasm. But crosscurrents to the Sun from Pluto and Mars are reminders to apply your force with precision. Impulsiveness breeds resistance from willful individuals who can undermine your efforts. Careful planning and purpose, though, should help you avoid these obstacles. The Full Moon in fair-minded Libra on **March 21** brings unsettled relationship issues out in the open. Use your best diplomatic skills to make your case without adding fuel to the fire.

MARCH 26 ★ *wandering off course*
A wobbly aspect between Mars and spacey Neptune can lead you on a wild goose chase. Retreat before exhausting yourself if you don't feel like you're on solid ground. You may find that artistic, altruistic, and spiritual pursuits are much more fulfilling than practical ones now.

MARCH 30 ★ *make work, not war*
A sharp 90-degree square between the willful Sun and active Mars can readily ignite conflict—a little nudge feels like a giant shove. A positive use of this high-energy aspect is to drive yourself forward on a productive path of your own choosing. You can get an amazing amount of work done when you take the lead and put your shoulder to the wheel. Ignore the distractions of whining co-workers and wimpy bosses. Well-managed passion can earn you respect and produce results mere mortals may never achieve.

APRIL

This is a busy month with the Sun, Mercury, and Venus blasting through your sign. The action starts on **April 2** when communicative Mercury bursts into Aries to fire up your mind with fast conversations and fresh ideas. The inspirational Aries New Moon on **April 5** marks the beginning of an annual cycle for you. This year it's tested by squares from energetic Mars and expansive Jupiter that are likely to push your ambitions to a much higher level. Although overextending yourself to reach the stars can be risky, it's better to create your own challenges than to stand still and spend all your energy protecting the status quo. Your desires can lead you into unfamiliar territory, so seek out experienced companions who can show you the way.

Mercury's entry into earthy Taurus on **April 17** brings a practical turn of mind that helps you find and manage resources more effectively. Some untested ideas may fall by the wayside as you seek tangible results rather than simply speculating about unrealistic possibilities. This pragmatic point of view is strengthened when the Sun enters Taurus and lights up your 2nd House of Money and Possessions on **April 19**. The Full Moon in shrewd Scorpio on **April 20** is another opportunity to discover sources of financial and emotional support. Acknowledging your needs, though, may be a challenge to your independent spirit. But the personal and professional rewards of deeper alliances are well worth the price. Constructive Saturn and potent Pluto in earthy Virgo and Capricorn align favorably with this Full Moon to set the stage for mapping a path to a major accomplishment.

> **KEEP IN MIND THIS MONTH**
>
> *Free your mind, open your imagination, and be creative for the first half of the month before turning your attention to more practical matters.*

KEY DATES

APRIL 2 ★ *keep calm and collected*

Jumping to conclusions can generate conflict with chatty Mercury in your sometimes combative sign. Simple statements of fact may be interpreted as challenges that require rebuttal. A difficult 135-degree aspect from Mars to the Moon's North Node adds an edge of competitiveness as well. Keep a cool head to deliver your innovative ideas in nonthreatening ways that invite dialogue instead of distrust.

APRIL 6 ★ *pleasure first*

Venus, the planet of love and pleasure, enters your sign on **April 6** to cast you in a more attractive light. Freshen up your appearance with a different look, and don't settle for the same old same old when it comes to romance. It's better to be pushy than passive, so put passion before politeness and make your desires known. If you rub someone the wrong way, a few apologetic words could make them purr. Keep them smiling and you can get away with just about anything.

APRIL 10 ★ *high-speed speech*

Your tongue is sharpened by a Mercury-Mars square that's a major asset for helping you make a point. Quick thinking allows you to come up with off-the-cuff answers that just might work. But verbal sparring is also possible now, with every comment sparking a comeback—some witty, some not. It's great to be clever, yet cutting remarks can damage a relationship if you're not careful where you aim them. Combine kindness with thoughtfulness to reduce the friction that turns words into weapons. Put the power of your mind into creative messages that motivate people instead of tearing them down.

APRIL 13–15 ★ *stay within the lines*

"Go for it" Mars bounces off Saturn, the planetary stop sign, in a testy 45-degree angle. This semisquare leaves little room for error and brings quick correction or punishment for any sloppiness of thought or deed. Stick to one task at a time— concentrated efforts produce powerful results that will help you overcome even the most daunting obstacles.

SUPER NOVA DAYS
APRIL 22–24 ★ *power to spare*

A cooperative trine between Mars and inventive Uranus on **April 22** sparks creativity that inspires you to do something you've never done before. A Venus-Mars square on **April 23** can bring the kind of clashes that excite as much as they irritate. You're easily annoyed if the wrong person teases you, but it could feel flirtatiously playful from someone you like. A high-octane Mars-Jupiter opposition on **April 24** makes everything bigger than life. You've got the power to sell your ideas with passion and back them up with action. But don't promise more than you can deliver if desire jumps too far ahead of common sense.

MAY

DELUGE OF DATA

Communication is your key to success this month as three planets enter jumping Gemini in your 3rd House of Information. Ideas start popping and data moves faster when Mercury hops into the sign of the Twins on **May 2**. Manage your messages to keep papers from piling up and your e-mail box from overflowing. Your mind is readily fascinated by so many subjects that you can lose track of your priorities. Just say no to gossip, stories, classes, and conversations that can't be applied to your major goals. The New Moon in determined Taurus on **May 5** enriches your 2nd House of Resources with a greater appreciation of your self-worth and plans for increasing your income. This isn't about a quick financial fix; instead, it can mark the beginning of steady progress toward greater prosperity.

Bountiful Jupiter turns retrograde in your 10th House of Career on **May 9** while your ruling planet, Mars, enters fiery Leo. The first event is a slow-moving shift that requires a more strategic approach to professional matters. The second, though, raises your confidence and willingness to take risks. It is appropriate to make bold presentations that are bound to impress people now. However, the full benefits of your performance may take months to impact your job. There's a fuzzy Full Moon in willful Scorpio on **May 19** that could incite some relationship confusion. This passionate event can push you past the bounds of reason or confront you with the irrational feelings of a trusted friend. Imprecise and imaginative Neptune's tense square to this Sun-Moon opposition blurs lines and skews judgment when it comes to intimacy and investments. What you see and feel may not necessarily be what you get.

> **KEEP IN MIND THIS MONTH**
>
> *Words alone don't equal commitment, so consider what you hear this month as interesting information rather than a solemn promise.*

KEY DATES

MAY 2–3 ★ *unfree speech*
Mercury's entry into curious Gemini on **May 2** should put more information on your plate, but tense aspects to this planet on **May 3** can complicate conversations. A quirky quincunx with Pluto and hard square to Saturn can undermine trust and stop a discussion cold. Others may be unwilling to reveal their feelings—and you, too, could be reluctant to relax and share openly. Patience is critical now, since pushing for answers will only raise resistance.

MAY 9-11 ★ *playing with fire*

Mars's entry into outgoing Leo on **May 9** should unleash your personality with even more punch than usual. Its movement into your 5th House of Romance is another reason to expect life to become more pleasurable now. But first you have to make it through an irritating quincunx between your ruling planet and Pluto on **May 11** that is more about crossing swords than opening hearts. Pride can be wounded, and passionate feelings are easily misinterpreted. If a nerve is touched, proceed gently to avoid deepening a wound.

MAY 18-20 ★ *living with luxury*

A highly active Venus can spice up your social life and stir an urge to splurge. On **May 18**, a lovely trine with Jupiter brings a feeling of luxury that invites you to indulge your senses. A clever quintile between Venus and Mars on **May 19**, though, helps you weave together loose ends in relationship and financial matters. However, a square between Venus and Neptune on **May 20** tends to put fantasy before facts. This aspect can be inspiring, but check your budget before investing your emotions or cash.

MAY 22 ★ *off the beaten track*

An edgy sesquisquare between active Mars and eccentric Uranus can be brilliant and inventive, but it has an impulsive and rebellious tendency as well. This is useful for finding methods that work outside the usual rules, yet can make following them much more difficult. It's easy to become irritated by an overly strict or cautious person, so avoid confrontations if possible.

MAY 26 ★ *delayed gratification*

Mercury and Neptune turn retrograde while Venus forms a punishing square to demanding Saturn. The backward cycle of communicative Mercury lasts until **June 15** and is an excellent time to reconnect with people from your past. Spiritual Neptune's five-month retrograde period is more subtle, gently waking dreams and ideals from within. The Venus-Saturn square, though, can manifest as a sudden shortfall in resources or an isolating social barrier. Restraining your desire for immediate answers can prove to others that you deserve their respect. Show your self-confidence with a willingness to work hard now for rewards that will come later.

JUNE

LIFE IN MOTION

Expect your enthusiasm to be rekindled by high-energy astrological events this month. The fun starts on **June 2** when the clever Gemini New Moon makes a free-flowing 60-degree sextile with your key planet, Mars. The sharp ideas spawned by this mentally active air sign are readily turned into action by Mars in creative Leo. Conversation comes easily, and meeting new people is a breeze. You're feeling more relaxed and playful, able to tease and be teased with grace and wit. Mercury, the communication specialist, is still moving backward, which usually produces mix-ups and mechanical breakdowns, so don't rely too heavily on any new information until it turns direct on **June 19**. Transformative Pluto backs into fellow fire sign Sagittarius on **June 13** for one last visit before reentering Capricorn in late November. This gives you one more chance to dig up hidden resources, purge old habits, and increase your power and potency.

The inspirational Sagittarius Full Moon on **June 18** brews up stimulating concepts and initiates an itch to travel. Expanding your horizons becomes a growing need, especially with Mars in an optimistic trine to the Full Moon. This can be a very playful time, as you're filled with anticipation about your next adventure. There is a countercurrent, though, when the Sun enters sensitive Cancer on **June 21**. This security-conscious water sign occupies your 4th House of Foundations, which could leave you feeling torn between the safety of familiar people and places and the desire for new experiences. Bring your well-tested values with you when you step out into the world. When at home, enliven your household with radical ideas, an exotic style, and a spirit of tolerance.

> **KEEP IN MIND THIS MONTH**
>
> *The excitement level is high, so turn down the volume just a bit to maintain control of all the energy you're feeling now.*

KEY DATES

SUPER NOVA DAYS
JUNE 4–6 ★ *creative momentum*
A friction-free sextile between the energetic Sun and initiating Mars on **June 4** is excellent for taking the lead without appearing as if you're taking over. You know how to motivate others, but you're capable of being very productive on

your own as well. Your creativity is high, and your charisma can light up a room. More control is required on **June 6** when Pluto's sesquisquare to Mars demands intense focus. You can be extremely efficient, especially when finishing up old business, as long as you concentrate on the task at hand without letting minor irritations escalate into full-scale combat.

JUNE 14-15 ★ *off the map*
This could feel like a lost weekend if you're pulled into someone else's world, exhausting your supply of time and energy. Mars on the karmic South Node on **June 14** suggests that lending a hand works best if you set some limits and stick to them. A Mars-Jupiter quincunx on **June 15** can also be inefficient, taking you on a wild goose chase of investing more and more effort with less and less in return. When you're off course, don't keep going in the same direction.

JUNE 18 ★ *erratic energies*
A Mars-Uranus quincunx provokes impulsive behavior that you might regret. It can be thrilling to be moving so fast—physically, mentally, or emotionally—but carelessness can spark a reaction that shakes you up. Find a safe outlet where you can blow off steam, rather than aiming at another person. Put your passion into playful activities where breaking the rules has no serious consequences.

JUNE 21 ★ *gentle persuasion*
A Mars-Neptune opposition is excellent for acting with compassion and imagination. Your touch is more sensitive, allowing you to advance your interests in subtle and delicate ways. However, if you force issues, or act under pressure, it's easy to exhaust yourself. Attending to the needs of others reflects your highest ideals, but it's no reason to lose your objectivity or common sense. You're vulnerable, too, and this isn't a sign of weakness but a sweet expression of your tenderness.

JUNE 29 ★ *satify yourself*
Mars in bold and brassy Leo makes a tight semisquare to Venus in cozy and quiet Cancer. Managing relationships can be complicated by this mix of strong and soft. Finding a comfortable groove you can stay in with someone could be challenging. Instead of trying to win approval or make others happy, start by checking in with yourself to know where you stand. When you're tuned in to your own needs, your solid foundation gives you the strength and flexibility to deal with others.

JULY

WORK HARD, PLAY HARD

Strive for excellence this month while contrasting planetary trends are such a powerful motivation. On **July 1**, Mars—your ruling planet—enters perfectionist Virgo, which adds discipline and focus to every task. Additional training and practice upgrade your skills and enhance the value of your work. Take the time to hone your talents to their highest levels rather than racing through your duties in a haphazard manner. The extra attention necessary to refine your methods will pay dividends in the long run. The New Moon in cautious Cancer on **July 2** and the Full Moon in practical Capricorn on **July 18** place security at the top of your to-do list at home and in your career. But if your approach to making your life safer is primarily motivated by fear, you could be limiting your chances for success. You're a fire sign, and you need sparks of excitement to sustain your interest in any lengthy process. Fortunately, it looks like those will be plentiful this month, too.

Three planets enter expressive Leo to encourage the playful side of your personality. Vivacious Venus moves into the Lion's sign on **July 12** to add some glamour to your life. Its passage through your 5th House of Romance, Children, and Creativity brings you more passion and enthusiasm in these areas. The Sun entering Leo on **July 22** engenders self-confidence that comes as much from the joy you feel as the abilities you're ready to show off. You can also expect to be bolder and braver when it comes to matters of the heart. Finally, mental Mercury joins the party on **July 26**, fueling your mind with fire that allows you to express your desires and sell your ideas with a greater degree of enthusiasm.

> **KEEP IN MIND THIS MONTH**
>
> *Great joy and hard work make excellent allies this month, so don't separate them into two separate categories of experience now.*

KEY DATES

JULY 1 ★ *tighten up*

Mars entering exacting Virgo spurs greater efficiency. Increase your physical and mental energy with a healthier diet and sensible exercise routine. No matter how great your talents, humbly accept that there's more for you to learn to maximize the return on your gifts. Taking one smart step backward to eliminate harmful habits will put you twenty paces ahead down the road.

JULY 6 ★ *managed growth*
A difficult-to-manage sesquisquare between active Mars and exuberant Jupiter tends to lead to overreaching today. Instead of doing all the work yourself, obtain support from others to lighten the load. If you're going to achieve your objectives now, strong leadership skills will make all the difference.

JULY 9–11 ★ *strategic strength*
An opposition between mobile Mars and stable Saturn on **July 10** presents you with clear-cut obstacles. If you resist, struggle persists and increases your frustration. But well-planned actions executed with patience and precision will produce lasting positive results. Play by the rules now, since you're likely to be caught if you make any questionable moves.

JULY 15–16 ★ *easy to fix*
Analytical Mercury and assertive Mars line up in a cooperative sextile on **July 15**. Insights and actions work well together to resolve small problems with ease. Emotional issues can be discussed with a high degree of self-control and sensitivity, allowing you to make a difficult point without adding fuel to the fire.

JULY 22 ★ *its showtime*
The Sun begins a month-long stay in your 5th House of Self-Expression, providing you with an excellent source of energy for creative projects. This is positive for opening up your heart and inviting in romance. It also awakens a spirit of play that helps you enjoy the company of children. You're ready for the spotlight. Step out and perform with a sense of pride that expresses your personality and talent.

SUPER NOVA DAYS
JULY 25–27 ★ *proud ambitions*
Mercury's entry into dramatic Leo on **July 26** infuses you with imaginative ideas and the confidence to express them boldly. However, an edgy 45-degree semisquare from the communication planet to Mars could incite verbal combat. Stubborn thinking can bog you down in a debate that no one wins. Work around differences of opinion now, if you can, to avoid wasting time. An optimistic trine between Mars and Jupiter encourages you to be overly ambitious. This enterprising aspect in practical earth signs should bring you the perfect blend of vision and execution that makes it possible to start turning an inspiring dream into reality.

AUGUST

MEET OTHERS HALFWAY

A Solar Eclipse on **August 1** in your lighthearted 5th House of Romance and Children indicates change in a personal way. If you let your emotions propel you forward without fully considering their impact on others, you're likely to receive feedback that alters your course of action. This new perspective may nudge you off stride at first, but it can also show you even more rewarding ways to express your creativity. Excessive pride can be a barrier to accepting this new information, but taking a step down now can reveal a path that will take you much higher later. A Lunar Eclipse in detached Aquarius on **August 16** unravels patterns with friends and groups that no longer suit your purpose. This event might express itself in distancing yourself from an old pal, or withdrawing from a team. However, its deeper meaning becomes apparent when you reconsider the way you fit into an organization and how you may need to change your position or your approach.

Mars crosses paths with potent Pluto on **August 17**, which often provokes power struggles. A situation may come to a boiling point, but the message of the eclipse and Mars's sign change on **August 18** is to maintain your cool demeanor rather than blowing your top. With your ruling planet entering airy Libra, it's clear that diplomacy is wiser than conflict. Mars's six-week stay in the sign of compromise and negotiation runs counter to your preferred "act first, explain later" way of dealing with people. This is a time when listening attentively helps you understand others' needs and expectations so that you can respond with fairness and kindness. The rewards include greater harmony through cooperation and more trust and intimacy in relationships.

> **KEEP IN MIND THIS MONTH**
>
> *Plan several moves ahead, like a good chess player, so that you can quickly adjust your reactions according to the changing circumstances.*

KEY DATES

AUGUST 1 ★ *true character*

Weekend plans may be eclipsed by last-minute events that require your attention. Be as generous as you can in responding to the needs of others, regardless of how inconvenient it can be for you. Demonstrating the quality of your character and the goodness of your heart is more important than just having a good time.

AUGUST 6-9 ★ *out of control*

An opposition between fiery Mars and electric Uranus on **August 6** is an explosive aspect, one that tends to shorten tempers and encourage impulsive actions. Turn your excess energy in a creative direction, though, and you can discover brilliant new ways to solve problems. Mars and Neptune form a quincunx on **August 8**, which can send you on a wild fantasy ride. Nebulous Neptune makes it nearly impossible for Mars to hit its target, so avoid wasting time if you're pushing without getting results.

SUPER NOVA DAYS
AUGUST 16-19 ★ *war and peace*

A Full Moon Eclipse on **August 16**, followed by an intense Mars-Pluto square on **August 17**, can be a call to battle as resentment urges you to take action. Avoid an exhausting struggle by aiming your passion with precision. A clear purpose and tight focus empower you to make a significant breakthrough. A fresh start is possible on **August 19** when Mars enters peace-loving Libra in your 7th House of Partnerships. Putting ongoing relationships on a different track or beginning new ones is in order now. This is also a good time to make a proposal or introduce a novel idea. A stylish appearance and a gracious attitude allow you to be more persuasive than ever.

AUGUST 23-24 ★ *keep it real*

Awkward sesquisquares from Mars to Chiron on **August 23** and the North Node on **August 24** may complicate your connections with others. You're likely to feel more vulnerable than usual, but it's your tendency to either keep going or disappear rather than admitting weakness or fatigue. Grumpiness is a sign that you need a break, so ask for one instead of carrying a burden that's too heavy for you now.

AUGUST 30 ★ *take it easy*

An efficient Virgo New Moon conjunct responsible Saturn in your 6th House of Work today indicates your need to take care of business. But Mars likes to be direct and Neptune lacks focus, so their clunky 135-degree aspect could divert you from your goals. Don't be too hard on yourself if you don't get as much accomplished as you wish. Give yourself a chance to escape the pressures of reality so that you're ready to take on life with renewed vigor over the days ahead.

SEPTEMBER

DEFINE YOUR GOALS

Work issues require extra attention this month. You might decide to do your current job differently or to map out a strategy for a major career shift. The energizing Sun crosses disciplined Saturn in the 6th House of Work on **September 3** and forms a hopeful trine with farsighted Jupiter in the 10th House of Career on **September 4**. Bumping up against limits with the first aspect can motivate you to create a wider view of your future with the second. Optimistic Jupiter turns direct in your 10th House on **September 7** while pushed by a forceful square from Mars, a combination that's bound to spur your ambitions. The exact trine of Jupiter and Saturn on **September 8** helps you balance high hopes and realism to develop an effective plan for advancing your public image. The higher you aim, the more precise you must be to ensure that this first step will support your aspirations.

The Full Moon in watery Pisces on **September 15** falls in your 12th House of Imagination, where it inspires spiritual insights and intuitive awareness. Let these flashes settle before making any sudden changes like quitting your job, moving to India, and joining an ashram. Impulsive Uranus's presence at this highly emotional moment can be so electrifying that you might want to radically alter your life overnight. The best ideas, though, will stand the test of time and should be applied with the care your future deserves. The Sun enters airy Libra and your 7th House of Partnerships on **September 22**, followed by the Libra New Moon on **September 29**. Working in tandem with others is high priority now, but it may require some give-and-take to overcome differences before learning to function together harmoniously.

> **KEEP IN MIND THIS MONTH**
>
> *Focus on what you are trying to accomplish rather than on your shortcomings to best overcome any self-doubt and ultimately reach your objective.*

KEY DATES

SEPTEMBER 7–8 ★ *push comes to shove*

A high-energy square between Mars and Jupiter on **September 7** gets your temperature rising. Major conflict can grow out of a minor issue, so tame the flames of your aggression if you want to avoid a fight. On the positive side, these punchy planets give you the courage to knock on doors and ask for what you want, even if you were previously refused. Chatty Mercury enters the picture on **September 8** with a conjunction to Mars that sets your mind on fire with progressive ideas and assertive conversation. The capacity to sell yourself and your ideas grows even stronger, but avoid being overly insistent if you encounter opposition.

SEPTEMBER 11–12 ★ *a charmed life*

A sweet and sassy conjunction between Venus and Mars late on **September 11** should spice up your social life. You have charm to spare and can be a magnet for creative, attractive people who turn work into play and bring more joy into your life. This is a good time to make peace with someone if a relationship has become less friendly of late. Even an old enemy may come on over to your side if you take the initiative to resolve your issues with an open mind and heart. Romance is possible and pleasure is virtually guaranteed when you slow down to enjoy the many delights available to you now.

SEPTEMBER 16 ★ *easily efficient*

Cooperation comes easily today, with active Mars aligning in a helpful trine with the North Node. You know which buttons to push to get others moving in the right direction without ruffling their feathers. Support comes to you from an unexpected source without you having to ask for it.

SUPER NOVA DAYS
SEPTEMBER 21–24 ★ *cooperation is key*

Mars trines spiritual Neptune on **September 21**, blessing you with a gentle touch and an ardent desire to serve others. This is excellent for the kind of creative work that lets you use your imagination and stand up for those who can't defend themselves. The Sun enters peace-loving Libra, marking the first day of fall, and lights up your 7th House of Relationships on **September 22**. This shift of seasons is likely to open doors to new connections in your personal and public lives. There's a greater focus on sharing, caring, and compromising now that might inhibit your freedom to act independently. But fair exchanges with gifted associates are well worth the price. On **September 23**, Mercury joins Mars again—the previous time was on **September 8**—just before turning retrograde the very next day. Avoid the temptation to get in the last word unless it's one of encouragement.

OCTOBER

ALL OR NOTHING

A more intense approach to relationships—and just about everything else—can be expected this month as your planet Mars sextiles Pluto on **October 2** and then plunges into Scorpio on **October 4**. It's time to cut the fat by eliminating people and activities that aren't fulfilling your needs. If you're unwilling to let go, you are likely to encounter individuals who force you to make tough choices anyway. Halfway measures won't suffice, so dig in and decide where you're going to invest your energy and where to pull back. When you focus on one task or one person, you can reach levels of fulfillment you haven't previously known. If you lack direction, the Full Moon in Aries on **October 14** will get your attention and open your eyes to where changes are needed. Communicative Mercury turns direct in your 7th House of Partnerships on **October 15**, which helps you discuss issues objectively with those close to you and reach out and make new connections.

Pleasure-seeking Venus enters fiery Sagittarius in your 9th House of Faraway Places on **October 18**. This lights up your sense of adventure, increases your desire to travel, and spurs interest in people from different cultures. The extroverted side of your personality will be appreciated now, and enthusiasm valued even more than precision. Express yourself openly and you will be especially appealing as a companion. Still, the Sun enters calculating Scorpio on **October 22** to join Mars in your 8th House of Intimacy and Shared Resources. This is a reminder to temper your spontaneity with a greater awareness of the interests of others. Acknowledge their gifts and respect their limits to create rewarding and enduring alliances.

> **KEEP IN MIND THIS MONTH**
>
> *An attitude of guarded optimism helps you sustain the necessary excitement to motivate yourself while working within the limitations of those around you.*

KEY DATES

OCTOBER 5–6 ⋆ *obstacle course*

You could feel trapped or slowed down on **October 5**, when restrictive Saturn forms a troubling semisquare with self-directed Mars. Concentrated effort is required to continue on your present course—but if the barriers are too high, consider changing your plans. On **October 6**, however, Mars and visionary Jupiter align in an inventive quintile that is ideal for coming up with unconventional solutions. So if you don't force an issue on Sunday, you may resolve it brilliantly on Monday.

OCTOBER 10 ★ *jumping the gun*
Mars and Uranus rattle your cage with an anxious sesquisquare that can all too readily trigger impulsive behavior. A desire for total freedom may stir rebellious acts more likely to increase tension than reduce it. It is fun to defy authority, but the cost of a moment's pleasure may be more than you really want to pay. Electricity is running through your system now that can be discharged with physical activity or creatively applied to solving problems. Take appropriate safety precautions if there's any danger involved.

OCTOBER 14 ★ *awakening awareness*
Today's Full Moon in your sign can be an "aha" moment, allowing you to suddenly grasp a pattern in relationships that you never previously noticed. The gap between attending to your own interests and responding to the needs of others may not be as great as you believed. Recognizing that it's totally appropriate to want both freedom and intimacy makes it easier to gracefully move from independence to partnership.

OCTOBER 24–26 ★ *chill out*
Mars forms a tough semisquare with "take no prisoners" Pluto on **October 24** that can escalate a small dispute into total warfare. Back off before one of you goes too far. Focus solely on the issue at hand rather than bringing up problems from the past, if you prefer resolution to conflict. Aggressive Mars forms a tense square to the Moon's Nodes on **October 26** that continues this potentially contentious theme. The message, therefore, is the same: Stay calm unless you want to fight. What feels like a provocation may be a needed wake-up call rather than an attack.

SUPER NOVA DAYS
OCTOBER 27–31 ★ *easy production*
Active Mars cruises comfortably between lucky Jupiter and karmic Saturn's trine by forming intelligent sextiles with the former on **October 27** and the latter on **October 30**. This is a highly efficient alignment during which your present efforts have an excellent chance of producing positive long-term results. You have the right balance between optimism and realism that allows you to work well on your own or with others. A Mars-Uranus trine on **October 31** ends your month with a brilliant twist.

NOVEMBER

SHAPE YOUR FUTURE

Three significant aspects among slow-moving outer planets make this a major month of transition. The effect of each one lasts for weeks, but the most noticeable events are likely to occur close to the peak dates given here. On **November 4**, structured Saturn, in your 6th House of Work, forms the first of three powerful oppositions to liberating Uranus in your 12th House of Destiny. Tension between responsibility and freedom may cause you to rebel against the boredom of your daily routine. Short-term crises can trigger flight from a job or a breakdown in discipline. If you seek meaningful change, slow down and plan an escape route that will lead you to a more manageable and spiritual life. This is just the first stage of a process that finishes in **September 2009**, so there's no need to take the leap before you clear a place to land.

Open-minded Jupiter, moving through your 10th House of Career, sextiles Uranus on **November 13**, enlightening your mind with an exciting image of the future. Optimism grows from an unexpected opportunity or a surprising vision of a more fulfilling professional life. A Taurus Full Moon in your 2nd House of Resources on the same day seeds your imagination with money-making ideas. Motivated Mars entering fellow fire sign Sagittarius on **November 16** gives you the energy to turn ideas into action. The shape of things to come is clearly outlined with the last of a series of creative trines between Jupiter and Saturn on **November 21**. The philosophical Sagittarius New Moon on **November 27** in your 9th House of Higher Education presents a learning opportunity or a chance to discover the world. The meaning of your life comes into clear focus, increasing your confidence and solidifying your commitment to achieving your goals.

KEEP IN MIND THIS MONTH

A conscious connection between purpose and possibility makes it easy for you to find and follow your star.

KEY DATES

NOVEMBER 3 ★ *healthy skepticism*

This busy day adds a spacey Mars-Neptune square and Mercury's entrance into intense Scorpio to the peaking Saturn-Uranus opposition. You may be asked to take on more responsibilities, but the cause is right and you have an exit strategy. Chatty Mercury turns highly persuasive in your 8th House of Intimacy. This is great for serious business or sex talk—as long as you keep your wits sharp.

NOVEMBER 12–13 ★ *altering alliances*

Vivacious Venus joins potent Pluto early on **November 12** before entering ethical Capricorn in your 10th House. A previous agreement about work may need to be renegotiated. The mind-expanding Jupiter-Uranus sextile on **November 13** changes everything, and you don't want to miss a great opportunity just to demonstrate your loyalty. A Sun-Neptune square symbolizes a charismatic person with unrealistic views, so if you're going to sacrifice yourself for a dream, do it for your own—not someone else's.

NOVEMBER 16 ★ *walk your talk*

Your ruling planet, Mars, fires into Sagittarius, where your natural enthusiasm reaches an extreme. Restlessness breeds urges to travel, expand your mind, and leave your present life behind. You are a powerful presenter of ideas and principles, making you a good teacher and salesperson. But now the only customer who truly counts is you. If you believe in something, don't just talk about it; do it.

SUPER NOVA DAYS
NOVEMBER 21–24 ★ *ready for launch*

The final Jupiter-Saturn trine on **November 21** is fueled by the creative Sun's entry into Sagittarius that same day. You are ready to commit to expanding your life. The meaning is clear, purpose is present, and there's no holding you back. Mercury moves into the sign of the Archer on **November 23**, giving you the fire of conviction and the art of persuasion to help you explain your mission. Your mind is made up and you're not interested in compromising now. Yet an overactive Mars-Jupiter semisquare on **November 24** can have you firing lightning bolts at innocent parties or spending your energy foolishly. Aim your passion carefully to advance your cause, instead of carelessly alienating others.

NOVEMBER 27–28 ★ *power of words*

The Sagittarius New Moon on **November 27**, conjunct verbal Mercury and impatient Mars, makes for fast thinking and forceful talking. Ideas burn so brightly that you may present them without considering the capacity of your audience, overwhelming individuals who aren't up to your speed. Warm up your listeners with some lightweight material before you break out the heavy artillery. Once you hone in on your target, then you can fire away more effectively.

DECEMBER

The year finishes with a powerful push that propels you full speed ahead into 2009. The action kicks off with an assertive Sun-Mars conjunction on **December 5**. Your enthusiasm can overwhelm the fainthearted or instigate arguments unless you have a constructive place to put excess mental and physical energy. A gentler cooling trend is initiated by sociable Venus's entry into friendly Aquarius on **December 7**. Cooperative friends remind you that you don't have to carry the load alone, but your instinct to act first and ask questions later may cause you to zoom right past people ready to lend you a hand. The Full Moon in high-strung Gemini on **December 12** can be extra intense as nervous energy pushes conversations beyond safe boundaries. Thoughtless words and sudden shifts of mood can detonate relationships. Pent-up feelings could explode if you feel too constrained. When you sense tension rising, step back and calm down before confronting its source.

The Sun's entrance into earthy Capricorn marks the Winter Solstice on **December 21**, setting traditional and practical matters on the table. Its passage through your 10th House of Public Status through the end of the year places you in a leadership position, whether you want it or not. The pressures of the season are further intensified by a Sun-Pluto conjunction on **December 22**. Repressed feelings can erupt from deep within, provoking power struggles. If you sense too much pressure to perform, ask for assistance before you harbor resentment or your frustration explodes, dampening the holiday mood. Mars enters practical Capricorn on **December 27** and along with the transformational New Moon could energize you to take the next step into your future.

> **KEEP IN MIND THIS MONTH**
>
> *Concentrate on one task at a time to avoid the potential for overextension. Invest your energy in building your confidence rather than tearing others down.*

KEY DATES

DECEMBER 5 ★ *self-direction*

Today could be fabulous or a fiasco, depending on what you do with it. The punchy Sun-Mars conjunction in your 9th House of Adventure is ideal for promoting a cause, hiking a mountain, or dancing until two in the morning. But without a healthy outlet for the fire you feel inside, you may strike out in anger or battle someone in authority. The key is to take charge of your life, even if it means temporarily abandoning others to direct your passion with play-fulness or for a higher purpose.

DECEMBER 11–12 ★ *risky business*
A Mars-Uranus square on the morning of **December 12** tightens your nerves like coiled springs. You are likely to burst with the energetic Gemini Full Moon opposing Mars, lifting emotional tides to a new height. Your newfound power can help you leap over obstacles with inventive moves no one's ever seen before. Yet the nar-rowing effects of a Sun-Saturn square, along with Mercury's entry into unforgiving Capricorn, leave little room for error. Be cautious unless you're certain that your bold actions will succeed.

DECEMBER 15–16 ★ *follow the rules*
Your planet, Mars, could run you into a wall of resistance on **December 15** with its tough square to demanding Saturn. Act within well-defined rules, however, and you can build a foundation that's likely to last. The pressure is off on **December 16** as Mars cozies up in a sweet sextile to imaginative Neptune, telling you to trust your intuition and improvise rather than following rigid guidelines.

DECEMBER 21–22 ★ *lighten your load*
The Sun enters ambitious Capricorn on **December 21** and sheds more light on your 10th House of Career and Community. Your intense drive for accomplishment will carry you well into the next year, yet a powerful conjunction between the Sun and Pluto on **December 22** reveals a need to eliminate outmoded responsibilities before taking on new ones. Pluto's potency can help you punch through to a higher level of success if you're willing to transform your public image and let go of act-ivities that distract you from reaching your goals.

SUPER NOVA DAYS
DECEMBER 27–28 ★ *power play*
A cautious Capricorn New Moon on **December 27** reflects your need to be serious, even during the festive holidays. Mars enters Capricorn the same day and joins penetrating Pluto on **December 28**. Your need for efficiency makes it easy to overlook how your actions might be affecting others. While you can be incredibly productive, burning bridges as you go might not be the best way to advance your interests. Additionally, a Venus-Neptune conjunction in your 11th House of Friends sweetens these days with spirituality and love.

TAURUS

APRIL 20–MAY 20

TAURUS OVERVIEW

Your world may be a kinder and gentler one this year, allowing you the time to appreciate what you have already created in your life. Of course there are still challenging issues to face on both a personal and global level, but at last you can reconsider goals you may have previously put aside. **It's a year of slow and steady progress that can set the stage for a long time to come.** The last couple of years have been rather stressful as Saturn the Tester tensely squared your sun sign from July 2005 to September 2007. If you met the tough resistance with your own unyielding determination, you may have overcome obstacles by making critical choices that reaffirmed the overall direction of your life. **Keep working hard and you should be able to enjoy the fruits of your labor throughout 2008.** If you experienced major setbacks, however, you might have had to start all over again, struggling to regain your lost stability. Now it's time to pick up the broken pieces and get yourself back on the right track, for karmic Saturn is harmoniously trining your Sun sign all year. Saturn is well known for delaying success, but it also rewards long-term planning and a serious routine.

Taurus is a fixed earth sign, so your emotional security depends upon having your basic needs met. Still, you seek pleasures beyond simple food and shelter. You may have a penchant for quality clothing and linens, comfortable furnishings, a nice car, good music, or fine wine. **It will be easier to satisfy your material desires now that the outer planet emphasis has shifted into the practical element of earth.** Expansive Jupiter spends the entire year in "achievement oriented" Capricorn, helping you to be realistic while considering opportunities for advancement. Solid Saturn is in earthy Virgo for a two-year visit, bestowing you with increased patience and efficiency. Even slow-moving Pluto enters Capricorn, starting a profound sixteen-year transformation of the beliefs that guide your biggest decisions. Accept the good news that these planets bring, for the cosmic energy is working with you this year and not against you.

The regulators, Jupiter and Saturn, form harmonious trines with each other throughout the year exact on January 21, September 8, and November 21. If possible, make your most important decisions around these times. Beneficent Jupiter in your 9th House of Learning supports originality and breakthroughs as it sextiles electric Uranus on March 28, May 21, and November 12, making this a great time to enroll in an unconventional course of study. The stabilizing resistance of Saturn gives way to a sudden awakening brought to you by Uranus as these two giant planets form the first of three oppositions on November 4, with the following two in 2009. **November may be the most dynamic month this year** as Jupiter, Saturn, and Uranus all pass through a series of mutual aspects, bringing the year to an early culmination while setting the tone for 2009.

SIMPLE PLEASURES

Your key planet, Venus, reveals the changing dynamics of your heart, yet the consistent message this year is one of security and integrity. If everything feels right, be ready to make that special commitment when loving Venus harmonizes with mature Saturn and opulent Jupiter from January 29 to February 1. A sensible approach to love will rule in the spring, especially when Venus enters your sign on April 30 and continues to stabilize your love life through mid-May. Your attractions become a bit more fragmented in June and July, but settle down again when Venus enters earthy Virgo on August 6. Do whatever you can to create harmony in your relationships in early September, for these efforts will have lasting impact. Excitement and uncertainty in mid-October turn into serious challenges by early November. But love will be easier to manage after November 12, when Venus enters Capricorn, creating the way for another long and lovely cycle of satisfaction.

STEADY PROGRESS

It's likely that you received a healthy dose of reality last year as somber Saturn opposed idealistic Neptune, continuing its long journey through your 10th House of Career. Now that the struggle between your dreams and life's limitations is subsiding, you must get on with the tasks at hand. Although you may feel more comfortable in your present work environment than you have in the past, it's essential to play your hand with intelligence and determination while you are holding the cards. Don't waste energy wondering where you are going or what you should be doing; you covered that ground last year. Just keep your eyes fixed on the distant horizon and do whatever you must each day to get closer, inch by inch if necessary, to your destination.

WATCH YOUR WALLET

There are many opportunities this year for you to improve your financial condition, yet your best bet now is to stay with tried-and-true methods. Caution and conservation will earn you more than the weekend trip to Las Vegas or a short-term purchase on the volatile commodities market. Working with the harmonious trine between ambitious Saturn and abundant Jupiter this year means finding the best balance between growth and consolidation. Take special care to make your purchases and investments count. Be particularly vigilant with your money toward the end of March; otherwise, you could find yourself in a precarious position by the first week of April, when Venus tensely squares dominant Pluto. It won't be easy to come out on top if you get into a power struggle at this time.

 NO SUDDEN MOVES

It's pretty straightforward, Taurus, for your body reliably responds to the changes you make in your routines. If too much stress has worn down your defenses, this is a great year to rebuild your immune system and reclaim your health. If you are already feeling in top shape, even the simplest improvements in your diet or exercise program can further enhance your quality of life. It's critical, however, not to turn everything upside down by trying to accomplish too much, too fast. Trendy supplements and unrealistic physical goals will not help you in your quest for increased vitality. In fact—aside from proper hygiene, nutritious meals, and basic exercise—rest and relaxation may contribute more to your overall recuperation than anything else.

 DESIGN FOR GROWTH

Chances are you made serious decisions recently involving your home and family. Take advantage of the new opportunities coming your way now that things are improving. Start slowly and cautiously, for moving too quickly will only create bigger problems down the road. You are preparing the earth in which your garden will grow over the years to come, so make sure you have a workable plan before planting even the first seeds or you will quickly run into trouble. The Solar Eclipse on February 6 can activate tension between your responsibilities at home and your career aspirations. Don't force resolution too quickly: Two more eclipses in August may require you to address the situation with finality, but anything before this time may prove premature.

TRAVEL TO LEARN

This could be an exciting year with "larger than life" Jupiter moving through your 9th House of Travel and Higher Education, yet you will probably accrue more miles for business than for pleasure. The somber nature of a trip could also involve taking care of family matters or fulfilling a promise by making a long-overdue visit. Obligations and responsibilities may be the motivating factors, but you still can have a fantastic time on one of your adventures as long as you plan in advance. With transformational Pluto also entering your 9th House this year, learning will be emphasized both in your travels and at home. In any case, prepare to have your horizons broadened. It's a big world, Taurus, and it's your turn to experience more of it.

MAGIC IN EVERY MOMENT

Although your spiritual values continue to evolve, you are able to derive significant meaning by simply staying aware of who you are, where you are, and what you are doing. The familiar adage "Be Here Now" surely applies to you these days. This year the greatest transformations happen not when your head is floating in the cosmic clouds, but when your feet are firmly on the ground. No matter how enlightened you are, there are still dishes to be washed, trash to be taken out, and bills to be paid.

RICK & JEFF'S TIP FOR THE YEAR:
Action Prevents Stagnation

Accepting your present circumstances could be crucial to your current happiness, but unfortunately it can also reinforce the status quo. You are tempted to be lazy and stay put, even if greener pastures wait nearby. Give yourself enough time to indulge your senses and experience pleasure, but remember that your real struggle this year is no longer about stabilizing your world. With the mundane aspects of your life in working order, it's vital that you don't unconsciously slip into an inescapable rut of predictable routines.

JANUARY

STRATEGIC DEVELOPMENT

Your inclination is to start slowly, gradually build momentum, and then hold a steady pace for a long time. This is exactly how 2008 begins, with energetic Mars retrograde throughout the month. The forward movement of your life is so sluggish that it seems you aren't getting anywhere fast. Keep in mind that it may take a while longer to put everything in order so you can accomplish your goals. Additionally, mental Mercury slows in its forward motion all month to begin a three-week retrograde cycle on **January 28**, contributing additional delays to your plans. This can still be a highly productive month. Be patient and focus your attention on adding value to your current ideas while fine-tuning your timetable. Once you begin to execute your strategy, you will be too busy for this kind of planning.

Practicality transforms into less pragmatic but more original thinking when Mercury enters quirky Aquarius on **January 7**. The dependable Capricorn New Moon on **January 8**, however, reminds you that you cannot leave your previous commitments unfulfilled, even if you are ready to think about something else. The emotionally secure Taurus Moon creates a few days of increased stability around **January 16**.

> **KEEP IN MIND THIS MONTH**
>
> *Frustrations may surface if you don't receive enough support right away. Take the extra time to improve your position before moving forward again.*

Instead of accepting the limitations of your current situation, maintain gentle but steady pressure as you lean into the resistance, for the Sun's entrance in Aquarius on **January 20** marks the beginning of a very dynamic week. Your creativity soars at the playful Leo Full Moon on **January 22**, yet you also may experience uncertainty or even a temporary loss of confidence due to a Mercury-Neptune conjunction. Don't change course; refine the one you're already on.

KEY DATES

JANUARY 2 ★ *powerful response*
Your will is being tested now as assertive Mars meets controlling Pluto. You need to stand strong. As crucial as it is for you to feel your own power, you must be careful. Instead of scaring anyone into submission, too much intensity will only stir up more resistance to your efforts. Hold tightly to what's most important, but don't try to browbeat others into accepting your plan.

JANUARY 6-8 ★ *protect your heart*

Your key planet, Venus, crosses intentions with stern Saturn on **January 6**, making you wonder why you work so hard for emotional satisfaction. Although this is a short-lived transit, it is serious enough for you to reevaluate your relationship goals and make necessary adjustments. The New Moon in conservative Capricorn on **January 8** can create additional obstacles that paint you into a corner. You may err on the side of isolation if you're already discouraged, for you know you can take care of yourself if needed. Protect your feelings, but don't pull away from others just because of your fear.

JANUARY 12 ★ *higher stakes*

Venus, the planet of money and love, tensely squares unorthodox Uranus, sending currents of desire through your body in ways that both thrill and agitate. You may find it difficult to settle into a routine—you're attracted to anything or anyone that excites you. Normally, you choose safety over fireworks, but today you may prefer the temporary flush of excitement. Avoid impulsive spending, for although your sensual needs are stimulated, this impetuousness can also play out when it comes to money.

SUPER NOVA DAYS

JANUARY 19-25 ★ *emotional seesaw*

A profound week of change rocks your world and stabilizes it in alternating waves of planetary pressure. The cosmic lovers Venus and Mars face off in an irresolvable opposition on **January 19**, pulling your heart one way and your physical needs another. The relationship tension is strong over the weekend, yet it can be lots of fun finding creative ways to resolve the stress. On **January 21**—just one day prior to the expressive Leo Full Moon—optimistic Jupiter trines realistic Saturn in one of the most important aspects of the year. This balancing act between the planets of reward and hard work focuses your attention on the overall direction of your life now—and will again refocus it on **September 8 and November 21**—setting a major theme for your year. Then, on **January 24**, sweet Venus conjoins "bad boy" Pluto just prior to entering cautious Capricorn. Touching an intense hidden reservoir of feelings can be exhilarating or destructive, depending on your willingness to deepen a relationship.

FEBRUARY

PATIENCE AT WORK

February begins positively as beneficent Jupiter receives a lovely kiss from sweet Venus in your 9th House of Big Ideas, clearing a path to better times. Good news can arrive in the form of love, money, or any type of pleasurable experience. It could take a few weeks to integrate this blessing into your life—assertive Mars only ended its retrograde phase on **January 30**, and it's still covering the ground it lost—so patience is required. Additionally, your best-laid plans may need revision, because Mercury the Communicator remains retrograde until **February 18**.

Two eclipses this month indicate major changes concerning your role in the community or on the job. The first, a high-strung Aquarian New Moon Eclipse, falls in your 10th House of Career on **February 6**. This is likely to create a sudden shift in the power structure at work. These changes may be caused by someone quitting or getting promoted, which results in additional responsibilities being delegated to you. On **February 17**, Venus leaves the concrete realms of Capricorn, joining several other planets already in your 10th House, placing additional emphasis on your professional life. Then, on **February 19**, the Sun enters imaginative Pisces, blending your dreams with the real world. The second eclipse, at the meticulous Virgo Full Moon on **February 20**, activates your 6th House of Work. With authoritative Saturn so close to the eclipse point, it's likely that you will see modifications to your daily work routine. It may be difficult to make the necessary adjustments right away, but you should be able to make the best of the new situation when verbal Mercury conjoins social Venus on **February 26**.

> **KEEP IN MIND THIS MONTH**
>
> *This month is chock-full of potential, but it's essential that you do your chores first. You will then be free to fully participate in everything else you want.*

KEY DATES

FEBRUARY 1-2 ★ *dream a little dream*

Your key planet, Venus, assures you of a particularly sweet time as it aligns with opulent Jupiter on **February 1**. Meanwhile, retrograde Mercury reactivates unfulfilled dreams as it aligns with imaginative Neptune on **February 2**. Recurring fantasies lure you away from reality, convincing you that anything you desire can now be yours. Maintain a sensible grasp on your duties and responsibilities, but enjoy the magical beauty while it lasts.

FEBRUARY 6 ★ *no holding back*

Original thinking about your place in the world challenges previous assumptions as the brilliant Aquarian Solar Eclipse activates wordy Mercury. But emotional scars are sensitive as wounded Chiron reminds you of your past. Only the truth can allow you to see how the opportunities of the present moment are different from a previous failure. And with unrestrained Uranus shocking lovely Venus into awareness, don't resist the speed at which your desires shift to match your current circumstances.

FEBRUARY 10 ★ *spiritual pursuit*

The Sun's conjunction with nebulous Neptune in your 10th House of Career can take the winds of your ego out of the sails of your ambitions. You can lose your way and wonder if your life makes sense. Since Neptune is more concerned with imagination than social status, use this time to take a short vacation from your real-world obligations. Include activities that increase your connection to your spiritual traditions through music, meditation, or nature. Indulge your dreams and honor the mystery of uncertainty.

SUPER NOVA DAYS
FEBRUARY 17–21 ★ *business first, pleasure later*

An unusual multiplanet configuration culminates on **February 17–19**—involving compelling Mars, restraining Saturn, and loving Venus—that marks three points on a five-pointed cosmic star. These magical quintiles highlight your creativity, focus your talents, and allow you to find a useful balance between the positive and negative forces acting on your life. Relying on your heightened intuition can help you alleviate the intense focus of the Virgo Full Moon Eclipse in your 5th House of Fun and Games on **February 20**. Don't try to avoid your responsibilities or you will feel quite guilty when Venus quincunxes Saturn on **February 21**.

FEBRUARY 24 ★ *head authority*

When the Sun makes its annual opposition to stern Saturn, you must stop, look, and listen—otherwise you will likely pay the price for your foolish lack of respect. Responding with anger is not the right answer, especially if the obstacles you now encounter require you to slow down. Combining determination and intelligence is a much better way to show that you have learned your lesson. You can still end up on top as long as you remember your limitations.

MARCH

DREAM CATCHER

Pay close attention to your dreams as planetary activity in imaginative Pisces emphasizes your 11th House of Friends, Hopes, and Wishes. Energetic Mars becomes more determined as it enters Cancer in your 3rd House of Communication on **March 4**, signaling a deeper connection between you and your immediate environment. You have more emotionally at stake, so it's crucial to be cautious about jumping into something new. The intuitive Pisces New Moon touches Uranus in your 11th House on **March 7** and suggests that friends will play a role in suddenly reawakening your dreams, as if they switch all the lights on while you're still sleeping. Once you remember what you've been hiding from yourself, you may turn your world upside down to reconnect with your lost vision.

While still in intellectual Aquarius, your ruling planet, Venus, encourages you to seek freedom of expression in love and money. When it enters compassionate Pisces on **March 12**, your ideals can blur with the object of your fantasy, opening the way to a new romance or rekindling an old one. This is reemphasized when logical Mercury joins the planetary pack in Pisces on **March 14**, shifting your thinking toward the unimagined possibilities before you without necessarily considering the practicalities. Then, on **March 20**, when the Sun enters impulsive Aries on the first day of spring, you become more motivated to make your dreams a reality. The creative Libra Full Moon in your 6th House of Health on **March 21** squares intense Pluto and assertive Mars, so you might have to fend off a minor illness or setback while maintaining your powerful presence at work.

> **KEEP IN MIND THIS MONTH**
>
> *You may be required to fight for the survival of your best ideas. Determination will bring success if you can combine your initial excitement with your strong will to succeed.*

KEY DATES

MARCH 2 ★ *love heals*

You may be overly concerned if anyone criticizes you today, yet your anxiety may have more to do with unresolved issues of self-esteem than it does with what's said. Release your burden; you have carried the weight of old wounds long enough. Make use of today's alignment between loving Venus and suffering Chiron by helping those in need instead of expecting others to take care of you.

MARCH 6-7 ★ *stand your ground*

On **March 6**, enriching Venus and compassionate Neptune conjoin in your 10th House of Public Status, casting a rosy glow over your professional aspirations. On **March 7**, the New Moon conjuncts freedom-loving Uranus in Pisces, further inspiring your fantasies. But your illusions may crash as assertive Mars opposes tyrannical Pluto, pitting your will against someone who resists your efforts. Although your tendency may be to acquiesce in the name of harmony, demonstrate your determination by holding your ground. Keep your dreams alive despite whatever problems you might face.

MARCH 13-16 ★ *sweet satisfaction takes time*

Sociable Venus sextiles passionate Pluto on **March 13**, intensifying your desires and making you more likely to express your needs. But you may change your tune and emotionally withdraw on **March 15**, when Venus opposes authoritative Saturn. You may feel as if you won't be satisfied no matter what you do, and thus wonder if your efforts are even worth it. Your persistence will pay off, for Venus goes on to harmoniously trine physical Mars on **March 16**. It may take a few days plus the power of your persuasion, but you will get exactly what you want.

MARCH 21-23 ★ *grudge match*

The Sun's tense square to invincible Pluto on **March 21** can reignite a power struggle that was in a dormant phase. Don't expect resolution yet, for the Sun forms an annoying quincunx with constrictive Saturn on **March 23**. Everything may be in flux, so don't expect the dust to settle soon.

SUPER NOVA DAYS

MARCH 28-30 ★ *just say yes*

The month ends in a flurry of activity surrounding the first of three supportive sextiles between buoyant Jupiter and erratic Uranus on **March 28**. This positive aspect opens doors that were previously shut, allowing you access to new and unexpected horizons, both socially and at work. Simultaneously, Venus conjoins Uranus, adding a romantic flavor, sensual pleasure, or even the possibility of a financial windfall. By **March 30**, though, the Sun tensely squares red-hot Mars. What began as an exciting experience can now turn into a petty ego dispute unless you hold your temper. Don't ruin a wonderful moment just because you are feeling insecure.

APRIL

OUT OF THE STARTING GATE

A lot of change occurs beneath the radar during the first part of April as planets join the action-packed Aries Sun in your 12th House of Imagination. Mercury fast-talks its way into Aries on **April 2**, followed by Venus on **April 6**. Your fantasies are highly active during this phase, fueled by your desire for seclusion. Although you are inspired to consider new projects, it may be challenging to actually get them off the ground. Instead of wasting energy by prematurely leaping before you look, think about taking a bit of time to further explore your imagination. Active Mars in passive Cancer also increases your inwardly directed focus. By midmonth, however, the emphasis begins to shift, encouraging more personal expression as Mercury, **April 17**, the Sun, **April 19**, and Venus, **April 30**, each enters solid Taurus, making this the best time for you to finally start plowing your field of dreams.

The loving action of Venus sparkles in the days around the headstrong Aries New Moon on **April 5**. Pay careful attention to what you want, but keep in mind that your spontaneity may need to be controlled or your atypical impulsiveness may stir up trouble. Social etiquette may stand in the path that leads to your satisfaction; you will likely pay a steep price if you disregard the rules now. Still, this is a time of fresh starts. Remain open and you can be led in an exciting new direction as long as you don't expect too much, too fast. A particularly stable time is indicated around the intense Scorpio Full Moon on **April 20**. You feel quite grounded and are able to work with the strong emotions that are overflowing into your life.

> ### KEEP IN MIND THIS MONTH
>
> *Avoid the temptation to expect immediate results, even when circumstances seem straightforward. Make yourself as comfortable as possible while waiting for the right time to act.*

KEY DATES

APRIL 2–3 ★ *no fighting*

Try not to force any issues now, for something you casually share can stir up a hornet's nest. Letting the hive settle back down is more sensible than inflaming the situation with unnecessary provocation. The culprit here is quicksilver Mercury, which moves into aggressive Aries on **April 2** and then dynamically squares powerful Pluto on **April 3**. Your mind is swift enough to find an emotionally sensitive button, push it, and move on to the next topic of conversation before anyone realizes what's happened. Unfortunately, a simultaneous quincunx to Saturn the Tester may not let you off the hook so easily. Don't be afraid to back down. You can favorably shift the energy with a well-intentioned apology.

APRIL 5–8 ★ *war and peace*
The animated Aries New Moon on **April 5** urges you to take risks, yet someone may accuse you of being too selfish. Sensual Venus is highly driven now, putting you directly in touch with what you desire. Venus enters fiery Aries and then forms a dynamic square with passionate Pluto on **April 6**, an irritating quincunx with Saturn on **April 7**, and a magical quintile with Jupiter on **April 8**. This is similar to Mercury's transits on **April 2–3**, but now you may have a deeper disagreement with a spouse or lover over core values. Be open to gestures of reconciliation or peace, since your differences won't be resolved by words alone.

APRIL 10–13 ★ *count to ten*
A pair of tense squares on **April 10** catalyzes frustrations that you have kept hidden. The two most massive objects in the solar system, the Sun and opinionated Jupiter, stoke the day with power that may be too much to handle. A second square between quick-thinking Mercury and assertive Mars can spark the highly flammable situation. Although your feelings are slightly settled by **April 12–13**, you must still be careful about overstating your position—or simply speaking at all.

SUPER NOVA DAYS
APRIL 20–24 ★ *tone it down*
Smoothly sailing through the days following the intense Scorpio Full Moon on **April 20** is a clear sign that you are heading in the right direction. However, any problems that arise can indicate where your life needs work. You may have all the proper tools you need to succeed, but an inflated opposition between overconfident Jupiter and passive-aggressive Mars on **April 24** can tilt your world out of balance—especially with Venus dynamically squaring both Jupiter and Mars. Be careful not to commit to more than you can do. Keeping the peace is not as important as keeping your sanity.

MAY

FOLLOW YOUR BLISS

The quality of your life is likely to noticeably improve with sweet Venus quite content while at home in Taurus until **May 24**, yet you will need to exercise caution toward the end of the month. A very deep wave of stabilizing energy flows through your life as "make it real" Saturn harmonizes with powerful Pluto, while picking up support from Venus on **May 1**. Mercury's entrance into interactive Gemini in your 2nd House of Money on **May 2** has you thinking about your earning power. But your life may not be so grounded, for idealistic Neptune aligns with the North Node on May 4, awakening unrealized dreams about your future.

The determined Taurus New Moon on **May 5** prompts you to take action, believing that the impossible is within reach. A magical quintile between the planets of material and spiritual wealth, Venus and Neptune, can convince you to do what you love and that the money will follow. Unfortunately, this isn't the case if your plans are built upon impractical visions. When physical Mars enters lively Leo in your 4th House of Home and Family on **May 9**, your energy shifts into high gear, and you generously focus your passion onto your personal life. Your feelings may hit a wall if a lover or friend cools to your advances as the relentless Scorpio Full Moon on **May 19** squares authoritative Saturn. You are a bit more light-hearted on **May 20**, when the Sun enters easy-going Gemini, followed by Venus on **May 24**. But Mercury the Messenger turns retrograde and Venus squares Saturn on **May 26**, so frustration could plague you through the end of month if you are too impatient.

> **KEEP IN MIND THIS MONTH**
>
> *You may face discouragement if you focus strictly on the material world. Create a higher spiritual ground on which to stand, however, and your tenacious efforts can overcome any obstacle.*

KEY DATES

MAY 1 ☆ *stubborn as a bull*

You are not in the mood to play games. Your key planet, Venus, now in sensible Taurus, grounds you as it harmonizes with both constructive Saturn and intense Pluto. You are quite determined to be understood and won't let anything stand in your way of getting what you want. Fortunately, choosing security over transient romance now does not mean giving up your chance for deeper passion.

MAY 5 ★ *ask for what you want*

It may not be as simple as writing your request and waiting for your dreams to arrive, but your New Moon is today, and your intentions go a long way. A tense sesquisquare to dictatorial Pluto suggests that a powerful person may oppose your plan, but a magical quintile to Mars shows your ability to transform a negative into a positive by being creative and productive.

MAY 12-14 ★ *shocking originality*

On **May 12**, the reliable Taurus Sun harmonizes with opinionated Jupiter and resourceful Uranus. Your original ideas are accepted by others because your actions are now integrated with your intentions. Even casual acquaintances may feel closer and more involved with your life. But challenging emotional under-currents can arise from a tense aspect between attractive Venus and unyielding Pluto on **May 13**, leaving you less certain about your choices by **May 14**. Holding your tongue for a few days will give you enough time for your confidence to return.

SUPER NOVA DAYS
MAY 18-22 ★ *go for it*

Charming Venus works magic on **May 18** as it trines opulent Jupiter and sex-tiles inventive Uranus, revisiting the territory illuminated by the Sun's passage through this point on **May 12**. You are in your own element now (practical earth), yet your thoughts (air) are fully connected to your feelings (water) and your actions (fire). Then the second Scorpio Full Moon of the year on **May 19**—the first one was on **April 20**—draws into your life people who demand a lot from you. Normally, you might retreat, but now you have the goods and deliv-er them with a smile. Expect your mind to be lit by intuition under an electric Jupiter-Uranus sextile, culminating on **May 21**. But even if you are a genius now, use your brilliance responsibly when the Sun crosses swords with karmic Saturn on **May 22**.

MAY 26 ★ *reality check*

Mercury turns retrograde today in your 2nd House of Resources, suggesting a delay in payment for work you already did or an annoying miscommunication about money. Additionally, plush Venus—now a bit scattered in Gemini—squares austere Saturn, requiring you to scale back your spending and your expectations of love.

JUNE

WORK SMARTER, NOT HARDER

Direct action is your best move this month, for you can easily justify nearly anything you do. Don't wait for a better time to start. Take advantage of four planets in your 2nd House of Resources during the clever Gemini New Moon on **June 3**, while assertive Mars is also supporting you. Your thoughts are smoothly transformed into deeds even with Mercury retrograde through **June 19**, which requires you to pay extra care to details, especially when communicating about money. All forms of trading, merchandising, and information exchange are emphasized. On **June 6-9**, don't be afraid to use a little force if necessary, but then be cautious or your plans can fall apart by **June 14**. You could be quite discouraged if you expect something for nothing. Smart thinking pays off during this time more than extra effort, because no amount of hard work will make a bad investment good. An enjoyable romance, too, is in the cards, as long as you can separate your illusions from what is real.

Life becomes overly complex during the Sagittarian Full Moon in your 8th House of Regeneration on **June 18**, and you may not find the courage to ask for what you want once sensual Venus enters quiet Cancer the same day. You might feel as if you are running around in circles without accomplishing much, especially on **June 20**, the Summer Solstice, when the Sun opposes powerful Pluto. You are being tested now, and if you can hold your position without exhausting yourself in the process, the hectic pace should slow over the next few days before intensifying again toward the end of the month.

> ### KEEP IN MIND THIS MONTH
>
> *Remember that the flighty Gemini influence this month can scatter your thoughts and distract you from your real work unless you are constantly vigilant of your every move.*

KEY DATES

JUNE 6-9 ★ *in the groove*

The Gemini Sun in your 2nd House of Values is squeezed by beautiful Venus on one side and retrograde Mercury on the other, creating a three-planet lineup that gives you an extraordinary ability to ask for what you want, even if you were previously turned down. Additionally, a supportive sextile from relentless Mars in Leo makes it easy to turn up the charm. You have all the moves it takes now; just don't waste them on trivial desires. Small acts of kindness can make these days quite memorable.

JUNE 12–14 ★ *embrace the buzz*

Sometimes you are so sure about what you want that you become rather inflexible. As the Sun and Venus tensely square electric Uranus on **June 12–13**, your senses may be rattled—shocking you, loosening you up, and reenergizing your love life in the process. Try staying flexible, for the jolt could be more upsetting than exciting if you are too rigid. Additionally, the Sun and Venus harmoniously trine imaginative Neptune on **June 13–14**. This makes it difficult to separate the facts from the fictions of your fantasies, although your dreams are ripe for the harvest. If your emotions are already on edge, don't wait for a storm. Make something wonderful happen.

SUPER NOVA DAYS

JUNE 18–21 ★ *avoid extremes*

You are being challenged to bring your feelings out in the open where they can be seen. The opinionated Sagittarius Full Moon on **June 18** is conjunct shadowy Pluto in the 8th House of Intimacy, so you may be disturbed by issues brewing beneath the surface. And with the Sun and Venus tensely opposing Pluto, you could become obsessive about uncovering what you believe to be hidden. Mental Mercury turns direct on **June 19**, giving a sense of urgency to the situation. And combative Mars opposes nebulous Neptune on **June 21**, adding to the confusion. Your smartest strategy now is to reduce the stress by being completely honest without attempting to control anyone else. The secrets will come out in their own time.

JUNE 30 ★ *drunk on power*

The resolve you now feel comes from hot-blooded Mars trining high-powered Pluto. This is Mars's last day in dramatic Leo, making you more willing than ever to fight for your cause. You are so firm in your current position that no one can talk you out of your beliefs. You know what needs to be done and you are prepared to do anything to reach your goals. Don't unconsciously override other people's feelings so you can get your way. It's better to use your energies to help everyone, not just yourself.

JULY

SWEET MODERATION

You are always ready for pleasure with sensual Venus as your ruling planet, and this month offers you extra opportunities to soak in the beauty that surrounds you. The emotional Cancer New Moon in your 3rd House of Communication on **July 2** sets the stage by making you more receptive to other people's feelings. Venus— also in your 3rd House—encourages romantic love to come your way, especially as you receive a power boost from its opposition to Jupiter on **July 3**. Additionally, your senses are aroused by Venus's harmonious trine to quirky Uranus on **July 6**, tempting you to take risks on your quest for satisfaction. However, trouble arises if you lose perspective. Turning an insignificant flirtation into a marriage proposal in your mind can lead to an awkward situation and great disappointment when feisty Mars runs into sobering Saturn on **July 10**. Inflated romances—financial investments, too—receive an overdue reality check.

Another shift occurs on **July 10**, when chatty Mercury becomes pensive as it enters moody Cancer. Then, on **July 12**, when Venus enters demonstrative Leo in your private 4th House, you are conflicted by your resistance to ask for what you want. The ambitious Capricorn Full Moon in your 9th House of Big Ideas on **July 18** can show you a sensible way to reach your destination, whether related to career or love. With optimistic Jupiter opposing thoughtful Mercury, however, you may commit to more than you can deliver. On **July 22 and July 26**, the Sun and Mercury, respectively, move into dramatic Leo in your 4th House of Roots, indicating that it's now time to focus on your personal life over your career.

> **KEEP IN MIND THIS MONTH**
>
> *It isn't necessarily selfish to do what makes you happy. You must achieve some degree of personal satisfaction before you can add joy to the lives of those you love.*

KEY DATES

JULY 2-3 ★ *splurge within reason*

The passive New Moon in protective Cancer on **July 2** blesses you with much-needed patience. You are willing to wait for what you want while nurturing those you love. By **July 3**, however, when sensual Venus opposes opulent Jupiter, you see fewer reasons to restrain yourself. It is easier than usual to overspend or overinduldge. Go ahead and have a wonderful time, especially if there's a special someone to share the fun—but keep an eye on your limits.

SUPER NOVA DAYS
JULY 9-10 ★ *back to the present*

A pair of oppositions emphasizes relationship issues as the Sun opposes "bigger than life" Jupiter on **July 9**, expanding your goodwill so far that you may promise anybody anything before thinking about the consequences. A second opposition on **July 10** between talkative Mercury and subversive Pluto packs your words with so much power, they can explode with emotional intensity, drawing you into a power struggle. But it's the conjunction between hot Mars and cold Saturn, also on the same day, that puts an end to your antics and forces you back into your place. Forget grand gestures and your desire to be on top. Instead, just be practical and focus all your energy on the obstacles you now face. Overcome the resistance that prevents you from being happy.

JULY 18-22 ★ *not so fast*

The serious Capricorn Full Moon on **July 18** reflects your need to apply yourself to get ahead. But a tense sesquiquadrate between rich Venus and crazy Uranus suggest that you are willing to gamble on a long shot, even if others think you've temporarily lost your mind. Mental Mercury opposes extravagant Jupiter on **July 19** and trines Uranus on **July 22**, driving you beyond your normal limits of common sense. Consider the mess you may have to clean up before you say whatever you think.

JULY 30-31 ★ *picky picky*

Beautiful Venus in your 4th House of Home and Family forms an irritating quincunx with unorthodox Uranus on **July 30**, followed by a tense opposition with dreamy Neptune on **July 31**. Your fussiness takes over, pitting you against friends or associates. With Neptune's involvement, circumstances at home can further confuse a work situation. Unfortunately, your solution may not match the desires of those around you, making the problem temporarily worse. Your position will likely change in the days ahead as the fog lifts; soften your stance, and you could be pleasantly surprised.

AUGUST

LET GO OF THE PAST

This month begins with a powerful roar as the New Moon on **August 1** eclipses the relentless Leo Sun in your 4th House of Home and Family. Personal issues move to the forefront, distracting you from your work. The real message here, however, is to acknowledge the importance of your roots, although family ties may produce their share of stressful situations. A fresh perspective can wash away past negativity, preparing you for the changes ahead, especially within the context of relationships. Emotions intensify early in the month as innocent Venus dances into the shadows of Pluto on **August 5**. The focus of your desires narrows as Venus enters discerning Virgo on **August 6**, but your need to communicate exactly what you want grows until mental Mercury trines Pluto on **August 9**, then slips into Virgo on **August 10**.

Fluctuating moods can complicate your life as sensual Venus and intellectual Mercury run into Saturn's austerity, forcing you to consider solitude as a viable alternative to the overwhelming confusion of love. But your isolation is temporary, for the Aquarius Full Moon Eclipse on **August 16** draws your energy from the subjective personal realms into the more objective issues of community and career. Venus harmonizes with opulent Jupiter, so the rewards will be yours if you have done your homework and learned your lessons well. Still, you may have to fight for what's important as combative Mars crosses swords with powerful Pluto on **August 17**. A second New Moon on **August 30** is in efficient Virgo, telling you to take responsibility for the life you have created for yourself. Oddly enough, it can be lots of fun if you're willing to work for it.

> **KEEP IN MIND THIS MONTH**
>
> *Stress arrives in successive waves this month, so it's a good idea to relax when you have the opportunity.*

KEY DATES

AUGUST 5–6 ★ *intensity creates results*
Dramatic actions based upon deep convictions have crucial relationship conse-quences now. Romantic Venus harmonizes with transformative Pluto on **August 5** and then enters earthy Virgo on **August 6**, staying there until **August 30**. Your love life becomes more practical—you may actually get what you want if you express your needs clearly. But an emphasis on clever Mercury, along with Mars's tense opposition to Uranus, has you exploding with new ideas. Maintain your composure.

Although a total breakdown should be avoided, a sudden disruption may be useful to get everyone's attention focused on the work at hand.

SUPER NOVA DAYS

AUGUST 13-17 ★ *lemons into lemonade*

Warm Venus and chatty Mercury conjunct severe Saturn on **August 13 and August 15**, respectively, raining on even the sunniest of parades. Dreams are spilling into reality as the Moon waxes toward the unpredictable energy of the Aquarian Full Moon Eclipse on **August 16**. It may seem as if someone is getting on your case and expecting you to take on more responsibility than you want. Don't promise more than you can deliver, even if you must give up some playtime to fulfill your obligations. But it turns out better than you expect as both Venus and Mercury harmoniously trine benevolent Jupiter by **August 17**, giving a positive and loving spin to even the most difficult situation.

AUGUST 21-24 ★ *worth the wait*

These can be a thrilling few days for love, yet you must be as flexible as possible to enjoy the excitement. Mental Mercury conjoins artistic Venus for a creative visit on **August 21** while the Sun illuminates Pluto's normally well-hidden depths. Something you previously overlooked can explode into awareness, freeing you from your safe illusions and thrusting you into a new relationship dynamic. The Sun enters analytical Virgo on **August 22**, adding intelligence to your decisions. Satisfaction may be delayed as Mercury and Venus quincunx nebulous Neptune on **August 23 and 24**, respectively. Make positive changes without expecting immediate results.

AUGUST 29-30 ★ *rediscover harmony*

You could feel one last kick as seductive Venus squares demanding Pluto on **August 29**, drawing you into a hot and heavy interaction that pivots on issues of control. As Venus enters gracious Libra in your 6th House of Daily Routines just hours prior to the Virgo New Moon on **August 30**, you enter a gentler phase that allows you to reestablish the balance that was lost in the wild emotional swings throughout August. The New Moon closely conjuncts conservative Saturn, telling you to slow down, postpone personal pleasures, and work hard toward regaining stability.

SEPTEMBER

September begins as a rather serious month, yet your desire to accomplish your goals is balanced by the encouragement you receive and the very real progress you make. The powerful planetary regulators, optimistic Jupiter and realistic Saturn, form a harmonious trine on **September 8**. Their stabilizing influence is palpable and greatly impacts the remainder of the year, replaying a familiar theme from their previous trine in late January. You may get a taste of Saturn's severity on **September 3**, followed by Jupiter's benevolence on **September 4**, filling you with pride about the work you do and the promises you keep. But there are counter-currents that arise as Mercury, Venus, and Mars travel together as a pack through fair-minded Libra. Between **September 7 and September 9**, they each square Jupiter, tempting you with unrealistic expectations and upsetting the otherwise healthy balance between ambition and achievement.

A series of irritating quincunxes from these same planets in your 6th House of Daily Routines to unorthodox Uranus from **September 16–19** can provoke rebellion if others attempt to rein in your uncharacteristically disobedient behavior. The wild Full Moon in escapist Pisces on **September 15** is conjunct Uranus and can drive you even closer to doing something you may later regret, relish, or both.

The Autumnal Equinox on **September 22** marks the Sun's entrance into "team player" Libra and your 6th House of Work, showing your willingness to labor quietly behind the scenes now. Lovely Venus turns secretive as it enters the hidden worlds of passionate Scorpio on **September 23**. Restless Mercury begins its three-week retrograde on **September 24**, re-emphasizing this inward shift. The creative Libra New Moon in your 6th House on **September 29** can help focus your mind on the tasks ahead.

KEEP IN MIND THIS MONTH

You have the chance to manifest your wildest dreams. Graciously accept what is offered without pushing your luck and asking for more.

KEY DATES

SEPTEMBER 3-4 ★ *balance preserves order*

Self-discipline and well-managed creativity can overcome serious obstacles now. The Sun's annual conjunction with resolute Saturn on **September 3** adds heavy responsibility to your day. Don't avoid any issues that surface, for they will only be more difficult to handle later on. When the Sun trines charitable Jupiter on

September 4, your load may be lessened as others jump in to help. Keep in mind that you need to balance your overly cautious attitude with an open mind so you don't miss the opportunities right in front of you.

SEPTEMBER 9-11 ★ *save your strength*

Your key planet, Venus, is stretched by Jupiter's big ideas and prodigious appetite on **September 9**, and then is further excited when it conjuncts fiery Mars on **September 11**. You might be tempted to throw your sensible plans to the wind as you are lured by the desire to indulge yourself in pleasurable activities. You can be quite creative and are prepared to fight for whatever you want. Just be careful that you don't exhaust yourself before you are able to enjoy the fruits of your labor. Remember, long-term goals should take precedence now over immediate gratification.

SUPER NOVA DAYS

SEPTEMBER 15-19 ★ *imagination versus realism*

These are a crazy few days when the dreamy Pisces Full Moon on **September 15** in your 11th House of Hopes and Wishes can push you to your limit. Chatty Mercury joins suave Venus, giving you the ability to express yourself with more confidence than you actually feel. The danger of overindulgence is still present, and the big Moon's alignment with high-strung Uranus only adds to the urgency of your needs. Both Venus and Mercury form annoying quincunxes with Uranus on **September 16 and 17**, highlighting your current distrust of what you are being told. Their easy trines to compassionate Neptune on **September 17 and 19**, however, suggest that if you keep a healthy perspective, your high ideals can fuel your dreams with reality.

SEPTEMBER 22-24 ★ *journey within*

Venus sextiles shadowy Pluto on **September 22**, arousing your deepest feelings while also giving you an excellent sense of control. Venus enters Pluto's sign, Scorpio, on **September 23**, where it remains until **October 18**, further emphasizing your relationship with others, especially regarding financial concerns and matters of the heart. This is not a light or easy time; you will need to delve into your fears to uncover the root causes of your behavior affecting these areas of your life. A lasting solution might take weeks, for interactive Mercury turns retrograde on **September 24**, requiring you to complete any unfinished business before moving on.

OCTOBER

TAKE YOUR TIME

The devil is in the details with picky Mercury moving through your 6th House of Work all month and retrograde until **October 15**. You may be asked to go back over a job that you already considered finished; making progress can be difficult until Mercury turns direct in the middle of the month. You could even feel trapped by your daily routine with its emphasis on getting every task done right, especially since you'd rather be doing more exciting things. You should notice a change of pace when Mars moves into passionate Scorpio on **October 4** and someone enters your life on a whirlwind of emotional intensity. Your key planet, Venus, harmoniously contacts both ambitious Saturn and confident Jupiter between **October 5 and October 7**. Don't coast through this period, but take advantage of the stabilizing results you can obtain just by being extra helpful. Venus awakens your creativity and activates your fantasy life when it harmonizes with unconventional Uranus on **October 10** and squares dreamy Neptune on **October 11**.

The enthusiastic Aries Full Moon on **October 14** falls in your 12th House of Secrets and is supported by a sextile from Neptune. Focus on developing compassion and seeking ways to express yourself more spiritually, in particular through service to others. Your world becomes brighter when Venus flies into adventurous Sagittarius on **October 18**, showing you new ways to enjoy yourself. The Sun's entry into Scorpio on **October 22** reminds you to stay aware of other people's feelings, even while you are having fun. The powerful Scorpio New Moon on **October 28** falls in your 7th House of Partnerships, intensifying your emotions and perhaps even changing the dynamics of your current relationships.

> **KEEP IN MIND THIS MONTH**
>
> *You have more time than you think to free yourself from a challenging situation.*

KEY DATES

OCTOBER 5–7 ★ *no free lunch*
A magnetic sextile from sexy Venus to upbeat Jupiter on **October 6** can raise your expectations, but its sextile to sensible Saturn on **October 7** prevents you from being too unrealistic. Jupiter pulls the Sun slightly off center as it dynamically squares it on **October 6**, encouraging you to feel expansive. Go ahead: Dream the impossible dream, but keep in mind that you'll have to follow your big ideas with hard work to achieve the desired results.

OCTOBER 10–11 ★ *be your own boss*

Unexpected twists and turns can lure you off the beaten path as charming Venus trines erratic Uranus on **October 10**. Instead of holding on to previous plans, stay open to the joy of surprises, without feeling restrained by too many rules. Trust your recent decisions and just keep heading in the same direction, even if you are a bit discouraged. Don't worry if you feel you're losing your way; Venus's dynamic square with confusing Neptune on **October 11** can temporarily fog even the clearest of intentions.

OCTOBER 14–18 ★ *aim high*

The impatient Aries Full Moon on **October 14** extends your recent bout with uncertainty or even self-deception, as it aligns with dreamy Neptune and prevents you from seeing the hard, cold truth of reality. Mercury turns direct on **October 15**, indicating that clarity is on the way, although you may need to allow a few more days for your mind to fully shift into forward gear. Your focus turns outward and upward as enticing Venus enters inspirational Sagittarius on **October 18**. Don't lower your expectations, even if you desire more than you think you deserve. The pleasure is in the journey ahead of you, rather than merely in the conquest of the summit.

SUPER NOVA DAYS
OCTOBER 28–31 ★ *make intimacy count*

These are fateful days as Venus in your 8th House of Intimacy harmonizes with the karmic Nodes of the Moon to help you overcome conflict between your home and your career. Mercury is in its trickster mode as it quincunxes erratic Uranus on **October 28**, followed by its trine to illusory Neptune on **October 30**. You may have a hard time distinguishing fact from fiction, yet you feel compelled to make a decision. The transformational Scorpio New Moon on **October 28** is given additional power by self-directed Mars—also in Scorpio—as it harmonizes with three outer planets. Maintain your composure and take enough time to connect with your feelings. Your emotional brilliance will shine through as long as you don't react too quickly.

NOVEMBER

CATERPILLAR INTO BUTTERFLY

November gets off to a rather rocky start as Venus in adventurous Sagittarius forms simultaneous squares to both karmic Saturn and rebellious Uranus. In an irrepressible expression of your true desires, resistance gives way as you blast into the future. Saturn and Uranus are in exact opposition on **November 4**, establishing a theme for change through next summer. Responsible Saturn in your 5th House of Play makes you more serious in love and more authoritative in your relationships with kids. But its opposition to eccentric Uranus also creates tension around the enforcement of rules, tempting you to help others break free of any expectations that hold them back. On **November 12**, beautiful Venus slips into the shadows, joining mysterious Pluto in urging you to express your deepest desires. Venus enters earthy Capricorn later the same day, giving you a more practical orientation to love and money throughout the remainder of the month.

The indulgent Taurus Full Moon on **November 13** brings confusion, as its square to Neptune stimulates fantasy and overwhelms you with unrealistic dreams. Meanwhile, the regulators—expansive Jupiter and contractive Saturn—are moving into their third and final harmonizing trine this year on **November 21**, giving a clear enough sense of reality for you to successfully manifest your goals. The Sun and Mercury enter philosophical Sagittarius on **November 21 and November 23**, respectively, motivating you to widen your vision and to move beyond simplistic objectives. Pluto enters strategic Capricorn on **November 26**, followed by the Sagittarius New Moon on **November 27**, empowering you with a new sense of confidence and indicating a long-term metamorphosis of your entire life.

> **KEEP IN MIND THIS MONTH**
>
> *Don't rest on your past actions. Creating a simple plan that gets you back to the basics can vastly improve your business and personal relationships.*

KEY DATES

SUPER NOVA DAYS
NOVEMBER 3–5 ★ *no immediate resolution*
Venus sends you mixed signals on **November 3**. Its dynamic square to somber Saturn can leave you feeling alone and undeserving of love, while a simultaneous square to erratic Uranus encourages you toward risky romantic

behavior. In your attempt to stabilize your feelings, you may act impulsively, making your situation even more precarious. Saturn's tense opposition to Uranus on **November 4** can place you between a rock and a weird place, with no apparent solution to your current dilemma. Adjust your personal preferences in order to prevent an important relationship from spinning wildly off course. The storm might begin to subside by **November 5**; still, the issues brought up now will need your attention over the months ahead.

NOVEMBER 10–13 ★ *be true to yourself*
The Sun forms a series of supportive aspects beginning on **November 10**. Remaining true to yourself allows others to come to your aid as long as you don't attempt to run the show. As much as you try, you cannot fully possess the object of your love without transforming it into something different from what you originally desired. The Venus-Pluto conjunction on **November 12**, along with a possessive Taurus Full Moon, can drive this difficult lesson home as you face the negative side of jealousy and control. Although the Sun-Neptune square on **November 13** may add uncertainty to your decision, don't let that stop you from taking action. A strong connection between beneficial Jupiter and eccentric Uranus can effect sudden positive change that is catalyzed simply by the sustained light of your awareness.

NOVEMBER 16–18 ★ *think success*
Mental Mercury's harmonious trine to brilliant Uranus on **November 16** may have you seeking shortcuts to finish your work quickly so you can start relaxing. Unfortunately, Mercury's stressful square with imaginative Neptune on **November 17** indicates your current tendency to believe your dreams instead of actual cues from reality. Still, you receive necessary support from both Jupiter and Saturn, so if you take care to separate out the unrealistic fantasies from the facts, your thoughts can effectively lay the foundation for whatever you choose to build.

NOVEMBER 27–29 ★ *return to common sense*
The friendly Sagittarius New Moon on **November 27** conjuncts wordy Mercury and sexy Mars, making you feel entitled to lots of fun. Additionally, Venus receives support from erratic Uranus on **November 28** and your antennae are extended, scanning the cosmos for a little more action—which can distract you from what you should be doing. But Venus harmonizes with stern Saturn on **November 29**, requiring you to put away your party shoes and take life and love more seriously.

DECEMBER

POWER AND PLEASURE

December begins well and ends on an even higher note, yet you may run into conflict toward the middle of the month with lingering intensity throughout the holidays. Beautiful Venus hooks up with abundant Jupiter in Capricorn on **December 1** for what may be considered the sweetest possible aspect. This indicator of pleasurable sensuality is highlighted by the Moon—also in the serious sign of Capricorn—placing a slight damper on your otherwise highly indulgent activities. The results can be quite rewarding if you focus your intentions toward reaching long-term goals instead of only on receiving immediate gratification.

Venus enters intelligent Aquarius on **December 7**—remaining there for the rest of the year, encouraging you to break free from social conventions and explore more individualized expressions of your heart. Meanwhile, a countercurrent develops as thoughtful Mercury tells you to play life by the rules, entering methodical Capricorn on **December 12**, followed by the Sun on **December 21**, and Mars on **December 27**. The Gemini Full Moon in your 2nd House of Money, also on **December 12**, accentuates the unresolved tensions from last month's Saturn-Uranus opposition. This can be unsettling, stretching your finances to the max or perhaps shaking your self-confidence with an emotional interaction that doesn't go your way. With the Sun conjunct assertive Mars, it's crucial to avoid letting an insignificant disagreement escalate into declared war. The cautious Capricorn New Moon on **December 27** is counterbalanced by Venus's conjunction with nebulous Neptune. This awakens your spiritual needs—in stark contrast with required holiday activities, which may be less than inspirational. A transformational Mars-Pluto conjunction on **December 28** can stir passions as you take dramatic steps to set your course for the year ahead.

> **KEEP IN MIND THIS MONTH**
>
> *Your drive for fame, fortune, or fun can get out of hand unless you practice restraint. Remember, short-term victories won't necessarily assure long-term success.*

KEY DATES

DECEMBER 1 ★ *sweet indulgence*

Love may be in the air as Venus enjoys its annual visit with bountiful Jupiter today. An old investment may finally pay off, or you might receive accolades, or a raise. Give yourself permission to have a really great time wherever you are.

DECEMBER 7 ★ *be experimental*

Often you choose to do the safe thing, continuing your same comfortable routine day after day. Now, however, as attractive Venus enters eccentric Aquarius in your 10th House of Career and Community, there are fresh winds blowing into your life for the following month. Don't waste energy analyzing why you are being pulled in a new direction; just be open to unusual experiences that reawaken your senses.

SUPER NOVA DAYS
DECEMBER 10-15 ★ *no sudden moves*

You feel the impetus of feisty Mars being illuminated by the Sun and you want to take action. On **December 10-12**, revolutionary Uranus hands you a fuse and matches, telling you to light it immediately. But by **December 12-14**, authoritative Saturn demands that you put down your weapons and slowly walk away from the source of the tension. In the midst of this dilemma, a noisy Gemini Full Moon on **December 12** overloads you with information. The key is realizing that no single action can fix everything. You are on a seesaw, so don't go too far in either direction. Make necessary adjustments without abandoning your basic plan. Still, by **December 15**, when red-hot Mars crosses paths with cold Saturn, your frustration can reach critical mass. Continue to make small changes without losing control.

DECEMBER 21-23 ★ *blind ambition*

Once you make up your mind, it takes quite a bit to keep you from your self-appointed destination. Now your power is even stronger as the Winter Solstice on **December 21** sees the Sun enter calculating Capricorn and then conjunct relentless Pluto on **December 22**. You may feel uncontrollably obsessive about your goals. It's wise to ride your power for all it's worth, but be careful not to trample over others on the road to success.

DECEMBER 27-28 ★ *beginner's mind*

Six planets in ambitious Capricorn during the New Moon on **December 27** drive you to reach the top of your game. But a fuzzy Venus-Neptune conjunction makes you unsure about your place in the world. Instead of acknowledging your vulnerability, a conjunction between assertive Mars and powerful Pluto on **December 28** can bring out your stubbornness. Allow yourself to question your basic assumptions so you can appreciate different points of view without always having to change your mind.

.

GEMINI

MAY 21–JUNE 20

GEMINI OVERVIEW

Rebuilding and realigning emotionally are your key issues this year with Saturn, the planet of hard, cold reality, in your 4th House of Roots and Foundations. Problems at home or in establishing a sense of safety and security can be resolved by reflecting on how you reached this point. Looking deeply into your personal history can be a painful process. Opening up old wounds may be the last thing you want to do. But this work, when done in a compassionate manner, will make you stronger and create a more solid foundation upon which to build your future. With the power of your own insightfulness or the support of a counselor or therapist, you can unravel knots that have inhibited the flow of your full creative potential. Regardless of the limits of the people closest to you or the barriers you encounter professionally, **you have the capacity to turn the course of your life in a more fulfilling direction.** This is not a process that can be rushed, because slow-moving Saturn in systematic Virgo requires changes of habit that can't be completed overnight. Taking small steps can test your patience, but consistent patterns of healthy self-awareness will eventually add up to a giant leap of consciousness that expands your opportunities for success.

Generous Jupiter is not giving away the store this year. This outgoing planet is somewhat restrained in practical and goal-oriented Capricorn, and its passage through your 8th House of Intimacy and Shared Resources is a graduate-level course in the meaning of relationships. **Being clear about your goals in a partnership is essential**, since anything less than a well-defined purpose can limit the benefits you collect. You receive the emotional and material rewards of joining forces when you know what you want and establish a plan to get it. In return, you need to commit to doing the hard work necessary to earn and keep the trust of others. If you are not willing to stick around when the going gets tough with someone, it may be wiser to not get started at all.

A Solar Eclipse on February 6 and a Lunar Eclipse on August 16 occur in your 9th House of Philosophy and Religion. Both are conjunct Neptune, the planet of ideals and dreams. These eclipses can strip away your illusions about a belief system or a revered teacher. However, a hunger for answers can lure you into following a new spiritual path that may not be all it seems. Connection with the divine does not require a human intermediary or a specific set of doctrine or rituals. If you feel abandoned in your faith or uninspired by your life, don't look for someone else to show you the way. **The magic of metaphysical meaning is all around you—in every cloud, tree, bird, and child.** If you allow your critical mind to step out of the way, and simply feel yourself in the world, you can experience the sense of communion that you seek.

TAKE IT TO THE NEXT LEVEL

This is a transitional year in relationships as Pluto starts to leave your 7th House of Partnerships, which it entered in 1995. The planet of transformation dips its toe into your 8th House of Intimacy from January 25 to March 23, and returns there for good on November 26. This is a long-term process that will deepen your connections to others. Powerful Pluto compels a reexamination of what you're getting from your partner in return for what you give. This raises the stakes in the game of love, making it less playful but potentially much more satisfying. Jupiter, the ruler of your 7th House, in serious Capricorn, underscores the importance of purpose and commitment to shared goals in partnerships. This optimistic planet's easy sextiles with inventive Uranus on March 28, May 21, and November 12 denote positive periods of unexpected changes that can recharge an ongoing union with a fresh perspective or connect you with someone new.

TEST THE WATERS

Aftershocks from last year's professional shakeup can keep your career in a state of flux. Fortunately, you do well under these dynamic circumstances. Shifting gears quickly allows you to jump on opportunities that overly cautious people are too slow to catch. Excitement and uncertainty may both be present, especially if you're working in a new field. Questions about whether you are on the right track may go unanswered until early November. Uranus in your 10th House of Career is opposed by stabilizing Saturn then, which lets you know if you want to maintain your current course. If you do, work should feel more settled. If not, start thinking about heading in another direction.

PARTNERING FOR PROFIT

Generous Jupiter and powerful Pluto in your 8th House of Shared Resources provide the potential for increasing income through strategic alliances. A joint venture with a financially savvy partner can be very rewarding, although a clear understanding of each one's role is a must. Avoid "get rich quick" schemes and fast talkers. The road to riches is not built overnight, but if you take your time and work steadily, there's a wide path to making more money open to you. If you're willing to shoulder more responsibility, a significant change in your economic future can begin.

 ## CHOOSE YOUR FOOD CAREFULLY

You tend to live in your mind a lot of the time, but paying more attention to your stomach can be the key to good health this year. Demanding Saturn in picky Virgo, the sign of digestion, forms a tough square to your Sun, which may make it difficult for you to assimilate certain foods. If you feel more nervous or uncomfortable than usual, take note of what you've eaten recently and you may notice a pattern. Cleaning up your diet is especially important now. Your tolerance levels for spicy items and rich sweets may be reduced, so temper your consumption of these. The state of order in your home is another key issue. Physical and emotional messes that you have been able to overlook in the past may now cause you trouble. Keeping your environment tidy reduces stress. Address emotional issues as they arise, rather than allowing them to build up until they manifest physically.

 ## MAINTENANCE REQUIRED

Responsible Saturn in your 4th House of Home and Family indicates that you are likely to have more work to do on the home front. Make time to maintain your living space. Investing in upkeep and repairs can save you money and aggravation, so don't wait for a leaky pipe to break before attending to it. Relationships with family members or roommates may become more complex as well. Domestic concerns can cut into time for work and socializing, but efforts made to better understand those closest to you are essential. It's not easy to turn a critical eye on your behavior and its impact on those you love. The point, though, isn't to prove anyone wrong, but to have the maturity to recognize problems and the desire and patience to resolve them.

INSPIRE YOUR MIND

Idealism and imagination motivate your travel plans in 2008. Spiritual Neptune in your 9th House of Higher Education and Long Journeys shows that the desire to nourish your soul is greater than wanting to shop for souvenirs or to drink a margarita by the pool. Religious and cultural sites that expand your consciousness and inspire your faith are fulfilling destinations. Learning is also meant to infuse you with a sense of the divine, rather than merely filling your head with facts. Courses that unravel the mysteries of existence or enhance your creative and artistic senses are most likely to prove worthwhile. Avoid career-oriented classes unless you have a deep personal interest in the subject matter.

EARTH LEADS TO HEAVEN

Spiritual truths may come through ordinary activities this year. Practical individuals who do not consider themselves sources of enlightenment can, in their own way, show you a great deal about the meaning of life. Wisdom-bearing Jupiter's presence in your 8th House of Transformation teaches you soul-stirring lessons through personal relationships. How you handle power, money, and sex could teach you more about higher truths than studying metaphysics or religion. Flashes of insight are most likely to occur when Jupiter sextiles brilliant Uranus on March 28, May 21, and November 12.

RICK & JEFF'S TIP FOR THE YEAR:
Commitment Brings Delight

In matters of faith, let your heart lead your mind and allow instinct to over-rule analysis. But in matters of the heart—whether romance, friendship, or family—careful thought can make the critical difference between fulfillment and disappointment. A goal-oriented approach to your desires may seem less than loving, and certainly not as much fun as dancing through life in a more carefree and casual way. But a deeper joy comes through the mature process of defining your needs, establishing a strategy to meet them, and then executing it. This is very grown-up stuff, yet acting like an adult can be the best gift to yourself and those you love.

JANUARY

ALIGNING THE PIECES

Dig deeper this month with active Mars backing into your sign on the last day of 2007 and your own planet, Mercury, slowing down and turning retrograde on **January 28**. The need to revisit tasks you thought were behind you may feel wasteful, but it's not. Getting the small pieces of your life in order serves the larger plan for defining your future, as indicated by a harmonious trine between visionary Jupiter and responsible Saturn on **January 21**. This is their third constructive alignment since March last year, with two more to come on **September 8 and November 21**. These highly positive aspects give you an opportunity to build more stability in your life. You are establishing more serious relationships that are rooted in integrity and an inner sense of purpose.

The Capricorn New Moon on **January 8** falls in your 8th House of Intimacy, which may require you to make some changes in relationships. This mature and patient sign signals a need to step up and clarify where you stand with others. Think about your goals—what you want, both personally and professionally—and then set a course to reach them. Giving up some spontaneity in order to define and manage partnerships more carefully will pay off in the rewards of greater satisfaction. The Full Moon in Leo on **January 22** is more emotional, even dramatic. Lively communication and fresh ideas are brewed up in your 3rd House of Information. Yet with your key planet, Mercury, turning retrograde the following week, it's best to digest new concepts slowly and express them with care. Jumping the gun in sharing them with others, or taking direct action yourself, may induce errors that can be avoided by operating at a slower speed.

KEEP IN MIND THIS MONTH

You need to process fast-flowing information with reflection and analysis. Weed out the waste and transform the best ideas into reality.

KEY DATES

JANUARY 6-8 ★ *crossed wires*

Hurt feelings and mixed-up communications can upset relationships on **January 6**. A clumsy quincunx between verbal Mercury and impatient Mars can force explanations that may be too complicated. If the message is not getting across, simplify it or change the subject for now. Your mind starts buzzing late on **January 7** when Mercury enters intellectual Aquarius before forming a testy semisquare with its ruling planet Uranus the following day. Brilliant ideas fly swiftly through your head, but may be too advanced for others to understand. Perhaps you're being too conceptual and not practical enough. Be patient with those too slow to catch on, and take a breath to calm yourself if your nervous system is overheating.

JANUARY 13-14 ★ *words as weapons*
Mercury caroms off a quincunx with strict Saturn on **January 13** into a contentious sesquisquare with assertive Mars on **January 14**. Frustration and impatience can wear you down and spur aggressive talk. Saturn demands that you work within well-defined limits, so aim your words and actions carefully to reduce friction. Mars likes to fight, but its less-than-comfortable aspect with Mercury can lead to circular arguments that push people apart rather than resolve their issues. Differences over details can provoke discussions that stray from the practical and become personal. If you can stick to the facts and keep emotions in check, a little conflict might actually be productive.

SUPER NOVA DAYS
JANUARY 19-22 ★ *smart and sexy*
A powerful opposition between the lovers, Venus and Mars, across the horizon of your chart adds charm and sex appeal on **January 19-20**. If you are in the mood to play, flirting should be fun. The Sun's entry into fellow air sign Aquarius on **January 20** can feel uplifting, raising your hopes and inspiring your mind to a more philosophical view of things. The Jupiter-Saturn trine on **January 21** helps align a long-term vision, but it's still too early to sketch in all the details. A conjunction between Mercury and diffusive Neptune on **January 22** is excellent for imagination, intuition, and spiritual insights. But don't take what you hear literally: Right now, words are mere impressions, images of possibility, rather than statements of fact.

JANUARY 28-30 ★ *diplomatic mission*
Mercury's retrograde turn on **January 28** is a reminder to double-check all details during the next three weeks. Mars turns direct, however, on **January 30**, gently shifting your will to act into forward gear. Impulsive moves at this time, though, may lead to spinouts, especially with a Mercury-Venus semisquare the same day that adds sensitivity to every conversation, requiring enormous tact to avoid wounding feelings.

FEBRUARY

SUDDEN INSPIRATION

Two eclipses and Mercury's shift to direct motion are this month's major astrological events. An Aquarius Solar Eclipse on **February 6** illuminates your 9th House of Higher Truth with inspiring views of a more fulfilling future. The close conjunction of idealistic Neptune and intellectual Mercury to this Sun-Moon alignment floods your mind with images not easily expressed in words. Whether these are illusions disguised as insights or true visions of a greater reality depends on what you do with them. If you cultivate this dream with thoughtful contemplation and conversation, it can blossom into reality. But if you think you now have all the answers you need, you're likely to become disillusioned and disappointed.

The creative power and will of the Sun scoops up Neptune's faith on **February 10** and then puts it into action with a constructive trine to Mars in Gemini on **February 14**. Compassion and kindness allow you to advance your interests in harmony with those of others. The greatest love of this Valentine's Day may be one of friendship and care for all humanity, rather than a rose-petal-filled romance. Venus, the planet of partnership and pleasure, enters innovative Aquarius in your expansive 9th House on **February 17**, suggesting that travel, unusual people, and original ideas will be sources of delight for you until mid-March. Mercury's direct turn the following day also frees your mind for fresh thinking and making new connections. The Sun's entry into watery Pisces on **February 19** in your 10th House of Career can bring emotional stress due to added work responsibilities. However, what might feel like an enormous burden can be managed by prioritizing tasks and engaging the support of others to help you complete them.

> **KEEP IN MIND THIS MONTH**
>
> *Your mind can see much more than you can describe now. Use music, dance, art, poetry, prayer, and nature to express this boundless vision.*

KEY DATES

FEBRUARY 2 ★ *healing words*

It may feel like Groundhog Day with your ruling planet, Mercury, passing over nebulous Neptune for the second time in a matter of weeks. This fuzzy combination often brings misunderstanding based on oversensitivity and lack of precision. Friends, classmates, and co-workers are your most likely source of mix-ups, yet this can also be a day of compassionate conversations that lift spirits and heal wounds.

FEBRUARY 6–8 ★ *mercury madness*

Retrograde Mercury conjuncts the Sun on **February 6**, which may require going back on your word or revising an agreement. The New Moon Eclipse in eccentric Aquarius on the same day pours in so much information that making sense of it all can be difficult. Don't try to understand everything; pick and choose among the bits of data to select one or two workable ideas. Mercury joins Chiron the Wounded Healer on **February 7**, revealing chinks in your intellectual armor, so avoid making factual statements if you haven't done your homework. Mental Mercury and potent Pluto form a harsh semisquare on **February 8** that's excellent for research or eliminating clutter, but may produce extreme reactions to relatively mild comments.

FEBRUARY 13–14 ★ *sour to sweet*

An irritable sesquisquare between Mercury and Mars can ignite verbal sparring on **February 13**. However, a more generous spirit arrives on **February 14** with a Sun-Mars trine capable of taming the wildest temper. Anger can turn to playful passion just in time to enjoy the romance of Valentine's Day.

SUPER NOVA DAYS

FEBRUARY 18–20 ★ *home repair*

Mercury's direct turn late on **February 18** begins a process of separation from the events of the past three weeks. What was delayed now begins to move forward as snafus transform into solutions. The Sun's entry into spiritual Pisces on **February 19** encourages idealism, but you will be expected to do the hard work required to turn fantasy into reality. Inspiration can carry you far, but be sure that you have the material support needed to achieve your goal. The Lunar Eclipse in perfectionist Virgo on **February 20** occurs in your 4th House of Roots. A thorough housecleaning to resolve unfinished emotional family business or to repair your physical environment is a wise investment in your future.

FEBRUARY 26 ★ *sweet talker*

A conjunction of chatty Mercury and sociable Venus is excellent for mixing business and pleasure. Information is shared in ways that make learning easy and enjoyable. You can express ideas so attractively that even those normally resistant will find you charming enough to listen to what you have to say.

MARCH

PRESSURE TO CHANGE

Active Mars reenters protective Cancer on **March 4** where it turned retrograde last November, and sweet Venus and intelligent Mercury move into dreamy Pisces on **March 12 and March 14**. The shift into water signs by these three planets normally brings a sensitive and softening touch to your life. However, intense New and Full Moons and the Sun's entry into fiery Aries on **March 20** make this anything but a mellow month. Shortly after Mars enters security-conscious Cancer, it opposes penetrating Pluto on **March 7**. The warrior planet is unlikely to find the safety it seeks when facing the dark Lord of the Underworld. There's a price to be paid for the comfort you desire—perhaps literally, since this opposition falls in your financial 2nd and 8th Houses. The rumble of discontent might rise to a roar since the New Moon in Pisces on the same day is conjunct Uranus. The Sun and Moon's annual meeting in the gentle sign of the Fish is often a spiritual affair, but revolutionary Uranus's presence upsets the applecart with explosive feelings and unexpected events. This occurs in your 10th House of Career and Public Responsibility, which can trigger conflict on the job and spur you to consider other opportunities.

The Sun enters fiery Aries on **March 20**, and the rising forces of spring stir impulses to start new projects. But the following day, the Full Moon in diplomatic Libra opposes the Sun, while Pluto—still within range of its own opposition to Mars—makes tense squares to both. This Grand Square builds pressure in groups and requires you to focus intently on your priorities. Concentrate your energy by streamlining procedures and, if necessary, discarding whatever is outdated and unneeded in your life.

> **KEEP IN MIND THIS MONTH**
>
> *Distractions reduce your efficiency now. Set aside ideas and activities that don't address your current needs so you can achieve your goals.*

KEY DATES

MARCH 1–3 ★ *think twice*

Your planet, Mercury, activates a tense Mars-Pluto opposition, with a dynamic aspect to the former on **March 1** and the latter on **March 3**. Passionate words and angry exchanges can damage relationships, so consider what you're going to say before expressing your opinions. You might, though, feel as if others are being aggressive and picky with you. Either way, this mental fire is much better used for problem solving than casting blame and criticism.

SUPER NOVA DAYS
MARCH 7–9 ★ *fight for what's right*
The sweet New Moon in Pisces on **March 7** may be soured by a mean Mars-Pluto opposition that can provoke fierce fighting and power struggles. This intense face-off between competitive Mars and "never say die" Pluto encourages bullies but can be better expressed by your heroic effort to reach a dream or battle for those who can't defend themselves. The exact Sun-Uranus conjunction on **March 8** brings a restless feeling that reduces the ability to compromise. You want to run your own show and be free of responsibility for others, but may also be brilliantly creative in a leadership position. A mushy Mercury-Neptune conjunction on **March 9** could muddy messages, yet offer intuitive insights when feelings are trusted more than logic.

MARCH 15–18 ★ *just the facts*
Clever Mercury helps you step in with bright ideas to resolve recent conflicts. Its sensible sextile to Pluto on **March 15** permits thoughtful discussion of delicate issues with clarity and tact. A socially insecure Venus-Saturn opposition on the same day needs this type of deeper wisdom to avoid wounded feelings. A happy trine, though, between Venus and Mars, the lovers, on **March 16** could make for a sensual Sunday. Mercury then hooks up with hard aspects to the decision makers, Jupiter and Saturn, on **March 17**, which can slow down inflated plans. Avoid over-selling, and back up your statements with facts.

MARCH 24 ★ *calming influence*
A conjunction between mental Mercury and sweet Venus today demonstrates your ability to get your message across with kindness, overcoming the objections of untrusting individuals. Peaceful thoughts, poetic words, and a pleasant disposition make major points for you now.

MARCH 27–28 ★ *problem solver*
Mercury conjuncts eccentric Uranus and sextiles hopeful Jupiter on **March 27**, overwhelming you with bright ideas that may be a little ahead of their time. Venus makes the same aspects on **March 28**, while Jupiter and Uranus form their own high-powered sextile. You could be on a thrilling creative high now, brimming with concepts that enable you to leap over hurdles. You're adept at solving personal and professional problems, and can take care of business and still have fun.

APRIL

CHANGE OF PACE

Your life feels as if it's running at two distinctly different speeds this month. Mercury, your ruling planet, picks up the pace when it joins the Sun in impatient Aries on **April 2**, provoking quick thinking and impulsive actions. The Aries New Moon in your 11th House of Groups and Friends on **April 5** is force-fed by a tense square from expansive Jupiter that can overload your social life and attract individuals who don't live up your expectations. Think carefully before jumping on board any new projects to avoid stretching yourself too thin. Loving Venus enters Aries on **April 6**, spurring more spontaneity in romance and in the pursuit of pleasure. Hasty decisions can prove costly, so invest your money and your hopes in small doses to avoid big disappointments.

The pace shifts on **April 17** when quicksilver Mercury moves into patient Taurus. The Sun's entry into this fixed earth sign on **April 19** reinforces the slowdown meant to give you time to assimilate the onrush of ideas spawned during Mercury's passage through Aries. Enthusiasm may diminish slightly, but your best ideas can flourish in a less hectic environment. Practical Taurus provides the resources to ensure that your sparks of inspiration are transformed from fantasy into reality. The Full Moon in transformative Scorpio on **April 20** falls in your 6th House of Health and Work, where you're reminded that less is sometimes more. A creative trine from Scorpio's ruler, Pluto, to the Full Moon represents addition by subtraction. Reduce the busyness of your daily routine to concentrate your efforts where they are needed most. Quieting your mind reveals under-developed abilities you can use to supply more power and productivity on the job.

> **KEEP IN MIND THIS MONTH**
>
> *Apply your natural versatility by adapting your reactions to the changing tempo of events unfolding before you now.*

KEY DATES

APRIL 2–3 ★ *heart of the matter*

Chatty Mercury fires into Aries on **April 2** to charge you up with fast talk and fresh ideas. But you may have to slam on the verbal brakes on **April 3**, when the communication planet runs into stressful aspects with tough guys Pluto and Saturn. There's no room for small talk or allowance for error when intense Pluto forms a hard square with Mercury. The power of one single word is enough to trigger strong responses that can terminate a conversation and undermine trust. A quirky

Mercury-Saturn quincunx tightens the mental screws with cynicism that inhibits the free flow of ideas. However, this mental squeeze can also reveal essential information as the pressure for precision cuts out the noise of what could be and what might be to address what's actually real. Look deeply and you'll find the kernels of truth that reveal the core of the issue, making your speech more potent and your actions much more effective.

APRIL 10-13 ★ *downsize it*

Mercury caroms from a square with volatile Mars on **April 10** that encourages haste to a sesquisquare with stern Saturn on **April 11** that demands patience. Self-control in word and deed avoids disappointment and earns respect. On **April 13**, Mercury's square with Jupiter elicits honest opinions that border on overstatement. For a more realistic picture, take whatever you hear and cut it in half. For credibility, reduce your words and the intensity of your argument by an equal amount.

SUPER NOVA DAYS
APRIL16-18 ★ *seek solutions*

You're at the top of your game with a smart Mercury-Sun conjunction on **April 16** that deepens self-awareness and empowers your speech with confidence. Mercury then enters solid Taurus on **April 17** to put more substance into your words and stability into your thinking. Your power of persuasion grows with Mercury's harmonious trines to potent Pluto and reliable Saturn on **April 18**. Knotty problems may be solved by your ability to look below the surface to uncover the underlying causes and then using your knowledge with cool efficiency.

APRIL 27-29 ★ *rapid recovery*

On **April 27**, Mercury connects with inventive Uranus to fill your mind with original concepts and unconventional conversations. This imaginative turn continues on **April 28** with a Mercury-Neptune square that pushes you even farther into unexplored territory. This aspect, though, exposes you to images that aren't easily translated into words, which can make misunderstanding and confusion more likely. Mercury's anxious square to the Lunar Nodes on **April 29** may complicate relationships with mismatched messages. However, a slick sextile between Mercury and assertive Mars makes for a quick wit that turns potential pitfalls into opportunities to display your playfulness.

MAY

TAKE THE SCENIC ROUTE

Normally, you might be reticent to take risks this month while the Sun is lolling around in your 12th House of Secrets prior to its passage into restless Gemini on **May 20**. However, Mercury's entrance into your sign on **May 2** can have you looking out toward the horizon and itching for change before you're ready. Serious Saturn turns direct in your 3rd House of Communication the same day, encouraging you to make a stand sooner than necessary. The sensual Taurus New Moon on **May 5** harmoniously trined with abundant Jupiter is a subtle call to enrich your life with new spiritual activity and greater material comfort.

Active Mars firing into expressive Leo in your 3rd House on **May 9** encourages tough talk and bold action. But a signal to slow down arrives the same day as Jupiter turns retrograde. Its backward shift in your 8th House of Intimacy and Transformation could require renegotiation with professional and personal partners. If the rewards you're seeking are significant, take your time pursuing them. But rushing ahead may throw you farther off track, requiring even more time to correct your course later. Another reason for caution is that the communication planet, Mercury, turns retrograde on **May 26**, beginning a three-week period of readjustment. Additionally, the Full Moon in passionate Scorpio on **May 19** forms a tense square with spacey Neptune, which could take you on a wild goose chase. The Sun's entry into flirty Gemini on **May 20** followed by lovely Venus on **May 24** are positive sources of energy and delight, yet savoring their sweetness instead of gulping them down will pay big dividends in the long run.

> **KEEP IN MIND THIS MONTH**
>
> *Restrain the impulse to leap into action until you have studied the situation so well that you can be certain that your plan will lead you to your desired destination.*

KEY DATES

MAY 2–3 ★ *weighty words*

Your planet, Mercury, flitting into its home sign Gemini on **May 2** gets conversations flowing and your mind racing. But roadblocks of details and doubters arise the next day to quickly slam the brakes on new ideas. Mercury's tense quincunx with suspicious Pluto and hard square to negative Saturn combine for challenging discussions that require you to back up every statement with facts. If you can satisfy your audience, though, you'll be rewarded with trust and respect.

MAY 7-9 ★ *do more, say less*

Discretion can suffer when a stressful sesquisquare between thoughtful Mercury and boundless Jupiter on **May 7** encourages you to express your opinions openly. Temper your enthusiasm to avoid saying something you shouldn't. Jupiter turns retrograde and Mars enters dramatic Leo on **May 9**, reinforcing the potential for overly optimistic speech. Be brave, bold, and creative, and let your actions do all the talking.

MAY 13-14 ★ *relationship squeeze*

Relationships require realism with a demanding Venus-Pluto sesquisquare on **May 13**. Feelings of dissatisfaction or rejection come close to the surface, but intimacy is gained by going deeper. An intense reevaluation of your desires and the cost required to fulfill them can strengthen a meaningful partnership or put an end to a weak one. A supersensitive Sun-Neptune square on **May 14** can have you licking your wounds, but you're not the only one who feels hurt now. Forgiving yourself and others is sure to heal hearts and raise hopes for the future.

SUPER NOVA DAYS
MAY 19-21 ★ *the next step*

The Scorpio Full Moon on **May 19** in your 6th House of Work could push you to your limits. If you feel unappreciated, take a day or two before expressing your feelings openly. Nebulous Neptune's hard square to the Full Moon can be tiring, so you may just need a break. The Sun entering your sign on **May 20**, though, can feel like a breath of fresh air. Making changes will be easier with an influx of energy. Still, don't overcommit; A Sun-Pluto quincunx on **May 21** is a reminder that something needs to go before you take you next major step forward.

MAY 24-26 ★ *return to the basics*

Sweet Venus sashays into your sign on **May 24**, which usually makes you feel more alluring. But its crunchy quincunx with Pluto and stingy square to Saturn the following two days could get you more criticism than cuddles. Love and approval demand adjustments that will increase your self-worth and upgrade relationships if you're willing to make real changes. Mercury's retrograde on **May 26** could seem like a step backward, but it's really an opportunity to retrace your steps and reset your life direction during the next three weeks.

JUNE

EXPLORE NEW DIRECTIONS

June gets off to a strong start with a friendly New Moon in Gemini on **June 3**. The annual Sun-Moon conjunction in Gemini is always a spur to action, but this one is especially rich with creative potential thanks to its conjunction with artistic Venus and supportive sextile from spunky Mars in expressive Leo. The message is to just play without any specific plans or defined goals, whether at home or at work, with others, or alone. It's your time to explore new avenues of fun and adventure in the most spontaneous ways possible. Retrograde Mercury joins the Sun on **June 7** to deepen your self-awareness, providing fresh insights into your purpose and potential. The Sagittarius Full Moon conjunct profound Pluto in your 7th House of Partnerships on **June 18** brings relationship issues to a head. Dissatisfaction can stir you to make major changes to attract someone new into your life or to radically alter the nature of an ongoing union. Try staying totally honest with yourself while remaining kind and considerate to others.

Your ruling planet, Mercury, turns direct on **June 19**, allowing ideas to start flowing more freely. With the complications of the retrograde cycle behind you, this is an excellent time to make new connections or launch new projects. The Sun enters protective Cancer on **June 20**, marking the Summer Solstice, the longest day of the year. This event occurs in your 2nd House of Resources, which can shed light on money-making possibilities and enhance your sense of worth for the next thirty days. Bottlenecks are possible on **June 26** as overconfident Jupiter runs into a restrictive sesquisquare with stodgy Saturn, and freedom-loving Uranus turns retrograde.

> **KEEP IN MIND THIS MONTH**
>
> *Give yourself plenty of chances to experiment with different attitudes and approaches instead of waiting for the one "right" way to appear.*

KEY DATES

JUNE 3 ★ *a breath of fresh air*

The Gemini New Moon is a trigger for change each year, but this one is especially rich with conjunctions to Venus and Mercury and a supportive sextile from Mars. These lively planets stimulate friendly relations, loving communication, and a youthful spirit. You can turn your life into a work of art with a brighter appearance and more carefree behavior. Let curiosity lead you to new people, places, and ideas. Any time lost from work will be amply compensated by the inspiration you get from a newfound sense of enthusiasm.

JUNE 7–8 ★ *the art of conversation*

Retrograde Mercury joins the creative Sun and Venus on **June 7** and sextiles active Mars on **June 8**, which makes for a loud and lively weekend. Laughter and lusty conversation makes you an entertaining companion. The warmth of your personality allows you to communicate powerful ideas in a convincing but nonthreatening way.

JUNE 13–14 ★ *discomfort zone*

Relationship complications are likely on **June 13** with an explosive Sun-Uranus square and penetrating Pluto retreating into your 7th House of Partnerships, where it digs up dirt until mid-June. Feisty Mars conjuncts the slippery South Node in prideful Leo on **June 14**, provoking arguments when people feel underappreciated. Sometimes, however, it takes a jolt of drama to readjust your connections and remind everyone that they're on the same team.

SUPER NOVA DAYS
JUNE 18–21 ★ *boiling waters*

A stressful opposition between Venus and Pluto during the Sagittarius Full Moon on **June 18** roils the waters of relationships. While changes are necessary, the situation might not be as extreme as it looks. Mercury's direct station on **June 19** can also magnify issues in your mind. The Sun's entry into caring Cancer on **June 20** and Mars's opposition to hypersensitive Neptune on **June 21** continues the emotional tsunami. If you can keep fear from carrying you too far, the rising tide of feelings can wash away the past pain and enhance your potential for intimacy. Deep movement within may also reveal underexploited talent that you can use to increase your sense of self-worth—and your income.

JUNE 26 ★ *delayed gratification*

It's one step forward and one step back with optimistic Jupiter in a sticky sesquisquare with pessimistic Saturn on **June 26**. This is the second in a series of three aspects that began in mid-March and finishes at the end of January next year. Patience and planning will be rewarded, but not overnight. This is a time to act strategically and make short-term sacrifices for long-term gains. Independent Uranus turning retrograde in your 10th House of Career reinforces the importance of impulse control now in the interest of greater gains later.

JULY

RESOURCE ASSESSMENT

Financial issues may take the forefront this month with the New Moon in Cancer on **July 2** falling in your 2nd House of Money. The Sun-Moon conjunction in this sensitive water sign is a reminder of how important emotions are to your income and your sense of self-worth. You're a thinker, but now the way to increase your cash flow and your self-esteem passes through your feelings. Quiet your mind and let your instincts lead you to an inner garden where your true riches lie. When you connect with your instinctive desires, your potential for material success will grow. The Capricorn Full Moon on **July 18** illuminates your 8th House of Intimacy and Shared Resources. This can provoke crises in partnerships that lead you to question your competence or commitment. The point, though, is to clarify what you want from others so that you can advance your personal and professional interests with their support.

Information will flow more easily now that your ruling planet, Mercury, is back up to speed after last month's lazy retrograde. Your mind is firing on all cylinders while Mercury is in home sign Gemini through **July 10**. Curiosity leads your thinking in a variety of directions, making conversations lighter and more interesting. Then Mercury enters quiet Cancer, which directs your mind inward and puts you in an introspective mood. You may not be so chatty as thoughts turn to more personal subjects that require deeper reflection. The mental tide changes again on **July 26** when the communication planet enters outgoing Leo. Bold ideas and dramatic speech spice your words with enthusiasm that's excellent for gaining attention. On **July 29**, Mercury joins Leo's ruling planet, the Sun—a powerful time to express yourself with creativity and confidence.

> **KEEP IN MIND THIS MONTH**
>
> *Even the most negative thoughts can produce positive results by bringing your attention to problems that need to be fixed right away.*

KEY DATES

JULY 1-2 ★ *inner treasure*

Assertive Mars enters corrective Virgo on **July 1** to highlight where adjustments are needed at home. Turn criticism in a constructive direction by cleaning up, reorganizing, and bringing healthier habits into your household. The Cancer New Moon on **July 2** may set off worries about resources, but its purpose is to stir you to look deeply within yourself; there you will discover untapped talents ripe for development.

SUPER NOVA DAY
JULY 10 ★ *power and persuasion*
Strong reactions are triggered by conversations today, thanks to an intense Mercury-Pluto opposition. However, you can have a powerful impact on others if you make a plan, choose your words carefully, and express them with clear intention. A conjunction between tough guys Mars and Saturn leaves no allowance for error and little interest in small talk. Focus your attention on one task at a time, though, and you can overcome almost any obstacle. Commit to do what it takes to reach your goal and you will make a major step toward achieving it now.

JULY 14-15 ★ *mixed messages*
Mercury bounces from clear-minded sextiles with Mars and Saturn that increase your efficiency to a shaky sesquisquare with spacey Neptune that fills you with illusions. Take care of business first and then allow your imagination to lift your mind far away from the worries of this world to dreams of magical and mystical places.

JULY 18-19 ★ *increased accountability*
The Capricorn Full Moon on **July 18** may expose you to demanding people. If their opinions matter to you, put aside the charm and deal with their concerns in a responsible way. This is a chance to earn respect and gain the support of powerful partners or associates. As long you are clear about what you're getting in return, an investment in hard work will pay off in the long run. An opposition between Mercury and Jupiter on **July 19** leans toward exaggeration, so be cautious in what you say and skeptical about what you hear. Still, a communication breakthrough regarding resources is quite possible now.

JULY 25-25 ★ *gaining allies*
A testy conversation can expose secrets with a crunchy Mercury-Pluto quincunx on **July 25**. It's best to either address issues directly or keep silent, rather than trying to finesse matters with incomplete answers, blame, or excuses. Mercury moves into expressive Leo on **July 26** while forceful Mars forms a high-energy trine with benevolent Jupiter. Big ideas presented in a well-organized manner can win you the admiration of influential allies. But for every promise that you make you will need a well-designed plan to keep the confidence of those who are ready to help.

AUGUST

SHIFTING PERSPECTIVES

This critical month starts with a Leo Solar Eclipse on **August 1**, rattling your 3rd House of Communication. The mighty may fall as grandiose statements and bold ideas fail to live up to your expectations. Fresh concepts that excite your mind require careful consideration and testing before you launch into a full-fledged campaign. Your ability to rally people to your side is strong, but make sure that the cause is worthy of your effort. A Lunar Eclipse in detached Aquarius on **August 16** is joined with nebulous Neptune in your 9th House of Higher Truth, another signal that enthusiasm doesn't necessarily equal reality. These eclipses are about changing your patterns of perception; being more skeptical now is not a turn toward cynicism, but a way to break with old ways of thinking to make room for the new. Fortunately, the New Moon in practical Virgo on **August 30** is rooted in your 4th House of Foundations and provides you with a blueprint for long-range growth. Its conjunction with stabilizing Saturn brings you clarity and discipline, while a trine to Jupiter in earthy Capricorn enriches your future with a realistic yet optimistic vision.

Passionate Mars leads a parade of planets into your 5th House of Romance, Children, and Creativity on **August 19**. Sophisticated sexiness and a playful attitude are reinforced when Mercury enters this house on **August 28**, followed by voluptuous Venus's arrival on **August 30**. You are able to grab attention and captivate your audience now without looking like a show-off. But don't use all this power to merely impress others; these transits can also enhance your creativity in all areas of your life.

> **KEEP IN MIND THIS MONTH**
>
> *Pressuring others is more likely to push them away than pull them over to your side. Maintaining your cool is actually much more appealing and persuasive.*

KEY DATES

AUGUST 6 ★ *high tension lines*

Nerves may be taut today with a tense Mars-Uranus opposition set to discharge explosions at home or at work. Mercury's edgy quincunx to electric Uranus and opposition to spacey Neptune can spin conversations in strange directions, mess with messages, and increase chaos. However, Venus's entry into fussy Virgo could bring out your inner Martha Stewart, leading you to make your environment more organized and attractive. Don't stress if you fall short of perfection.

AUGUST 9-10 ★ *sharper mental image*
Your planet, Mercury, combines comfortably with potent Pluto and less skillfully with jovial Jupiter on **August 9**. The former brings focus that sharpens your mind and empowers your words. The latter, though, tends toward overreaching, so avoid saying yes to an opportunity that might not be as good as it sounds. Your ruling planet, Mercury, enters Virgo, its other home sign, on **August 10**, which is ideal for taking a critical look at your life, enabling you to reduce the clutter in your head and in your surroundings.

SUPER NOVA DAYS
AUGUST 15-17 ★ *out with the old*
A heavy-duty Mercury-Saturn conjunction on **August 15** stimulates serious thinking, but can also induce a negative attitude. Notice what needs repair without falling into despair, and then fix problems instead of just fixating on them. The Aquarius Lunar Eclipse on **August 16** washes away old fantasies to make room for new dreams fed by a generous Venus-Jupiter trine. A stressful square between combative Mars and indomitable Pluto on **August 17** may produce conflict, but also supplies you with extra power to finally overcome stubborn obstacles. Additionally, a brilliant Mercury-Jupiter trine supports mental balance, good judgment, and constructive conversation.

AUGUST 21-23 ★ *mellow out*
Sweet talk can be expected with a gentle Mercury-Venus conjunction on **August 21**. The tone shifts with the Sun's entry into sensible Virgo on **August 22**, increasing responsibilities on the home front and bringing your mind back to basics. Mercury opposes Uranus and then quincunxes Neptune on **August 23**, taking you on a journey from brilliant but disconnected conversations to a more relaxed state of mind that helps you unwind from the demands of the day.

AUGUST 27-30 ★ *looking good*
Mercury's square to Pluto on **August 27** gives you a glimpse below the surface to see the inner workings of your mind or someone else's motivations. Mercury shifts into friendly Libra on **August 28**, when being nice tends to push doubt into the background. Venus, the love planet, enters Libra on **August 30**, launching your most social month of the year, encouraging you to improve your image, and inviting romance into your life.

SEPTEMBER

STRATEGIC PLANNING

Visionary Jupiter goes direct on **September 8** just in time to make its second harmonious trine of the year with realistic Saturn, helping you clarify long-range plans, especially related to work. Additional training or education could be the key to advancing your career and earning the respect you desire. Transformative Pluto shifts into forward gear on the same day, underscoring the deep urge to enhance your position. The Sun's conjunction with Saturn and trine to Jupiter on **September 3–4** could foreshadow these changes, making the early part of the month a key time for strategic thinking. However, a volatile Full Moon in Pisces on September 15 could shake things up on the job, for its conjunction to unpredictable Uranus and a tense square to Pluto are likely to rock your boat. Avoid making any quick decisions, though, since a crisis could subside as quickly as it surfaces.

The Sun's entry into diplomatic Libra on **September 22** falls in your 5th House of Romance, Children, and Creativity, which is bound to open your heart and lift your spirits. Take time to play instead of pressuring yourself to constantly drive forward. A light-handed approach may actually prove more productive than pushing the pedal to the metal. Besides, your key planet, Mercury, is slowing down and comes to a standstill on **September 24**, marking the beginning of its thrice-annual retrograde cycle. It will move backward until **October 15**, a signal to carefully manage what's already on your plate instead of loading yourself up with more. The New Moon in Libra on **September 29** also spurs romantic feelings, but a challenging square from overenthusiastic Jupiter warns against going too far too fast.

> **KEEP IN MIND THIS MONTH**
>
> *Aim high but move slowly. The farther you want to go, the more cautious you need to be at this point in your journey.*

KEY DATES

A strident square between assertive Mars and adventurous Jupiter on **September 7** may push you farther than you need to go. Passion can provoke fights, flirtations, or competitiveness that could get out of hand. This is no time to be shy, yet holding back your emotions just a little bit can allow you to remain in control. Mental Mercury joins Mars and squares Jupiter on **September 8**, adding verbal fuel to the fire with overblown ideas and more information than anyone can use. Sensible Saturn's stabilizing trine with Jupiter may help you find balance, but you will have to be patient for it to last. Pleasure-seeking Venus's supercharged square with Jupiter on **September 9** may lead to excessive appetites for food, fun, and fooling around. A little self-indulgence is appropriate as long as you don't spend more money or time than it's worth.

SEPTEMBER 14–15 ★ *surprising turn of events*

A conjunction between communicator Mercury and graceful Venus in peaceful Libra on **September 14** cuddles you with comforting conversations and pleasant thoughts. But the intuitive Pisces Full Moon on **September 15** can spark a shocking breakthrough in awareness about your responsibilities and professional goals. Electric Uranus's conjunction to the Moon stirs restlessness that makes it difficult to feel settled now. A crisis could spur a sudden change of leadership or a shift of duties over the next few days.

SEPTEMBER 19–24 ★ *going to extremes*

A flowing trine between gentle Neptune and chatty Mercury makes it easy to share your dreams on **September 19**. Yet there's a turn in your personal weather with a heavy-duty Sun-Pluto square arriving on **September 20**. Controlling people can temporarily undermine your trust. Happily, a healing trine between independent Mars and compassionate Neptune on **September 21** helps you find common ground to repair relationships. The Sun's entry into the partnership sign of Libra and loving Venus's helpful sextile with Pluto on **September 22** support emotional recovery. Still, Mercury meets up with impulsive Mars on **September 23** as Venus enters intense Scorpio, perhaps prompting another wave of conflict before Mercury turns retrograde on **September 24** and a cooling-off period finally begins.

SEPTEMBER 28–29 ★ *new ways to play*

Retrograde Mercury trines Neptune again on **September 28**, reactivating your imagination and adding sweetness to your words. Then, on **September 29**, the New Moon in indulgent Libra plants fresh ideas for pleasure in your 5th House of Self-Expression. This is an excellent time to try out a new look and a different approach, whether to make yourself more alluring to others or simply to stimulate a spirit of playfulness.

OCTOBER

PROFESSIONAL PRESSURE

Assertive Mars enters fervent Scorpio in your 6th House of Work and Service on **October 4**, beginning a period during which more effort and greater productivity are demanded of you. You might feel pushed to the limit and could be tempted to push back to the point where you either quit or are shoved out the door. Don't let short-term stress undermine your professional future, though; you'll have more creative ideas on the subject later this month. The Full Moon in spontaneous Aries on **October 14** in your 11th House of Groups fires you up with support from a new colleague or pal. Your ruling planet, Mercury, ends its retrograde cycle and goes forward on **October 15**, which can feel like a significant turn in the right direction. Information that you've been waiting for may finally start to flow, and you are more confident in your public-speaking and networking skills.

An emotional uptick is almost certain when loving Venus in adventurous Sagittarius enters your 7th House of Partnerships on **October 18**. The planet of pleasure and approval in this part of your chart is a major boost for relationships, helping you to attract exotic individuals who open your heart as well as your mind. The Sun's entry into intense Scorpio on **October 22** and the New Moon in this sign on **October 26** should increase your creativity regarding employment issues. A change of job or starting your own part-time business is more likely to succeed when you're motivated by the desire to do something positive than when you're simply escaping something negative. You have untapped resources and underused talents that can help you improve your current situation or fuel your move to a new one.

> **KEEP IN MIND THIS MONTH**
>
> *Don't isolate yourself when you're feeling down. People will support you, or at least listen, when you share your feelings.*

KEY DATES

OCTOBER 6 ★ *more is not always better*

The usually temperate Sun in Libra can lead you down the path of excess with a tight square to indulgent Jupiter. Your appetite for food, play, or recognition may be extreme. Retrograde Mercury joins the Sun and also squares Jupiter, which tends toward exaggeration or unyielding opinions. You have every right to express yourself and to enjoy life's pleasures, but a little bit goes a long way now. Be prepared to back up your statements with facts if you want to maintain your credibility.

Expressing yourself calmly, even in the midst of a disagreement, can earn you trust that will enhance personal and professional relationships.

SUPER NOVA DAYS
OCTOBER 13-15 ★ *flirt or fight*

A sticky semisquare between chatty Mercury and socially sensitive Venus on **October 13** can lead to misunderstandings and hurt feelings. Don't take what you hear too seriously—words may sound more critical than intended. The inventive Aries Full Moon on **October 14** can blur the lines between romance and friendship, as well as between flirting and fighting. You may simply be teasing while another person thinks you're being serious. Signals can be muddy, so be direct about your intentions to avoid confusion. Mercury turns direct on **October 15**—a powerful time for clear thinking. However, your best ideas should be kept to yourself. Let them percolate inside instead of diluting them through long-winded explanations.

OCTOBER 21-22 ★ *passsion play*

It's time to put an end to childish things and foolish flings. The Sun in the last degree of your 5th House of Romance forms a constructive sextile with Pluto the Cleaner on **October 21**. Put your attention where your passion is and cut out activities that don't touch your heart. Intensity makes you a compelling person, able to motivate others by the power of your words and the example of your commitment. The Sun enters Scorpio on **October 22**, enlightening you to direct your consciousness with greater purpose. But resourceful Scorpio may lead you to question your life and to consider finding a more rewarding career.

OCTOBER 25-26 ★ *inner struggle*

A testy square between pushy Mars and the Moon's Nodes can arouse conflict on **October 25**. The real battle, though, is within. You're learning to be less sensitive to others' judgments as you pursue truth in your own terms. Pushing someone away may be what it takes to head you off in this positive direction. Another square between detail-oriented Mercury and big-picture Jupiter on **October 26** is likely to stir debate. A sense of humor allows free expression without anger or wounded egos.

NOVEMBER

ADVENTURES IN RELATIONSHIPS

November releases a torrent of energy as three major aspects, two planetary changes of direction, and three planets enter uplifting Sagittarius to light up your 7th House of Relationships. The action starts on **November 1** when spiritual Neptune slips into forward gear to make faith more visible and turn inspiration into action. Stable Saturn and unconventional Uranus form the first of five oppositions on **November 4** across your 4th House of Family and 10th House of Career that may redefine your definition of security. Combining fresh ideas with a long-term strategy enlivens your career and rattles your home life. Enthusiastic Jupiter making its third helpful sextile to Uranus on **November 13** brings encouragement from someone you trust, yet the Full Moon in solid Taurus on the same day counsels patience—tense squares from nebulous Neptune to the Sun, Moon, Mars, and Mercury suggest that illusion trumps reason now.

Impulsive Mars stimulates new connections by entering your 7th House of Relationships on **November 16**, followed by the Sagittarius Sun's regal march into this house on **November 21**. Fun-loving individuals kick up more excitement, but even if they don't show up, you will have the energy to take the initiative with others now. The last of five Jupiter-Saturn trines on the same day supplies good judgment to balance your heightened enthusiasm. Your ruling planet, Mercury, joins the Sagittarius party on **November 23** with an optimistic voice that helps you promote yourself with conviction and humor. On **November 26**, penetrating Pluto plows back into serious Capricorn, where it will deepen relationships until 2024. More immediately, electric Uranus turns forward on **November 27** to spark sudden breakthroughs in your professional life.

> **KEEP IN MIND THIS MONTH**
>
> *Overselling yourself could harm your credibility. Temper your excitement now with a more controlled way of communicating your strengths.*

KEY DATES

NOVEMBER 4 ★ *deep thinking*

This busy day starts with a sloppy Mars-Neptune square that can waste your time and energy. If you're not making progress in one direction, working harder will only take you farther off track. Fortunately, sharp thinking can save you with an insightful sextile between intellectual Mercury and profound Pluto, followed by Mercury's entry into Pluto's home sign of Scorpio. The Saturn-Uranus opposition could bring conflict with authority figures, but reflects the possibility of long-term professional change.

NOVEMBER 12-13 ★ *partnership pressures*

Loving Venus joins dark Pluto before entering Capricorn on **November 12**, which can complicate relationships with controlling or withdrawn partners. State your feelings clearly, but avoid strong criticism; a Mercury-Pluto semisquare on **November 13** intensifies words, and a sensitive Sun-Neptune square increases vulnerability.

SUPER NOVA DAYS
NOVEMBER 16-17 ★ *high intelligence*

You are as sharp as a tack on **November 16** with incisive Mars entering your 7th House of Partnerships and mental Mercury making three clever aspects. It forms a brilliant trine with inventive Uranus, followed by sensible sextiles to hopeful Jupiter and realistic Saturn. The key to using all this intelligence effectively is to be radically honest with yourself. As long as your beliefs are grounded in your body, rather than flying off the top of your head, your insights and communication skills should be top notch. A Mercury-Neptune square on **November 17**, though, could muddy the waters with foggy thinking and incomplete information.

NOVEMBER 23-25 ★ *fiery talk*

Mercury's entry into Sagittarius on **November 23** opens new channels of information and new venues in which to communicate them. The fire behind your words may grow even hotter on **November 24**, when a semisquare between assertive Mars and gigantic Jupiter can turn a little spark into a blazing inferno. Apply this intensity to a worthy cause, rather than using its enormous power in a petty squabble. A Mercury-Sun conjunction on **November 25** connects ego and intellect, sharpening self-understanding and increasing your powers of persuasion.

NOVEMBER 27-28 ★ *too hot to handle*

Your head stays hot with opinionated Mercury fueled by a tense semisquare from Jupiter on **November 27**, followed by the same stressful aspect between the Sun and Jupiter the next day. Mercury also conjuncts Mars the Warrior on **November 28**, which signals intellectual impatience, irritability, and aggressiveness on the negative side, but sharp and concise thinking on the plus side. Rebellious Uranus turning direct on **November 27** adds to your sense of urgency. Conflict with partners and friends can be expected, but the strong words and feelings shared can also push relationships to a higher level.

DECEMBER

TRANSFORMATIONAL HOLIDAYS

The holiday season may be less than jolly with the planetary tensions building this month. A near opposition between controlling Saturn and freedom-loving Uranus is kicked up by faster-moving planets that can trigger this explosive force. The action starts when assertive Mars, blazing its way through your 7th House of Relationships, joins the Sun on **December 5**. The competitive feelings stirred, however, can be turned from conflict to productivity if you have a partner who shares your passion. The Sun squares Uranus on **December 10**, followed by Mars in the same tense aspect on **December 12**. The combined forces of the willful Sun, impatient Mars, and incendiary Uranus are not inclined to compromise. Pushing people to their limits or feeling yourself pushed by others is to be expected.

The Full Moon in restless Gemini on **December 12** adds emotional fuel to the fire; rising tension can strain even the most stable of relationships. Mercury's conjunction with penetrating Pluto the same day adds pressure to every conversation. To reveal your truth or not is the question. If you speak openly, couch it with kindness to maintain trust. The Sun's square to Saturn on **December 12**, along with Mars's square to the ringed planet on **December 15**, leaves little margin for error. Be vigilant in your actions and noble in your intentions to avoid frustration. The Sun's entry into ambitious Capricorn on **December 21** is followed by its conjunction with Pluto on **December 22**, which can instigate power struggles. Mars repeats the pattern on **December 27–28**, bringing the intensity to an even higher pitch. The shrewd Capricorn New Moon on **December 27** conjunct Pluto and Mars in your 8th House of Shared Resources calls for transformation in financial or intimate relationships.

> **KEEP IN MIND THIS MONTH**
>
> *Take full responsibility for your feelings to avoid turning frustration into arguments that could undermine the support you need from others.*

KEY DATES

DECEMBER 5–7 ★ *twists and turns*

Communicative Mercury runs the gauntlet of a square with eccentric Uranus on **December 5**, a square with stodgy Saturn and a sextile with spiritual Neptune on **December 6**. The first brilliant but edgy aspect comes on the day of the combative Sun-Mars conjunction, making it difficult to avoid differences of opinion. The Mercury-Saturn square slows communication, demands facts, and requires restraint.

Mercury's sextile with Neptune provides needed forgiveness and understanding. Sociable Venus enters your 9th House of Higher Mind on **December 7**, bringing pleasure to the learning process and attraction to unconventional individuals.

SUPER NOVA DAYS
DECEMBER 10–12 ★ *explosive words*

The Sun's and Mars's squares to unpredictable Uranus on **December 10 and December 12** make the air crackle with electricity. Cooperation suffers as the need for independence grows. Impatience may be seen as arrogance and evoke anger in return. Mercury's entry into authoritarian Capricorn and conjunction with pressure-packed Pluto on **December 12** reveals secrets that may force changes in relationships. One careless word can incite an avalanche of reaction. Use the power of your mind to reflect deeply and communicate precisely to control this process of transformation.

DECEMBER 15–16 ★ *a rock and a soft place*

Macho Mars runs into Saturn's wall of resistance with a tough square on **December 15**. Pushing harder won't help, but being smarter will. Narrow your focus and act with discipline to move ahead where it counts most. If you prepare properly, you can break new ground now. A gentle sextile between Mars and Neptune on **December 16** can reward you with an easier flow when you allow intuition to guide your actions.

DECEMBER 24–26 ★ *earning trust*

Chatty Mercury's smart sextile with inventive Uranus on **December 24** produces bright ideas and attracts intelligent individuals with whom you may find an instant rapport. Mercury's creative trine with practical Saturn on **December 26** gives you a down-to-earth way of communicating that builds your credibility with others.

DECEMBER 31 ★ *conversational riches*

The year ends on a joyous note as your ruling planet, Mercury, joins generous Jupiter in a stimulating intellectual dance. The union of the planets of fact and philosophy enriches you with hope, vision, and optimism. Your ability to impress others with your knowledge is helpful as long as you don't come across as a know-it-all. Even if you are an expert in the area under discussion, allow space for others to speak as well. Connections can be strengthened when monologue gives way to dialogue in a mutually supportive exchange of ideas.

CANCER

JUNE 21–JULY 22

CANCER OVERVIEW

Relationships open your life and widen your horizons this year, but the reality of what follows may not live up to your exaggerated expectations. Exercising caution and using common sense could be your best weapons against disappointment, because some opportunities won't prove quite as amazing as they first seem. A feeling of infinite possibilities in January quickly turns into hard work as you successfully scale the mountain of ambition to reach your goals. When Saturn was in your sign just a few years ago—from May 2003 to July 2005—you had to get serious and make a stand for what was then most important to you. In 2006 and 2007, you began to firmly establish yourself in a new direction. In September 2007, Saturn entered practical Virgo, and stays here in your 3rd House of Communication throughout 2008. **Now you must organize your thoughts clearly enough to present them to others.** Putting your personal information in order, deciding how to make better use of your time, and establishing positive working relationships enable you to progress methodically along your path to success.

Your long-term goals broaden, yet your expanding vision widens slowly and surely in a way that keeps you feeling safe throughout the process. **Optimistic people enter your life and encourage you to move beyond your established boundaries of safety.** Jupiter in cautious Capricorn this year suggests that growth will not come easily. As it travels through your 7th House of Partnerships, it indicates that your spouse, friends, and co-workers will confront you with their realistic assessments of your progress, motivating you to learn, grow, and be open to options as they appear. But Jupiter does not operate alone this year, for Pluto, the slowest moving of all the astrological planets, has tentatively moved into Capricorn—also in your 7th House—signifying that **you are taking the first small steps toward a much larger transformation that will take years to fully unfold.** Although this metamorphosis will surely affect your most intimate relationships profoundly, all interactions with others will deepen along with your newfound emotional intensity.

Compassionate Neptune continues its journey through your 8th House of Shared Resources that began in 1998, melting away boundaries that might prevent you from experiencing increased levels of intimacy. But don't fool yourself, for Neptune can also pull the wool over your eyes. As a Crab, you are particularly sensitive to eclipses, which affect you for months before and after their occurrences. Since nebulous Neptune is closely involved with three out of four eclipses this year—on February 6, August 1, and August 16—confusion can create avoidable problems. **Enter into emotional and financial negotiations with caution;** things could unravel quickly unless everyone is clear about expectations and commitments. Due diligence is essential, so put extra effort into digging out all the needed facts and separating the useful information from the unrealistic promises.

 ## INTENSIVE CARE

There is little question about the increased importance of relationships for you, with both Jupiter and Pluto spending time this year in your 7th House of Partnerships. Of course their activity can include a variety of relationship types, including more formal business associations. However, the spotlight is on your 8th House of Intimacy throughout the year from both Neptune, the planet of forgiveness, and Chiron, the planet of healing, along with three out of four of this year's eclipses. Memories of emotional hurt can tempt you to stay safely hidden behind your protective outer shell. The greatest growth will occur by leaning into your fears, overcoming your resistances, and healing old wounds, allowing you to interact with others much more intimately.

 ## NO SHORTCUTS ALLOWED

Optimistic Jupiter and realistic Saturn promise solid gains this year, but only if you are willing to focus on long-term goals. No allowances are made if you get distracted by "get rich quick" schemes or shortcuts to success. Self-directed Mars, the ruler of your 10th House of Career, entered sensitive Cancer in late September 2007, initiating new projects and stimulating your enthusiasm for professional advancement or recognition in your community. Plans stall through January and February as Mars retrogrades, forcing you to finish old business before moving on. Mars's return to Cancer on March 4 signals the reactivation of projects previously set aside. Still, you may be more interested in your personal affairs until Mars begins an upward climb through your chart beginning in late summer and carrying you through the spring of 2009.

PREEMPTIVE RESPONSIBILITY

The Sun rules your 2nd House of Money and Resources. When it's eclipsed by the Moon on February 6 and on August 1, you might experience unexpected changes in your financial condition. The electric Aquarius Solar Eclipse on February 6 involves Mercury and Neptune, so it is possible to misread a situation that can cost you later if you're not vigilant. The dramatic Leo Solar Eclipse on August 1 falls in your 2nd House, indicating more changes of fortune. If you have become too complacent about your spending habits, you might wake up to an unpleasant surprise. But if you manage your resources prudently, then this eclipse suggests an acknowledgment and even monetary rewards for your work.

 ## ECLECTIC THERAPIES

Your 6th House of Health is ruled by Jupiter, which spends the entire year in hardworking Capricorn. Establishing healthy routines can have long-lasting positive effects. Pay extra attention to your waistline during January, while Venus—associated with sweets—moves through your 6th House. The healing Pisces New Moon on March 7 accentuates a supportive sextile between Jupiter and electric Uranus, which rules the nervous system. Beginning any kind of energy therapy makes sense at this time, in particular, acupuncture and chiropractic medicine might be beneficial. This sextile is exact on March 28, May 21, and November 12, increasing the potential benefits you can derive from continuing this kind of work on a regular basis throughout the year.

 ## EMBRACE THE INTENSITY

Venus, the ruler of your 4th House of Home and Family, joins controlling Pluto in your 7th House of Partnerships on January 21. Your deepest feelings may surface in a way that sets a sequence of events into motion, ultimately bringing about dramatic transformations in your personal life. As pleasurable Venus aligns with extravagant Jupiter on January 31, you move through a period of greater ease. Circumstances heat up over the summer when Mars in gracious Libra enters your 4th House on August 19, followed by Mercury and Venus on August 28 and August 30, respectively. Focusing on family issues greatly influence what happens over the months ahead. Venus makes an unusual second conjunction this year with Pluto on November 12, creating a sense of jealousy that can have challenging consequences if you don't address any unresolved issues prior to this time.

BOOK AHEAD

Jupiter is the traditional ruler of your 9th House of Travel and Education. This year, since confident Jupiter and strategic Saturn spend so much time harmoniously trining each other, you are graced with determination and discipline, giving you the stability you need in order to explore new places and ideas. Solid communication and sensible planning are key factors in your willingness to travel throughout the year. If possible, enroll in a course of study or time a major trip to correspond with the exact Jupiter-Saturn trines around January 21, September 8, or November 21. Avoid unnecessary travel when these two planets form anxious sesquisquares on March 18 and June 25, when even well-formulated plans can run into trouble.

FACTS FIRST

The intelligent Virgo Full Moon Eclipse on February 20 falls in your 3rd House of Communication, reemphasizing the need for accurate information to help you along your spiritual path. Take meticulous notes if you attend a lecture or workshop or you might be unable to remember something important. The lively Leo New Moon Eclipse on August 1 falls in your 2nd House of Self-Worth and is conjunct mental Mercury, so don't be afraid to talk about your personal values. This can increase your self-esteem as you gain clarity while receiving valuable guidance from those you trust.

RICK & JEFF'S TIP FOR THE YEAR:
Moderate the Extremes

Although your temperament is often less than consistent, your change-ability itself is constant, for you are intimately linked to the cyclic waxing and waning of the Moon's light. This year, however, Jupiter opposite your sign in grounded Capricorn can teach you about the benefits of practices that can help you sustain your feelings over longer periods of time. Adding time-tested tools such as yoga, meditation, or other relaxation techniques can help stabilize your life. By acting with more common sense, instead of fearful insecurity, you can minimize the effects of your mood swings and smooth over the rough spots in your emotional cycles.

JANUARY

STARTING SLOWLY

The year begins with an intense struggle as retrograde Mars opposes relentless Pluto on **January 2**. Although you first might try to avoid conflict, feelings are aroused and you're ready to jump into the fray. There is, however, a growing sense of frustration, for Mars—retrograde until **January 30**—directs you to keep some energy in reserve. By **January 6**, a tense square between warm Venus and cold Saturn is yet another signal for you to withdraw. Nevertheless, when someone requests help, you must meet your obligations, for the responsible Capricorn New Moon on **January 8** falls in your 7th House of Partnerships. A glimmer of hope shines through and a fresh perspective invigorates you as Mercury moves through the intelligent sign of Aquarius for the rest of the month.

Pleasure-seeking Venus squares eccentric Uranus on **January 12** as unconventional desires explode into consciousness, distracting you from the normal routines of your life. Fortunately, life gets on a more productive track by **January 16**, when the stable Taurus Moon forms a Grand Earth Trine with optimistic Jupiter and pessimistic Saturn—and this is no time to be lazy. The exact Jupiter-Saturn trine occurs on **January 21**, just prior to the dramatic Leo Full Moon on **January 22**. You can see your future, create a sensible plan, and begin moving toward your goals with uncanny accuracy and unstoppable determination. Passions rise as loving Venus conjuncts powerful Pluto on **January 24**, just before they both enter the serious world of Capricorn and your 7th House, bringing relationship issues to the forefront of your life. Mercury the Messenger turns retrograde on **January 28**, indicating that progress will be thwarted if you try to move ahead too fast.

> **KEEP IN MIND THIS MONTH**
>
> *The stage is being set for steady, long-term growth, so take enough time to strategize before starting more than you can finish.*

KEY DATES

JANUARY 6–8 ★ *look within*

Romantic Venus squares restrictive Saturn on **January 6**, tempting you to guard your heart to protect yourself from rejection. Others might make matters worse by putting too much emotional pressure on you. No one can ease your loneliness unless you look at your own suppressed feelings. The serious Capricorn New Moon on **January 8** signals a new start, so take action to rectify an uncomfortable relationship situation.

JANUARY 12 ★ *storms of desire*
A few days ago you were deep inside your shell, but today as Venus squares electric Uranus, you are ready for an emotional risk. It's not that you're in denial of your fear; you are just caught up in the excitement. Be careful that you don't unintentionally close the door on someone close to you as you try to make something new happen. Remember, your needs are somewhat distorted now, so let the dust settle for a few days before doing anything you may regret.

JANUARY 16 ★ *brick by brick*
It's a simple matter to push outward now and build upon the foundations that you already created, but don't get discouraged if it feels as if you aren't progressing; measurable results will follow soon enough. And although you may be content with your current lot, don't get too comfortable. Work steadily toward your goals and graciously accept the support of your friends and associates, even if you think you are doing fine without them.

SUPER NOVA DAYS
JANUARY 21–24 ★ *emotional triage*
You may feel stress in your personal life, even though the long-term prognosis is much better than it seems. Joyous Jupiter's happy trine to pragmatic Saturn on **January 21** creates an underlying harmony that trumps any uncertainty caused by the confusing Mercury-Neptune conjunction on **January 22**. However, you could be in emotional turmoil by **January 24** as sweet Venus hooks up with shadowy Pluto. Unfulfilled needs are surfacing and can stand in the way of your happiness. Although the stakes are high, your determination is strong. You can produce the most positive effect if you stay focused on the big issues and look beyond your transient personal desires.

JANUARY 28–30 ★ *temporary retreat*
Self-doubt could resurface, prompting you to be especially hard on yourself. With warm Venus trining cold Saturn on **January 29**, it may also be a challenge to feel close to anyone else. A time-out may be just what you need to sustain something worthwhile. It may take time to fully understand what's happening as Mercury turns retrograde on **January 28** and Mars turns direct on **January 30**.

FEBRUARY

REALITY CHECK

February is a month of great change, hosting a pair of eclipses that can alter your view of reality and thrust you into your future whether you are ready or not. The first, a Solar Eclipse on **February 6**, can be rather disorienting. This intelligent Aquarius New Moon gains additional mental strength from a conjunction to chatty Mercury—but you aren't just talking about abstract concepts, for it's also conjunct Chiron the Wounded Healer. Discussing old emotional hurts can free you from the pain of the past. However, you may not be able to distinguish true memories from fantasies, because it's also conjunct nebulous Neptune. The Sun's conjunction with Neptune on **February 10** presents you with a chance to connect with a creative vision unrestrained by your day-to-day responsibilities.

Interactive Mercury ends its retrograde phase on **February 18**, just prior to the Sun's entry into compassionate Pisces. The second eclipse on **February 20** is a practical Virgo Full Moon in your 3rd House of Communication. With the Moon conjunct realistic Saturn, clarity returns and your illusions crash to the ground. Although you may be discouraged, there is no doubt about what's happening and what you must do. The two eclipses set the tone for the entire month, perhaps longer, representing a transition from unrealistic dreams to a more concrete relationship with your world.

The Sun's annual opposition to Saturn on **February 24** forces you to focus your attention on overcoming obstacles in your path. It's imperative that you do not succumb to hardships during this time. Once you know what you're up against, you can put all your efforts toward managing whatever is in your way.

> **KEEP IN MIND THIS MONTH**
>
> *Spend the first part of the month exploring all the possibilities that you can imagine. Then pick out the most practical and work toward achieving a goal of lasting value.*

KEY DATES

FEBRUARY 1–2 ★ *beautiful as a dream*

A lovely conjunction between luxurious Venus and opulent Jupiter on **February 1** falls in your 7th House of Partnerships, setting the stage for a wonderful day. Respect your physical and financial limits or you could indulge until you don't feel so well. The best use of this transit is to find pleasure in romance rather than in the material realm. But logical Mercury hooks up with dreamy Neptune on **February 2**, affecting your ability to think clearly. If you aren't sure about what to do, ask a trusted friend for advice, because he or she can give you a much-needed jolt of perspective.

SUPER NOVA DAY
FEBRUARY 6 ★ *seek the source*
The Aquarius New Moon Eclipse falls in your 8th House of Deep Sharing, drawing you into the mysteries of intimacy that involve complicated inter-relationships and unresolved feelings. Although intelligent Mercury is conjunct the eclipse, your logic is overridden by sudden flashes of curiosity, compelling you to investigate unfamiliar emotional terrain as you look for the root cause of what's happening. Trust your intuition, whatever twists and turns your research places in front of you.

FEBRUARY 10 ★ *nothing is real*
The Sun's annual conjunction with nebulous Neptune can inspire you to delve even farther into nonphysical dimensions. Whether you choose to communicate with spirits, journey into science fiction and fantasy, or develop a growing interest in psychology, you are being lured into the hidden worlds of consciousness. Don't let anyone tell you that you are trying to escape the real world, for this is about dis-covering personal meaning while you have the chance to find it.

FEBRUARY 20 ★ *self-repair*
Today's discerning Virgo Full Moon is a Lunar Eclipse, so your critical thinking may temporarily be hidden. Even if everything seems okay, you can pick up subtle signals that tell you otherwise, encouraging you to help those in need. But so much of your energy is flowing out toward everyone else, there is little left for you. Take care of yourself or you won't have anything left to give. For now, fixing what's broken has to start with a realistic reevaluation of your own needs.

FEBRUARY 24–26 ★ *make your point*
You may run into a wall as the Sun opposes authoritative Saturn on **February 24**. Something or someone is blocking your progress, and you must take a stand to overcome the obstacle. Don't retreat until you are heard. Be confident that you can present your ideas in a positive and creative way, for talkative Mercury hooks up with charming Venus on **February 26**. People will like your style even if they disagree with your point of view.

MARCH

It's a whole new ball game this month with dynamic Mars entering tenacious Cancer on **March 4**. Your adrenaline surges—although it may be difficult to apply your newfound enthusiasm. You may be overwhelmed by your fantasies, not knowing which way to turn as beautiful Venus conjuncts dreamy Neptune on **March 6**, followed by an intense Mars-Pluto opposition. Also, the imaginative Pisces New Moon on **March 7** adds more uncertainty to your heightened emotions. But with erratic Uranus nearby, you may be ready to explode with feelings. Be gentle, for this is an opportunity to process emotions buried deep within.

Venus enters compassionate Pisces on **March 12**, moving toward a harmonious trine with Mars on **March 16**. You are apt to act on your feelings now, rather than expressing them as detached intellectual ideas. It isn't easy to talk about your insecurities, for Mercury enters shy Pisces on **March 14** and bumps into Saturn on **March 17**. You may have to keep your thoughts to yourself until taking action as Mercury harmonizes with assertive Mars on **March 18**. The Sun's entrance into Aries on **March 20** marks the Spring Equinox, a time when intentions are pushed forward, but this may conflict with your desire to proceed with caution. The sociable Libra Full Moon on **March 21** can be quite stressful with squares to Pluto and Mars. It may feel like there is no resolution to your current problems, yet this is a critical transition point. March culminates with intense activity as smart Mercury, sensual Venus, and strange Uranus conjoin between **March 27 and March 28** while receiving a sweet sextile from optimistic Jupiter. There is no need to wait for a better time to begin the journey that awaits you.

> ### KEEP IN MIND THIS MONTH
>
> *Avoiding conflict will only make you angrier with others and disappointed with yourself. Risking rejection is a much better plan than burying your head in the sand.*

KEY DATES

SUPER NOVA DAYS
MARCH 6–9 ★ *honest disclosure*
You may be confused about your needs as pleasure-seeking Venus conjuncts mystical Neptune on **March 6**. Your judgment may be clouded for a few days, but the real issue is your tendency now to act first and think later. The dreamy

Pisces New Moon on **March 7** is electrified by a conjunction with Uranus, prompting you to react impulsively, without considering the consequences. Passions are running strong, for feisty Mars forms a tense opposition with powerful Pluto, provoking power struggles and churning emotional turmoil. You must find a way to express what is bothering you. You can be kind and gentle in your disclosure, but you must be real. If, however, you avoid the pressing issues, you may confront even bigger ones on **March 8** as the catalytic Sun-Uranus conjunction unexpectedly releases social restraints.

MARCH 15–17 ★ *compassionate warrior*

Relationship tensions can initiate a process that heals a challenging situation now. Venus's opposition to somber Saturn on **March 15**, followed by Mercury's on **March 17**, can create a layer of isolation between you and others. Repressed fear may hold you back from embarking on the journey of a lifetime, but Venus and Mercury also trine assertive Mars, giving you the courage to take action. If you feel blocked, don't blame anyone else; it's your own issues that need your attention. Remember, everything is less scary with the light of awareness shining on it.

MARCH 21 ★ *go deep*

The harmony-seeking Libra Full Moon finds little satisfaction today as it dynamically squares destructive Pluto and energetic Mars. Additionally, a Sun-Pluto square inflames the emotional intensity even further. Passions may be riled—but don't compartmentalize your feelings, even if you long for a quieter frame of mind. There are few easy solutions now; however, if you can find the courage to go along with the whirlwind, your life can be enriched by this experience. Everything will begin to settle down in a day or two.

MARCH 28–30 ★ *no holds barred*

You are acutely aware of what you want now and are willing to go for it. Even if you tend to be shy, conjunctions of Venus and Uranus on **March 28**, coupled with a Sun-Mars square on **March 30**, give you the potential to surprise yourself and others by acting inconsiderately. A more eccentric side of you is struggling to get out, and a powerful sextile between confident Jupiter and unorthodox Uranus can make this easier than ever. If you've been waiting for the right moment to break out of your shell, this is your chance.

APRIL

MOVE AT YOUR OWN SPEED

Your stress level could be high as April begins, making it difficult to find balance between your desire for personal expression and the pressures you feel from your career or family responsibilities. You are being pushed along too fast; you want to dig in your heels and tell everyone to leave you alone. As quick-thinking Mercury enters impulsive Aries on **April 2** and dynamically squares transformative Pluto on **April 3**, you could become compulsive in your resistance to inevitable change. Your suspicion is that no matter what you do now, you just won't get it right. Surround yourself with positive people so you can maintain your confidence. The Aries New Moon on **April 5** falls in your 10th House of Public Status, again emphasizing the gap between your goals and your current commitments. Venus joins the headstrong Aries pack on **April 6** in your 10th House and squares Pluto, possibly reactivating a recent power struggle.

When the Sun squares extravagant Jupiter and mental Mercury squares forceful Mars on **April 10**, you again try to balance personal needs with external demands. Your angst settles as Mercury enters placid Taurus on **April 17**, followed by the Sun on **April 19**. The emotionally powerful Scorpio Full Moon on **April 20** falls in your 5th House of Creativity and is supported by a practical Grand Earth Trine, allowing you to express your most intense feelings in a playful manner. Applying your fantasies constructively is the best use of a gentle sextile between Venus and Neptune on **April 26**. Then Venus enters easygoing Taurus on **April 30**, reconnecting to the Grand Earth Trine and again smoothing your path. Don't get too comfortable or you could waste the great potential inherent in this moment.

> **KEEP IN MIND THIS MONTH**
>
> *Your actions now can propel you forward, although you still must be careful not to overextend yourself even when everything looks so promising.*

KEY DATES

APRIL 5–6 ★ *be professional*

The accent is on your public life as the action-packed Aries New Moon on **April 5** falls in your 10th House of Career. But your need for independence can create conflict with your work and community responsibilities. You are more assertive with sexy Venus entering Aries, but asking for what you want doesn't always mean you'll be satisfied. Venus crosses swords with shadowy Pluto on **April 6** and you might not be able to stop yourself from demanding more than you need, even if this isn't your usual style. If you go too far out on the limb now, you may need to quickly retreat to regain your lost security.

APRIL 10 ★ *not so fast*
You are often tentative in your emotional expression, but a pair of dynamic squares today encourages you to take a risk. The powerful Sun-Jupiter square graces you with the energy you need, but you still might find yourself in over your head if you don't pay attention to deadlines. The argumentative Mercury-Mars square makes you uncharacteristically impulsive, yet if you jump before you understand what's happening, it may be difficult for you to clean up the mess you create. Back away from petty disagreements; open conflict will not bring you any closer to your goals.

SUPER NOVA DAYS
APRIL 20–24 ★ *sweet simplicity*
The magnetic Scorpio Full Moon on **April 20** may prevent you from being too lighthearted, yet you are still quite serious about having fun. A series of harmonious trines through **April 22** give you the emotional tools to balance your needs with reality. And even if trouble is brewing, you are adamant about your action plan. It can get quite intense as innuendos fly, but incomplete statements don't really hide anything at all now. As Venus squares Mars and Jupiter on **April 23**, you may be tempted to lose your patience, but rash actions won't help. Remember, you should be untangling emotional knots, not making them worse. With Mars still in nurturing Cancer in your 1st House of Self, opposing expansive Jupiter in your 7th House of Others on **April 24**, it's all too easy to say yes to someone's great idea before you think it through completely.

APRIL 28–29 ★ *enlightened detachment*
A slippery quincunx between fiery Mars and nebulous Neptune on **April 28** has others misreading your intentions now, but a Mercury-Jupiter trine allows you to move beyond the misunderstanding. Then, as Mercury squares Neptune on **April 29**, reality slips through your fingers when you see a way out of the dilemma. Unfortunately, denial is not a solution. Remember that spiritual enlightenment is within reach if only you can detach your desires from your feelings.

MAY

SURPRISES IN STORE

May starts smoothly as beautiful Venus harmonizes with opulent Jupiter and taskmaster Saturn on **May 1**. Then communicator Mercury slips into noisy Gemini in your 12th House of Imagination, marking a time of heightened spirituality and greater internalization of your mental processes. The sensible Taurus New Moon on **May 5** falls into your 11th House of Groups, indicating that the weeks ahead can be quite active socially, even if you prefer more time alone. But then Mars enters generous Leo on **May 9**, remaining in your 2nd House of Money and Resources throughout the rest of the month, strengthening your drive to improve your fiscal condition.

The Sun creates a harmonizing trine with confident Jupiter and a supportive sextile with exciting Uranus on **May 12**, magnifying the potential associated with a new project. These opportunities are revitalized around **May 18** when Venus reactivates Jupiter and Uranus. The passionate Scorpio Full Moon on **May 19** falls in your 5th House of Pleasure, challenging you to balance your physical desires with your need for metaphysical growth. Venus's tense square with spiritual Neptune turns this Full Moon into a truly inspirational day as long as you are willing to open your heart.

The Sun enters curious Gemini on **May 20**, signaling another shift into mental realms. But the optimism of Jupiter's sextile to Uranus on **May 21** is somewhat counteracted by Saturn's squares to the Sun and Venus on **May 22 and May 26**, respectively, blocking your path and creating delays. Additionally, Mercury turns retrograde on **May 26**, beginning a three-week period of reevaluation and reconsideration. Avoid unnecessary frustration by resisting temptations to push yourself faster than circumstances now allow.

> **KEEP IN MIND THIS MONTH**
>
> *Prioritize your goals and create a practical plan so you won't end up frittering away the vast potential in front of you.*

KEY DATES

MAY 1 ★ *self-contained*

Your self-sufficiency could allow you to withdraw deeper into your shell today, and you are tapped into powerful emotional issues that can teach you something important about yourself. Others may think you are retreating, but it might just be your way of forcing them to show their cards. There's no need to explain your motives; your patience will be rewarded.

MAY 5 ★ *watch your back*

The Taurus New Moon reminds you to surround yourself with family and friends who can help you find your way through the upcoming changes. But you must be somewhat cautious, for domineering Pluto is sesquisquare the Moon, increasing the stakes and insinuating that someone else might not share your goals. Take practical advice to heart, but steer away from convoluted schemes that don't further your progress.

MAY 11-14 ★ *dazed and confused*

Energetic Mars forms an irritating quincunx with shadowy Pluto on **May 11**, evoking memories of being controlled by others and prompting you to overreact now, even if the current situation isn't as threatening as it seems. But your uneasiness doesn't last long, for the Sun harmonizes with beneficent Jupiter and brilliant Uranus on **May 12**, gracing you with an opportunity to enjoy yourself with your friends. You may feel a bit confused on **May 14** when the Sun crosses paths with nebulous Neptune, making it difficult to tell the difference between your thoughts and someone else's fantasies.

SUPER NOVA DAYS
MAY 18-21 ★ *the power of now*

Your desire for a romantic adventure is heightened as Venus harmonizes with opulent Jupiter and unorthodox Uranus on **May 18**. Emotional extravagance may not be your regular style, but the magnetic Scorpio Full Moon on **May 19** excites you with playful dreams that spill over into your waking life. You are truly inspired, and you're up for just about anything. Don't waste energy attempting to hold back the floodgates of your imagination. Jupiter's sextile to Uranus on **May 21** excites the very core of your soul and tempts you with one possibility after another.

MAY 26 ★ *fix it yourself*

It may feel like your easy progress is grinding to a halt as intellectual Mercury and dreamy Neptune both turn retrograde. You might want to hide in a cave because you are uncomfortably vulnerable. Your tendency is to seek solace by retreating, for you know your friends cannot help you. You got yourself into this dilemma, and now you'll have to get yourself out of it. Although you might feel pressure to fix everything at once, you have more time than you think.

JUNE

ANYTHING IS POSSIBLE

June should be highly productive, but the real gains may not be apparent until later in the month. The action starts with the Sun, Mercury, and Venus all in your 12th House of Endings, underscoring the importance of finishing old projects before beginning anything new. Communicator Mercury is retrograde until **June 19,** reminding you of all the phone calls and e-mails that need your replies. The restless Gemini New Moon on **June 3** is also in your 12th House, reemphasizing this hidden flurry of activity. The harmonizing effect of this New Moon lasts through the Sun's conjunction with Venus on **June 9.** Then, however, both Venus and the Sun form irritating quincunxes with overindulgent Jupiter, expanding your sense of what's possible and making it difficult to know what is real and what you want.

A sensible balance to your life continues to elude you as both Venus and the Sun dynamically square wild Uranus on **June 12–13,** followed by trines to Neptune on **June 13–14.** You are up for anything, yet you aren't exactly sure how to proceed. But the philosophical Sagittarius Full Moon on **June 18** is conjunct Pluto, giving you a chance to resolve relationship tensions one way or another. The end of Mercury's retrograde phase on **June 19,** coupled with the Sun's entry into your sign on **June 20,** renews your vitality as you look ahead. Venus's supportive sextile to stabilizing Saturn on **June 21** can transform even the darkest night into the nurturing growth of summer ahead. The last days of June are marked by a harmonious trine between assertive Mars and powerful Pluto, rejuvenating you with an unending source of energy in order to move your life in the direction of your dreams.

> **KEEP IN MIND THIS MONTH**
>
> *Don't be surprised if a relationship situation becomes temporarily overwhelming. Just remember that the intensity should wane once you honestly confront the issues.*

KEY DATES

JUNE 3 ★ *hidden agenda*
Intelligent Mercury and attractive Venus cluster around the thoughtful Gemini New Moon in your 12th House of Secrets, tempting you to share your innermost fantasies with someone you trust. But you make everything appear less complex than it is, for you are playing a shell game with reality now. A feeling arises, you say something about it, and then you pretend that it never happened. Even if you withhold your real intentions, at least don't hide them from yourself.

JUNE 7-9 ★ *prosperity consciousness*

You can make real gains in your pursuit of spiritual awareness on **June 7**, but you must fight the tendency to keep your wisdom all to yourself. A supportive sextile from Mercury to Mars in your 2nd House of Money on **June 8** can be good news for your personal finances. The Venus-Sun conjunction on **June 9** reminds you that the power of the mind can positively impact your overall wealth, increasing the size of your bank account along with your self-esteem.

JUNE 12-13 ★ *risk for love*

Venus, the planet of money and love, dynamically squares nonconformist Uranus on **June 12** and then harmoniously trines visionary Neptune on **June 13**. You are eager to move outside your comfort zone, for you are attracted by the thrill of being free from your normal self-restraint. Although you may face disappointment later on, it will be worth the risk. Open your heart to the beauty that surrounds you; even if it feels fleeting, enjoy it while you can.

SUPER NOVA DAYS
JUNE 18-20 ★ *your time to shine*

The adventurous Sagittarius Full Moon on **June 18**, mixed with Venus's opposition to shadowy Pluto, demands that you confront deep psychological issues. The Sun's entry into Cancer marks the Summer Solstice on **June 20** and continues to toss you about on the seas of change. Fortunately, the weeks ahead can bring you a heightened sense of belonging, deepen your current relationship, or even introduce a new love interest into your life as Venus enters nurturing Cancer on **June 18** and Mercury turns direct on **June 19**. Don't slip back into your shell, even if you think you must protect your heart. Let your emotions flow naturally.

JUNE 30 ★ *move with integrity*

You may feel an irrepressible urge to have your way as assertive Mars harmonizes with unstoppable Pluto. You can unconsciously manipulate co-workers to do your bidding, yet coercion for your own selfish benefit is likely to backfire. As much as you want change, remember that you will be most effective by acting from your heart and not from your head.

JULY

Communication is a major theme during the month of July, but it isn't always easy or straightforward. Unflappable Mars enters fussy Virgo on **July 1**, moving into your 3rd House of Communication, where it stays the entire month. This encourages you to assert yourself—yet you will likely do so cautiously, and only when you are sure that you are right. Chatty Mercury in talkative Gemini squares eccentric Uranus on **July 5** and trines fuzzy-thinking Neptune on **July 6**, exciting you intellectually but making it difficult to be precise in verbal or written form. Part of the problem is that Venus trines Uranus the same day, enticing you to reach so far conceptually that you are unable to effectively make your point. Mercury enters moody Cancer on **July 10**, intensifying your thoughts and increasing your emotional attachment to them. In contrast, beautiful Venus enters dramatic Leo in your 2nd House of Self-Worth on **July 12**, motivating you to show off your generosity. And the Sun's brilliant trine to Uranus on **July 14** ensures that the spotlight will be shining on you.

The sobering Capricorn Full Moon on **July 18** in your 7th House of Partnerships may require you to step outside your comfort zone to address the current situation responsibly. The Sun enters lively Leo on **July 22**, the same day that Mercury trines eccentric Uranus. Your spirits lift and you are ready to move into new territory, yet the days ahead could threaten your sense of security. Mercury enters Leo on **July 26** and conjuncts the Sun on **July 29**, again re-emphasizing the need for communicating your ideas without being overwhelmed by your feelings.

> **KEEP IN MIND THIS MONTH**
>
> *Although the main emphasis is on rational communication, you don't always need to separate your personal needs from your more intellectual pursuits.*

KEY DATES

JULY 2-3 ★ *self-help*

The emotionally sensitive Cancer New Moon on **July 2** sets the stage for sweet times ahead as pleasure-craving Venus opposes opulent Jupiter on **July 3**. You may appear passive, but your desire to nurture others is strong, for you want those you love to enjoy themselves. Keep in mind, however, that it's not selfish to look after yourself. You could end up resenting others if you don't take care of your own needs. Still, be careful not to be so enamored with the potential of sweet indulgence that you grow lazy and inadvertently allow important obligations to pass unfulfilled.

JULY 9-10 ★ *call the bluff*

The Sun's opposition to gigantic Jupiter on **July 9** magnifies your ambitions, making it tough to fit your goals into the circumstances of your life. But Mars inches closer to a difficult conjunction with restrictive Saturn that's exact on **July 10**, forcing you to acknowledge someone else's authority. You are eager to get on with your journey, but first must meet the demands being placed on you close to home. Narrow your scope of vision to improve your chance for success, but don't shut down too much. The current situation may hinge on feelings that are not out in the open. You can change the entire game by laying your cards face up on the table.

SUPER NOVA DAYS
JULY 18-22 ★ *break through your shell*

The emotionally cautious Capricorn Full Moon on **July 18** can unveil serious relationship conflicts. Don't attempt to avoid direct discussion, or the unresolved issues will only come back to haunt you later. You must remain present even if you would rather withdraw from the tension. Your courage builds as cunning Mercury opposes confident Jupiter on **July 19**. The facts are not as important as your opinion these days, so be certain to express your beliefs. Get behind your cause and let your friends know exactly what you think. Your optimism can even turn reckless as Mercury trines irrepressible Uranus on **July 22**. Go ahead and take a chance as long as it's reasonably safe. This momentary shot at freedom could very well be worth the risk.

JULY 26 ★ *decisive action*

Your mind turns to the practical issues of finances as Mercury in action-oriented Leo moves into your 2nd House of Money. You are less fearful now, because you can visualize a path that leads you toward greater stability. Enterprising Mars trines broad-minded Jupiter, encouraging you to be so enthusiastic that you are game for nearly anything. Fortunately, your common sense will prevent you from doing something you may later regret, so trust your own judgment.

AUGUST

A MARATHON OF CHANGE

August is a power-packed month that brings issues to a climax, rewards the hard work you have done, and clearly demonstrates what you have yet to accomplish. It begins with a fiery Leo New Moon Eclipse on **August 1** and ends with a critical Virgo New Moon on **August 30**. Little can stand in the way of your desires when alluring Venus harmonizes with intense Pluto on **August 5**. Even the wave of common sense that washes over you as Venus enters precise Virgo isn't enough to counteract the wild opposition between decisive Mars and radical Uranus on **August 6**. Fortunately, clarity returns as logical Mercury trines Pluto on **August 9** and enters Virgo on **August 10**. Then Venus and Mercury move toward conjunctions with taskmaster Saturn on **August 13 and August 15**, respectively, setting heavy responsibilities onto your shoulders. You must stand up and deal with a potentially frustrating situation, overcome any obstacles, and examine your resistance so you can accomplish your goals.

The eccentric Aquarius Full Moon Eclipse on **August 16** is conjunct psychic Neptune, allowing you to see through the mists of your own dreams. A harmonizing trine between sweet Venus and beneficent Jupiter graces this emotionally intense time with great potential for success. Mars makes a difficult square with Pluto on **August 17**, indicating a potential struggle for control as a powerful person tries to block your efforts. Don't succumb to external pressures; use Mars's entry into strategic Libra to regroup and consider a change of tactics. The Sun's trine to Pluto on **August 21** adds conviction to your actions, but Mercury and Venus oppose Uranus on **August 23**, heralding a few more surprises before the month is over.

> **KEEP IN MIND THIS MONTH**
>
> *Fear of change might upset you, but retreating will not be helpful. Flexibility in the face of adversity will always be your greatest ally.*

KEY DATES

AUGUST 1 ★ *healthy abundance*

The dramatic Leo New Moon Eclipse on **August 1** falls in your 2nd House of Values and can quickly define problems with your self-esteem as well as with your bank account. Money issues that surface may be tied to your lack of confidence. If you believe, even subconsciously, that you deserve the finer things in life, then you are much more likely to receive them.

AUGUST 5–6 ★ *powerful forces at work*

You can tap into profound emotional issues on **August 5** as seductive Venus harmonizes with passionate Pluto, giving you a chance to explore your hidden desires. Oppositions from Mercury and Mars to unorthodox Uranus and spiritual Neptune on **August 6** excite you with a taste of freedom while also confusing your thinking process. This can be a thrilling yet unsettling mix as you throw caution to the wind without fear. Although it's probably the right time to break free, careful communication coupled with some self-restraint can ease this transition.

SUPER NOVA DAYS

AUGUST 13–17 ★ *the good, the bad, and the intense*

The paradox of the quirky Aquarius Full Moon Eclipse on **August 16** can provoke explosive emotional tension if you try to ignore your true feelings. On the one hand, you may feel discouraged and ready to give up as congenial Venus and quick-witted Mercury are opposed by pessimistic Saturn on **August 13** and **August 15**, respectively. On the other hand, they are harmoniously trined by generous Jupiter on **August 16–17**, turning a bleak situation into a successful venture. A stressful square between aggressive Mars and defiant Pluto could indicate a struggle for dominance that ends in an emotional standoff. There will be no sweet victory for anyone unless you are willing to avoid unnecessary escalation. You have the power of logic working on your behalf, so trust your judgment while always taking the high road.

AUGUST 23 ★ *wide emotional swings*

Both Mercury and Venus oppose nonconformist Uranus today, rousing your inner rebel. Your heart is alternately attracted and repulsed as love and fear take turns spinning your navigational compass. Keep an open mind and be ready for surprises. Once you make the necessary adjustments to your thinking, everything can settle back down within a couple of days.

AUGUST 29–30 ★ *release the past*

Attractive Venus in picky Virgo squares Pluto on **August 29** as relationships can become a source of discomfort. Pain arises from the memory of previous emotional traumas that are connected with current experiences. An exacting Virgo New Moon on **August 30** conjuncts karmic Saturn, clearing the air so you can forgive and forget. It's time to move forward without holding on to your past.

SEPTEMBER

BALANCING ACT

An emphasis on your 4th House of Home and Family this month encourages you to stabilize your foundation, yet a pressing need to keep the personal and professional aspects of your life in balance can produce moments of significant stress. An annual conjunction between the Sun and responsible Saturn on **September 3** harmonizes with a long-term trine between expansive Jupiter and contractive Saturn on **September 8**. This second of three stabilizing trines between these cosmic regulators this year can smooth over the rough spots in your life, but can be so effective that you may become bored with the sameness of your life. The personal planets—cerebral Mercury, aesthetic Venus, and energetic Mars—are traveling together in a cluster through social Libra, motivating you to create harmony within your family. And although the strong Jupiter-Saturn trine graces your life with lovely balance, on **September 7–9** the personal planets all dynamically square Jupiter, now moving through disciplined Capricorn in your 7th House of Others. You could find yourself struggling to maintain your position as a persuasive partner encourages you to venture outside your cozy cave of safety.

The Sun's yearly opposition to brilliant Uranus on **September 12**, however, provokes you to express hidden feelings and secrets, possibly igniting a few days of turmoil. The intuitive Pisces Full Moon on **September 15** is closely conjunct spontaneous Uranus, tempting you to act before you think. Neptune is trined by Venus on **September 17**, by Mars on **September 21**, and by Mercury on **September 28**, soothing your anxieties and replacing restlessness with comfort. The sweet Libra New Moon on **September 29** ends the month with the same 4th House emphasis on your home, family interactions, and childhood memories, all familiar and comfortable territory.

> **KEEP IN MIND THIS MONTH**
>
> *Unexpected events may require immediate attention, but don't change your overall direction— the distractions will fade, allowing you to continue on your way.*

KEY DATES

SEPTEMBER 7–9 ★ *eye on the prize*

The influential trine between Jupiter and Saturn on **September 8** should bring you a sense of equilibrium. However, Mars, Venus, and Mercury all square excessive Jupiter during these days, overwhelming you with an endless list of chores. Your schedule might indeed fall apart—but don't worry too much. While it's crucial that you extinguish the brushfires, don't be distracted from your long-term goals, even if they're very ambitious—you needn't resolve every issue that arises now.

SUPER NOVA DAYS
SEPTEMBER 15–19 ★ *internal compass*
The visionary Pisces Full Moon on **September 15** falls in your 9th House of Big Ideas, yet its conjunction to Uranus, the planet of sudden action, can change everything overnight. If you are feeling overly optimistic about an upcoming project or adventure, you may be unexpectedly reeled back to shore. It's time to take out your maps and use your navigational skills to determine your exact location and your desired destination. However, a series of annoying quincunxes with Uranus throughout the week turns a simple problem into a complicated string of events, requiring you to make one adjustment after another. If your commitment wanes or you lose your way, stop long enough to check you compass and get your bearings.

SEPTEMBER 20–22 ★ *the illusion of control*
The Sun's dynamic square to defiant Pluto on **September 20** fills your day with duties and obligations that are beyond your control. Your goals may be in conflict with someone who tries to tell you what to do. Keep in mind that others are likely to be on your side; they're not really against you. If you are too involved in an ongoing power struggle, the Sun's entry into diplomatic Libra on **September 22**, the Autumn Equinox, in your 4th House of Security will remind you of your need to keep your personal feelings separate from your professional interactions. Additionally, potent Mars harmonizes with diffusive Neptune on **September 21**, dissipating your motivation. Although you may fear getting lost in someone else's agenda, your intuitive energy is running strong enough to show you a path back to clarity.

SEPTEMBER 28–29 ★ *imagination matters*
Trickster Mercury trines psychic Neptune on **September 28**, immersing you in your dreams. Don't expect to be rational while explaining your actions to others now, even though the Libra New Moon on **September 29** can help you understand both sides of the equation. Use these days to develop a logical framework for your current activities, but don't toss out what comes to you in an intuitive flash. Instead, find a way to blend the best of your fantasies with your present reality.

OCTOBER

CLOSER TO SUCCESS

Your experiences diversify throughout October as the planets—which were clustered in easygoing Libra last month—now separate. Venus is already in emotional Scorpio; Mars joins it, moving into Scorpio in your 5th House of Love and Creativity on **October 4**, a comfortable visit for your fellow water-loving Crabs. You are in your element now, for the cosmic lovers, Venus and Mars, in Scorpio encourage you to assert yourself in more playful ways, although you are also fully capable of passionately defending a serious position. Seductive Venus rekindles the long-term stabilizing Jupiter-Saturn conjunction as it sextiles the former on **October 5** and the latter on **October 7**. You are clear these days about what you want, but a dynamic square from the Sun and Mercury to Jupiter tempts you to go overboard and turn an insignificant desire into the cornerstone of a building. Venus's trine to erratic Uranus on **October 12** and square to nebulous Neptune on **October 11** fuels your attractions with the fires of your fantasies; there's no stopping you from pursuing them now.

The spontaneous Aries Full Moon on **October 14** falls in your 10th House of Career as you are thrown into the spotlight, perhaps doing more outside your home than you wish. Venus enters adventurous Sagittarius on **October 18**, followed by the Sun's entry into Scorpio on **October 22**, coaxing you even farther out of your shell. And although the magnetic Scorpio New Moon in your 5th House on **October 28** revitalizes you with the potential for pleasure, you may already feel the pressure of the **November 4** opposition between repressive Saturn and irrepressible Uranus. It may be impossible to make any major decisions just yet.

> **KEEP IN MIND THIS MONTH**
>
> *You are preparing to step into something new, but must decide what to leave behind so you can pursue the opportunities ahead.*

KEY DATES

OCTOBER 2-4 ★ *grin and bear it*

Mars the Warrior forces its way into Scorpio on **October 4**, announcing a dramatic shift of strategy. Diplomacy and negotiation can transform into subtle manipulation in the darker worlds of hidden actions and secret alliances. This change is heralded by an opportunistic sextile between Mars and Scorpio's key planet, Pluto, on **October 2**. You can feel your resentment swell, knowing that you will have to handle an unpleasant issue. It's best that you express any anger as kindly as possible, for it's likely to fester and infect you with negativity if you keep it to yourself. Acting with conviction and honesty can quickly sweeten a sour situation.

SUPER NOVA DAYS
OCTOBER 10-15 ★ *truth and consequences*
Sexy Venus in passionate Scorpio harmonizes with unpredictable Uranus on **October 10**, teasing you with unprecedented freedom of expression. If you hide your needs, you may miss a chance for shared intimacy along with the security you desire. Venus squares confusing Neptune on **October 11**, possibly throwing you into a temporary state of despair as you try to resolve your dilemma. The impulsive Aries Full Moon on **October 14** can clarify your needs in the struggle to find a comfortable balance between assertiveness and acceptance. Mercury turns direct on **October 15**, releasing your thoughts from fears of the past. Any decision now is better than none, so just pick one and accept the consequences.

OCTOBER 22 ★ *joyful flow*
The Sun's entry into watery Scorpio in your 5th House of Fun and Games isn't all light and easy, but it does illuminate your path to creative self-expression. You are ready to retreat from professional activities in favor of spending more time playing with your kids, mentoring younger people, or pursuing your inner child. This isn't just a matter of age; it's about being more spontaneous and recapturing the joy of romance and the thrill of doing what brings you pleasure.

OCTOBER 28-31 ★ *it's getting better all the time*
The Scorpio New Moon on **October 28** in your creative 5th House is reassuring, for it renews your spirit and strengthens your resolve to put your life on a track to happiness. But an annoying quincunx between chatty Mercury in socially correct Libra and maverick Uranus accentuates the differences between what you feel and what you can actually say out loud. Support arrives from your dreams as Mercury harmonizes with imaginative Neptune on **October 30**. Fortunately, dynamic Mars arrives with a brilliant yet doable plan, supported by hardworking Saturn and inventive Uranus on **October 30-31**.

NOVEMBER

AT THE EDGE OF A NEW WORLD

Deep cosmic waves rattle your home, shake the foundations of your life, and open your future to previously unseen possibilities. As great as these changes may be, they will not happen overnight; in fact, it may be well into next year before you fully understand where your life is leading you. Saturn has been blessed by a harmonious trine to buoyant Jupiter for most of 2008, but now there could be trouble brewing as hardworking Saturn opposes rebellious Uranus on **November 4**. Uranus's irrepressible urges run into an immovable wall of circumstances; responsibilities that were acceptable only a short time ago now prevent you from being true to yourself. The Sun shines light on this conflict as it sextiles Jupiter and Saturn, and trines Uranus on **November 10–11**.

The overall intensity increases around the sensual Taurus Full Moon on **November 13**, with Venus conjunct intense Pluto on **November 12** before moving into Capricorn in your 7th House of Relationships. This Full Moon is even more significant because Jupiter sextiles Uranus in the last of three windows of opportunity—the first on **March 28**, the second on **May 21**—opening a door to new relationships while revitalizing old ones. Mars's entry into upbeat Sagittarius in your 6th House of Daily Routines on **November 16** increases your busyness at work, but your temperament is positive as Mercury harmonizes with Jupiter, Saturn, and Uranus. Don't waste time worrying about what isn't okay; instead, enjoy the stability while it lasts. The Sun and Mercury enter Sagittarius on **November 21 and November 23**, respectively, filling your life with too many chores to finish, yet the confident Sagittarius New Moon on **November 27** motivates you to set goals for your next journey.

> **KEEP IN MIND THIS MONTH**
>
> *Maintain your daily routines as best you can. It makes sense to fulfill your current responsibilities, even if you are seeking to radically change the direction of your life.*

KEY DATES

SUPER NOVA DAYS
NOVEMBER 3–4 ★ *unexpected catalyst*
Pressure at work can make you feel like you can't do anything right as friendly Venus squares stern Saturn on **November 3** and unstable Uranus on

November 4. But the larger issue concerns Saturn's opposition to Uranus, also on **November 4**. Tensions have been increasing for a while, and now something must give. Retreating into the safety of your shell won't work. There is such a great sense of urgency that you could make yourself sick if you try to suppress your discontent. Your discouragement is great and your patience is short. For now, many small changes may be better than turning your whole world upside down.

NOVEMBER 12-13 ★ *night into day*
Friendly Venus joins dark Pluto on **November 12,** scaring you with the intensity of your unexpressed passions. Even if it feels hopeless, you are unlikely to change your mind once your heart is set. The determined Taurus Full Moon on **November 13** gives you reason to dig in your heels as you try to hold your world steady. Good news arrives in the form of an unexpected opportunity as benevolent Jupiter sextiles astonishing Uranus the same day. Just when you were ready to give up, the heavens open and even your most outlandish dreams seem possible.

NOVEMBER 21-23 ★ *just compensation*
The third and final trine between enthusiastic Jupiter and ethical Saturn on **November 21** stabilizes your work relationships and harmonizes communication with friends and family. This continues a theme that began on **January 21** and was rekindled on **September 8**. If you worked diligently throughout the year, organized your plans, and built sturdy bridges toward your future, now you reap the benefits of your efforts. Success won't be the result of momentary good luck, but rather the culmination of steady progress. If you face any setbacks, rest assured they can be overcome with a practical strategy, a strong work ethic, and lots of determination.

NOVEMBER 27-29 ★ *baby steps*
It's easy to make commitments that you won't keep now, as the overconfident Sagittarius New Moon on **November 27** conjuncts flattering Mercury and impulsive Mars, emboldening you to promise more than you can deliver. With the Sagittarius emphasis, you are likely to exaggerate your abilities, but Venus's trine to realistic Saturn on **November 29** can bring you back to your senses. Although you may attempt to inflate a little thought into a grand plan, it may not work. You will do best if you think small, act for the present moment, and leave the outrageous ideas for another day.

DECEMBER

BE TRUE TO YOURSELF

December begins with a lovely conjunction between attractive Venus and jolly Jupiter, setting a festive atmosphere for the holidays. Your friends and associates encourage you to step out beyond the safety of your cocoon into the world. But this optimism doesn't last, because an irritating quincunx between reality-driven Saturn and dreamy Neptune affects you all month. You can feel the weight of responsibility as you try to lose yourself in the spirit of the season. Taking your obligations seriously may be necessary, but acting like Scrooge doesn't make anyone feel good. The Gemini Full Moon on **December 11** in your 12th House of Spirituality can be rather intense as impulsive Mars squares Uranus, setting off fireworks and urging you forward, even if you aren't getting the support you want. You will know if you overstepped your bounds when Mars comes up to square restrictive Saturn on **December 15**. If you must apply the brakes, do it willingly; otherwise, your resentment will show, and others will be even less supportive.

The Sun joins shadowy Pluto on **December 22**, making these long winter nights even longer, forcing you to look into the darkest recesses of your dreams with the potential to transform negativity into wondrous beauty. Mars's entry into earnest Capricorn on **December 27,** just prior to the Capricorn New Moon, quiets the holiday celebrations long enough for you to review the previous year, list your current ambitions, and calculate your chances for future success. Fortunately, an uplifting conjunction between Mercury and Jupiter on **December 31** broadens your thinking, clears the clouds from your skies, and allows you to look forward to the New Year with great hope and anticipation.

> **KEEP IN MIND THIS MONTH**
>
> *Be prepared to take a stand for what is in your heart if sharing your dreams arouses any resistance in others.*

KEY DATES

DECEMBER 1 ★ *pleasure principle*
A beneficial Venus-Jupiter conjunction brightens your 7th House of Partnerships, and everyone seems to be extra friendly. They may entice you with sweet indulgences, contributing to your sense of contentment. This rewarding transit can also indicate that extra money coming your way, so it wouldn't hurt to ask for a raise if you think you deserve one. You are likely to treat yourself to a luxury today, so try to stay within your budget.

DECEMBER 5-6 ★ *silent treatment*

It's often difficult for you Crabs to express your anger, making you the champions of passive-aggressiveness, and the Sun-Mars conjunction on **December 5** brings this weakness to the forefront. You might be quite irate with someone's actions, yet your tendency is to withdraw rather than explode. Communicator Mercury crosses paths with authoritative Saturn on **December 6**, making it even harder to get your point across if you lose your temper. Gently express your hurt as clearly and patiently as possible, and hope for the best.

SUPER NOVA DAYS
DECEMBER 12 ★ *still waters run deep*

Your feelings are more erratic than ever as the Sun and Mars dynamically square rebellious Uranus on **December 10 and December 12**, respectively. You can get sucked into a philosophical or political debate before you know it. The intellectually curious Gemini Full Moon on **December 12** encourages you to seek answers by discussing pertinent issues, but language alone won't take you where you need to go. Although eloquent Mercury's conjunction with passionate Pluto can intensify your words, deeper emotions are not easily communicated. Don't try so hard, or you will end up only frustrating everyone involved.

DECEMBER 21-22 ★ *innevitable metamorphosis*

The joy of the holidays is counterbalanced by the regenerative Sun-Pluto conjunction on **December 22**, just one day after the Winter Solstice. You can sense that your world is irrevocably changing and there isn't anything you can do to stop the process. Transforming your fear into hard work may be quite productive, but it doesn't get to the underlying issue. There's no need to struggle so much; letting go of the caterpillar is required before you can become a butterfly.

DECEMBER 27-28 ★ *stake your claim*

You may feel as if others have trapped you in a box as the restrictive Capricorn New Moon on **December 27** falls in your 7th House of Public Life. You don't seem to have much of a choice, with everyone depending on you now. But Venus's conjunction with spiritual Neptune, and Mars's conjunction with "change agent" Pluto, force you to raise the stakes, show your vulnerability, and risk rejection. Others will see that you aren't really withdrawing, so they won't have to be so aggressive with their demands.

LEO

JULY 23–AUGUST 22

LEO OVERVIEW

Your primary focus this year is likely to be on practical matters as Jupiter and Saturn, the planetary regulators, are both in realistic earth signs. Expansive Jupiter's drive for more in life is managed by patient yet ambitious Capricorn. This "lucky" planet's passage through your 6th House of Work shows that good fortune must be earned through your direct efforts. Talent, skill, and social connections all have value, but without clear intention and commitment on your part, they are unlikely to take you where you want to go. **For the most part, gains accrue when you make a plan and stick to it.** This slow and steady path to success may lack some of the drama and flair you tend to enjoy. However, there are more than a few bright moments along the way that make your sacrifice worthwhile. Jupiter's three synthesizing sextiles with inventive Uranus in imaginative Pisces on March 28, May 21, and November 12 are periods when intuitive flashes and surprisingly supportive people allow you to take great leaps forward.

Saturn, the planet of hard, cold reality, filters out distracting fantasies through Virgo's tightly woven screen of practicality. The cost of random thoughts and ill-conceived ideas is higher than usual this year. Instead of feeling constrained within these narrow limits, though, this is your chance to focus your attention and raise your abilities to a higher level of competence. **Develop your expertise in one area at a time instead of scattering your attention across broad fields of interest.** Serious Saturn is in your 2nd House of Resources all year, a reminder to honor your gifts, including your precious time, by not squandering them carelessly. This planet that says no but means yes demands that you humbly serve your talent through practice and training to express it to its highest potential. Last year, Jupiter and Saturn formed favorable trines to each other in visionary fire signs that framed an inspiring vision for the future. They repeat these creative aspects this year in earth signs to turn those ideals into something real. Passionate Pluto's first steps into constructive Capricorn from fiery Sagittarius are another signal of the elemental shift from the realm of concept to the world of form.

A progressive Aquarius Solar Eclipse on February 6 and an Aquarius Lunar Eclipse on August 16 may suddenly and irrevocably shift the shape of your relationships. Letting go of partners or close friends due to differences of beliefs or aspirations is not easy. Yet holding on to people out of loyalty or a shared illusion may be too costly to bear. **Don't confuse sentiment with commitment, or compassion with a contract.** Aquarius, which occupies your 7th House of Partnerships, requires more personal space and a respect for individuality that could lead to a parting of the ways. Face matters of the heart with cool intelligence rather than hot emotion to see situations more clearly and make the best decisions possible.

 ## DREAMCATCHER

A lot of hard work and a little bit of magic are the keys to your heart this year. Generous Jupiter, the ruler of your 5th House of Romance, is in strategic Capricorn, where planning produces results. Aim high when it comes to love, since settling for the middle can sink your hopes to the bottom. You have an opportunity to build a ladder to heaven, but must be willing to do the arduous work necessary to make it happen. Jupiter is in your 6th House of Self-Improvement, motivating you to study your emotional patterns and daily habits, and then changing or eliminating whatever gets in the way of your happiness. Two eclipses in your 7th House of Relationships represent a changing attitude or even a change of partner. The Solar Eclipse on February 6 is conjunct Neptune, the planet of ideals and illusion. It's time to wake up to the reality of your present situation, rather than maintaining hopes or fantasies that stop you from addressing issues in a concrete way. Neptune is prominent again during the Lunar Eclipse of August 16, another reminder to temper relationship dreams with a major dose of realism. Still, Neptune joins the Moon's North Node in your 7th House of Partnerships on May 8, which can put you in a magical zone of soul connection that heals your relationship wounds. Forgiveness and faith open the way for unconditional love.

 ## INVEST IN YOUR FUTURE

Transformational Pluto pokes its nose into your 6th House of Employment in late January, backs out in mid-June, and returns for a long-term engagement at the end of the year that is likely to alter the course of your professional future. Positive changes on the work front can result from training in new technologies or developing unconventional areas of expertise thanks to intelligent sextiles between expansive Jupiter and inventive Uranus on March 28, May 21, and November 12. Jupiter's presence in your 6th House this year signals advancement at work achieved by taking on more responsibilities. Continuing your education and spending extra time and energy on the job are solid investments now.

 ## REDUCE, RECYCLE, REUSE

A cautious approach to finances makes sense with restricting Saturn in your 2nd House of Resources this year. Maintaining what you already own is wiser than purchasing the latest, greatest version of equipment that may not be worth the cost. Avoid extravagant expenses, especially around the Lunar Eclipse on February 20, falling in the money house of your chart. However, healthy trines between forward-looking Jupiter and Saturn on January 21, September 8, and November 21 can provide economic stability and a clear vision of how best to spend your time and money to achieve your long-term goals.

 ## LONG-TERM STRATEGY

You love the joys of the flesh, Leo, but self-discipline in diet, exercise, and life-style is required to keep you in good shape this year. Opulent Jupiter in your 6th House of Health tempts you to be excessive in your appetites, which is clearly not ideal for your physical well-being. But instead of following the latest diet scheme or just making up your own plan, read books, take a class, or talk to a health professional to create a comprehensive approach to staying fit. Dropping calories without managing nutrition carefully could diminish your energy. Potent Pluto's visits to the health zone of your chart make this a transitional year. Slowly and steadily establish permanent healthy patterns to reduce illness and increase vitality through fundamental changes in your habits and daily routine.

 ## EMPTY THE CLOSETS

Old wounds stirred up last year continue to play an important role in your home life early this year. Penetrating Pluto, the ruler of your 4th House of Roots, revealed family vulnerabilities with tough semisquares to pained Chiron that could reoccur in late January. Baring unexpressed hurts is never easy, but can be a powerful step toward healing. Aggressive Mars makes hard aspects to Pluto on January 2, March 7, August 16, and December 28— days when a little pressure can trigger a blow-up. Use the intensity of these times for emotional and physical cleanup that allows you to turn your deepest desires into action.

OPEN ROAD

This year is quite favorable for learning and globe trotting, but avoid hitting the road or undertaking a serious course of study before January 30 when Mars, the ruler of your 9th House of Higher Education and Travel, turns direct. If you must do either sooner, having a partner with you will make it much easier. The travel bug may bite on May 9, when initiating Mars enters your sign. Temper your instinct to go first-class, since you might ignore obvious budget considerations at this time. This transit may also provide an opportunity to share your beliefs with others; just stay open-minded to keep from coming across as a know-it-all.

SPIRIT IN ACTION

Your spirituality will grow more through real-world activities than contemplation or study this year. Jupiter the Guru occupies practical Capricorn in your down-to-earth 6th House where service to others teaches you much more than living in a monastery, reading volumes of sacred text, or praying several times a day. Use your leadership skills to organize activities that uplift those in need. Every act of conscious kindness raises your awareness while contributing directly to the well-being of humanity.

RICK & JEFF'S TIP FOR THE YEAR:
Moderate the Extremes

Raising your public profile would seem to put more weight on your shoulders, so it's natural to unconsciously resist making yourself more visible. Yet the more you accomplish this year, the more secure you'll feel. Instead of sensing the burden of responsibility that success often brings, your inner strength will grow with a sense of accomplishment. This builds up your foundation, increases your power, and gives you more options in life. Hard work won't slow you down or narrow your choices; in fact, it will open you up to greater freedom to create the future you desire.

JANUARY

JUGGLING WORK AND PLAY

The two key issues of career and relationships share center stage in your life this month. Professional concerns are triggered by the ambitious Capricorn New Moon on **January 8** that falls in your 6th House of Work. You may be burdened with additional responsibilities, but this may also be an occasion to earn respect by demonstrating your loyalty and competence. Seize any opportunities for training that upgrades your skills or supports a desire to start your own business. On **January 21**, optimistic Jupiter and conservative Saturn form the third in a series of harmonious trines that began last March. The first two aspects were in creative fire signs, while this one and the final two—which follow on **September 8 and November 21**—are in practical earth signs. The message is to ground your high hopes with concrete action, patience, and commitment.

Curious Mercury crosses into your 7th House of Partnerships on **January 7**, attracting unusual individuals and opening your eyes to alternative views of relationships. The Sun's entry into the 7th House on **January 20** opens your heart to deeper intimacy as you express your feelings and share love more generously. The proud Leo Full Moon on **January 22**, though, dramatizes emotions growing out of the contrast between self-interest and compromise. Whatever is agreed to may need to be renegotiated later, since Mercury the communication planet turns retrograde on **January 28**, beginning a three-week period of review and revision. Impulsive Mars awakens from its own retrograde slumber on **January 30** in your 11th House of Friends. A pushy pal may encourage you to act before you're ready. Resist the pressure to move quickly; spend your extra energy playfully instead of rushing an important decision.

KEEP IN MIND THIS MONTH

Pace yourself personally and professionally this month. Impatience is a sign of uncertainty; demonstrate self-confidence by moving slowly and steadily.

KEY DATES

JANUARY 6-8 ★ *ahead of your time*

Bright ideas are popping on **January 6** with a mentally sharp sextile between inventive Uranus and your ruling planet, the Sun. But no matter how clever you are, a tense square between withholding Saturn and sociable Venus can keep you from getting the kudos you deserve. Earning approval requires diligence now as well as patience. Mercury's entry in heady Aquarius late on **January 7** keeps your mind spinning, especially when the speedy planet forms an edgy semisquare with Uranus on **January 8**. Unconventional thoughts spark brilliant conversations, but new concepts could be too radical for others to accept.

JANUARY 12–13 ★ *stay on your toes*

A heightened sense of vulnerability can complicate relationships this weekend. The watery Pisces Moon in your 8th House of Intimacy offers both closeness and uncertainty. Pisces's two ruling planets, Jupiter and Neptune, form an awkward semisquare on **January 12** that adds to the misty mood. The desire for smooth connections can be shattered by a tense square between Venus and unpredictable Uranus, triggering sudden changes that chill the atmosphere one minute and charge it with excitement the next. Staying flexible to adapt to surprises will make everyone more comfortable. The Sun forms a demanding sesquisquare with ambitious Saturn on **January 13** that spawns power struggles. Setting limits with others is helpful, but mutual respect is essential to maintain harmony.

SUPER NOVA DAYS
JANUARY 19–21 ★ *adult playtime*

Passions rise with romantic Venus in your 5th House of Love Affairs, heated up by an opposition from sexy Mars on **January 19**. Even if you don't have a dream lover, your playful personality ensures that you'll have a good time. The Sun's entry into your 7th House of Partnerships on **January 20** shows that you're ready to move forward in relationships. Unconventional Aquarius in this house shows that an open mind may be your key to happiness. A tense Sun-Uranus semisquare on **January 21** can flip an emotional switch. Stay calm; wait a couple of days to avoid overreacting to what may just be a passing storm.

JANUARY 28–30 ★ *think now, act later*

Mercury's retrograde turn on **January 28** is a time to back up and reflect on recent events before pushing forward. However, an impatient Sun-Mars sesquisquare on **January 29**, one day before the warrior planet turns direct, spurs action rather than contemplation. Affectionate Venus slides from a slippery semisquare with dreamy Neptune on **January 29** to a constructive trine with responsible Saturn on **January 30**, indicating a quick journey from fantasy to reality that puts your feet back on the ground in matters of love, money, and self-worth.

FEBRUARY

A HELPING HAND

This is a time to eliminate, adjust, and reorganize before going forward with confidence as a pair of eclipses plus communicative Mercury's retrograde cycle can keep you off balance for much of this month. Keep your ambitions in check and master what you already have on your plate before adding more. The Solar Eclipse in quirky Aquarius on **February 6** is conjunct illusory Neptune in your 7th House of Partnerships. You may be told entrancing stories laced with promises to change your world, or could find yourself pitching ideas that you know aren't completely accurate. A magical person may turn out to be a mere mortal, which might be as much of a relief as it is a disappointment. It's a time to take back your projections, stop idealizing others, and recognize your own inspirational gifts.

Loving Venus's entry into your 7th House on **February 17** cracks open a door to a new kind of relationship rooted in equality and mutual respect. Mercury, also in your 7th House, turns direct on **February 18**, sparking mental connections with others and facilitating negotiations in your personal and professional life. The Sun slips into watery Pisces on **February 19** in your 8th House of Intimacy just prior to a Lunar Eclipse in your 2nd House of Resources on **February 20**. A reexamination of finances could be needed to shore up your cash flow. Yet you may find outside support if you're open enough to express your needs and humble enough to accept help. Don't lose your pride, but be willing to bend it a little if that's what it takes to meet your needs.

> **KEEP IN MIND THIS MONTH**
>
> *Check out all bright ideas before making any commitments. A little research will eliminate false leads and head you in a more productive direction.*

KEY DATES

FEBRUARY 5-6 ★ *compassion conversation*
The Sun's conjunction with Wounded Healer Chiron on **February 5** gives you a chance to share your concerns with a sympathetic individual. Retrograde Mercury's passage over the Sun on **February 6** offers deep insights into relationships, clarifying your thoughts and helping you communicate them more precisely. The Solar Eclipse on the same day in your 7th House of Partners is another chance to bring the magic back into relationships. A supportive sextile between Venus in earnest Capricorn and unconventional Uranus in forgiving Pisces can

soften judgments, suspend rigid relationship rules, and show you alternative ways to enjoy life's pleasures.

FEBRUARY 10 ★ *beautiful illusion*
The Sun's annual conjunction with nebulous Neptune dissolves ego boundaries and brings both closeness and confusion. Identity is not clearly defined, which increases your sensitivity to others. But the line between real communion and projected illusion is hard to find. Opening your heart is probably safe, but watch your wallet and avoid making any serious commitments now. You may have found real inspiration upon which a relationship can grow, but this could also just be a dream that becomes a nightmare if you set aside all reason and common sense.

FEBRUARY 14 ★ *hot valentine*
A happy trine between the Sun and energetic Mars animates you with a passionate and playful spirit this Valentine's Day. But you could be feeling so friendly and open that a private evening for two is too quiet for your taste. Invite friends to join the party or go out dancing; the pulse of the crowd will surely make your heart beat faster.

SUPER NOVA DAYS
FEBRUARY 17–20 ★ *increasing intimacy*
Venus entering your 7th House of Relationships on **February 17** makes you even more captivating, while Mercury's return to forward motion on **February 18** gives you even more to say. However, the Sun entering your 8th House of Intimacy on **February 19** rouses tender feelings below your charming exterior. Uncertain about how far to go, you may want to retreat or keep things superficial. Yet penetrating Pluto's smart sextile with the Sun indicates that it's safe to go deeper. The Lunar Eclipse on **February 20** conjunct no-nonsense Saturn in your 2nd House of Resources signals a need for tighter financial discipline.

FEBRUARY 24 ★ *half a loaf*
Today's Sun-Saturn opposition presents you with obstacles that can't be ignored. You might not get the emotional or material support you want, so you may have to face this challenge on your own. Patient negotiations can help you overcome differences of values that block cooperation. Compromise will work much better than engaging in an exhausting power struggle where neither side wins.

MARCH

UNEXPECTED OPPORTUNITIES

Surprising turns in the road of relationships could leave you feeling disoriented, but if you grasp new opportunities instead of retreating to old familiar positions, the payoff can be great. The emotional Pisces New Moon in your 8th House of Intimacy on **March 7** is conjunct unpredictable Uranus, which is likely to shake personal and professional connections. Agreements with lovers, friends, or business associates can fall apart, but there's no reason to panic. Generous Jupiter forms a supportive sextile to the New Moon that blesses you with surprising solutions. Venus, the partnership planet, and communicative Mercury enter Pisces and your 8th House on **March 12 and March 14**, increasing sensitivity in your exchanges with others. This creates a delicate environment in which even the mildest criticism feels like a sharp rebuke. Being tender, though, may make this a period of sweetness when shared pleasures can reach new heights.

Serious Saturn opposes Venus on **March 15** and Mercury on **March 17**, followed by a difficult sesquisquare to Jupiter on **March 18**, dampening your enthusiasm. What looks like a stop sign, however, is only a warning flag reminding you to slow down and think carefully before moving ahead. You're likely to feel revitalized by the Sun's entry into your 9th House of Higher Thought and Faraway Places on **March 20** and the Full Moon in your 11th House of Friends on **March 21**. Nevertheless, purging Pluto's powerful square to the Sun on **March 21** and Saturn's clumsy quincunx to it on **March 23** leave you little room for error. Eliminate distractions to sharpen your focus and increase productivity. A smart sextile between Jupiter and Uranus on **March 28**—repeating in May and November—sparks an abundance of brilliant ideas from unexpected sources.

> **KEEP IN MIND THIS MONTH**
>
> *Subtle moves can produce big reactions, so use less force and more intuition to avoid the need for a major course correction.*

KEY DATES

MARCH 6–8 ★ *relationship surprises*

Inspiring individuals raise your hopes as a romantic Venus-Neptune conjunction and an optimistic Sun-Jupiter sextile broaden your horizons on **March 6**. The spiritual Pisces New Moon in your 8th House of Intimacy on **March 7** is conjunct explosive Uranus, shattering illusions about others or unexpectedly triggering a breakthrough in relationships. A no-nonsense opposition between Mars and Pluto on the same day, though, can cause conflict if you're feeling overburdened by work. Avoid wasting energy on power struggles and seek ways to increase efficiency by eliminating any unhealthy habits.

MARCH 15-18 ★ *talk it out*

An opposition between sober Saturn and joyful Venus on **March 15** puts a serious spin on relationships. Although a discussion of values and needs might be helpful, you could prefer to clam up for the time being, yet an urgency to clarify issues can mount with a Mercury-Saturn opposition on **March 17**. Any desire you have to avoid a tough conversation, however, is likely to be overcome by strong emotions fueled by the Moon's passage through your sign. An easy trine between chatty Mercury and instigating Mars on **March 18** allows you to communicate with enough finesse to untangle a knotty situation. This is also the day of the first of three shape-shifting sesquisquares between hopeful Jupiter and pessimistic Saturn that repeat on **June 26 and January 30, 2009**. These aspects signal a reevaluation of work and money that leads to a major change in your career direction.

SUPER NOVA DAYS
MARCH 20-23 ★ *resetting priorities*

The Sun's entry into fellow fire sign Aries on **March 20** marks the Spring Equinox and begins a new astrological year by igniting a spark of excitement in your 9th House of Adventure. A fresh interest in understanding the world motivates you to sign up for a course in religion, philosophy, or metaphysics. A desire to explore new territory has you reading travel magazines and Web sites. This fast-rising enthusiasm, though, can be quickly subdued when encountering roadblocks represented by hard aspects between the Sun and Pluto on **March 21** and the Sun and Saturn on **March 23**. Your ruling planet's challenging hookups with the two toughest planets can create conflicts with authority figures. The unbearable tension pressures you to restructure your priorities and eliminate inessential activities that deter you from your goals.

MARCH 28-30 ★ *the good fight*

Electric Uranus charges you up with a conjunction to Venus and a sextile to Jupiter on **March 28**, awakening new forms of pleasure and expanding your mind. A hard-driving, combative square between the Sun and Mars on **March 30** is a call to battle, better used for self-improvement than putting someone else down.

APRIL

PEERING OVER THE HORIZON

Fresh insights into the meaning of your life could spur you in a new direction this month. Intellectual Mercury kicks off the action by leaping into your 9th House of Higher Truth on **April 2**, followed by sociable Venus on **April 6**. These eye-opening transits can attract lively people who heat up your sense of discovery and adventure. This desire to expand your horizons escalates when your ruling planet, the Sun, forms a high-tension square with boundless Jupiter on **April 10**. A tendency to overcommit is possible, so temper any promises you make with a strong dose of realism to maintain your credibility. Be on the alert for fast-talking friends or colleagues who push you to leap without looking. Getting encouragement is great, Leo, but not when it comes from a questionable source.

The Sun enters stubborn Taurus and your 10th House of Public Responsibility on **April 19**, which can lock you into a committed position. This is another reason to restrain yourself from allowing unbridled enthusiasm to carry you beyond the capacity to meet your obligations. You can earn respect and even advance your career with the Sun in this house of your chart, but the greatest gains come when you operate with both feet solidly on the ground. The passionate Scorpio Full Moon on **April 20** can trigger an emotional crisis at home. The demands of family members or your own lack of fulfillment can arouse instinctive responses that may seem raw and unreasonable. However, you're digging into your root chakra, the deep survival point within, to connect with powerful primal forces that are strong enough to fuel personal and professional transformation.

> **KEEP IN MIND THIS MONTH**
>
> *You learn best by doing, so continue your education with courses based on direct hands-on experience, rather than just sitting and listening to someone else.*

KEY DATES

APRIL 5-6 ★ *shoot for the moon*

The New Moon in excitable Aries late on **April 5** lights a brushfire in your 9th House of Travel and Education that stirs an urge to move mentally and physically. However, tense squares to the New Moon from Jupiter and impatient Mars can arouse angry or excessive behavior. Don't waste these powerful forces on arguments or self-indulgence; apply your adrenaline to pursue your highest aspirations. Innocent Venus enters Aries on **April 6** but almost immediately crosses paths with controlling Pluto, proving that impulsive attractions may be more complicated and costly than anticipated.

APRIL 10 ★ *curb your enthusiasm*

You could be very bold today as confident Jupiter squares the Sun and a spicy Mercury-Mars square encourages feistiness. The key to managing this stable of racehorses is to keep a firm grip on the reins of your emotions. You have the ability to promote your ideas, knock over obstacles, and cut through the chitchat to get yourself heard. But remaining calm at the center of this storm can be the difference between making an impression and just making noise.

APRIL 13–16 ★ *punchy presentation*

A sweet sextile between the Sun and spiritual Neptune infuses your dreams with inspiration on **April 13**. Yet a tendency to go overboard requires self-restraint with a tense Mars-Saturn semisquare on **April 14** that resists fantasy while rewarding discipline and productivity. A conjunction between informative Mercury and the Sun on **April 16** sharpens your mental focus and enables you to communicate with clarity and power, making you a very convincing speaker.

SUPER NOVA DAYS
APRIL 19–21 ★ *skillful manager*

The Sun enters reliable Taurus on **April 19** prior to the Full Moon in magnetic Scorpio on **April 20**. You may be at peace in public, but strong feelings are brewing inside that could boil over into a confrontation. Fortunately, a constructive trine between the Sun and regenerative Pluto helps you transmutes discontent into positive change. The Sun's trine with stable Saturn on **April 21** gives you a sure sense of direction, as well as the maturity and patience to manage people and resources with creativity and wisdom.

APRIL 23–24 ★ *personality plus*

Your level of passion, playfulness, and spontaneity is very high now. Vivacious Venus aspects lusty Mars and bawdy Jupiter on **April 23**, while the Moon in Sagittarius lights up your 5th House of Romance. However, the sheer force of your personality could overpower a timid individual. Mars opposes Jupiter on **April 24**, which can turn minor battles into major wars. Overdoing everything is definitely a risk, but with the abundance of energy available now, this is not the time to sit on the sidelines.

MAY

SEVERAL TURNS OF DIRECTION

There's a major cosmic shuffle this month as four planets change directions. Serious Saturn turns direct on **May 2**, giving structure to plans that have been floating in the background for almost six months. This forward turn in your 2nd House of Resources gets financial matters moving ahead. Philosophical Jupiter, though, begins a four-month retrograde cycle in your 6th House of Work and Habits on **May 9**. This is a good opportunity to bring your skills up to date or to review personal and professional systems to make them more efficient. Mercury and Neptune both turn retrograde on **May 26**. The fast-moving messenger planet's twenty-four-day reverse period often produces problems with data, details, and technology. This retrograde occurs in your 11th House of Friends and Groups, making team activities more subject to error, although it could also bring a reconnection with a pal from your past. Spacey Neptune's backward turn in your 7th House of Partners is very subtle, but suggests that your greatest sources of inspiration for the next five months can be found within yourself.

The Taurus New Moon on **May 5** adds responsibilities in your 10th House of Career, and the Full Moon in Scorpio on **May 19** awakens strong emotions at home that may be more fantasy than reality. You get a major boost of energy when active Mars enters your sign on **May 9** for the first time in almost two years. This dynamic planet raises your metabolism and has you acting more decisively while it's in Leo through **July 1**. The creative and heroic aspects of your personality sizzle, helping you get new projects off the ground and express yourself more passionately.

> **KEEP IN MIND THIS MONTH**
>
> *Take the risk to follow your passion instead of spending your time putting out fires or passively waiting for opportunities to arise.*

KEY DATES

MAY 2-3 ★ *back to basics*

Mercury's leap into its chatty home sign of Gemini on **May 2** spawns tons of bright ideas. Yet it's wise to narrow your focus, because strict Saturn turns forward on the same day and joins pressure-packed Pluto in making stressful aspects to Mercury on **May 3**. Communication bogs down, and minor events require more effort than expected. Simplify, streamline, and stick to the basics to avoid complications now.

SUPER NOVA DAY
MAY 9 ★ *heart of a lion*

Mars the Warrior strides into your sign to amplify your power and boost your confidence. This is a good time to start projects, especially those requiring physical energy. Participating in sports, dance, yoga, and outdoor activities can improve your fitness level considerably. Your strong personality takes on another degree of intensity, motivating yourself and others to perform at the highest level. You're wearing your heart on your sleeve now, and there's no hiding your intentions. This direct approach encourages people to trust you, although there is a risk that some will find you overbearing.

MAY 12-14 ★ *a peek into the future*

The Sun forms productive aspects with visionary Jupiter and inventive Uranus on **May 12**, kicking your intuition into high gear. You have a knack for sensing what's coming next, especially related to work and career issues. A cranky sesquisquare between Venus and Pluto on **May 13**, though, points out where resources are lacking and can attract distrustful people who may be disinclined to share your optimism. The Sun's square with idealistic Neptune on **May 14** feeds your imagination, which can supply you with creative answers or allow you to escape into your own fantasy world.

MAY 20-22 ★ *tightly wound*

This is an intense period of mixed signals, with a romantic Venus-Neptune square and the Sun's entry into clever Gemini on **May 20** promising a good time for all. The second of three exciting Jupiter-Uranus sextiles on **May 21** sings with possibilities, but the tune can be quickly quieted by hard aspects between the Sun and skeptical tough guys Saturn and Pluto that day and the next. Your patience may be tested, but avoid impulsive reactions that can work against your best interests.

MAY 26-27 ★ *relationship repairs*

Mercury's retrograde turn on **May 26** combines with an uncertain Venus-Saturn square that could inhibit your sense of self-worth. Expect serious negotiations in relationships that demand a realistic and down-to-earth approach. Blaming others or feeling guilty is not likely to restore trust. Both sides are responsible for the current situation, and working together is the best way to resolve it. If you get snagged in sticky details, an expansive Sun-Jupiter sesquisquare on **May 27** helps you see the big picture.

JUNE

RETURNING HOME

Your ruling planet, the Sun, jumps from curious Gemini in your sociable 11th House of Friends to cautious Cancer in your private 12th House of Secrets on **June 20**. This marks the Summer Solstice, beginning a relatively quiet period in which solitude is likely to seem more attractive to you. Your usual outgoing nature, though, gets plenty of planetary support earlier in the month with a spicy sextile between the Sun and active Mars on **June 4**, an atomic-powered Mars-Pluto sesquisquare on **June 5**, and an erotically charged Venus-Mars sextile on **June 6**. Sensual pleasures, emotional indulgences, and shopping sprees with friends are signaled by a luscious Venus-Sun conjunction on **June 9**, followed by judgmentally questionable quincunxes from Venus and the Sun to excessive Jupiter on **June 10–11**.

The uplifting Sagittarius Full Moon on **June 18** falls in your 5th House of Fun and Games, but its close conjunction with Pluto and square to Uranus indicates radical changes rather than sweetness and light. Venus opposes Pluto the same day, and cuddles up in Cancer in your 12th House of Endings. The Sun repeats the same pattern on **June 20**, which can tempt you to live in a robe and slippers 24/7 until your emotional wounds are healed. Nevertheless, you can benefit by some time away from the front lines of life and love. While talk-ative Mercury's forward turn on **June 19** can keep your phone ringing and your e-mail box full, you're not obligated to respond to every message. There's an inner call to the quiet part of yourself where you can hear the sound of your soul. You're not retreating from the world now, Leo, but hopefully are reconnecting with nature, spirituality, and the source of your existence.

> **KEEP IN MIND THIS MONTH**
>
> *Give yourself permission to shift from social to solitary and back again, depending on your mood; both modes of operation greatly enrich your life.*

KEY DATES

JUNE 3-4 ★ *light-handed leadership*

The jaunty Gemini New Moon on **June 3** can feel like a party with its conjunctions to talkative Mercury and flirtatious Venus along with an uplifting sextile with Mars. Your head can be spinning with conversations, invitations, and obligations, but your strong leadership abilities attract the support you need from others. Remember, asking for help isn't a sign of weakness. The exact Sun-Mars sextile on **June 4** allows you to take command with such style and grace that you make work seem like play.

SUPER NOVA DAYS
JUNE 11–14 ★ *fruitless show of force*

Inept authorities and misapplied faith can throw you off stride with an awkward Sun-Jupiter quincunx on **June 11**. If you're not making progress with someone, don't push harder. There's a tendency to act with more confidence than merited, so question opinions—your own or others'—that aren't validated by solid facts. Venus and the Sun form squares with twitchy Uranus on **June 12–13** that can destabilize relationships. Attractions shift in the blink of an eye, and money can disappear in a flash. Happily, a gentle Venus-Neptune trine can save the day by putting everyone in a forgiving mood. This pause for peace is essential, since aggressive Mars in Leo joins the karmic Lunar South Node on **June 14**, which could lead to a clash of egos in a futile attempt to gain dominance.

JUNE 18–21 ★ *emotional extremes*

Pluto's opposition to sweet Venus on **June 18** can elicit extreme reactions in relationships. Jealousy, fear, control, and manipulation may expose the dark underbelly of love, but if real damage is avoided, partnerships may be strengthened by this therapeutic exercise. Venus then enters sensitive Cancer to lick her wounds, and the Sun follows the same path on **June 20**, bringing the courage and consciousness that repair broken hearts. Meanwhile, macho Mars passes from a jittery quincunx with Uranus on **June 19** that could trigger nervous behavior to a calming opposition with Neptune on **June 21** that can take the edge off but might lead to wasting time by chasing illusions or escaping reality.

JUNE 25–26 ★ *worthy sacrifice*

A solid Sun-Saturn sextile on **June 25** gives you a steady platform to build dreams spawned by an imaginative Venus-Neptune sesquisquare. Jupiter and Saturn, the regulators, make their second sesquisquare on **June 26**, which may cause you to adjust your long-term plans. The first in this series started this process on **March 18**, while the third and final aspect will crystallize professional issues next year on **January 30**. Take a strategic approach now, trading immediate rewards for future gains.

JULY

CREATIVE MANAGEMENT

This month is a complicated journey leading you from finances to fun. Money matters enter the foreground when active Mars moves into your 2nd House of Resources on **July 1**. Conflict about cash may drive you to work harder, perhaps even seeking an additional source of income. The fretful Cancer New Moon on **July 2** in your 12th House of Privacy can reinforce insecurities, but its message is to look within for calming inspiration rather than letting fear drive you to act impulsively. A conjunction between active Mars and patient Saturn on **July 10** can tighten the monetary screws, so if you're under pressure, channel your anxiety into creating a solid plan. Commitment to increasing your value through training and discipline can earn you more control over your future income. Mental Mercury's opposition to scary Pluto and entry into timid Cancer the same day may increase your apprehension, but reality is much less dire than it seems.

Attractive Venus entering your sign of the Lion on **July 12** begins to swing the pendulum in a more positive direction. The revival of your fundamentally creative and playful spirit makes you feel especially appealing. Others notice and are ready to reward you with the attention and affection you crave. The ambitious Capricorn Full Moon on **July 18** in your 6th House of Work stirs feelings about respect. If you're not getting it, this is a time to speak up or consider a job change. Don't be too proud to express your needs if they're not being met. The Sun's entry in shining Leo on **July 22** brings a warming trend that validates just how fabulous you really are. If you're not fulfilling your potential yet, honor your gifts by doing whatever you can to develop them.

> **KEEP IN MIND THIS MONTH**
>
> *Turn negative thoughts and self-doubt into positive affirmations and constructive actions. Even the smallest first steps can lead to rewarding long-term results.*

KEY DATES

JULY 3–5 ★ *sweet indulgence*

An expansive Venus-Jupiter opposition can increase your appetites in the midst of Cancer New Moon worries on **July 3**. Some sweet pleasures are well deserved, but overeating, overspending, or overestimating others should be avoided. A nononsense semisquare from Saturn to Venus on **July 4** will make the cost of excess immediately obvious. But then new ideas start jumping with an electric Mercury-

Uranus square on **July 5** in your 11th House of Pals. Friends pop in and out, suddenly changing plans, so let go of your need to control the agenda for less stress and more fun.

SUPER NOVA DAYS
JULY 9-10 ★ *over the edge*
An opposition between the Sun and adventurous Jupiter on **July 9** urges you to look forward, but all the other signals insist that you manage what you already have before putting more on your plate. Mercury's opposition to Pluto on **July 10** demands singular concentration that will make you a clear thinker and compelling communicator. The conjunction of hardworking Mars and Saturn in your 2nd House of Self-Esteem on the same day can feel restrictive, but its purpose is to focus you on your most valuable talent. Pledge to develop it to the highest potential.

JULY 14-15 ★ *mind in transition*
A combination of inventiveness and practical thinking works in your favor on **July 14** as the Sun trines brilliant Uranus while clever Mercury sextiles earthy Saturn. But the Sun's hard aspects to pointed Mars and fuzzy Neptune on **July 15** can make it difficult to hit your target. Sometimes your aim is true, other times it is off, so approach each activity as a separate event to prevent overconfidence from leading you astray.

JULY 21-22 ★ *ready to roar*
The Sun is squeezed by a quincunx with pressurized Pluto on **July 21** that can leave you feeling bullied or misunderstood. This uncharacteristic loss of personal authority, though, won't last long since the courageous Sun enters your heroic home sign on **July 22**. Expect a rise of enthusiasm in the days ahead. This is your season, Leo—a time to take risks, show your heart, and demonstrate the creativity that makes you an inspiring leader and a lovable powerhouse.

JULY 26 ★ *super-efficient*
A free-flowing trine between energetic Mars in your 2nd House of Self-Worth and hopeful Jupiter in your 6th House of Skills gives you the strength to accomplish a long list of tasks today. Controlled intensity enables you to work hard and still have plenty of fuel left for play. You can be a terrific teacher now; your ability to produce both quantity and quality to get any job done is a shining example to others.

AUGUST

LETTING GO TO GET AHEAD

This incredible month is supercharged by two eclipses, two New Moons, and the Sun's continuing passage through your dynamic sign. The action starts on **August 1** with a Solar Eclipse in flamboyant Leo that can have you rethinking your life's purpose. Rational Mercury joined with this Sun-Moon conjunction can provide plenty of reasons to hold on to a position or set of beliefs that just isn't working. Digging in your heels, though, is not the answer; letting go somewhere is a must. Persistence, one of your greatest strengths, may be a weakness now. The Full Moon on **August 16** is a Lunar Eclipse in your 7th House of Partnerships designed to change the shape of relationships or alter your public image. Fantasy-filled Neptune's conjunction with this Aquarius Full Moon may send you chasing rainbows in an unrealistic pursuit of the perfect mate or allow you to minimize problems with your partner. A more positive story, though, is a tale of compassion and forgiveness that heals relationship wounds and restores your faith in love.

Your thinking becomes more practical with the Sun's entry into earthy Virgo on **August 22** in your 2nd House of Income. Intense conversations follow when Mercury squares Pluto on **August 27** a day before entering harmonious Libra. Venus repeats the exact same pattern on **August 29–30**. Their presence in this gracious and communicative sign would appear to settle tensions and make compromise possible. However, the New Moon in analytical Virgo on **August 30** is conjunct unyielding Saturn, which is not interested in making light of anything. Happily, generous Jupiter in a favorable trine to Saturn and the New Moon gives you a broad, strategic vision that points you toward a successful financial and professional path.

> **KEEP IN MIND THIS MONTH**
>
> *Turning loss into gain when it's time to let go makes it possible to take one step back and leap ten steps ahead.*

KEY DATES

AUGUST 1 ★ *the power of change*
It's easy to accentuate the negative as Mercury forms an agitated sesquisquare with penetrating Pluto during today's dramatic Leo New Moon Eclipse. The trick to riding this transformational wave, instead of being wiped out by it, is to find one key thing that you can change. A small shift of thinking or an adjustment to your behavior begins a powerful process that can move your life in a positive direction.

AUGUST 6 ★ *step back from the edge*

The mood may be prickly today with mental Mercury and active Mars forming hard aspects to impatient Uranus and super-sensitive Neptune. Stay clear of any disputes—even your best intentions can be misinterpreted and add more fuel to the fire. Venus's entry into Virgo normally encourages discretion, but it's not easy maintaining your cool in this high-intensity atmosphere. The Sun's stressful quincunx with Jupiter could provoke overreactions, so it's best to take whatever you hear now with a huge grain of salt.

SUPER NOVA DAYS
AUGUST 13-17 ★ *mining for gold*

A stingy Saturn-Venus conjunction on **August 13** can put a pinch in your wallet or raise doubts about your worth. Income and self-esteem can rise from a low point with objective analysis and hard work. Punishing words could accompany a Mercury-Saturn conjunction on **August 15**, but the Lunar Eclipse on **August 16** is the major story. The Moon's conjunction with idealistic Neptune is reinforced by a generous Venus-Jupiter trine, shining love and light in the midst of major changes. A down-to-the-bone Mars-Pluto opposition on **August 17**, however, indicates that you're going to have to dig hard and deep for all that gold you see in front of you now.

AUGUST 22-23 ★ *breaking the rules*

The Sun's entry into practical Virgo on **August 22** is countered by high-tension oppositions from Mercury and Venus to Uranus on **August 23**. Unconventional ideas, individuals, and fashion choices typically don't fit modest Virgo's style, but you should enjoy the creative possibilities available when you are no longer bound by tradition or self-restraint.

AUGUST 27-30 ★ *untapped resources*

You must narrow your mental and social focus with squares between Mercury and Pluto on **August 27** and Venus and Pluto on **August 29**. Eliminate excess information and conversation, and cut out pleasures that are becoming too costly. A deeper examination of what you give for what you get can lead to restructuring relationships and altering your spending patterns. Hidden resources may be uncovered that can be used to increase your income and liven up your love life.

SEPTEMBER

SUDDEN CHANGES

The big gears of Jupiter and Saturn that shape your future—especially in your career—take a significant turn this month. On **September 8**, the planets of aspiration and accomplishment make their next-to-last trine in a series that began early last year. This provides you with the good judgment to adjust your course one more time before the last trine locks in long-term patterns on **November 11**. You can pour some of your playful and enthusiastic spirit into the mix when your ruling planet, the Sun, joins Saturn on **September 3** and trines Jupiter on **September 4**. A broad perspective sharpens your sense of strategy, allowing you to assess challenges skillfully and chart a course to success. Jupiter, the Guru or Teacher, turns direct on **September 8**, signaling your readiness to learn from those with more experience and to generously share your knowledge with others.

The sensitive and spiritual Pisces Full Moon in your 8th House of Intimacy on **September 15** is conjunct unpredictable Uranus, which can bring shocks or breakthroughs in relationships. Financial partnerships may be shaken, but alternative sources of support could arise unexpectedly if a previous commitment falls through. Hope may fade due to unfair pressure from the Sun's square with manipulative Pluto on **September 20**. But the Autumn Equinox, marked by the Sun's entry into fair-minded Libra on **September 22**, provides the data, logic, and diplomacy needed to restore your sense of balance. Feelings, though, count as much as facts with loving Venus entering emotional Scorpio on **September 23**. To get the whole story, let your gut inform you as much as your head. Furthermore, Mercury, the information planet, turns retrograde in your 7th House of Alliances on **September 24**, which calls for rethinking and renegotiating during the next three weeks.

> **KEEP IN MIND THIS MONTH**
>
> *Convert enemies into allies by thinking fast on your feet to catch opportunities that come when you least expect them.*

KEY DATES

SEPTEMBER 3-4 ★ *reasonable doubt*

The Sun's snuggle with crusty Saturn on **September 3** could put you in a grumpy mood as self-doubt or financial worries are exaggerated. You're looking at a worst-case scenario rather than at an objective picture. A trine between jolly Jupiter and the Sun on **September 4** is bound to lift your spirits, even if you're not quite ready to display your optimism openly. Your exuberance may be tempered by recognizing how much work lies ahead of you to achieve your goals, but this low-key form of enthusiasm earns you credibility. You seem solid and sure of yourself, rooted in reality rather than carried away by your own promotional hype.

SUPER NOVA DAYS
SEPTEMBER 7-8 ★ *spirited debate*
Assertive Mars is normally cool in diplomatic Libra, but its stressful square to Jupiter on **September 7** motivates you to be more outspoken than ever. Verbal Mercury joins the fray on **September 8** with a conjunction to Mars and a square to Jupiter that intensifies communications. Jupiter's direct turn increases your tendency to exaggerate, making compromise unlikely. Additionally, Pluto's direct turn can release long pent-up feelings. The potential for damage, though, is moderated by the wisdom of the Jupiter-Saturn trine.

SEPTEMBER 12-14 ★ *disconnect and reconnect*
An opposition between the Sun and Uranus on **September 12** can shorten your fuse and spark impulsive behavior. Breaking free from someone close to you, suddenly changing the rules of a relationship, or finding yourself attracted to a person who is not your usual type feels dangerous but exciting. The Sun's quincunx with forgiving Neptune on **September 14**, though, can soften hard edges and allow you to repair recent damage caused by thoughtless actions.

SEPTEMBER 20-23 ★ *reveal yourself*
The Sun-Pluto square on **September 20** applies pressure through power struggles. Unburden yourself by letting go of inessential obligations. The Sun in social Libra on **September 22** reminds you that you need to share your concerns with those who care instead of keeping everything to yourself. Venus's tough semisquare with Saturn just before entering passionate Scorpio on **September 23** is a reminder that love requires work and that intimacy includes showing vulnerability.

SEPTEMBER 29 ★ *stick to the basics*
The evenhanded Libra New Moon in your 3rd House of Information opens your eyes to new facts, faces, and ways of looking at the world around you. Just keep things simple while Mercury is retrograde to avoid cluttering your mind with data that complicates communication and gets in the way of understanding.

OCTOBER

TRANSFORMING YOUR PAST

As a fiery Leo, your preference is to be creative and outgoing, but now the planets are tugging your attention back to the unfinished business of the past. This deep reflective work is challenging, but the benefits you get from untying psychological knots and finishing off old business are worth the effort. Retrograde Mercury in your 3rd House of Communication through **October 15** continues the process of reexamining and restating positions that began last month. Active Mars dives into emotionally deep Scorpio on **October 4**, stirring the deep waters of your 4th House of Home and Family. You may tap into feelings of resentment or distrust with roots that go all the way back to your childhood. Yet touching a sore spot can be a significant and necessary step in releasing repressed emotions and empowering you to be yourself.

The Full Moon in pioneering Aries on **October 14** lights a spark of adventure in your 9th House of Faraway Places. Expanding your horizons with travel or additional education is appealing, but overconfident Jupiter's stressful square to the Full Moon suggests that the cost may be greater than anticipated. Adorable Venus enters adventurous Sagittarius in your 5th House of Romance on **October 18**, which is likely to put you in a playful mood. Laughter and lust go together as a good sense of humor allows you to be seductive in a lighthearted way. Then the mood thickens when the Sun enters intense Scorpio on **October 22**. The Scorpio New Moon on **October 28** casts light into the shadows of family history, but harmonious aspects from Mars to wise Jupiter and stable Saturn on **October 27 and October 30** give you the tools to transform emotional trauma into constructive action.

> **KEEP IN MIND THIS MONTH**
>
> *Once you clear your heart of what is no longer needed, you can utilize your precious resources to focus on manifesting your dreams for the future.*

KEY DATES

SUPER NOVA DAYS
OCTOBER 4-6 ★ *strong opinions*

Mars's entry into relentless Scorpio on **October 4** is intensified by its semi-square to restraining Saturn on **October 5**. You hate confinement, but may feel yourself hemmed in by complex tasks or controlling individuals. Retrograde

Mercury joins the Sun on **October 6**, and both form squares with Jupiter. You know what you want, but could express it with so much force that others feel intimidated. Your natural sense of authority can make simple comments sound like judgments from above. By all means, speak your mind, but consider the possibility that others' ideas are useful, too, and soften your tone if you want your message to be heard.

OCTOBER 12–15 ★ *new mind-set*

A cranky quincunx between the Sun and erratic Uranus on **October 12** may put you on edge. Unreliable individuals or impulsive tendencies elicit rapid reactions that aren't necessarily on the mark. It's best to look before you leap, and then look again to realize that taking a deep breath and standing still might be wiser right now. A soothing trine between the Sun and Neptune during the impetuous Aries Full Moon on **October 14** helps you stay cool in volatile situations. Spiritual connections arise unexpectedly to open your heart and increase your faith in humanity. Mercury's direct turn on **October 15** gets information flowing again, providing you with fresh perspectives and fascinating conversations.

OCTOBER 18 ★ *the cat's meow*

This could be a sexy Saturday with pleasure-loving Venus dancing into your 5th House of Self-Expression, amplifying your already vibrant personality. Your generous side is showing, and you can attract plenty of attention with your openhearted approach. Being direct and honest about your feelings is a welcome invitation to participate in your life that most people will gladly accept. However, there may be an insecure soul or two who feels threatened by your bold display of self-confidence. Don't hold yourself back on their account; it's all about fun now, so jump in with delight.

OCTOBER 21–25 ★ *gathering force*

You collect power and influence with a strong but subtle sextile between the Sun and Pluto on **October 21**. Then the Sun enters Pluto's home sign, Scorpio, on **October 22** to deepen your well of potency. Scorpio's traditional ruler, Mars, forms a stressful semisquare with Pluto on **October 24** that readily provokes power struggles. Avoid unnecessary conflict to focus on more fundamental issues where concentrated effort can allow you to overcome intractable obstacles. The Sun's semisquare with stern Saturn on **October 25** can be bothersome, especially when dealing with narrow-minded people. Manage your own life and do your best to ignore their petty concerns.

NOVEMBER

SOLID FINANCIAL GROWTH

Three major outer planet aspects mark a changing of the guard this month. Taskmaster Saturn makes the first of a series of oppositions to explosive Uranus on **November 4** that won't finish until **July 2010**. This face-off between the forces of order and revolution in your resource-rich 2nd and 8th Houses can reshape your financial future. The impulse to break away from your current methods of earning money can feel risky, but could lead to a breakthrough that allows you to meet your obligations in a more stimulating way. Jupiter's smart sextile with Uranus on **November 13** is the last of three that previously occurred in late March and May. Bright ideas about work and health can provide you with instant answers to longstanding questions. Jupiter then makes its final trine to Saturn on **November 21** in a set that began in **March 2007**. This positive alignment of the planets of hope and reality stabilizes your vision of the future, especially related to your career.

The Full Moon in solid Taurus on **November 13** squares squishy Neptune and falls in your 10th House of Public Responsibility. Idealism or a desire to avoid conflict can load you down with obligations you may be hard-pressed to meet. Being inspired to do great things is wonderful, Leo, but not if you're exhausted by taking on too much. The Sun enters fellow fire sign Sagittarius on **November 21**, and Mercury follows suit on **November 23** in your 5th House of Self-Expression, placing you directly in the spotlight. You could receive even more attention on **November 27** when the enthusiastic Sagittarius New Moon also illuminates your creative streak and your flair for drama.

> **KEEP IN MIND THIS MONTH**
>
> *A clear sense of your long-range goals will guide you well, so don't let petty details get in the way of your big-picture view.*

KEY DATES

NOVEMBER 3-4 ★ *social insecurity*

Social awkwardness is possible with Venus's hard square to the Saturn-Uranus opposition on **November 3**. One side swings to safety and commitment, the other to freedom and adventure—a contrast that can produce uncertainty in relationships or finances. A wandering Mars-Neptune square on **November 4** can feel like a walk in the fog, so don't keep pushing forward if you can't see where you're going. Perceptive Mercury's entry into Scorpio, though, can turn on your inner radar to help you out if you let go of logic and allow intuition to guide you. The

Saturn-Uranus opposition can suddenly crank up tension with bosses or bossy people, but you're not the only one sensitive to being bullied. Be sure to treat others with the same consideration you wish for yourself.

SUPER NOVA DAYS
NOVEMBER 10-13 ★ *bottled lightning*
The Sun's harmonious aspects to Jupiter and Uranus on **November 10** generates brilliant ideas, and its strengthening sextile with practical Saturn on **November 11** ensures that you'll be able to apply them successfully. Pleasing Venus passing over dark Pluto just before entering calculating Capricorn on **November 12** could cast doubt on a relationship. Others seem particularly ungenerous, which may force a reevaluation of your expectations. On **November 13**, the Sun's square to Neptune blurs reality, instilling you with dreams or distracting you with illusion.

NOVEMBER 16-17 ★ *clear turning cloudy*
Your ability to impress others increases as punchy Mars shoots into boundless Sagittarius on **November 16**, boosting your enthusiasm while Mercury sextiles Jupiter and Saturn to earn you credibility. High energy and clear thinking promote your interests. But conversations can get slippery on **November 17** when mental Mercury squares dreamy Neptune and your feelings may submerge the facts.

NOVEMBER 21-23 ★ *love and honesty*
The Sun entering your 5th House of Romance on **November 21** emphasizes your warm, generous, and creative side. The more you give, the more you get—so don't hold back now. The Jupiter-Saturn trine puts current events in a bigger framework, giving you perspective that's perfect for long-range planning. Chatty Mercury's shift into your 5th House on **November 23** spurs you to speak frankly.

NOVEMBER 25-26 ★ *kill them with kindness*
A Sun-Mercury conjunction on **November 25** focuses your mind and empowers your words, making you a compelling speaker. Tempering opinionated comments with kindness may be needed to keep you from overwhelming others. Penetrating Pluto reenters ambitious Capricorn on **November 26**, beginning a long stay in your 6th House of Work and Service that will eventually change the way you do your job, manage your health, and handle your daily routine.

DECEMBER

HOLIDAY MADNESS

The month starts sweetly with a luscious Venus-Jupiter conjunction in your 6th House of Details on **December 1**, adding more joy to your daily routine. Charming Venus enters your 7th House of Relationships on **December 7**, enlivening an ongoing partnership or opening the door to a new one. This is a good time to try out a fresh look, since people tend to find you irresistible now. Yet despite this potential for more delight in your life, the holiday season might prove quite stormy. The presence of Mars, Saturn, and Uranus at the Full Moon in noisy Gemini on **December 12** turns this usually mild event into a potential crisis point. Impatient Mars conjunct the Sun in your 5th House of Play is electrified by a square from Uranus and constrained by another square from Saturn. The sudden urge to leap into love or creativity in unique and unusual ways breaks down barriers to self-expression and shows off your originality. But stern Saturn's presence allows no room for error, so carefully choose how and where you push the limits.

The strategic Capricorn New Moon on **December 27** is as intense as the earlier Full Moon, bringing the year to a powerful conclusion. This event in your 6th House of Work challenges you to take a fresh look at your job. Mysterious Pluto and assertive Mars reinforce the New Moon, which could put a chip on your shoulder. You're not in a compromising mood and may struggle with authority figures. Simmering resentment can rise to the surface and produce emotional conflict at home. Your passion, though, can drive you to finally let go of a job or habit that holds you back, clearing the way for a more potent and fulfilling expression of your talents.

> **KEEP IN MIND THIS MONTH**
>
> *Respond to tension by making big changes in your life instead of uselessly trying to hold on to what you don't even want anymore.*

KEY DATES

DECEMBER 5-6 ★ *it's showtime*
Communication is quirky with Mercury's squares to electric Uranus on **December 5** and somber Saturn on **December 6**. Fast thinking and brilliant ideas are quickly cooled by reality's limitations. But a supportive sextile from spiritual Neptune to Mercury on **December 6** softens the blow with compassionate words that keep hope alive. A Sun-Mars conjunction on **December 5** heats up your 5th House of Romance and Creativity, igniting a flame of desire that compels you to take bold

action. Take the lead, Leo, when it comes to love, play, and entertaining. The performer in you is ready to hit the stage.

SUPER NOVA DAYS
DECEMBER 10-12 ★ *beyond the law*
Eccentric Uranus is squared by the Sun on **December 10** and Mars on **December 12**. This one-two planetary punch is not likely to put you in a mood to compromise. You want freedom and may even break some rules to get it, but you'd better be prepared to accept the consequences. Mercury enters law-enforcing Capricorn on **December 12**, where it joins exacting Pluto to expose your secrets. Conversations will not be light, so measure your words carefully. Saturn's square to the Sun that day also signals accountability, so if you've gone out of bounds, you will hear about it. Positively, this character-building aspect indicates your commitment to developing your abilities to their highest potential.

DECEMBER 15-16 ★ *from work to play*
Hard work and precious rewards go together with a tough Mars-Saturn square on **December 15**, followed by an inspiring Venus–North Node conjunction on **December 16**. The first aspect can be frustrating, because high levels of concentration and effort are required to inch forward. The second, though, is like finding bread crumbs along the trail of emotional and spiritual fulfillment. Revel in your joyful discovery with a friendly and open-minded individual.

DECEMBER 21-22 ★ *ambition over celebration*
The Sun's entry into Capricorn and your 6th House of Employment marks the Winter Solstice on **December 21**, followed by its conjunction with unyielding Pluto on **December 22**. Work pressures may mount beyond reason, making it clear that you must streamline your life. Prioritize your tasks so that you have time for holiday festivities, rather than scattering your attention among a variety of tasks.

DECEMBER 27-28 ★ *time out for pleasure*
Mars marches into industrious Capricorn on **December 27** like a conquering army and then finds reinforcements with its conjunction to potent Pluto on **December 28**. You are an unstoppable force, but a divine and delightful conjunction between Venus and Neptune in your 7th House of Partnerships is a reminder to slow down and enjoy the sweetness available for sharing at the end of this eventful year.

VIRGO

AUGUST 23–SEPTEMBER 22

VIRGO OVERVIEW

This is a karmic year for you as Saturn, the gatekeeper of reality, moves steadily through your sign, testing the integrity of the foundations upon which you continue to build your life. It may sound trite, but you just might get what you deserve. Some areas of your life may fulfill your fantasies beyond your wildest dreams, while others will present you with one test after another, requiring you to work vigilantly with relentless self-discipline. Although Saturn can be rather strict, punishing laziness and sloppiness, it can also be quite reassuring when it rewards your diligence. Be aware that if problems do arise, they aren't necessarily a sign of failure. As Saturn works its way through critical Virgo, it simply points out where more effort is needed. Rather than growing discouraged over what you didn't do or what you should have done, **this is the time to refocus your best intentions and take care of the serious business at hand, instead of waiting for a better time.** But all is not difficult this year, for Saturn can also bring more certainty into your life. If your efforts are sincere, then your perseverance will bring you closer to personal success. It's not only about receiving what you've earned; it's also about setting your long-term goals and creating the necessary strategies to materialize your dreams.

The good news is that you are blessed with continued support all year as optimistic Jupiter counteracts the realism of somber Saturn. Jupiter is in Saturn's sign, Capricorn, systematically expanding your horizons and gracing you with a positive attitude that helps you overcome any obstacles. Key times for initiating actions that have long-lasting effects are January 21, September 8, and November 21—dates when the supportive Jupiter-Saturn trine is exact. Since Jupiter is in your 5th House of Self-Expression, your creativity is at a peak during these times, although you probably won't be overly demonstrative. Instead, what pays off is your commitment to perfection and your desire to be involved with meaningful projects. On the other hand, you may experience some creative blocks when Jupiter forms tense sesquisquares with Saturn on March 18 and June 25. **Keep in mind that unresolved pressures can be channeled into productive work**, assuming you can manage your frustration and keep your eyes on the goal.

New opportunities replace previous disappointments, positively impacting your personality, romantic relationships, and professional partnerships. The overall shift is reassuring, yet it can slow the pace of your life. Jupiter, Saturn, and Pluto were all in more spontaneous fire signs last year; now they are in sensible earth signs. As an analytical and thoughtful earth sign, Virgo, you are inclined to return to basics when given a chance. Transformative Pluto edges into ambitious Capricorn on January 25, testing the viability of the ground upon which you must stand for the next fifteen years. This can signal a long-term metamorphosis that can affect your creative expression, your connection with children, and your romantic relationships.

SURPRISE PACKAGE

You may be normally cautious in matters of love, for serious Saturn rules your 5th House of Romance. There is, however, good news on the horizon as buoyant Jupiter moves through your 5th House this year, promising more laughter and love. Sensual Venus visits your 5th House January 24–February 17, tempting you to be more playful and encouraging you to relax and just be yourself. Your attractions and desires are further intensified by passionate Pluto on January 25. Although you are blessed with the potential of much joy, there may also be unusual surprises in store for you in 2008, especially when unpredictable Uranus sextiles Jupiter on March 28, May 21, and November 12. Stay open to new experiences all year, even if love does not arrive as expected.

GROWTH MANAGEMENT

This is a time of consistent career growth, although greater changes may be more likely toward the end of the year. It's as if you know that a big shift is imminent, so you tend to go out of your way to make your current situation last longer. Saturn is most stable from mid-March through early May, and again from late August through mid-September. Make the most of these times by accomplishing as much as you can, even if your career is going very well. Do not wait for the additional stresses that may come later—late October and early November—to take action. If you prepare well throughout the year, you will be able to make great strides toward your goals.

MONEY CHANGES

Venus rules your 2nd House of Resources, and it makes two conjunctions this year with possessive Pluto—on January 24, and again on November 12—transforming your relationship to money and your personal possessions. Your need for financial security is intensified, prompting you to work harder than ever to get what you want. Venus also makes two conjunctions with opulent Jupiter on February 1 and December 1. Rewards can come to you in the form of a raise or a sweet opportunity, but remember that there is no substitute for concentrated effort throughout the year. Financial issues can heat up as assertive Mars enters your 2nd House on August 19, followed by Mercury on August 28, and Venus on August 30. Approach money issues carefully rather than impulsively shooting from the hip throughout September and October.

 MIND OVER BODY

Saturn and Uranus, co-rulers of your 6th House of Health, both receive supportive aspects from beneficial Jupiter, indicating a year of overall good health. But their mutual opposition in early November can bring up unresolved problems if you don't pay attention to the warning signs. An Aquarius New Moon Eclipse on February 6 and an Aquarius Full Moon Eclipse on August 16 both involve illusive Neptune. If something is bothering you, get the necessary tests, for knowing the facts can prevent needless worry. Neptune's recurring presence creates a problem along with a solution. Murky data can make a clear diagnosis difficult, but the healing capability of your imagination is strong. Whatever you call it, positive thinking can strongly impact whatever ails you.

 PURPOSEFUL PLAY

It has been said that your home is your castle—but this year, your home is more like your sandbox. Jupiter, the ruler of your 4th House of Home and Family, encourages you to have fun even as it moves through goal-oriented Capricorn in your 5th House of Self-Expression. Although you may not go over the creative edge, this is still a great year to lighten up and enjoy yourself at home, whether that means spending quality time with children or connecting with your own inner child. Remodeling or updating your decor can be quite a thrilling adventure, rather than the chore it might be at other times. Worry less about what others think and give yourself permission to play.

PROACTIVE PLANNING

There may not be many surprises in the department of travel, for your 9th House of Voyages is strongly grounded throughout the year. Plan an educational trip for personal growth around April 17, when your ruling planet, Mercury, enters your 9th House and forms a harmonious Grand Earth Trine with disciplined Saturn and regenerative Pluto. Avoid discretionary travel, if possible, when "not so speedy" Mercury is retrograde January 28–February 18, May 26–June 19, and September 24–October 15. If travel is necessary during these times, make sure to go over the details an extra time, but still be ready for unexpected snafus along the way.

PLANT NOW, HARVEST LATER

Your spiritual path may take you through rather mundane territory this year, for you are planting seeds in your garden of personal growth—ones that you will be tending for many years to come. But there is also a highly motivating tension that builds to a crescendo on November 4, as conservative Saturn moves toward an opposition with radical Uranus, setting the stage for a quantum leap of awareness later in the year and on through 2009. Even if you feel comfortable in your old patterns, this is ultimately the time to break free from them as sweeping changes revitalize your life.

RICK & JEFF'S TIP FOR THE YEAR:
Take Control of Your Life

You may not be one to impulsively jump into something new before carefully reviewing your plans. You have recently survived a period of stress, and as your life now smoothes out, you may be tempted to just go along for the ride. But this is not a year for laziness, because your current efforts have major consequences later on. Risk more and do more instead of being satisfied with the status quo. Taking responsibility one day at a time can build stability, but remember that even the strongest foundation must be able to shift with circumstances. Staying flexible will increase your ability to withstand the pressures of change.

JANUARY

READY, STEADY, GO

The increased emphasis on work this month demands your full attention, and you are ready to go. However, you may be somewhat distracted as retrograde Mars in versatile Gemini forces you to revisit old familiar territory. This assertive planet is moving through your 10th House of Career, directing your energy into your public life—at work or in the community. The issues you must face pull you in two directions on **January 2** as Mars opposes intense Pluto. Making a statement at work can be a struggle while something significant is bothering you at home. Your key planet, Mercury, enters progressive Aquarius in your 6th House of Work on **January 7**, prompting you to seek new and more efficient ways of doing your job. Mercury, though, slows down throughout the month, turning retrograde on **January 28**, reducing the speed of your analytical mind. The ambitious Capricorn New Moon in your 5th House of Self-Expression on **January 8** moves you into a new cycle of creativity, yet you are also acutely aware that success requires a major commitment of time and effort.

Although there can be increasing tension between you and your partner that stems from your conflicting needs for emotional closeness and personal space, a wave of stability builds gradually throughout the month. The dramatic Leo Full Moon on **January 22** falls in your 12th House of Spirituality, reminding you of the necessity of solitude so you can reconnect with your inner self. Your sense of reserve continues through the end of the month as communicator Mercury turns retrograde on **January 28**. In contrast, "action planet" Mars turns direct on **January 30**, signaling movement into new territory over the weeks ahead.

> **KEEP IN MIND THIS MONTH**
>
> *Impulsive behavior can create problems. Although you may be raring to go, you really must lay the groundwork before rushing into anything new.*

KEY DATES

JANUARY 2 ★ *avoid extremes*

As warrior Mars opposes Pluto, you could easily overreact today to a perceived threat to your reputation. It's vital that you get your fears and doubts under control. The more you struggle, the worse it could get. Fortunately, if you can temper your consternation with faith, a magical quintile between beneficial Jupiter and radical Uranus can spark a new perspective that frees you from the conflict.

JANUARY 6-8 ★ *necessary detachment*

You may feel lonely or isolated around **January 6** when warm Venus crosses paths with austere Saturn. Even the best relationships can cool under this influence, so don't make any drastic decisions for a few days. Mercury's entry into intelligent Aquarius on **January 7** can trick you into believing anything. The practical Capricorn New Moon on **January 8** gives you the clarity you need to figure out your next move.

JANUARY 12-13 ★ *worth the wait*

The pace picks up on **January 12** when Venus squares erratic Uranus, but this also awakens restlessness, especially if your partner or co-worker fails to deliver on a promise. When mental Mercury forms an annoying quincunx with restrictive Saturn on **January 13**, you may discuss what happened and attempt to patch up any damage done to your relationship. But it's difficult to know how effective your attempts are until later in the week. Be patient yet persistent in creating a longer-lasting resolution to stress.

SUPER NOVA DAYS
JANUARY 20-22 ★ *focus on the distance*

Your situation is likely more stable than you realize when an expansive Jupiter trines contractive Saturn on **January 21**—a pattern that will recur on **September 8 and November 21**. Develop a strategy for immediate action that is also farsighted enough to carry you through the year. A down-to-earth approach to your own success helps relieve the high anxiety that can be stimulated by the idiosyncratic Aquarius New Moon on **January 22**. Luckily, you have the assistance of Mercury as it conjuncts spacey Neptune, stimulating dreams and taking the edge off your thinking.

JANUARY 28-30 ★ *think before you leap*

Your key planet, Mercury, turns retrograde in quirky Aquarius on **January 28**, initiating a three-week period of reevaluating your assumptions about your habits and daily routine. Active Mars turns direct on **January 30**, saying go, while Mercury wants you to think about it more. Meanwhile, attractive Venus in your 5th House of Romance harmonizes with responsible Saturn to bring you a reasonable attitude about love. Move slowly and surely toward that which makes you happy.

FEBRUARY

POWER OF INTENT

This month begins on an optimistic note with one of the sweetest possible aspects as alluring Venus joins up with confident Jupiter in your 5th House of Love and Romance on **February 1**. It is in cautious Capricorn, however, so even if opportunities for pleasure abound, you are still careful about overstepping your limits. In fact, you might doubt the wisdom of your actions as retrograde Mercury conjuncts illusory Neptune, reactivating recurring fantasies that began on **January 22** at their previous conjunction. The rejuvenating potential of the high-strung Aquarius New Moon Eclipse on **February 6** in your 6th House of Health is reaffirmed as Mercury conjuncts Chiron the Wounded Healer on **February 7**. Nevertheless, be wary about falling down the slippery slope of negativity as you remember something painful that happened a long time ago. You may remain less than certain about the impact you are having through **February 10** when the Sun illuminates dreamy Neptune.

Your fantasies shine this month, but it still can be a challenge to discern reality through the mists of illusion. Still, your normally acute analytical abilities regain focus, picking up additional energy as Mercury turns direct on **February 18**. You are standing at the edge of significant changes as your ruling planet, Mercury, ends its current retrograde cycle. For the past three weeks you have continued to think and rethink your plans without necessarily being able to implement them. Frustration may have tempted you to make rash decisions, complicating your life by disturbing its normal pace. The Virgo Full Moon Eclipse on **February 20** brings new responsibilities into your life and gives you good reason to let go of the past to make room for what's coming next.

> **KEEP IN MIND THIS MONTH**
>
> *Your nerves may be a bit frazzled, potentially making you anxious over even the littlest of things. It's essential to include relaxation time in your daily routine.*

KEY DATES

FEBRUARY 2 ★ *beyond the horizon*
Your logic usually serves you well, but you are challenged today as mental Mercury backs into whimsical Neptune. Forget about detail-oriented work that requires focused thinking. Instead, give yourself permission to dream, for this may be the best way now to reconnect with your creative spirit.

FEBRUARY 6 ★ *the power of positive thought*
An intellectually brilliant Aquarius Solar Eclipse on **February 6** draws the healing powers of Chiron and Neptune into the spotlight. You have a tremendous opportunity now to enhance your body by improving your diet, your exercise routine, and the intention of your thoughts. The predominance of mind over matter is reemphasized as your ruling planet, Mercury, passes between the Earth and the Sun, sharpening the clarity of your ideas. It may be difficult for you to put concepts into words with Mercury retrograde, yet the simple act of contemplation can salve your pain and soothe your weary spirit.

FEBRUARY 10 ★ *dream weaver*
It's difficult to be as reliable as everyone expects today, while the Sun joins diffuse Neptune and shines its light into your subconscious world of fantasy. Your dreams are talking to you and you need to listen, even if what you hear is not easily integrated into your ordinary life. You might need to withdraw socially for a while to attend to your own spiritual process. Remember that your intuition now holds the key to manifesting your dreams.

SUPER NOVA DAYS
FEBRUARY 17-20 ★ *around the next corner*
The long-lasting effects of the Lunar Eclipse in Virgo on **February 20** can alter the fabric of your life. Its conjunction with Saturn the Taskmaster requires that you take deliberate action, so get to work. Although it will take a few days for Mercury to pick up speed in its forward movement, your stated intentions have great power on **February 18** when it actually changes direction. Additionally, sensual Venus joins the Aquarius pack of planets on February 17 and the Sun slips into compassionate Pisces on **February 19**, reconfirming Mercury's forward shift and signaling a clean break from the past.

FEBRUARY 24-26 ★ *concrete desires*
This is not a light and easy time, yet you can crystallize your dreams by integrating them with your reality as the Sun opposes karmic Saturn on **February 24**. Fortunately, clever Mercury joins up with beautiful Venus on **February 26**, increasing your charm and your sociability, encouraging you to express your heart's desire, even if gratification may still be delayed awhile longer.

MARCH

FOCUS ON YOUR FRIENDS

You could experience a gradual shift away from your need to get ahead and toward a more active social life this month, as your friends and associates encourage you to realize dreams not related to your career. Mars visits nurturing Cancer in your 11th House of Friends and Wishes from **March 4 until May 9**. Assertive Mars opposes dominant Pluto on **March 7**—as it did last year on **September 21** and again on **January 2**. Although the circumstances could be very different now, deeper issues are being raised about how you must struggle to maintain your position in the world or give up your power and submit to the will of others. This time, however, you can literally imagine your way through a difficult situation as charming Venus and communicator Mercury join fantastic Neptune on **March 6 and March 9**, respectively. The intuitive Pisces New Moon on **March 7** in your 7th House of Partnerships joins unpredictable Uranus, making you very aware of unresolved tensions between yourself and others. Unexpected assistance arrives with the Sun's annual conjunction with Uranus on **March 8**, giving you the impetus to stand up to any challenges.

The Moon's passage through industrious Virgo on **March 19–20** can overwhelm you with the amount of work you must do, culminating on a stressful Libra Full Moon on **March 21** that can stretch your finances, increase relationship demands, and reactivate the memory of a recent power struggle. But the Vernal Equinox on **March 20** reminds you that hope springs eternal. And although the month ends with a conflictive square between the Sun and Mars, this noisy show of annoyance or anger will quickly settle in the days that follow.

> **KEEP IN MIND THIS MONTH**
>
> *Be ready to make your stand, for you have a chance to convert an overload of stress into the success you desire.*

KEY DATES

MARCH 4 ★ *change old patterns*

Self-directed Mars slips into emotional Cancer in your 11th House of Groups, motivating you to involve others in your activities. You could experience déjà vu, for Mars entered Cancer back on **September 28, 2007**, prior to retrograding into Gemini on **December 31, 2007**. It isn't a great idea to set off on your own during this period, although your tendency now is to advance like the Crab, slowly and cautiously. Be careful about withholding any anger, for passive-aggressive behavior will not serve you well. You'll be happier if you can remember to put your feelings out in the open.

MARCH 9 ★ *otherworldly guidance*

Clever Mercury makes its third and final conjunction with spiritual Neptune today—the first was on **January 23** and the second on **February 2**. Normally, you are highly analytical in your thinking, but this aspect diffuses your mental acuity as it softens your logic with intuition. Instead of seeking solutions by throwing more facts into the mix, let the invisible forces guide you to your answer.

MARCH 12–16 ★ *believe in yourself*

Venus and Mercury leave your familiar 6th House of Health, Work, and Daily Routines for the emotionally richer relationship grounds of your 7th House of Partnerships on **March 12 and March 14**, respectively. You are surely traveling into new territory now, but when Venus opposes stubborn Saturn on **March 15** while trining Mars on **March 16**, you may feel that a friend or partner is not being supportive. Don't get discouraged, because increased self-confidence can improve your ability to convince someone else to be your ally.

MARCH 17–18 ★ *try new tactics*

Your key planet, Mercury, runs into an opposition with resistant Saturn on **March 17**, sending you back to the drawing board without the approval you need, and making you wonder about your actions over the past few days. Fortunately, Mercury then harmonizes with impulsive Mars on **March 18**, encouraging you to do whatever is necessary to fine-tune your thoughts and create a new strategy before communicating your plan to anyone else.

SUPER NOVA DAYS
MARCH 27–28 ★ *outside the box*

Mercury and Venus continue to travel together, connecting with wild and crazy Uranus on **March 27–28**. Additionally, optimistic Jupiter's supportive sextile to these three planets widens your horizons and can bring an important teacher or romantic interest into your life. If you have paid attention throughout the month and attended to the necessary details, this is your chance to reap the rewards. Initiating bold and brave action now will increase your chance for success.

APRIL

OUT OF THE STARTING GATE

April begins with a bang as your ruling planet—Mercury, the Messenger of the Heavens—smashes its way into fiery Aries on **April 2**, only to cross words with powerful Pluto on **April 3**. You can easily say more than intended, for your delivery style now is like a machine gun, with one idea rapidly firing after another. Give others time to digest what you say before moving on to the next thought. Stylish Venus follows Mercury into Aries on **April 6**, also running into a dynamic square with Pluto as deeper desires enter the equation. Passions rise and interactions with others can get destructive unless you pay close attention and express your feelings kindly and without blame. Remember, assertive Mars is in nonconfrontational Cancer all month, urging you to avoid conflict. But passive aggression won't work, because unexpressed feelings will eventually erupt, forcing you to work out your emotional differences anyhow.

Mercury enters tenacious Taurus on **April 17**, establishing a wonderfully stabilizing Grand Earth Trine with Saturn and Pluto on **April 18**. Although you might feel too comfortable to take risks, your ability to organize complex ideas into sensible action plans creates an opportunity that should not be missed. The intense Scorpio Full Moon on **April 20** firms up your resolve to make something happen, for you cannot marginalize your powerful feelings. Good news arrives as communicator Mercury trines Jupiter on **April 28**, but it may not turn out as imagined, for the Trickster Messenger then squares confusing Neptune on **April 29**. Still, the month closes with optimism and anticipation as lovely Venus enters sensual Taurus on **April 30** and you get ready to settle in to some serious enjoyment.

> **KEEP IN MIND THIS MONTH**
>
> *Instead of luxuriating in the calm between the storms, use this time to prepare yourself to handle any situation that unexpectedly arises.*

KEY DATES

APRIL 3 ★ *conflict of intentions*

Your natural affinity to the thinking planet, Mercury, can bring struggle as it squares off with deep, dark Pluto. Unfortunately, someone else might be eager to engage your intensity. You might not be the best judge of what's appropriate today, for Mercury's current quincunx to Saturn makes it difficult to know when to stop. Even if resolution is elusive, you're still likely to learn something from this intellectual journey.

APRIL 5-7 ★ *emotional surrender*

The ardent Aries New Moon on **April 5** falls in your 8th House of Intimacy, setting the tone for the weeks ahead and motivating you to delve into unexplored areas of vulnerability. Venus squares powerful Pluto on **April 6** and quincunxes Saturn on **April 7**, so others may secretly resist you even if you believe that they know what you want. Remember, building an emotional barrier to protect yourself can do more damage than just letting feelings flow naturally.

APRIL 13-14 ★ *talk is cheap*

You are normally somewhat reserved, so you may be challenged when your key planet, Mercury, is activated by exaggerating Jupiter on **April 13**. You are thinking bigger, talking more, and stepping outside your comfort zone. Mercury's supportive sextile from intuitive Neptune on **April 14** puts your fantasies within reach, but tension between Mars and Saturn requires that you work extra hard to bring your dreams to life.

SUPER NOVA DAYS
APRIL 18-22 ★ *creative confidence*

Your originality shines, and taking bold action can be highly productive as Mercury and the Sun create Grand Earth Trines with Pluto and Saturn **April 18-21**. These powerfully stabilizing days around the artistic Libra Full Moon on **April 20** are immediately followed by energetic Mars's trine to unconventional Uranus. With your key planet, Mercury, now in determined Taurus, you must take the bull by the horns and make something happen. If you don't, you'll be managing situations instead of creating something extraordinary. Consider your options and then narrow your focus by picking the very best one.

APRIL 28-29 ★ *the view from above*

You still know where you are going, even if you don't know how to get there. Mercury's harmonious trine to fortunate Jupiter on **April 28** implies success, but your thoughts are carried away by lofty ideals. Confusion could arise as Mercury's square to nebulous Neptune on **April 29** turns your mind into a camera that cannot focus and you become frustrated by trying. Free your imagination from the restraints of common sense and let yourself gently return to Earth over the days ahead.

MAY

BOTH SIDES NOW

You could be dancing around the maypole, for this month begins idyllically as lovely Venus—now at home in her own sign of sensual Taurus—forms a comfortable Grand Earth Trine with Saturn in Virgo and Pluto in Capricorn on **May 1**. It's a rare event when innocent Venus can hook up with these two tough characters in such a positive manner, giving you the ability to stabilize intense feelings and to sustain something worth preserving. But your key planet, Mercury, leaps into its other favorite sign, dualistic Gemini, on **May 2**, setting the stage for the next couple of months when you will be forced to look at everything in two ways. You prefer to use Mercury's analytical abilities to help you discern what information is useful and discard the rest. But while Mercury is in noisy Gemini, you may be less inclined to eliminate any data, for all information contributes to your widening perspective. Choosing between a small amount of precise information and an overload can present a dilemma as you communicate with others throughout the month.

The simplistic Taurus New Moon on **May 5** in your 9th House of Big Ideas reminds you again of the difference between focused intentions and creative explorations. The complex Scorpio Full Moon on **May 19** in your 3rd House of Communication may have you longing for simpler days. The cacophony continues as the Sun enters versatile Gemini on **May 20**, followed by Venus on **May 24**. But the Sun's square to Saturn on **May 22**, followed by Mercury turning retrograde on **May 26**, can initiate your much-needed journey back to basics.

> **KEEP IN MIND THIS MONTH**
>
> *Know that you're standing in a field of power now, even if you express yourself imperfectly. The force is within you.*

KEY DATES

MAY 2–3 ★ *say the right thing*
Saturn the Taskmaster is apparently stationary in the sky on **May 2** as it ends its retrograde phase, strengthening your resolve to succeed and increasing your self-discipline. But mental Mercury's entrance into scattered Gemini the same day slams into a square with Saturn on **May 3**, stopping you in your tracks and forcing you to realize that a few precise words have more impact than a long speech.

MAY 9-12 ★ *invisible friends*

Energetic Mars is very hot as it enters shining Leo in your hidden 12th House on **May 9**, but the fires of inspiration may dwell within your imagination, rather than burning brightly on stage for everyone to see. Supportive aspects from the Sun to optimistic Jupiter and surprising Uranus on **May 12**, along with the Moon's return to your own sign, grant you the emotional support you need, especially when dealing with those who may be less committed than you.

SUPER NOVA DAYS

MAY 18-20 ★ *no quick answers*

You could feel confident enough to express unconventional feelings as loving Venus harmonizes with optimistic Jupiter and radical Uranus on **May 18**. But the passionate Scorpio Full Moon on **May 19** makes it nearly impossible to maintain good judgment about your irrational needs. You may feel frustrated when Venus's square to fuzzy Neptune on **May 20** places practical answers just out of reach, causing you to lose your rhythm as you try to go about the business of your day. This is a chance to step outside your logical mode and rely on your intuition. Still, your attempts to find simple solutions fade as the Sun enters Gemini in your 10th House of Public Status and you become more aware of what you must sacrifice to pursue your career goals.

MAY 26-29 ★ *share your past*

You may feel as if icy emotions are aimed at you when warm Venus in lighthearted Gemini squares cold Saturn on **May 26**. Perhaps your friendly smile is returned by a scowling frown and you wonder if you acted inappropriately. This could bring up old memories to share as Mercury the Messenger moves into a harmonious trine with Chiron the Wounded Healer on **May 29**. You may talk about your emotional hurt and reveal an increasing vulnerability as you speak. Move beyond your personal pain if you want to be of real assistance. Your concern for everyone else will be seen as a mediating voice of reason. While telling your story can be cathartic to you, in the right context it can be an important lesson for someone else.

JUNE

IN THE PUBLIC DOMAIN

June is a goal-oriented month for you, starting with the Sun, Venus, and Mercury in your 10th House of Career, joined by a versatile Gemini New Moon on **June 3**. Yet with your key planet, Mercury, retrograde, it may not seem like you are making much headway. Even after it turns direct on **June 19**, the Winged Messenger takes a couple of weeks to regain its normal speed. Don't get frustrated, for progress is being made whether or not it's apparent. As stylish Venus catches up to the Sun in Gemini, Mercury retrograde backs into the pair of planets, conjuncting both the Sun and Venus on **June 7**. Relying on your fast wit and sweet charm can help you get what you want.

Venus moves into opposition with dark Pluto as the Moon waxes full in Sagittarius on **June 18**. This potentially explosive Full Moon can provoke conflict, even if you believe your words are soothing rather than argumentative. Passions quickly rise to the surface, yet when you understand someone else's point of view, true love has the opportunity to shine in a way that deepens intimacy beyond your expectations. Mercury's retrograde phase ends on **June 19**, just before the Sun moves into its opposition to Pluto on **June 20**. You are determined now to make a stand, and even if others resist your efforts you may be reluctant to negotiate. This is also the Summer Solstice, indicating the beginning of a more nurturing time for you, especially as Venus forms a supportive sextile with Saturn in Virgo. You are graced with a more realistic perspective on love that allows you to respond in a more caring and enduring manner.

> **KEEP IN MIND THIS MONTH**
>
> *Although the first part of June may be less than peaceful, your patience and perseverance will pay off as long as you don't lose sight of your ultimate destination.*

KEY DATES

JUNE 3 ★ *fools rush in*

The Gemini New Moon usually scatters your energy, but a supportive sextile from relentless Mars in Leo gives you enough endurance to complete whatever you start. Retrograde Mercury's square to Uranus is a high-frequency buzz, flashing you answers even before the questions are finished. You could be brilliant now, but you may have more to lose than gain if you jump to the wrong conclusion.

JUNE 8–10 ★ *secret weapon*

Mental Mercury in your 10th House of Career sextiles assertive Mars in your 12th House of Secrets on **June 8**, as sweet Venus kisses the Gemini Sun. This paradoxical mix shows how your desire to be effective in the world can be supported by the creativity within the secret realms of your imagination. Remember, you don't have to say everything you know in order to get your point across. The Moon waltzes through your sign on **June 9–10**, bringing emotions closer to the surface. Still, you wonder whether it's more important to share your feelings or to keep them buried so you can appear more appropriate.

JUNE 12–13 ★ *spiritual fulfillment*

Venus's square to unpredictable Uranus on **June 12**, followed by its trine to Neptune on **June 13**, stimulates your sensual desires and encourages you to seek satisfaction, whether or not you conform to the expectations of others. The softer side of this combination comes into play when beautiful Venus trines imaginative Neptune, allowing you to rely on a deeper spirituality and intuition to know what to say about love.

SUPER NOVA DAYS
JUNE 18–20 ★ *save something for tomorrow*

The cavalier Sagittarius Full Moon in your 4th House of Security gains strength from its conjunction with dark Lord Pluto on **June 18**. Despite all the effort you have put in at work for the past few weeks, emotional pressures require you to ask uncomfortable questions. This is a pivotal time as Mercury turns direct on **June 19**, followed by an intense Sun-Pluto opposition on **June 20**. Your needs are strong, so be careful about asking for too much, too soon. You are better off keeping your feelings to yourself until your passions settle down.

JUNE 25–30 ★ *natural talent*

Trickster Mercury is quintile quicksilver Mars on **June 25–28**, gracing you with a rare opportunity to think of original solutions to ongoing problems. This is a charismatic and intellectually creative aspect that allows you to present your ideas in a convincing and thoughtful manner. Your energy continues to rise as Mars moves toward a harmonious trine with Pluto on **June 30**, giving you the stamina to accomplish more than you thought possible.

JULY

GAINING TRACTION

You enter a high-energy zone on **July 1** as "action planet" Mars visits your sign through **August 19**, yet it may be challenging to filter this planet's impulsive expressions through the focused precision of critical Virgo. You may feel anxious as the heat of Mars pushes up against resistant Saturn through **July 10**, requiring you to slow down. Don't run roughshod over the obstacles in your path, for little progress will be made until you take them seriously. If you successfully transmute your frustration and channel your physical energy into hard work, then the rest of the month will be much easier to handle. Your key planet, Mercury, is in emotional Cancer on **July 10–26**, turning your analytical approach into a softer and more nurturing manner.

The gentle Cancer New Moon on **July 2** falls in your 11th House of Friends and is sweetened by its proximity to loving Venus. This lunation is further encouraged by an opposition to confident Jupiter, so getting more involved with a group or organization may be one way to connect with something greater than yourself. Plant the seeds now by taking action as a team player, and then watch this part of your life grow through the coming weeks. The earthy Capricorn Full Moon on **July 18** sets the practicality of personal love or self-expression against the needs of your wider community. You can see exactly where you don't fit in and may need to take steps to define new boundaries. The superconductive trine between Mars and Jupiter on **July 26** floods your system with optimism and enthusiasm, fueling your hard work with high energy through the rest of the month.

> **KEEP IN MIND THIS MONTH**
>
> *Conserve and pace your energy. This can be a very productive period as long as you don't exhaust yourself before you reach the finish line.*

KEY DATES

JULY 5–6 ★ *high-wire act*

Details may fall by the wayside as mental Mercury triggers electric Uranus on **July 5**. Instead of having everything in order, you are out on a ledge without the safety net of your usual facts and figures. Your grasp on reality is further loosened by Mercury's smooth trine to dreamy Neptune on **July 6**. You are likely to enjoy the unexpected changes, for sweet Venus harmonizes with Uranus the same day, allowing you to easily move beyond old social limits. This isn't about idle daydreaming; using your imagination to sprout wings has positive practical consequences.

SUPER NOVA DAYS
JULY 9-10 ★ *talk it out*

An opposition from the Sun to expansive Jupiter on **July 9** intrigues you with creative and romantic possibilities. Meanwhile, Mercury's cosmic tug-of-war with Pluto drives your thoughts into the hidden recesses of your subconscious mind, bringing unpleasant material into the open. Letting the messenger planet do its work is crucial, for you'll be better off after a difficult issue is discussed. Still, it may not be easy, for the Mars-Saturn conjunction on **July 10** can make you feel as if you're facing insurmountable obstacles. Channeling anger into constructive dialogue is the best way to relieve the stress. Skillfully handling these turbulent days can ultimately have a calming effect on your home and career, especially with Mercury swimming in the supportive emotional waters of Cancer for the next couple of weeks.

JULY 18-22 ★ *hope floats*

The days following the intellectually challenging Aquarius Full Moon on **July 18** are filled with optimism and hope as sudden realizations resolve relationship tensions. Mercury in your 11th House of Friends opposes joyful Jupiter on **July 19** in your 5th House of Love and Creativity, emboldening you to take on a new project or even to make a heartfelt promise to someone special. Your choices will be good ones as long as you remember your limitations, for Mercury's trine to erratic Uranus on **July 22** can spark an unrealistic sense of possibilities. Don't take any unnecessary risks unless you have carefully weighed the consequences.

JULY 26 ★ *go for the gold*

You have had some time now to get used to fiery Mars in your sign: It has instilled you with the courage to act more decisively throughout the month. Now, as the warrior planet harmoniously trines buoyant Jupiter, your optimism swells even more. The Moon in solid Taurus forms a stabilizing Grand Earth Trine with Jupiter and Mars, adding realism to an otherwise over-the-top day. Listen to the inner coach who's telling you that you can win this one if you calculate your moves and then give it your very best.

AUGUST

WINDS OF FATE

A dramatic Solar Eclipse in your 12th House of Destiny can jump-start your month with a fateful series of events that have long-lasting consequences. With Mercury and Venus also in your private 12th House, others may not even realize what you're going through now. Venus's entry into Virgo on **August 6**, followed by Mercury on **August 10**, feels a bit like a homecoming, but it's challenging to manage all the planets currently in your sign—the heat of Mars, the responsibility of Saturn, the desires of Venus, and the sharp intelligence of Mercury. There may be too much happening, making it difficult to keep everything under control. You don't have much of a choice, however, when Venus conjoins Saturn on **August 13**, followed by Mercury on **August 15**. Both of these conjunctions stop you in your tracks, forcing you to improve some aspect of yourself that is not up to standards. The Aquarius Full Moon Eclipse on **August 16** overwhelms you with emotions, erasing any lingering doubts about the intensity of these times.

The Sun's entry into efficient Virgo on **August 22** can deliver a boost of brilliance, providing you with much more clarity. The tense opposition from Mercury and Venus to radical Uranus on **August 23** brings the message home; a clean break is surely one of your options. Mercury and Venus enter Libra on **August 28 and August 30**, respectively, reaffirming your desire to bring your life back into balance. A rare second New Moon this month falls in your 1st House of Personality. No matter how much change you have experienced this month, this Virgo New Moon is the stamp of finality that you need in order to move on.

> **KEEP IN MIND THIS MONTH**
>
> *Your stress level is high, so it's crucial to look beyond differences of opinion. Otherwise, unexpected conflicts might turn even the smallest disagreements into major meltdowns.*

KEY DATES

AUGUST 1-2 ★ *leap of faith*
The creative Leo New Moon Eclipse on **August 1** in your 12th House of Soul Consciousness emphasizes your desire to reconnect with your inner world. In a flash of awareness, you realize the need to delve into your own imagination to discover how past experiences are still affecting your current choices. Your spiritual journey may not be an easy one, but the ramifications of metaphysical work can be quite profound.

AUGUST 5-6 ★ *out of balance*

The love planet, Venus, enters your sign on **August 5**, and satisfaction depends upon your ability to be clear about your needs in intimate relationships. Physical Mars's opposition with "wild and crazy" Uranus on **August 6**, followed by mental Mercury's opposition to foggy Neptune the same day, messes with your powers of critical analysis. Postpone decisions for a few days, until you can tell what's truly important. In the meantime, maintain your center by making a wish list for your future.

SUPER NOVA DAYS

AUGUST 10-16 ★ *no going back*

Mercury visits Virgo **August 10-28**, emphasizing all aspects of communication and delivering a heightened awareness of your own thoughts. This is a great time to hone your mental skills, but focusing on your specific fields of interest may require that you become more comfortable saying no. A Venus-Saturn conjunction on **August 13** can feel like a wave of discouragement, but you can better assess which commitments are worth keeping now. Then, as Mercury joins sobering Saturn on **August 15**, you are ready to turn your heart's desires into reality by talking about your personal goals. The good news is that you truly understand the consequences of your decisions. The unconventional Aquarius Full Moon Eclipse on **August 16** confirms that you cannot turn back from the choices you recently made.

AUGUST 23 ★ *mental fireworks*

Today Uranus shocks both alluring Venus and your ruling planet, Mercury, creating brilliant flashes of desire in your mind. It's thrilling and unsettling, and you'll need all your attention just to keep up with your own thoughts. So many ideas flow through quickly that in the end, you might be left with nothing but a fleeting memory. Let the most outrageous ideas slip away while keeping only a few of the best ones for later.

AUGUST 27-28 ★ *change of perspective*

Your feelings intensify as Mercury squares powerful Pluto on **August 27**, but everything can shift in a moment once you share what you've been hiding. It's time to find a more evenhanded way of dealing with conflict as Mercury enters Libra the Scales on **August 28**. Instead of simply speaking the truth, now you must also be diplomatic with your response.

SEPTEMBER

CONSOLIDATE YOUR GAINS

September begins on a heavier note as the Sun, now moving through efficient Virgo, makes its annual conjunction with austere Saturn on **September 3**. You must take responsibility for your entire life—the successes and the failures. Last month may have been a wild ride filled with surprise, but it also opened a new path for you. This month, however, is a time of integration, affording you the opportunity to take advantage of what you've learned and to confidently apply this new perspective to your life. The second of three harmonizing trines between optimistic Jupiter and realistic Saturn on **September 8** sets the tone not only for this month, but for the remainder of the year as well. Both Jupiter and Pluto turn direct the same day, fueling this powerful wave of stability. Expanding your life slowly according to your well-organized plans can bring you closer to your idea of personal success while also allowing you greater latitude of self-expression.

In general, your flow of new ideas, as well as any forward progress, may seem slow throughout the month as your ruling planet, Mercury, gradually grinds to a halt, finally turning retrograde on **September 24**. This month is less about breaking new ground than it is about preparing the soil on which you stand for a garden that is yet to be grown. The fantasy-driven Pisces Full Moon on **September 15** can bring a surprising change within a relationship, for it conjuncts unpredictable Uranus in your 7th House of Partnerships. The fair-minded Libra New Moon on **September 29** in your 2nd House of Values is a reminder to consider all perspectives before you decide which ones best fit your principles and personal needs.

> **KEEP IN MIND THIS MONTH**
>
> *Instead of worrying about how you can fix everything all at once, reevaluate your life and develop a strategy to preserve what's already working.*

KEY DATES

SEPTEMBER 3-4 ★ *deliver more than promised*

Serious Saturn restrains the brilliant Sun on **September 3**, piling responsibilities onto your shoulders. Even if you're uncertain about what you're doing, trust your common sense—it won't mislead you now. The Sun's lucky trine to hopeful Jupiter on **September 4** graces you with a positive attitude, no matter how hard you must work. Aside from the possibility of promising more than you can deliver, your current efforts should bring the desired results.

SEPTEMBER 7-9 ★ *realistic expectations*

Realism tempers your "I can do anything" attitude when the Jupiter-Saturn trine culminates on **September 8**. However, there are real obstacles to overcome between **September 7 and September 9** as mental Mercury, sensual Venus, and energetic Mars each, in turn, squares extravagant Jupiter. You can all but assure your success by consciously resisting the temptation to set your sights too high. Overspending, overcommitment, and overindulgence are traps that could have negative consequences later on.

SUPER NOVA DAYS
SEPTEMBER 12-15 ★ *the price of freedom*

The Sun loses focus as it shines opposite radical Uranus on **September 12**, sending waves of excitement through your system as you react to your new-found freedoms. Mercury's conjunction with charming Venus on **September 14** helps you get away with otherwise unacceptable behavior, especially if you stay conscious of other people's feelings. The psychic Pisces Full Moon on **September 15** is conjunct Uranus, rattling you with sudden awareness. Even if you are uncomfortable with an unexpected change of rules, just acknowledge what you learn and get on with your daily routine.

SEPTEMBER 20-24 ★ *resource reassessment*

The Sun's square with intense Pluto on **September 20** may indicate an emotional problem caused by something that remains unsaid. The Autumn Equinox on **September 22**—bringing the Sun into Libra in your 2nd House of Self-Worth—is a turning point: Hidden financial issues may be brought out into the open so that you can deal with them directly. This is reemphasized by Mercury's retrograde turn on **September 24**, requiring you to go back over money issues even if you thought they were already resolved.

SEPTEMBER 28-29 ★ *dream a little dream*

Retrograde Mercury forms an easy trine with fanciful Neptune on **September 28**, acting as a transition to ease you into a softer and dreamier frame of mind. The lovely Libra New Moon on **September 29** reinforces the rose-colored image you now have of the world. Don't worry if your analytical powers are not as sharp as usual. Use this time to explore your fantasies and indulge your imagination instead.

OCTOBER

YOU ARE WHAT YOU THINK

Mercury the Messenger is not only your key planet but also the key to this whole month. Until **October 15**, Mercury is retracing ground it covered in September, pulling your thoughts back through familiar issues and requiring you to reconsider previous concerns. Mercury spends all of October in Libra the Scales in your 2nd House of Money and Resources, making this a time to balance your accounts and put your possessions in order. Using diplomatic finesse to discover common ground in the midst of conflict eases tensions and strengthens your ability to negotiate. Breaks from this pattern occur when Mercury forms an annoying quincunx with conceptually brilliant Uranus on **October 1**, creating such a shock of excitement that you could find yourself in a state of nervous frenzy, making it difficult for you to concentrate on your work. This stimulating aspect is repeated on **October 28**, indicating the need to find calming activities to prevent the stress caused by high anxiety. Mercury squares extravagant Jupiter on **October 6** and again on **October 26**, setting up another theme for the month. A tendency to exaggerate is possible, so remember to make your usual checklist to ground yourself with the important details that you might otherwise overlook.

The competitive Aries Full Moon on **October 14** falls in your 8th House of Shared Resources, reminding you that you must cooperate with others, even if your personal styles are vastly different. The magnetic Scorpio New Moon on **October 28** falls in your 3rd House of Immediate Environment and is energized by Mars's trine to rebellious Uranus, daring you to express yourself in a surprisingly reckless manner.

> **KEEP IN MIND THIS MONTH**
>
> *Instead of being sure that what you know is enough, remain open to receiving new information that can change your mind, however unexpected and unconventional the source.*

KEY DATES

OCTOBER 4-6 ★ *find a balance*

Mars enters emotional Scorpio in your 3rd House of Communication on **October 4**, intensifying even the most casual of conversations. But the waves of change now are more than personal, pulling you into social or political realms as the Sun and Mercury—both in evenhanded Libra—dynamically square bold Jupiter on **October 6**. You may be overstepping your boundaries and moving in the direction of excess.

Sweet Venus's supportive sextile to Jupiter on **October 5** increases your desire to overindulge, so voluntarily cut back before you overdo it.

OCTOBER 10–11 ★ *no quick fixes*
You are just itching to break out of your routine as seductive Venus in Scorpio trines rebellious Uranus on **October 10**. If you are feeling relationship conflict, resolution can come as a total surprise thanks to an unexpected new perspective. Moving outside the box allows you both to get what you want, but Venus squares confusing Neptune on **October 11**, making it tough to know what's real. Using your astute powers of concentration can prevent you from believing that all is well when in fact it is not.

SUPER NOVA DAYS
OCTOBER 14–16 ★ *soft focus*
The impulsive Aries Full Moon on **October 14** is diffused by a harmonizing Sun-Neptune trine, allowing you to be less analytical and more creative. You may suffer from an unusual lack of motivation as you slip past a deadline. Mercury turns direct on **October 15**, but it will take a couple of weeks for it to regain enough speed to feel like you're moving forward again. Let go of your self-criticism; the increased pressure you place upon yourself will only encourage rash thinking and poor judgment. Allow enough time for your best ideas to germinate, and they will bear fruit right on schedule.

OCTOBER 18 ★ *wanderlust*
When charming Venus enters open-minded Sagittarius on **October 18**, you might be inclined to expand your horizons, but your innate shyness can hold you back. It's challenging for you to let go of your need to have everything in order prior to receiving pleasure. However, this is a good moment to set your regular habits aside and accept the adventure and love that may arrive at your doorstep.

OCTOBER 30–31 ★ *the strength of flexibility*
Mars forms a supportive sextile with restraining Saturn on **October 30** and an easy trine with unrestrained Uranus on **October 31**, giving you the ability to smoothly manage the powerful tension between your need for structure and your desire for independence. Take every possible chance to gracefully release relationship tensions instead of holding on to them tightly.

NOVEMBER

EYES ON THE DISTANT FUTURE

Don't underestimate the long-term impact of what occurs this month, for the stage is being set not only for the remainder of this year, but in fact for several years to come. Hardworking Saturn stands tensely opposed to surprising Uranus on **November 4**, a powerful aspect lasting through July 2010. It is likely you are already feeling on edge, itching to turn the most repressive parts of your life upside down and backward if necessary to gain your independence. Your frustration may not produce immediate results, but it offers clues to issues that must be resolved in the months and years ahead. It's likely that personal relationships will undergo major changes, dramatically affected by your current feelings of restless-ness and an increasing need for freedom.

Fortunately, confident Jupiter relieves some of the tension this month as it harmonizes with the Saturn-Uranus opposition. Jupiter's third supportive sextile with Uranus on **November 13**—the first was on **March 28**, the second on **May 21**—allows you more latitude of self-expression as long as you respect the previously established rules and boundaries. Jupiter's easygoing trine with serious Saturn on **November 21** is the third in a series that began on **January 21** and was repeated on **September 8**.

It reaffirms the changes you've made through-out the year based upon slow and steady growth. The Taurus Full Moon on **November 13** com-pletes a practical Grand Earth Trine involving Jupiter and Saturn, yet imaginative Neptune's involvement suggests that you must rein in your illusions to manifest your dreams. The optimistic Sagittarius New Moon on **November 27** gives you great hope for the future and blesses you with the support of close friends and family.

KEEP IN MIND THIS MONTH

It's difficult to gauge the relative importance of specific events now, so treat each one—no matter how insignificant it seems—as a life-changing moment.

KEY DATES

NOVEMBER 3-4 ★ *face the music*

Family dynamics can be a source of tension as your relationship houses are pulled by a tug-of-war between traditional Saturn and progressive Uranus on **November 4**. Disagreements about money could arise—especially if you've neglected your fiscal responsibilities—as valuable Venus squares both Saturn and Uranus on **November 3**. Underlying stress won't disappear until you give it your undivided attention.

SUPER NOVA DAYS

NOVEMBER 10–13 ★ *overcome your fears*

The Sun's supportive trines and sextiles to optimistic Jupiter, persistent Saturn, and inventive Uranus on **November 10–11** are like a dose of high-potency vitamins, giving you the power to change your life as long as you are willing to take a chance. When sweet Venus conjuncts intense Pluto on **November 12**, however, you are brought face-to-face with your subconscious fears. Fortunately, you have an opportunity to conquer a self-imposed limitation that has prevented you from reaching your goals. The down-to-earth Taurus Full Moon on **November 13** fills you with much-needed determination while feeding the exciting Jupiter-Uranus sextile. Visualizing your future exactly as you desire it is a great start, but you must follow through with determination and diligence.

NOVEMBER 16 ★ *the sky's the limit*

Your key planet, Mercury, forms an easy trine with electric Uranus today, sending waves of unconventional thought through your brain. Your current mental activity touches the edges of brilliance, yet it may be tricky capturing the ideas before they fly off. Meanwhile, assertive Mars enters adventurous Sagittarius, encouraging you to reach for the farthest horizon instead of being satisfied with a closer destination. Don't sell yourself short now; you can do more than you ever thought possible.

NOVEMBER 23 ★ *freedom of speech*

Mercury the Communicator aims high as it enters uplifting Sagittarius in your 4th House of Home and Family on **November 23**, making you quite the philosopher on this Thanksgiving Day. Typically, you are more interested in the practical applications of your analytical thinking, but right now you aren't overly concerned with the real world. Let your thoughts roam and partake in theoretical discussions without having to be responsible for taking any action at all.

NOVEMBER 28–29 ★ *mixed bag of feelings*

Sensual Venus sextiles outrageous Uranus on **November 28** and trines disciplined Saturn on **November 29**, creating a sensible path to your most unconventional desires. Even if you want to try something totally out of the box, you still have the ability to impress others with your reliability and your no-nonsense approach to handling your responsibilities.

DECEMBER

STRESS MANAGEMENT

December begins with a wonderful conjunction between beautiful Venus and broad-minded Jupiter on **December 1** in the resourceful sign of Capricorn, allowing you to approach an investment—financial or emotional—with extra common sense. But the sweet pleasures of the Venus-Jupiter conjunction are not long lasting, for the Sun drives toward its annual conjunction with the warrior planet, Mars, on **December 5**. This alignment in well-intentioned Sagittarius can give you good reason to initiate actions that move you closer to your goals, but can also stir up trouble at home or in a relationship. Your communication may be a bit on edge, for Mercury's squares to unpredictable Uranus on **December 5** and to respectful Saturn on **December 6** make it difficult for you to lead a discussion to a logical conclusion. Instead, you uncharacteristically fire off thoughts before you think about their consequences and then a moment later hesitate to say what's on your mind because you are afraid it might be inappropriate.

The scattered Gemini Full Moon on **December 12** falls in your 10th House of Career, increasing the stresses you already feel about your job. This Full Moon is square Saturn and Uranus, demonstrating the tenuousness of your hard-earned stability in life. Your originality sparkles as you participate in exciting discussions about unconventional ideas on **December 24**, supported by mental Mercury's sextile to Uranus the Awakener. Mercury's harmonious trine to Saturn on **December 26** helps you settle the energy and ground your erratic thoughts. The well-behaved Capricorn New Moon on **December 27** falls in your 5th House of Fun and Games, so be sure to fill up your calendar with holiday festivities.

> **KEEP IN MIND THIS MONTH**
>
> *Allowing for imperfection in yourself and others doesn't mean you have to sacrifice your high standards. Maintain a healthy perspective and positive results will follow.*

KEY DATES

DECEMBER 1 ★ *make time for fun*

You might need to remind yourself to be practical today as buoyant Jupiter encourages sweet Venus to bring you more pleasure. You may have work to finish, but you are likely thinking about something that's a lot more fun. This can turn out to be a joyous time if you plan your social activities for later in the day.

DECEMBER 10-12 ★ *where is the love*
These stressful days are highlighted by the restless Gemini Full Moon on
December 12. The Full Moon is tensely aspected to impulsive Mars, stern
Saturn, and unpredictable Uranus, challenging you to balance holiday enthusiasm with the reality of your current responsibilities. You may already feel
the tension by **December 10**, when the Sun squares Uranus, but it's mental
Mercury's conjunction with intense Pluto on **December 12** that can heat up
the situation to the boiling point. If a casual comment sets off a disruptive
discussion, clear the air of bad feelings and move on.

DECEMBER 15 ★ *change your mind*
You might be at odds with your family over upcoming holiday plans as assertive
Mars squares austere Saturn, yet you need to take the most responsible course of
action. Even if you are discouraged, keep in mind that things aren't as bad as they
seem. While you may not see an immediate resolution to your dilemma, trying too
hard will only make matters worse. Instead, work with the obstacles in your path
and rest assured that your consistent positive attitude, coupled with sincere effort,
will bring relief. Switching your focus to a nonadversarial mode can make all the
difference in the world.

DECEMBER 21-22 ★ *shine light into the dark abyss*
The Sun enters pragmatic Capricorn, marking the Winter Solstice on **December 21**
and joining Pluto on **December 22**. You may know what you want and how to get it,
but your uncontrolled power could hurt someone you love unless you remember to
consider their needs as well as your own. Don't hold on to negative feelings. The
sooner you acknowledge your fears, the better it will be for everyone involved.

DECEMBER 27-31 ★ *resolve to succeed*
Mars enters ambitious Capricorn on **December 27** and conjuncts Pluto on
December 28, giving you an irrepressible drive to significantly improve your life
as you look back over the previous year. Use this powerful alignment, combined
with Mercury's uplifting conjunction with confident Jupiter on **December 31**, to
set your goals for the year ahead. Instead of wasting this energy by falling into
dreamy fantasies, choose realistic goals that give you something tangible to work
for in the future.

LIBRA

SEPTEMBER 23–OCTOBER 22

LIBRA OVERVIEW

Expect a tricky balancing act throughout the year between your innate need for relationship and the attention you must place on your inner development. Saturn, the planet of making it real, entered your 12th House of Spiritual Mystery on September 2, 2007, and will spend all of 2008 in this part of your chart. Your most precious accomplishments may not receive full recognition with Saturn in this behind-the-scenes house, but this can also give you a break from some of your worldly responsibilities. **Taking more time to tend to your inner life is a good way to gain strength, heal old wounds, and reassess your life purpose.** This is a period of preparation, Libra, when you're readying yourself for an enormous step forward, beginning with Saturn's entry into your sign on October 29, 2009. Still, you're far too sociable to cut people out of your life. In fact, even with the challenging changes, **you might be ready for a rebound when it comes to love.**

Two eclipses in your 5th House of Love and Creativity can shift the landscape in these vital areas of your life. The Solar Eclipse on February 6 is joined with inspirational Neptune to raise hopes for a more sublime emotional connection, and a harmonious trine to Mars may even provide a willing playmate. Neptune, unfortunately, tends more toward fantasy than reality, which could lead you astray in the pursuit of a more perfect union. The Lunar Eclipse on August 16 is also joined with magical but illusory Neptune, repeating the fantasy-chasing theme. It's certainly healthy to open your heart and mind to more fulfilling forms of love, yet if common sense is lost in the process, you could wind up with less than you expected. **The magic lies within you, so create through your own acts of art, style, and self-expression where you can direct the process and control the outcome.**

Expansive Jupiter in practical Capricorn implies that rewards must be earned by disciplined effort as you gain wisdom through your hard work. Last year, Jupiter formed two strategic trines with Saturn in fire signs that may have sparked a new vision for your future happiness. The planets of hope and reality form three more trines on January 21, September 8, and November 21, but this year they are in earth signs, validating your great ideas with a commitment to a concrete plan. Still, 2008 begins while initiating Mars is moving retrograde, so it's best to wait until it turns direct on January 30 to kick your activities into high gear. The "action planet" becomes even more influential when it's in your sign from August 19 through October 3. It's an excellent period to demonstrate your abilities as a creative self-starter. Working, living, or playing solo is not your idea of fun, but knowing that **you can be productive without the support and approval you normally enjoy can free you from having to compromise** your actions and accommodate yourself to the will of others.

 ## NOTHING BUT THE BEST

You're a romantic, Libra, so even if disappointment in a relationship puts you on your guard for a while, it tends to drop again as soon as your heart begins to heal. The two eclipses in your 5th House of Romance this year, though, can signal a change of direction that's likely to impact you for years to come. If you've spent your life trying to make others happy without asking for much in return, it's time to stop. Vulnerable Neptune's proximity to the eclipses suggests that the cost of silence is too high and can leave you feeling disillusioned about love. Instead of always compromising, treat yourself as the precious person you are—one worthy of all the love you're willing to give and even more. You have a good chance to connect with someone new who inspires you or to bring a higher level of idealism into a current partnership, but what's most important now is how generous this person is to you. Good intentions and promises mean nothing unless they are backed up by sincere action. The secret to a successful love life is to expect the best for yourself and reject anyone who doesn't give it to you.

 ## A SURPRISING TWIST

The seven-year transit of inventive Uranus through your 6th House of Work receives a boost from intelligent sextiles by visionary Jupiter on March 28, May 21, and November 13. These are periods when sudden opportunities arise to expand your professional horizons. You might get an unexpected promotion, a chance to shift to a more intriguing field, or a spark of inspiration that leads you in a totally new direction. There are real possibilities to break through boundaries that have been keeping you from finding satisfaction in your job. Learning different skills or acquiring specialized education, especially in areas where you never thought you could succeed, is key to a more exciting and rewarding employment.

BURIED TREASURE

Pluto, the ruler of your 2nd House of Resources, crosses the bottom of your chart this year, which can lead to a complete reassessment of financial matters. It could help you uncover lost or discarded assets, so scouring your basement, attic, or garage for hidden treasures might prove quite profitable. Income may be gained through real estate, especially if you can apply your good taste and creative abilities to increase the value of distressed properties. Your family is another possible source of material gain—either via inheritance or by your reclamation of a talent passed down by one of your ancestors.

LAUGHTER IS THE BEST MEDICINE

Variety is more than the spice of life: It could be your key to physical well-being in 2008. Unconventional Uranus in your 6th House of Health indicates a need for diversity to break up any rigid structures of routine that can sap your energy. Instead of sticking to one familiar diet or form of exercise, experimenting with several different ones can work to your benefit. Neptune, the ruler of your 6th House, is making a long-term transit of your 5th House of Play, reminding you that expressing yourself joyfully is a core element of reaching peak performance. Dance, sports, and adventures in the great outdoors are just some of the ways to combine fun with fitness.

FAMILY TIES

Optimistic Jupiter's passage through your 4th House of Home and Family makes this a great year for domestic growth. Spending time and energy to improve your living space is a worthwhile investment; the possibility of moving into a larger domicile also makes sense. However, this isn't about building a palace or paying for flashy furniture and decorations. A more utilitarian approach with a focus on quality and convenience will serve your needs more effectively. Jupiter, the Guru or Teacher, in this house can also turn your attention to family history. Whether it's research into your ancestral past or a reexamination of your childhood experiences, a growing understanding of where you came from will definitely help you get where you want to go.

THE ROAD PREVIOUSLY TRAVELED

Giant Jupiter, the long-distance travel and learning planet, is in your 4th House of Roots, which rewards you when you return to familiar places instead of seeking out exotic new ones. Trips that connect you with history, especially of your own family, can be enriching. It's best to stick close to home from the first of the year until January 30 while assertive Mars moves backward in your 9th House of Faraway Places, and again from May 26 until June 19 when Mercury is retrograde in this part of your chart. Educational pursuits are most worthwhile when they are well organized. A smattering of classes here and there or a course taken casually with a friend is probably not going to be entirely satisfying this year; rigorous programs geared toward developing specific skills will be a better fit.

PRACTICE MAKES PERFECT

With solid Saturn passing through your 12th House of Soul Consciousness, this is a great year for serious spiritual work. The reality planet in earthy Virgo requires dedicated practice to develop this important area. Patience and concentration will deeply enrich your inner life. Pay attention to details to align yourself with your higher purpose. Small steps taken on a journey of commitment can carry your spirit as far as you want to go. Study the works of masters whose lessons may be demanding—but will faithfully guide your inner development.

RICK & JEFF'S TIP FOR THE YEAR:
Work for Your Dreams

Take yourself very seriously this year, for your aspirations are not merely hopes and your dreams are not just passing whims. They are seeds of your future to be planted in the earth, nourished by your conviction, and grown by your actions. You hold in your hands the power to take control of your destiny and change the shape of your future. There will be moments to play, of course, and times to fantasize. But respect those inspiring images by doing what you can to manifest them in the outer world rather than just allowing them to stay in your head.

JANUARY

YOU FIRST

Start the New Year with serious commitment, Libra, as the New Moon in Capricorn on **January 8** plants a seed of ambition in your 4th House of Security. Don't broadcast your big plans until you've done enough work to be certain they will take root. Action will feed your dreams, but too many words can dissipate its power. Patience is more than a virtue now; it's a necessity for reaching your goal. The Sun's entry into futuristic Aquarius on **January 20** illuminates your 5th House of Romance and Creativity and can lighten your mood with play and enrich your life with joyous spontaneity. Aquarius encourages originality, so experiment with new ways to express yourself personally and professionally. A fresh look or attitude will spice up your love life even if conservative friends don't appreciate your change of style.

On **January 21**, hopeful Jupiter and realistic Saturn make the third in a series of harmonious trines that began in March 2007 and will finish on **November 21**. This is an excellent opportunity to assess your progress toward long-term goals, and make any necessary adjustments to get back on course. The bold Leo Full Moon on **January 22** in your 11th House of Groups can put you in a leadership position or provide you with a boost from a friend or colleague. However, don't let flattery charm you into taking on more than you can handle. Venus, your ruling planet, joins purging Pluto on **January 24**, which signals the need to focus on one or two core issues instead of scattering your attention across a variety of projects. Go-getter Mars turns direct in diverse Gemini on **January 30**, further tempting you to divide your energies, but it's best to avoid distractions now.

> **KEEP IN MIND THIS MONTH**
>
> *Don't forget to tend your personal needs despite a growing ambition to make your creative mark on the world.*

KEY DATES

JANUARY 6–7 ★ *speak up smartly*

A tense square between sociable Venus in your 3rd House of Communication and stifling Saturn on **January 6** could make you feel put down or underappreciated. It's a good idea to express yourself honestly—but do this discreetly to avoid creating further conflict. Chatty Mercury enters your 5th House of Self-Expression on **January 7**, which helps you present your ideas in an intelligent and entertaining manner. However, Mercury's retrograde cycle in this house from **January 28 until February 18** may require some backtracking in matters of the heart.

JANUARY 12 ★ *experimental emotions*

Social plans may change suddenly with a challenging square between Venus and electric Uranus. Your likes and dislikes can rapidly switch, attracting you to unusual individuals or objects and turning you off familiar ones. Hair-trigger reactions can destabilize relationships and spur spending sprees. Exploring new tastes and desires, though, can be healthy as long as no one is hurt.

JANUARY 19–21 ★ *creative juice*

Passions are powerful with a super-stimulating opposition between romantic Venus and impulsive Mars on **January 19**. Flirting and fighting are possible as interactions are intensified in both directions. Your usual well-mannered demeanor readily gives way to more extreme behavior. This force, though, can also be applied positively, making this a good time to utilize your artistic abilities instead of engaging in the complications of relationships. The Sun's entry into your 5th House of Love and Creativity on **January 20** adds confidence, helping you to carry yourself proudly, but your idealism and generosity make it easy for you to share the stage. Responsibility kicks in strongly on **January 21** with the Jupiter-Saturn trine, but don't let others' panic push you to overreact. Slow and steady gets the job done now.

SUPER NOVA DAY
JANUARY 24 ★ *down to the core*

Sweet Venus joins dark Pluto on **January 24** before both march into demanding Capricorn. This conjunction can reveal underlying doubts about your self-worth and raise questions about control and power in relationships. It can be a descent to the depths of desire that evokes obsessive attractions—and yet it's also a chance to deepen your understanding of what you really want compared with what you're willing to give in return. This might not feel especially loving or generous, but a greater awareness of how you operate with others is worth the price. You are getting to the heart of the matter, the core of love, and questioning the quality of intimacy you have with others. Reevaluating your partnership patterns can be painful, but you can be repaid with a renewed appreciation for yourself that will bring more balance into all your relationships.

FEBRUARY

CHANGE FOR THE BETTER

This is a month of emotional extremes, making objectivity more important than ever. The fun starts on **February 1** when your planet, Venus, makes a conjunction with generous Jupiter and expands your horizons of delight. Their union in your 4th House of Home and Family suggests that entertaining at your place or spending to upgrade your environment is a wise investment. An Aquarius Solar Eclipse on **February 6** in your 5th House of Love and Play can fill you with hope, but nebulous Neptune's presence at this New Moon blurs the boundaries between fantasy and reality. You need to dream, Libra, and to allow your aspirations for love and harmony to grow. Yet if the delicate cord between the ideal and the real is broken, the disillusionment can be painful. Stretch yourself in the pursuit of greater happiness, but fill in the gap between where you are now and where you want to go with logic that helps you to complete the journey.

Sweet Venus enters your 5th House on **February 17**, casting you in a very attractive light. Your talents take center stage as you charm your audience. Mercury the Communicator turns direct on **February 18** to recover ideas and information that may have been misrouted during the past three weeks. A Lunar Eclipse on **February 20** is joined by karmic Saturn in your 12th House of Confinement, which can stir up old fears and unpleasant memories. If you encounter doubts, delays, and disappointments, dig deep—you will find the resources to overcome them. Regenerative Pluto's powerful trine to Saturn and the Virgo Full Moon indicates that emotional resurrection is close at hand. Disaster can be transformed into triumph.

> **KEEP IN MIND THIS MONTH**
>
> *Moderate the mood swings of short-term highs and lows by keeping your eyes on the future, where the peaks and valleys will be mere bumps in the road.*

KEY DATES

FEBRUARY 1–2 ★ *host with the most*

The Venus-Jupiter conjunction on February 1 brings out your inner party planner. Your ability to manage complex events demonstrates your leadership skills while entertaining others and boosting your self-esteem. Retrograde Mercury slides past dreamy Neptune on **February 2**. It's an ideal union for imaginative fantasy—but vexing when it comes to handling details and clear communication.

FEBRUARY 6 ★ *gifts from the past*

Retrograde Mercury conjunct the Sun and Moon during today's eclipse deepens your thoughts and recovers long-forgotten creative ideas. Reflecting on the activities that have inspired you in the past can help you choose which ones you wish to pursue in your future. Vivacious Venus is sextile inventive Uranus as well, to help you shake free of any self-esteem issues that stand in the way of love. Unusual forms of fun and a quirky new playmate can add sparkle to your social life.

FEBRUARY 13-14 ★ *hometown getaway*

An awkward quincunx between Venus and Mars, the lovers, on **February 13** is not the perfect setup for Valentine's Day. Venus in Capricorn wants a fixed plan, while Mars in Gemini prefers the freedom to improvise. Differences of style may not be resolved quickly; stay flexible to avoid conflict. A lusty Sun-Mars trine on **February 14**, though, can save the day with high energy and enthusiasm. Make time for a little adventure, whether with a partner, a friend, or all by yourself. Foreign cultures can provide exotic experiences through food, movies, or music without you having to leave the country.

SUPER NOVA DAYS
FEBRUARY 17-19 ★ *lighten your load*

Venus's entry into Aquarius on **February 17** frees you to express yourself with less restraint. A more open attitude toward love and fashion encourages experimentation with less self-criticism and concern about the opinions of others. Mercury's shift to forward motion on **February 18** encourages frankness and progressive thinking. The Sun's entry into impressionable Pisces and your 6th House of Employment on **February 19**, though, increases your sensitivity on the job. Patterns that didn't faze you in the past can touch a nerve now. Rules are wearisome and bosses less tolerable. This is no time to ignore the physical and emotional toll of your daily routine. The Sun's helpful sextile with Pluto points out what habits need to go and the best ways to eliminate them.

FEBRUARY 26 ★ *heartfelt expression*

Mental Mercury joins loving Venus, enabling you to see relationships with clarity and articulate your needs more artfully. Strong analytical skills and a broad perspective on your current situation make it easier for you to solve problems. Bright conversations please you and illuminate your clever wit.

MARCH

ADVANCE YOUR INTERESTS

This month's planetary dynamics demand more activity on your part, but it's definitely better to be led by your own ambitions than to tread water in someone else's pond. Independent Mars gets the ball rolling when it enters protective Cancer in your 10th House of Career on **March 4**, loading extra responsibilities at home and work onto your shoulders. The message, Libra, is not to just smile and cooperate, but to consider blazing your own trail, either personally or professionally. The Pisces New Moon on **March 7** falls in your 6th House of Work and Service, signaling a time to choose between exhaustion and inspiration. Rebellious Uranus is conjunct this New Moon, adding uncertainty on the job and, perhaps, stressing your nervous system. Before you invest more of yourself to hang on to the status quo, consider alternative ways you could apply your energy to free yourself from this pressure.

Your key planet Venus's entry into compassionate Pisces on **March 12** may tempt you to give ground to keep the peace, yet its purpose is to encourage you to be kinder to yourself and to balance work with pleasure. The Sun enters impulsive Aries and your 7th House of Partnerships early on **March 21** and opposes the Libra Full Moon later in the day. This Full Moon in your sign forms tense squares with potent Pluto and impatient Mars in a powerful Grand Square. It can bring relationship issues to a head and give you that last push you need to take your life in a new direction. If you're not ready for a major change, it's time to go into training to build up your mental, physical, and spiritual stamina in preparation for an ambitious move in the near future.

KEEP IN MIND THIS MONTH

Put your own health and safety first. No job is worth wearing yourself out, unless you are being driven by a higher purpose than profit.

KEY DATES

MARCH 1 ★ *relationship options*

A testy semisquare between gracious Venus and controlling Pluto could back you into a corner. The excessive demands or withholding behavior of someone you normally trust can undermine your confidence in this person or cause you to question yourself. A deeper understanding of your own desires will help you decide whether to retreat or forge ahead.

MARCH 6-7 ★ *unpredictably brilliant*

Venus joins boundless Neptune spinning relationship dreams and fantasies on **March 6**. Your artistic vision may be sublime now, but a realistic view of love and money could be lacking. A stressful opposition between assertive Mars and dominating Pluto on **March 7** can load you up with work; apply triage to do the most vital ones first. The New Moon's conjunction with eccentric Uranus on the same day can spike your life with chaos. However, this New Moon activates a super-smart sextile between inventive Uranus and strategic Jupiter—although not exact until later in the month—it fires your intuition with surprising solutions now.

MARCH 13-15 ★ *all over the map*

A savvy Venus-Pluto sextile on **March 13** gives you a strong but subtle power of persuasion, while a highly productive Mars-Saturn sextile on **March 14** can vastly increase your efficiency. Mercury enters Pisces in your 6th House of Employment on the same day, blending the fruits of your imagination with your accomplished diplomatic skills. Venus semisquares jolly Jupiter early on **March 15**, spurring spending and romantic optimism, but an opposition from stern Saturn to your ruling planet later in the day jerks you back to reality and responsibility in relationships.

SUPER NOVA DAYS
MARCH 20-21 ★ *climb your own mountain*

The Sun's entry into courageous Aries on **March 20** marks the Spring Equinox and opens a door to your 7th House of Relationships. But instead of jumping into a new project or taking the initiative in a partnership, carefully calculate your next move, as the Libra Full Moon on **March 21** is too powerful to be used naively. Your usual trust in others can backfire if your defenses are down. Macho Mars and militant Pluto square the Full Moon in your sign, requiring toughness and resiliency on your part. You can meet others halfway, but only after they've proven their trustworthiness and if it's in your best interest to compromise.

MARCH 28 ★ *influencial charm*

Venus joins Uranus as the two form a supportive sextile with Jupiter. You combine a sense of excitement with reliability that earns you admiration and attention. This is a good time to stretch your social boundaries and take risks in expressing yourself within a group or in a one-to-one relationship.

APRIL

TAKE IT TO THE EDGE

Relationships, your favorite theme, stay in the foreground this month as the life-giving Sun transits both your 7th House of Partnerships and your 8th House of Intimacy. The action heats up with verbal Mercury's entry into the 7th House on **April 2** to intensify communication with others. Sharp differences of opinion spark debates that can threaten harmony. It's vital that you speak up for yourself, rather than remaining silent to keep the peace. The New Moon in ardent Aries on **April 5** is also in your 7th House, planting seeds of new possibility in partnerships. Challenging squares from active Mars in defensive Cancer and expansive Jupiter in ambitious Capricorn expose conflicting needs: holding on to what you have versus pushing ahead for something more. Loving Venus, your key planet, enters Aries and squares Pluto on **April 6**, which can drive romantic issues to extremes. Letting go of old expectations may be required to open the way to the next level of intimacy.

The Sun's entry into earthy Taurus and your 8th House of Shared Resources on **April 19** is normally stabilizing, but the passionate Scorpio Full Moon on **April 20** keeps emotions churning as you dig more deeply into the underpinnings of partnership. Reexamining your own needs, and the needs of the people you love, can begin to transform the nature of your connections. However, your awareness of a problem does not require its immediate resolution. Give yourself time to assimilate new insights and feelings about desire and intimacy before making any radical moves. Venus entering patient Taurus on **April 30** helps you ground your emotions and find the common sense needed to guide you in reassessing your relationships.

> **KEEP IN MIND THIS MONTH**
>
> *The deep fear of loss or lack of love is not a bottomless pit where you will stay, but a turning point from which you can rise to greater heights.*

KEY DATES

SUPER NOVA DAYS
APRIL 5–7 ★ *impulse control*
The exciting Aries New Moon on **April 5** is packed with responsibilities, especially if you're playing the rescuer role. Assisting others is noble, but make sure they're working as hard as you. Spend energy advancing your own agenda—this can be a breakthrough time for connecting with the public

or launching a new project. Venus firing into active Aries on **April 6** can trigger love at first sight. But whether you fall for a person or an irresistible object, karmically accountable Pluto's tough square to Venus indicates a need to evaluate your financial and emotional investments very carefully.

APRIL 13–14 ★ *keeping it real*

With the squishy semisquare between Venus and idealistic Neptune on **April 13**, you'll feel like you're wearing rose-colored glasses—especially with a Mercury-Jupiter square that often leads to exaggeration. Stretching your mind and heart is fine at times, but a semisquare between sharp Mars and strict Saturn on **April 14** will quickly impose the limits of reality to end ill-conceived dreams. Come down to earth and focus on a task that requires your immediate attention.

APRIL 19 ★ *small bites*

The Sun's entry into Taurus is rich with sensual potential. Indulging yourself with touch, taste, and sound soothes your soul and sweetens a relationship. But a crunchy sesquisquare between soft Venus and hard-nosed Saturn signals a need to control your appetite. Pleasure is best taken in small bites to avoid emotional indigestion or financial regret.

APRIL 23–24 ★ *too much is just right*

Passion fires you up on **April 23** with a hot square between the lovers, Venus and Mars. Both attraction and anger can be dramatic, especially with enormous Jupiter opposing Mars and squaring Venus on **April 24**. Excessive behavior may be unavoidable and too much fun to miss. This is a time to exceed the speed limit on the highway of love and the road to recreation. Choose the game you want to play and put all of yourself into it. You may not attain your goal, but you'll have a lot of fun trying.

APRIL 30 ★ *relationship preview*

Libra's ruling planet, Venus, enters your 8th House of Shared Resources, increasing your capacity to receive more love and approval from others. You may encounter individuals who lack generosity, however, and you might be tempted to accept whatever crumbs they offer. This is no time to underestimate yourself. You are worth at least as much as you give and should accept nothing less. Don't allow the stubbornness of someone else to stop you from speaking openly about your desires and, if necessary, renegotiating the terms of your relationship.

MAY

FINANCIAL FOCUS

The dependable Taurus New Moon on **May 5** in your 8th House of Deep Sharing puts you in a good bargaining position, thanks to a supportive trine from generous Jupiter. If you have a clear plan, your ability to gain the material and emotional support you need from others should be enhanced now. Some romantic magic is possible, too, what with blissful Neptune's conjunction with the Moon's North Node in your 5th House of Love. Serious Saturn goes direct on **May 2**, but expansive Jupiter turns retrograde on **May 9**, a complex combination requiring you to completely assimilate any gains before cautiously pushing ahead. Mental Mercury's appetite for information grows upon entering its airy home sign, Gemini, on **May 2**. However, its hard aspects to restraining Saturn and Pluto on **May 4** complicate data flow, a slowdown that will occur again when the Messenger turns retrograde on **May 26**. Keep in mind that you need to maneuver carefully to ride the waves of change when planets turn in different directions.

The Scorpio Full Moon on **May 19** in your 2nd House of Resources could bring financial issues to a boil. Yet nebulous Neptune's square to this Sun-Moon opposition may produce more fiction than fact. Careless spending, faulty calculations, and unrealistic dreams can be more costly than anticipated. Still, faith or forgiveness could get you through a tight spot, and inspiration may open your eyes to your own untapped talent. The second brilliant Jupiter-Uranus sextile of the year on **May 21** offers unconventional insights and flashes of intuition that can allow you to make a rapid course correction. The first two occurrences of this aspect may not be fully appreciated until the last one on **November 13**.

> **KEEP IN MIND THIS MONTH**
>
> *Spending a modest amount of money on a small indulgence or two can satisfy your cravings without necessarily breaking the bank.*

KEY DATES

MAY 1-2 ★ *recovered wealth*

Venus forms constructive trines with no-nonsense Saturn and Pluto on **May 1**, creating a potent and practical Grand Earth Trine. Your sense of judgment about objects and people is excellent, especially when it comes to finding value that others overlook. You are able to increase the worth of material things with repairs or restoration and can even save a relationship that seems to have lost its way.

Opportunities for learning or travel could open with mobile Mercury's entry into your 9th House of Higher Thought and Faraway Places on **May 2**. Focusing your attention on a single subject, though, may not be appealing, so don't sign up for any long-term courses unless you've been planning to do so for a long time.

MAY 9–11 ★ *choose your battles*
On **May 9**, assertive Mars strides into bold Leo in your 11th House of Friends and Groups. Your confidence, creativity, and courage could put you in a leadership position—or perhaps a pushy pal shoves you into the spotlight. Stay alert, for a Mars-Pluto quincunx on **May 11** can entangle you in a struggle with someone who doesn't fight fair. Be prepared to use all your force to prevail or, if you can't win or want to avoid conflict, cut your losses and back away.

SUPER NOVA DAYS
MAY 18–20 ★ *active sixth sense*
Expect pleasant surprises on **May 18** when attractive Venus aligns favorably with optimistic Jupiter and inventive Uranus. Your innate understanding of human nature helps you turn an uncomfortable situation into a surprisingly enjoyable one. Trust your instincts, even if they lead you in an unconventional direction—you are blessed now with higher intelligence. A square between Venus and Neptune on **May 20**, though, is less reliable. Your logic might be blurred by misplaced faith or vulnerability. You may even be misled by some-one who is strong on image but weak on substance. The Sun's entry into curious Gemini the same day tells you to ask questions and get the facts instead of making false assumptions.

MAY 24–26 ★ *earning respect*
Sweet Venus's entry into fellow air sign Gemini on **May 24** usually signals a friendly and playful social environment, yet a testy quincunx from manipulative Pluto on **May 25** suggests that all is not as it seems. Confirmation comes on **May 26** when Saturn's square to Venus defines relationship problems more clearly. If you're feeling underappreciated, it's natural to be less confident and, perhaps, avoid confrontation. A simple, honest statement about your expectations, though painful, can be a powerful step toward regaining the respect you deserve.

JUNE

A CURIOUS TURN OF MIND

This month highlights journeys of the mind and body for you. Ideas are bubbling and your feet are itching as the chatty Gemini New Moon joins with Mercury and Venus on **June 3** in your 9th House of Travel and Higher Education. You are ready for fresh stimulation to overcome the predictability of your daily routine. Planning a voyage, signing up for a class, or connecting with foreign ideas and cultures can scratch that itch. Gemini's intellectually curious ruling planet, Mercury, is still retrograde, so the precise picture of where these urges might take you isn't likely to come into focus until the Messenger turns direct on **June 19**. Powerful Pluto backs out of Capricorn in your 4th House of Foundations on **June 13** to make one last visit to judicious Sagittarius. It will stir deep thoughts in your 3rd House of Data Collection before turning direct on **September 7** and passing back into your 4th House on **November 26**. Use this time to review major plans, especially those related to your home and family.

Pluto's presence at the Full Moon in Sagittarius on **June 18** adds a dark tone to a typically lighthearted lunation. This opposition of the Gemini Sun and the Sagittarius Moon illuminates your 3rd House of Learning and is rich with bright new ideas. But Pluto challenges your mind to dig more deeply and extract the meanings hidden behind hopeful words and playful conversations. Inventive Uranus is square this Sun-Moon opposition, adding an explosive element that prompts hair-trigger responses and unexpected events. Uranus, though, also brings brilliance in the form of lightning strikes of intuition that shatter your perceptions and open your mind to a totally new reality that could free you from the past.

> **KEEP IN MIND THIS MONTH**
>
> *Give the world time to catch up to what your mind envisions now. A bold leap of awareness can take years to come down to earth.*

KEY DATES

JUNE 6-7 ★ *smooth operator*

A sweet sextile between Venus and Mars on **June 6** aligns desire and action to help you get what you want from others. Your will is strong, yet you have a delicate touch that helps you motivate people gracefully and with purpose. Groups bring out your creative skills, making you a valuable member of any team. Retrograde Mercury conjuncts the Sun and Venus on **June 7**, indicating an excellent time for reopening discussions involving unfinished business. You may change your mind about a previous agreement, but you're unlikely to alter your thinking again. Trust your perceptions: Right now you have a very clear sense of your needs and aspirations.

JUNE 12-14 ★ *winds of change*
Anxious squares from Venus and the Sun to eccentric Uranus on **June 12** can upset your mood and your schedule. Uncertainty in relationships is possible, with rapid shifts of attitude that can take you far from your comfort zone. But these aspects also symbolize a desire for new kinds of people, objects, and activities. You are simply experimenting now, and no long-term commitments are necessary. Loving Venus forms a supportive trine with spiritual Neptune on **June 13** that helps you glue the pieces back together. A sense of wholeness increases trust and allows forgiveness. However, aggressive Mars joins the Moon's South Node in your 5th House of Romance on **June 14**, intensifying your emotions with powerful feelings of attraction or repulsion—and little else in between.

SUPER NOVA DAYS
JUNE 18-21 ★ *opposites attract*
Venus opposes passionate Pluto and then enters watery Cancer on **June 18**, which is sure to push some emotional buttons. Avoid quick judgment: Your reactions may be too extreme. Mercury turns direct on **June 19**, and then the Sun follows Venus's path opposing Pluto and entering Cancer on **June 20**, the Summer Solstice. This intense planetary mix brings another wave of powerful feelings, along with the urge to make a profound change. There is a break in the emotional weather, though, on June 21 as solid Saturn forms a stabilizing sextile with Venus. Additionally, an opposition between pushy Mars and passive Neptune describes the pursuit of a fantasy or an exhausting struggle that can be avoided with patience and common sense.

JUNE 25-26 ★ *slow and steady*
A Venus-Neptune sesquisquare on **June 25** blurs judgment on personal matters, but is balanced by the strength of a Sun-Saturn sextile that adds stability to your professional life. Revolutionary Uranus turns retrograde on **June 26**, while the ill-fitting sesquisquare between visionary Jupiter and taciturn Saturn slows down any big plans. Don't let aggressive individuals provoke you into hasty action. An impulsive move now can cost you a great deal of time and frustration later.

JULY

GROWING AMBITION

Making your world safer is a key issue this month with the New Moon and Full Moon occurring in the security houses of your chart. The powerful Cancer New Moon on **July 2** is in your 10th House of Career, stimulating fresh ideas about your professional future. Attractive Venus conjunct the New Moon—and generous Jupiter opposite it—brings recognition of your talent and encourages your lofty aspirations. You're not ready to shift jobs right away, but seeds for change planted now can lead you to more rewarding work in the future. Mars, the planet of initiative, enters your 12th House of Privacy on **July 1**, making this a time to operate behind the scenes, tie up unfinished business, and develop the spiritual awareness needed to support your next big move.

Your ruling planet, lovely Venus, sashays into expressive Leo in your 11th House of Groups on **July 12**, which may raise your profile as a leader or key player on a team. This contrasts with Mars going into stealth mode earlier in the month and leaves you feeling pulled between the pleasure of being with others and the need for quiet time alone. The enterprising Capricorn Full Moon on **July 18** illuminates your 4th House of Roots, stirring an urge to take on new challenges. Memories of parental advice can prod you forward with their high expectations or hold you back with their doubts and fears. The needs of current family members could prove demanding, too. Ideally, this is when the New Moon's seed of ambition takes hold: You feel the desire for success growing inside you and commit to nourishing it with all your might.

> **KEEP IN MIND THIS MONTH**
>
> *Fear and self-doubt are not signals to curtail your ambition, but points of focus to show where you need to apply more effort to get ahead.*

KEY DATES

JULY 3-4 ★ *checks and balances*

Relationships are complicated as socially sensitive Venus passes from an optimistic opposition with Jupiter on **July 3** to a restricting semisquare with Saturn on **July 4**. The first transit awakens a spirit of generosity that could leave you burdened with extra responsibilities. You may even overestimate someone or spend more than you should. The second transit brings contraction and accountability. You are likely to get a quick wake-up call if you go too far or expect too much.

SUPER NOVA DAYS
JULY 9-10 ★ *not much choice*

A wide-open Sun-Jupiter opposition on **July 9** can fill you with hope and promises. It's appropriate to be optimistic, but remember that careful steps are required before you reach the top of the mountain. A sharp-edged conjunction between go-go Mars and stern Saturn on **July 10** leaves no room for slack, because you have very specific tasks that must be done now. Even if you have a chance to escape a tough job, there's more to be gained by buckling down and finally finishing it off. Mental Mercury opposes purging Pluto and enters Cancer, repeating the message that completing what's already on your plate is essential before starting anything new.

JULY 12 ★ *return to self*

You may feel emotionally squeezed early in the day when your planet Venus forms a complex quincunx with insatiable Pluto. This can represent a final showdown before you finally give up on meeting unreasonable demands and turn your attention back to fulfilling your own needs. Venus's passage into proud Leo follows, burning away self-doubt—with the joyful support of friends, who remind you of how wonderful you really are.

JULY 22-23 ★ *meeting as equals*

Your public profile should rise during the next few weeks as the Sun follows Venus into expressive Leo and your 11th House of Groups on **July 22**, but the moody Moon in your 6th House of Work and Service can leave you feeling more like a servant than a star. This feeling will pass quickly when the Moon shifts into fiery Aries on **July 23** and you are ready and able to engage others on your own terms.

JULY 26-27 ★ *fearless leader*

Intellectual Mercury enters creative Leo on **July 26** to fill your head with dramatic ideas that beg to be expressed. Fortunately, you have the tools to turn them into reality: A highly productive trine between Mars and Jupiter in practical earth signs shows you how to get the job done. Venus conjunct the karmic South Node on **July 27** may attract individuals with strong opinions who impress you with their self-confidence and charisma. However, trust your own instincts to guide you instead of following someone else's lead.

AUGUST

MAKING MAGIC

This high-powered month is charged up with two eclipses, two New Moons, and three planets entering peace-loving Libra. The New Moon in dramatic Leo on **August 1** creates a Solar Eclipse in your 11th House of Groups that shakes things up with friends or colleagues. An overbearing individual can go too far, forcing you to take a stand. As hard as you try to compromise, the only way out may be to end the relationship. You may also need to reduce a grandiose project to a more manageable size in order to simplify your life. The unconventional Aquarius Full Moon Eclipse on **August 16** occurs in your 5th House of Romance, opening your heart to a profound experience. However, dreamy Neptune's conjunction with the Moon brings a dose of fantasy that can cloud your judgment. Put faith in your own creative abilities rather than in someone else's promises. There is a place for magic in your life now, but surprisingly it's something you can produce for yourself.

"Action planet" Mars raises your energy level when it enters your sign on **August 19**, urging you to be more assertive and to take the initiative with others. You know how to advance your interests with a friendly grace that gets you ahead without irritating anyone else. Mercury the Messenger enters fair-minded Libra on **August 28**, sharpening your thinking and enhancing your communication skills. Venus joins the party on **August 30**, when it highlights your beauty and charm through **September 24**. A small change in appearance can dramatically increase the favorable attention you receive and boost your confidence. The meticulous Virgo New Moon in your private 12th House on **August 30** aligns favorably with goal-oriented Jupiter and Saturn, providing you with the perspective you need to map out long-term happiness.

> **KEEP IN MIND THIS MONTH**
>
> *When you like what you see in the mirror, others will as well. Trust your naturally good taste to determine the look that suits you best.*

KEY DATES

AUGUST 5-6 ★ *stormy weather*

Your confidence rises on **August 5** as Venus aligns with promising Jupiter and powerful Pluto. However, it's best to avoid overindulgence: On **August 6**, your ruling planet moves into refined Virgo, where excesses are not well tolerated. Explosive oppositions from Mars to unpredictable Uranus and from Mercury to nebulous Neptune are far from calm. Miscommunications can trigger emotional outbursts, so make sure you have the facts before leaping into action.

SUPER NOVA DAYS

AUGUST 13-17 ★ *forces of change*

A Venus-Saturn conjunction on **August 13** adds a serious tone to your day. Rewards or approval may not come easily; the message is to be specific about your desires and work hard to fulfill them. A soft Sun-Neptune opposition on **August 15** feeds your fantasies, but a strict conjunction between Mercury and Saturn demands critical thinking and concise communication. Sweetness returns on **August 16** with a generous trine between Venus and Jupiter that can provide enormous satisfaction, even with the unsettling Full Moon Eclipse. A volcanic Mars-Pluto square on **August 17** stirs deep feelings about power and control. Directing this intensity with precision can give you the strength to resolve long-standing problems.

AUGUST 19 ★ *your turn*

You are primed to plunge into action as Mars enters your sign to fill you with a surge of energy and a strong dose of passion. If you are passive now, you may find yourself in a defensive position or fighting someone else's battle. This is an excellent time to begin a personal project that you can do on your own.

AUGUST 22-24 ★ *social inconsistency*

The Sun moves into your 12th House of Secrets on **August 22**, which normally spurs a desire for less social interaction. But with artistic Venus opposite surprising Uranus on **August 23**, this is not a time to follow conventional patterns. You need the freedom to come and go as you please, rather than maintaining a constant presence with others. Nervous tension may build friction in relationships, but this can be overcome on **August 24** when forgiving Neptune aligns with Venus, allowing you to finally put the past behind you.

AUGUST 27-30 ★ *pushed to the edge*

Conversations intensify as communicative Mercury squares domineering Pluto on **August 27**. Mercury moves into Libra on **August 28**, opening the way for more objective discussions. Then, on **August 29**, Venus repeats the pattern by squaring Pluto, pushing relationships to extremes. Your innate capacity to compromise is diminished as an "all or nothing" attitude prevails. This struggle can expose your deepest desires, which you can then manage in a more balanced way when Venus slips into reasonable Libra on **August 30**.

SEPTEMBER

WORKING IT

Work is a primary issue this month, but the good news is that opportunistic Jupiter in ambitious Capricorn turns direct in your 4th House of Roots on **September 7**. This can set off an inner process of expansion that encourages you to aim higher professionally. Investing in a home office or buying equipment to launch your own business is a smart move. Jupiter and Saturn, the planetary planners, form a constructive trine on **September 9** that effectively combines hope and pragmatism to help set a long-term strategy. This fourth contact in a series that began in **March 2007** is a time to adjust your plans before a final commitment is made at the last trine on **November 21**.

Conditions are less stable during the sensitive Pisces Full Moon on **September 15**, which occurs in your 6th House of Daily Routines. The raw emotions, vulnerability, and vivid imagination of this event are jolted to a higher level of intensity by electric Uranus's conjunction with the Moon. You could be shocked by unexpected shifts on the job or in your health. However, this is also a time when a sudden flash of insight can free you from self-limiting ideas about your abilities and old habits that stand in the way of a more exciting professional life. A reevaluation of your assets is appropriate when Venus enters compulsive Scorpio and your 2nd House of Resources on **October 23**. Chatty Mercury turns retrograde the same day, beginning a three-week period in which you should review recent events, fill in missing details, and reconnect with people from your past. The New Moon in your sign on **September 29** provides a gentle push forward that encourages you to be more socially and physically engaged.

> **KEEP IN MIND THIS MONTH**
>
> *Short-term crises can lead to long-term opportunities when you are able to let go of your unnecessary fears and visualize future opportunities.*

KEY DATES

SEPTEMBER 3–4 ★ *eyes on the prize*

The Sun slams into Saturn in your 12th House of Confinement on **September 3**, which can make you want to withdraw from the world. However, you can do some excellent work without any interruptions. The creative Sun's energizing trine to hopeful Jupiter on **September 4** gives you a picture of a more rewarding future. This is not mere fantasizing or escapism; it's a real source of insight into your potential. There are plenty of sources of distraction ahead, though, so don't over-load yourself with peripheral activities that could keep you from your goals.

SEPTEMBER 9-11 ★ *personality plus*
Pleasure prevails with a fun-loving square between Venus and Jupiter on **September 9**. You may toss good judgment out the window to play with friends or in a romantic pursuit of questionable nature. The desire to fill your heart can spur you to lose sight of your basic values and perhaps spend more than you should. It is appropriate to broaden your tastes and feed your senses, but keeping this within reasonable bounds right now can save you from regret later. A Venus-Mars conjunction on **September 11** continues the sensual theme. Whether you are seductive or shy, your ability to charm others wins friends and influences people.

SEPTEMBER 14-17 ★ *intermittent bliss*
Talkative Mercury's conjunction with lovely Venus on **September 14** is great for sweet talk or discussing a difficult issue in a kind and thoughtful way. It can be hard to maintain your cool during the explosive Pisces Full Moon on **September 15**. If an edginess reveals your less-than-gracious side, take a break until you calm down enough to carry on a constructive conversation. Venus caroms off crazy Uranus with a quirky quincunx on **September 16** that can jolt self-confidence and rattle a relationship. Fortunately, a healing trine between Venus and spiritual Neptune on **September 17** shows a way back to common ground with others and wholeness within yourself, restoring peace and harmony in your world.

SUPER NOVA DAYS
SEPTEMBER 20-23 ★ *take your time*
A tense Sun-Pluto square can undermine trust and provoke power struggles on **September 20**. Repressed emotions surging to the surface feel destructive, but can be a necessary step toward self-empowerment. A Mars-Neptune trine on **September 21** shows that you can be assertive and compassionate at the same time. The Autumn Equinox is marked by the Sun's entrance into your sign on **September 22**, helping you find your balance while a sextile between Venus and Pluto gives you access to deeper levels of intimacy. These aspects will serve you well when the love planet enters profound Scorpio on **September 23**. Its semisquare with strict Saturn and Mercury's retrograde turn, however, counsel patience above all.

OCTOBER

DOLLARS AND COMMON SENSE

Life becomes increasingly intense this month, driving you to earn more money and further develop your talents. Ardent Mars enters unyielding Scorpio and your 2nd House of Resources on **October 4**, prodding you to look more deeply into your financial matters. Reducing expenses to help pay off interest-heavy debts, for example, may require self-restraint now, but it will pay dividends later. The creative Sun's entry into Scorpio on **October 22** will shed more light on money issues and, perhaps, reveal underexploited abilities that you can develop to increase your sense of self-worth. The Full Moon in autonomous Aries on **October 14** opposes the Sun in accommodating Libra to put the issue of independence versus partnership on the table. Voluminous Jupiter square the Full Moon may push this polarity to extremes, leading to a showdown in which the choice appears to be giving in or going it alone. The real lesson is that successful partnerships require both a respect for the individual and a willingness to compromise from time to time.

Ideas flow freely when talkative Mercury turns direct in charming Libra on **October 15**. Venus, the relationship planet, wants more openness and honesty when moving into outspoken Sagittarius in your 3rd House of Communication on **October 18**. You are ready to speak more frankly about your desires and could even surprise yourself if you don't hold back. You need more than safety, security, and the same old boring routine. The New Moon in relentless Scorpio on **October 28** intensifies your focus on increasing your cash flow. Carefully refining your budget and developing your assets over time can produce lasting changes.

> ### KEEP IN MIND THIS MONTH
>
> *Tame impulsive urges, but use the intent behind them to point you in the right direction so you can create a strategy to reach your goals.*

KEY DATES

SUPER NOVA DAYS
OCTOBER 4–6 ★ *deal maker*
Mars enters emotionally intense Scorpio on **October 4**, moving you past politeness to get to the bottom line. Tense semisquares between Mars and realistic Saturn and Venus and penetrating Pluto on **October 5** force you to define your needs and protect your interests. Getting down to brass tacks

involves tough-minded negotiations that don't necessarily show your generous side. Fortunately, a hopeful Venus-Jupiter sextile the same day reveals additional options that allow you to take a stand without shutting the door on a possible win–win solution. Keep optimism in check, because squares from the Sun and Mercury to unrestrained Jupiter on **October 6** can make you too unselfish and undermine your recent gains.

OCTOBER 10–11 ★ *unique pleasures*
A harmonious trine between joyful Venus and inventive Uranus on **October 10** can spark your social life with an unusual event, individual, or attitude. A Mars-Uranus aspect adds to your adventurous spirit, but could connect you with an unreliable, unpredictable person. A supersensitive square between Venus and Neptune on **October 11** is romantic and idealistic, but you could be easily fooled. If you make yourself vulnerable to someone, ensure that he or she is worthy of your trust.

OCTOBER 18 ★ *the great beyond*
Venus shoots into heroic Sagittarius to widen your horizons of delight. A semisquare with "more is better" Jupiter adds rocket fuel to launch your hopes beyond the realm of reason. Going too far in the pursuit of pleasure or in your need to please others is almost too easy now. Avoid the temptation to have it all and do it all at once. You are glimpsing an amazing future; give yourself some time to reach it.

OCTOBER 24 ★ *power play*
Passionate Mars in Scorpio forms a difficult semisquare with purging Pluto just two days after the Sun entered this emotionally complex sign. You may feel marginalized now and unsure how to fight back without losing your temper. Focusing on the specific issue, rather than an individual personality, will allow you to unleash your power with a precision that produces change without doing harm.

OCTOBER 26–27 ★ *in the lead*
A square between little Mercury and giant Jupiter on **October 26** can turn a small difference of opinion into a major discussion. Exaggeration and miscalculation are possible, so stick to the basics to avoid becoming swamped in extraneous information. A highly energetic Mars-Jupiter sextile on **October 27** gives you the muscle and the motivation to be even more physically and socially involved. Your enthusiasm is showing in the best possible way. Wherever you go, others want to follow.

NOVEMBER

STRATEGIC PLANNING

You have the power to change the shape of your future with three major planetary aspects occurring this month. On **November 4**, conservative Saturn makes the first of five oppositions to radical Uranus in a series that finishes in July 2010. This stressful face-off connects your 12th House of Spirituality and your 6th House of Work, triggering upsets on the job due to boredom, lack of fulfillment, or an over-bearing boss. While this can arise as a sudden crisis, it's not one you want to try to solve impulsively because your actions will have lasting consequences. A supportive sextile between optimistic Jupiter and Uranus on **November 13**, however, sparks insights that eventually might produce a more exciting career. The third major aspect, a trine between strategic Jupiter and Saturn on **November 21**, is the last in a series, giving you a new perspective that effectively combines optimism with reality to help you chart your course for the future.

Your ruling planet, Venus, enters responsible Capricorn and your 4th House of Roots on **November 12** to solidify your base with a sense of purpose and discipline. Yet a parade of planets moving into energetic Sagittarius in your 3rd House of Communication this month is bound to provide distractions. Active Mars arrives first on **November 16**, followed by the willful Sun on **November 21** and chatty Mercury on **November 23**. Your deeply rooted sense of fair play and need for harmony may be challenged by a desire to assert yourself. Passion for your beliefs makes you an entertaining and persuasive speaker, writer, and teacher; with a playful rather than combative attitude, you can have fun impressing others with your wit and wisdom.

> **KEEP IN MIND THIS MONTH**
>
> *Speaking the truth can ruffle someone's feathers—but it's a price you should be willing to pay to claim your power.*

KEY DATES

SUPER NOVA DAYS
NOVEMBER 3-5 ★ *emotional contradictions*

Venus in Sagittarius forms tough squares to Saturn and Uranus on **November 3**. Saturn brings seriousness and restraint, and sometimes a lack of appreciation. Uranus, on the other hand, is a breakout planet that can provoke you to take social, romantic, or financial risks. You are feeling the pull between duty and freedom represented by the exact Saturn-Uranus opposition on **November 4**. It's best not to leap into action, however. A misleading Mars-Neptune square can waste your energy and leave you fighting phantoms. Calm your emotions and calculate your next move carefully—or simply take some time off to heal your spirit and gather strength. Mercury plunges into Scorpio to reveal secrets, uncover hidden resources, and intensify conversations. A sweet sextile between loving Venus and all-encompassing Neptune on **November 5** offers compassion and forgiveness, restoring your faith in relationships.

NOVEMBER 12-13 ★ *digging deep*

Venus conjuncts profound Pluto early on **November 12** just before entering Capricorn to put a more serious spin on relationships. Unsettled issues stir deep feelings, even resentments, but facing them is healthier than denial. Respect is needed with Venus in ethical Capricorn, but it's something you have to give yourself before you can expect it from others. Venus in your 4th House of Home prompts you to make your environment more attractive and efficient. The Full Moon in sensual Taurus on **November 13** falls in your 8th House of Intimacy, increasing your desire to connect. Yet a square to the Sun-Moon opposition from hazy Neptune blurs the line between fantasy and reality to create magic, confusion, or both.

NOVEMBER 16-17 ★ *clouds in your coffee*

Mental Mercury's intelligent sextiles with Jupiter and Saturn add precision to your thinking and communication on **November 16**, even as active Mars's entry into adventurous Sagittarius unleashes an urge to toss aside restraints and play. Imaginative Neptune is squared by Mercury and semisquared by Venus on **November 17**. Heightened sensitivity may enhance your creative powers, but fantasies can cloud your judgment and blur details.

NOVEMBER 27-29 ★ *jumping jack flash*

The New Moon in Sagittarius on **November 27** emboldens you with fresh perceptions and strong opinions. Electric Uranus turns direct, bringing additional excitement. Facts can be fudged in the interest of making your case, which is fine as long as you won't be held accountable for minor errors. A clever sextile between Venus and Uranus on **November 28** rewards you with unexpected fun, while a Mercury-Mars conjunction increases the already rapid pace of communication. You get your feet back on the ground on **November 29** with a solidifying sextile between Venus and Saturn that clarifies your values and earns you trust.

DECEMBER

Powerful patterns during this month's Full and New Moons will spice up the season with intensity and potential conflict. The Full Moon in noisy Gemini on **December 12** generally kicks up conversations characterized by relatively benign differences of opinion. This one, though, is supercharged by a Grand Square involving five planets. The Sagittarius Sun is joined by aggressive Mars in your 3rd House of Communication, giving force to your ideas. Uncompromising Uranus and restrictive Saturn form tense squares to the Sun, Moon, and Mars that readily provoke arguments. The opposition between freedom-loving Uranus and law-enforcing Saturn intensifies this entire complex. You could experience brilliant breakthroughs of awareness; the challenge is in maintaining enough cool to keep discussions from boiling over. Fortunately, forgiving Neptune forms a creative trine to the Full Moon that can help you find common ground with those whose beliefs appear to be in direct opposition to your own.

The Sun's entry into traditional Capricorn on **December 21** marks the Winter Solstice as it crosses the bottom of your chart. You feel a deep sense of responsibility, but it's important to lighten your load before taking on any more obligations. A Sun-Pluto conjunction on **December 22** shows that it's time to let go of old expectations that don't support your current goals. The New Moon in Capricorn on **December 27** is conjunct tough guys Mars and Pluto, stirring up pugnaciousness in stark contrast with your normally peaceful and accommodating ways. Family members could simply be too demanding or push you too far. Don't repress your anger; focus it intently and you can channel its force to clear the air and finally put the past behind you.

> **KEEP IN MIND THIS MONTH**
>
> *The price of peace may be giving up on your own convictions. Consider this high cost before seeking compromise.*

KEY DATES

DECEMBER 1 ★ *inner strength*

A conjunction between artistic Venus and exuberant Jupiter in your 4th House of Home and Family is ideal for beautifying your living space. Adding one special picture or decorative item can be enough to make a difference. Your confidence is running strong today as well, but it's the quiet kind that you feel inside and don't need to show off to anyone.

DECEMBER 5-6 ★ *war of words*

Tension mounts on **December 5** with a Mercury-Uranus square tightening up your nervous system and a Sun-Mars conjunction placing you on a battlefield. You are in no mood to fight and would prefer to mind your own business and ignore the source of irritation. Still, this is your chance to kindly but firmly break news that you have been reluctant to share. Conscientious Saturn's square to Mercury on **December 6** demands that you face facts and speak honestly. Fortunately, gentle Neptune's sextile with chatty Mercury enables you to express your truth with compassion, hopefully making it easier to hear.

SUPER NOVA DAYS
DECEMBER 11-13 ★ *fasten your seat belt*

Quirky Uranus receives a semisquare from Venus on **December 11** and a hyperactive square from Mars on **December 12**—a pair of aspects bound to shake up relationships. Differences of taste and values are dramatized with the explosive Full Moon, when every desire for change encounters the limits of fear or habit. At the same time, mental Mercury enters strict Capricorn and instantly encounters penetrating Pluto, increasing worry and distrust. Give yourself time to absorb the situation rather than trying to sort things out immediately. A Venus-Saturn sesquisquare on **December 13** signals that self-trust must happen first and that patience is your ally in addressing these complex issues.

DECEMBER 21-22 ★ *descent to awareness*

On **December 21**, the Sun enters ambitious Capricorn, a sign that seeks higher ground. But an intense Venus-Pluto semisquare can send your feelings plunging with disappointment or betrayal. The Sun then joins Pluto on **December 22** to take this emotional abyss to a deeper level. Be kind to yourself, but don't flinch when you see what's lurking in your depths. Getting to the bottom of your needs and desires clears up a murky situation and begins the process of recovery and transformation.

DECEMBER 26-28 ★ *hope springs eternal*

An irritating Venus-Saturn quincunx on **December 26** may seem to hold satisfaction at bay. But active Mars enters efficient Capricorn on **December 27** to get you on a proactive track, while a romantic Venus-Neptune conjunction dissolves old disappointments in the refreshing waters of new hopes for love.

SCORPIO

OCTOBER 23–NOVEMBER 21

SCORPIO OVERVIEW

A big year lies ahead of you, complete with a few surprises that can complicate your life, yet fortunately you have the tools to integrate change with great ease. Optimistic Jupiter, realistic Saturn, and exciting Uranus create a major theme as you are ready to see opportunities through a practical filter, enabling you to steadily move toward your desired goals. Together, Jupiter and Saturn form a significant repeating pattern of harmonious trines—exact on January 21, September 8, and November 28—that balances your drive to succeed with the continued focus you need to reach your goals. Your sign, Scorpio, is safely nestled between these cosmic regulators, with confident Jupiter encouraging you to **expand your thinking to grow beyond your present level of awareness**, while practical Saturn simultaneously concentrates your energy inward so you conserve valuable resources. Saturn in your 11th House of Friends and Wishes requires you to **work cooperatively rather than venturing out on your own**. You may not have the patience for the frivolous activities of others, yet being part of a team can help you be much more productive. Additionally, Saturn expects you to honor your hopes and distant dreams, not just meet your daily obligations.

This is a transitional year for you, beginning with an intense standoff between your two key planets, fiery Mars and domineering Pluto. As a Scorpio, you are particularly sensitive to the movements of Pluto. Your life was transformed when Pluto was in Scorpio between 1983 and 1995. Then, as Pluto moved through opinionated Sagittarius, you reexamined your core beliefs, discarding ideas, values, and possessions that no longer served you well. On January 25, this tiny concentrated bundle of planetary intensity leaves Sagittarius to enter hardworking Capricorn in your 3rd House of Communication. There it will force you to reevaluate the validity of your intellectual foundations.

A Jupiter-Uranus sextile—exact on March 28, May 21, and November 12—creates a positive environment for you to communicate more spontaneously, especially in matters of love or with children. **Tensions increase through the autumn** as restrictive Saturn engages in a cosmic tug-of-war with erratic Uranus—exact on November 4—in yet another long-term cycle that strongly influences your life through 2010. The viability of previous commitments is set against your need for individual self-expression, and although Jupiter blesses you with buoyant optimism through most of November, Mars's square to

Saturn and Uranus on December 12–15 can drive your frustration to the surface, provoking you to take radical action to put your life back on track. All in all, **this is a year for you to make great strides forward in accomplishing your goals as long as you don't ride roughshod over the feelings of people around you.** With the year long Mars-Pluto theme that is exact on January 2, March 7, August 17, and December 28, it's crucial to express your feelings constructively and calmly, especially to those you love.

CALM BEFORE THE STORM

The cool Virgo Full Moon Eclipse on February 20 activates your love houses, yet its close proximity to serious Saturn throws obstacles in your path to pleasure. Manage these issues wisely and you can solidify a significant relationship. Generous Jupiter, the traditional ruler of your 5th House of Love, brings steady growth to romance as it moves through cautious Capricorn all year. Its trine to somber Saturn can quiet your excitement, which could be a dilemma since you are naturally intense. But it may also be a relief, for you have likely grown weary of romantic dramas due to unstable Uranus's extended journey through your 5th House, which began in 2003. Fulfilling commitments is important, but you may not be able to hold back your irrepressible need for more independence as Saturn moves toward its life-changing opposition with Uranus—exact on November 4.

TEAM PLAYER

It's important to work with others rather than alone as career-minded Saturn moves through your 11th House of Teamwork. Although you may be naturally inclined to remain separate from the group, discipline involving ongoing interactions with your associates can keep you moving along the right track and improve your chances for success. The steadying Jupiter-Saturn trine strengthens the ideas upon which you build your career path, but eclipses also play an important role in your success this year. In particular, the dramatic Leo Solar Eclipse on August 1 falls in your 10th House of Public Status, and its proximity to mental Mercury suggests the necessity for bold communication. Nevertheless, be sure to discuss your plans with others before making major decisions on your own.

NO FREE LUNCH

Beneficent Jupiter, the ruler of your 2nd House of Money, is somewhat restrained this year as it moves through pragmatic Capricorn and is further limited by ongoing aspects with frugal Saturn. At first glance, this might sound like bad news—but it does indicate steady financial growth as long as you don't make any foolish moves. Avoid temptations to invest impulsively; if something appears too good to be true, it probably is, especially when over-confident Jupiter sextiles unreliable Uranus around March 28, May 21, and November 12. Keeping a tight rein on unnecessary expenditures during these times can really pay off as you increase your bank account with your hard work and smart long-term planning throughout the year.

 LET'S GET PHYSICAL

Physical exercise is more important this year than ever before, regardless of your age and previous level of activity. The year begins and ends with energetic Mars, the ruler of your 6th House of Health, contacting transformational Pluto, making it critical to channel your overly intense feelings into action. If you work out regularly, it may be time to push yourself to the next level. On the other hand, if you don't have a daily regimen, join a gym, enroll in a yoga class, or start taking regular walks. The positive impact this will have on your health cannot be overstated. What's most important now is to realize that you have a chance to renew and regenerate, but it will take real commitment on your part, along with the necessary self-discipline to stick to your new routine.

 SAFE HAVEN

Mercury's entry into your 4th House of Home and Family on January 7 can flood your mind with ideas for bringing more excitement and innovation into your personal life. Venus enters quirky Aquarius in your 4th House on February 17—staying there through March 12—indicating your potential for sharing good times with unconventional friends in the privacy of your own place. But it is dreamy Neptune in your 4th House all year that continues to remind you that your home is a place to retreat from the noise of the outer world. Here you can entertain the infinite possibilities of your imagination.

REVISIT YOUR PAST

Rather than expending excess energy on vacations this year, you are more likely to travel with a specific purpose in mind as Jupiter, the planet of distant horizons, harmoniously trines practical Saturn. Mars enters your 9th House of Travel on March 4, remaining there through May 9, firing you with the desire to get up and go. However, its movement through self-protective Cancer suggests that you may return to a favorite spot from the past or revisit a childhood home instead of heading off to someplace new. Although it may not be your first inclination, don't be afraid to follow a whim and go somewhere different for a change.

INNER GROWTH, OUTER WORK

Your physical and metaphysical growth are exceptionally intertwined this year as Pluto, the planet of metamorphosis, pushes you into new territory while facing strong resistance from repeated tense aspects with "action oriented" Mars. Your challenge is to express yourself creatively rather than avoiding the stress. Imaginative Neptune's involvement in three out of four eclipses this year suggests the important role spiritual practice plays in unlocking the doors of potential. You can facilitate transformation by working on subtle inner planes while improving your mastery over physical limitations. It's more crucial than ever to blend your dream work, meditation, and the power of positive thought with all your actions in the outer world.

RICK & JEFF'S TIP FOR THE YEAR:
Shorten Your To-Do List

Although you are eager to test the ground in a new world, temper your optimism with reason and caution. Even if you feel a great sense of urgency about making sweeping changes to the fundamental underpinnings of your life, remember that you don't have to make them all at once. In fact, shifting several routines too quickly can create turmoil that is more detrimental than helpful. Instead of scattering your energies, prioritize your needs and initiate only a few changes that will have lasting impact. Remember, what you set into motion now may take many years to reach fruition.

JANUARY

DELAYED SATISFACTION

The opening days of January pack a punch of adrenaline, but it's misleading, for your movement may be stymied throughout the month. Your two key planets, energetic Mars and fixed Pluto, form a tense opposition on **January 2**, bringing resistance from a mighty opponent. This sets the stage for power struggles through **March 7**, when Mars again faces Pluto. Mars is retrograde until **January 30**, potentially turning your frustration into anger while forcing you to revisit ground covered last September. You cannot escape the pressure that comes from interacting with others now: Mars in your 8th House of Shared Resources emphasizes the partnerships you must maintain to enrich your life. Optimistic Jupiter harmonizes with realistic Saturn on **January 21**, the first of three such trines that repeat on **September 8 and November 21**. Stability is your key to success, making January a prime time to create a long-term strategy for achieving your goals by year's end. The earthy Capricorn New Moon on **January 8** is one more reminder of the importance of cautious practicality over reckless abandon.

As if there weren't enough planetary pressure preventing your professional progress, intelligent Mercury crawls along slowly until it turns retrograde on **January 28**, disrupting your thoughts and plans. The dramatic Leo Full Moon on **January 22** brings out your extreme nature, especially as sensual Venus pushes toward a conjunction with potent Pluto on **January 24**, stirring your passions and driving you to experience emotional heights. However, the ecstatic feelings may rebound, pushing you into darker places that you also wish to explore. You may be disappointed if someone is not yet willing to go there to share in the discovery.

KEEP IN MIND THIS MONTH

Your strong urge to merge with someone special takes longer to happen than you wish. Handle your frustration with a long-term perspective and not by seeking short-term gratification.

KEY DATES

SUPER NOVA DAY
JANUARY 2 ★ *fight to the finish*
You may be feeling suspicious as self-directed Mars—now retrograde and less effective than normal—meets tyrannical Pluto in a cosmic standoff. If someone

is undermining your efforts, it might seem as if your reputation or even your survival is at stake. Whether or not this is true, it's time to step up and confront the issues, for if you try to keep everything light and breezy you'll only make matters worse. Look back to **September 21,** 2007, for the possible origin of this conflict. If you respond out of fear, you'll only fuel the drama. Adding a bit of self-control to your passion can be an unbeatable combination, especially since full resolution may not occur until **March 7,** when Mars direct repeats the aspect for the third and final time.

JANUARY 9–13 ★ *practical magic*

These days are blessed by an unusual pattern: Mental Mercury, physical Mars, and wise Saturn mark three points of a magical five-pointed star. Mars biquintiles Mercury on **January 9** and quintiles Saturn on **January 13,** revealing the charisma and creativity bubbling up from the deep pool of your imagination. Even the most original thoughts can now be applied in the real world, though you must take the initiative to express the best ones. Still, be careful—sweet Venus squares wild Uranus on **January 12,** attracting you toward love and freedom simultaneously. Don't set aside your ambitious aspirations to act on every unconventional desire that runs through your mind or you'll find more trouble than you can manage.

JANUARY 19–21 ★ *build a bridge*

Relationship discord mounts as Venus and Mars, the cosmic lovers, pull you in opposite directions on **January 19.** Anxiety can build walls between you and your partner, but the tension can be handled if you are willing to listen to what someone else wants. Remaining open to a new perspective gives you a way to process the stress—either emotionally or physically—and create the romantic magic you were seeking all along. Fortunately, you receive additional support from the stabilizing Jupiter-Saturn trine on **January 21,** strengthening your commitment to love.

JANUARY 22–24 ★ *a walk on the dark side*

The fixed Leo Full Moon on **January 22** falls in your 10th House of Public Status, so everyone will likely know exactly how you are feeling. But a conjunction between mental Mercury and foggy Neptune suggests that you may not be able to clearly explain your mood. Beautiful Venus joins dark Pluto on **January 24,** driving your intense desires out from the shadows of your mind. Although your stress levels may be high, this is not a permanent condition. Facing your fears is not as dangerous as suppressing them.

FEBRUARY

TIGHTEN YOUR PLANS

You may feel somewhat scattered this month as self-directed Mars moves ahead in versatile Gemini. And although you are eager to push your life forward on a variety of fronts, mental Mercury is retrograde until **February 18**, tying your thoughts to the past. Nevertheless, you may be quite optimistic as the month unfolds, for lovely Venus joins beneficial Jupiter on **February 1** in earthy Capricorn, where they tempt you with the sweet fruits of pleasure. You can have what you want as long as you honor your commitments and play by the rules. Still, you may be caught off guard as the quirky Aquarius New Moon Eclipse on **February 6** in your 4th House of Roots changes your mind about what security means to you. You may be suddenly inspired to shake up stagnant energy at home—even if done with the best of intentions, this could stir up a hornet's nest of fear. Painful memories of old family conflicts can resurface, possibly causing you to overreact and aggravate the situation.

You are nudged into new territory when Venus enters progressive Aquarius on **February 17**, Mercury turns direct on **February 18**, and the Sun enters compassionate Pisces on **February 19**. These transitional days prepare you for the focused thinking you must do during the analytical Virgo Full Moon Eclipse on **February 20**. The Sun's annual opposition to responsible Saturn on **February 24** can illuminate the shortcomings of a current strategy by revealing obstacles to your development. Don't just give up: Accept whatever difficult news you hear with grace while promising yourself to do whatever is necessary to reach your destination.

> **KEEP IN MIND THIS MONTH**
>
> *Instead of racing off in several directions without a cohesive strategy, reevaluate your plans to take into consideration the unexpected information you receive throughout the month.*

KEY DATES

FEBRUARY 1–2 ★ *inner voices*
Beautiful Venus's conjunction with optimistic Jupiter on **February 1** encourages you to gloss over the more serious problems of the day because your life appears to be looking up. This can be quite healing, allowing you to take a mental holiday away from the issues that have been troubling you. But retrograde Mercury's conjunction with imaginary Neptune on **February 2** can confuse boundaries, stimulate fantasies, and make it difficult to sustain your confidence. Put off big decisions for now, but pay close attention to your dreams for the guidance you need.

SUPER NOVA DAYS
FEBRUARY 6-7 ★ *change the rules*
An emotionally revealing Aquarius Solar Eclipse on **February 6** in your 4th House of Home and Family can bring a shock, but you will be better off once you are armed with the truth. Fortunately, harmonious trines to "action hero" Mars in clever Gemini help you dance through a recurring family drama. Additionally, a magical quintile between Mars and authoritative Saturn on **February 7** issues you a much-needed reality check. Although you could bump into walls of restraint, they won't stop your progress. The transformative nature of the quintile gives you the tools to change the rules instead of fighting against them.

FEBRUARY 13-14 ★ *integrity counts*
Your desires may remain unfulfilled with sexy Venus quincunxing aggressive Mars on **February 13** in an irritating emotional standoff as you attempt to gain control of an unmanageable situation. You are awkwardly torn as you search for an elusive balance between withholding your feelings and saying too much. Luckily, the Sun harmoniously trines Mars on **February 14**, so others will appreciate your directness if you combine it with honesty. Even if you are sure that you were right all along, an overt gesture of reconciliation is worth more than a thousand well-intended thoughts.

FEBRUARY 20 ★ *choose logic*
The intuitive Pisces Sun lights up your life, yet the practical Virgo Full Moon Eclipse on **February 20** sets your pragmatic logic against the whims of your heart. The Moon is conjunct austere Saturn in your 11th House of Dreams and Wishes, adding an inarguable sense of reality to your thinking. Trust these thoughts, for your sound judgment can now show you the best path forward.

FEBRUARY 24 ★ *rise to the challenge*
Although you want to go out and play, the Sun's tense opposition to Saturn may require you to wait. Even if you can't join in the fun, this temporary barrier can provide just the right amount of resistance to force you to concentrate. Don't give others a reason to judge you negatively; just focus on taking one small step at a time in order to reach your goal.

MARCH

CRAZY LOVE

You have had time enough to prepare; now you need to swing into action. Mars's entry into emotionally protective Cancer on **March 4** in your 9th House of Big Ideas indicates the close connection between your feelings and your behavior this month. Avoid the temptation to isolate yourself behind a hard outer shell. Taking a calculated risk can catalyze your life and set your long-term plans into motion. But your will may be pitted against someone else's as Mars opposes domineering Pluto on **March 7**. Happily, romantic Venus enters Pisces in your 5th House of Fun and Games on **March 12**, followed by Mercury on **March 14**, emphasizing the importance of expressing yourself spontaneously. Rediscovering the joy of your inner child can turn this month into quite a memorable one. But it's not all laughter, for both Venus and Mercury oppose restrictive Saturn on **March 15–17**. Acknowledging your responsibilities, realizing your shortcomings, or just coming to grips with the stark reality of a current situation can be depressing at first, but facing the truth can surprisingly also set you free.

You are highly motivated to overcome any feelings of low self-esteem as Venus and Mercury move on to support assertive Mars on **March 16–18**. The Sun's rejuvenating entry into enthusiastic Aries on **March 20** marks the Spring Equinox, illuminating your 6th House of Health and Work. You are excited about tackling what's next, but the indecisive Libra Full Moon on **March 21** can temporarily overwhelm you with conflicting feelings about your relationships. Mercury and Venus, still traveling through psychic Pisces together, join explosive Uranus on **March 27–28**, blasting you with sudden awareness and leading you toward a truth you have been avoiding.

> **KEEP IN MIND THIS MONTH**
>
> *Passive acquiescence is no more an option than telling everyone exactly what you think. Soften your extremes by choosing a path of moderation and kindness.*

KEY DATES

SUPER NOVA DAYS
MARCH 7–8 ★ *the high price of self-expression*
Even the smallest disagreements can escalate into serious struggles as touchy Mars opposes potent Pluto on **March 7**, firing up your passions so

strongly they cannot be suppressed. You are ready to play for keeps if a powerful opponent attempts to undermine your efforts. However, it may be difficult to keep everything in perspective, for you are easily provoked right now as the imaginative Pisces New Moon joins reckless Uranus in your 5th House of Self-Expression. When the Sun joins Uranus on **March 8**, a flash of inspiration suddenly shifts your perspective. Although it still may be a challenge to let go of your fears, at least a more humorous approach can move the energy into a healthier place.

MARCH 14–18 ★ *healthy outlets*
You may feel a bit defeated as friendly Venus and sweet-talking Mercury stand opposed to stern Saturn on **March 15 and March 17**. You needn't, though, for a readjustment to your plans may leave you in better shape than before. Assistance arrives from the supportive sextile between energetic Mars and Saturn on **March 14**, giving you the organizational skills you need, along with sufficient fortitude to meet any resistance. Additionally, Venus's and Mercury's trines to Mars on **March 16 and March 18** can smooth over the rough spots. Try balancing your responsibilities with playful activities involving children. Expressing your own inner poet through creative or romantic pursuits can also reduce the current pressure.

MARCH 21 ★ *conflict management*
This can be an intense day as the combative Aries Sun and the diplomatic Libra Full Moon cross paths with passionate Pluto, putting you at odds with someone in your immediate environment. If it feels like others are working against you, give them good reason to support you instead of fanning the fires of conflict. It may be better to get physical and sweat it out as the Moon wanes over the next few days. Venting your frustration will only make matters worse.

MARCH 28–30 ★ *magnetic appeal*
Your amorous attractions break out of their constraints on **March 28** as Venus conjoins radical Uranus in your 5th House of Romance. Together they form a supportive sextile with optimistic Jupiter, filling you with an outrageous confidence that emboldens you to extend your reach and take advantage of an unusual opportunity. But the Sun's dynamic square to manipulative Mars on **March 30** produces disagreements over something that won't really matter in the long run. Find constructive ways to express your negativity so you can end the month on a positive note rather than wasting energy in needless conflict.

APRIL

BATTEN DOWN THE HATCHES

April brings an odd mixture of practical solutions to complex problems that can stabilize your life. At times, however, you may have so much enthusiasm about the potential of what lies ahead that you can get yourself in trouble by taking on more than you can handle. The excitement begins as mental Mercury talks its way into eager Aries on **April 2**, followed by stylish Venus on **April 6**. Both of these planets immediately encounter dynamic squares to potent Pluto, demanding that you justify your new ideas before taking them any farther. The Aries New Moon on **April 5** in your 6th House of Health and Daily Routines dares you to start spring cleaning, whether it involves chores around the house or healthy new habits.

Throughout early April, you're called upon to reduce stress by taking the initiative anywhere you can, often with small steps that can bring about larger changes over time. But as the Moon waxes full, Mercury enters dependable Taurus on **April 17**, followed by the Sun on **April 19**, creating Grand Earth Trines with constructive Saturn and powerful Pluto. The Scorpio Full Moon on **April 20** can be an intense confirmation of the path you've chosen. Common sense combined with cautious optimism allows you to capture the importance of this moment in a cohesive plan that can solidify a significant relationship. Things seem to be going your way, yet a high-energy trine between Mars and surprising Uranus spurs you to act impulsively due to unrealistic overconfidence influenced by Mars's opposition to fearless Jupiter on **April 24**.

KEEP IN MIND THIS MONTH

You may need to temper your desire for immediate satisfaction by keeping your eyes on the distant prize.

KEY DATES

APRIL 3-6 ★ *boiling point*

The impatient Aries New Moon on **April 5** urges you to get your feelings out into the open; however, you may feel forced to say something you would prefer keeping private. Your mind—influenced by quicksilver Mercury in speedy Aries squaring compulsive Pluto on **April 3**—is thinking faster than your heart can process the data. Attractive Venus squares Pluto on **April 6**, drawing you farther into a complex web of feelings. You must find ways to bring positive change into your life or the volcanic emotional pressures could erupt and complicate an already tense situation.

APRIL 10 ★ *out of proportion*

The Sun squares expansive Jupiter, tempting you with opportunities that look too good to be true. Your optimism can fuel your actions, helping you accomplish more than usual as long as you don't take on too much. Be careful, for communicator Mercury squares pushy Mars, triggering you to say more than you intend, possibly stirring an argument driven by ego and not by necessity. Channel your aggression into cooperative efforts instead of divisive ones.

SUPER NOVA DAYS
APRIL 18–21 ★ *conscious intent*

You could lose a few days of harmony if you let yourself get overwhelmed by the passionate Scorpio Full Moon on **April 20**. Fortunately, the intensity is ameliorated by trines from logical Mercury and the Sun to heavyweights Saturn and Pluto. Mercury completes a Grand Earth Trine on **April 18**, concentrating your intentions on meaningful activities. The Sun illuminates this same grand trine on **April 20–21**, adding the strength of conviction to your words. Power is a double-edged sword, though, and you could inadvertently hurt someone if you wield it unconsciously. Play for keeps, but do it with awareness and humility.

APRIL 22–24 ★ *let freedom ring*

Your enthusiasm builds as impetuous Mars opposes overconfident Jupiter on **April 24**. Your fervor can take you over the top, but you may also feel the frustration of Venus squaring both Mars and Jupiter on **April 23**. Surprisingly, it's unconventional Uranus that comes to your rescue as it trines Mars on **April 22**, allowing you to act independently in a manner that is not abrasive or obsessive. Instead of rebelling against a person or an idea, explore your options with passion and common sense.

APRIL 28 ★ *free falling*

An irritating Mars-Neptune quincunx makes it difficult to know how much force you should apply to resolve a conflict. Being forthright won't necessarily help you achieve your goals: The likelihood of rejection could outweigh the benefits of disclosure. Once you accept the lack of clear direction now, the tension could dissipate, allowing you to move toward resolution over the days ahead.

MAY

RELATIONSHIP STRUGGLES

Venus in sensual Taurus this month reactivates the Grand Earth Trine that influenced your life on **April 18–21**. A quiet satisfaction belies the dramatic intensity beneath the surface, as this trine involves somber Saturn and evolutionary Pluto. Your decisions now can have long-lasting ramifications. But as Mercury dances into flirty Gemini on **May 2**, you often find yourself engaging in lively conversations, distracting you from the serious work at hand. Powerful waves are churning as both Saturn and Jupiter change apparent directions in the sky, reinforcing the resolute Taurus New Moon on **May 5** in your 7th House of Partners. The New Moon's stressful sesquisquare to immovable Pluto indicates that you may be working at cross purposes with a close friend or partner. Although your tendency is to dig in your heels when faced with change—especially as Mars moves into proud Leo on **May 9**—you'll be better served by compromise and a willingness to change your mind.

Both the willful Sun and romantic Venus get boosts of confidence from trines to Jupiter on **May 12 and May 18**, respectively, as your desires intensify and your mood swings widen and deepen. The passionate Scorpio Full Moon on **May 19** may overwhelm you, making it difficult to know what's real. With Venus square Neptune, your fantasies become so enticing that you may choose them over reality. However, the Sun's entry into cerebral Gemini in your 8th House of Intimacy, combined with the long-term effects of Jupiter's sextile to unconventional Uranus on **May 21**, opens your mind to a whole new array of opportunities ahead.

KEEP IN MIND THIS MONTH

Love may be near, but additional preparation and even sacrifice could be required before you achieve the intimacy you seek.

KEY DATES

MAY 1 ★ *deep connection*

You can experience love that truly matters today as Venus harmonizes with passionate Pluto and stabilizing Saturn. Don't miss an opportunity for deep emotional contact, for interactions today will likely have enough substance to withstand the tests of time. Valuable Venus in your 7th House of Others can also be ideal for making an investment, especially if you go in with a partner. Whether in romance or business, you are especially effective as long as you are willing to accept the outer responsibilities while doing the inner work.

MAY 9–11 ★ *back away from the edge*

Active Mars is all fired up and ready for the show as it enters expressive Leo on **May 9** in your 10th House of Career. Managing your workload now is critical—don't exhaust yourself. But as Mars quincunxes Pluto on **May 11**, you may be annoyed with the way things are going. Instead of taking your irritation out on someone at home, channel it into an attack plan for the week ahead. There's no need for a showdown; the tensions will diffuse on their own.

MAY 14 ★ *unreality check*

A subtle yet dynamic square with the practical Taurus Sun illuminates dreamy Neptune, luring you into your rich fantasies. You might actually believe that you can be logical enough to think your way through a current relationship or family dilemma, yet the best answers will come from intuitive realizations. Pay attention to your imagination, for spiritual solutions can be just what you need now.

SUPER NOVA DAYS
MAY 19–22 ★ *make a choice*

You are standing at a crossroad, and the decisions you make now can have great consequences. The magnetic Scorpio Full Moon on **May 19** infuses you with unresolved emotions. Squares to Saturn and Neptune suggest that your dreams have escaped from the night and must be reevaluated in the light of day. If you have been overly optimistic, it's time to accept the facts. Still, surprises are possible—even likely—on **May 21**, when the long-lasting sextile is exact between beneficial Jupiter and brilliant Uranus. These are crazy days, but if you're totally carried away by unreachable ideals, the Sun's harsh square with austere Saturn on **May 22** can be an unwelcome reminder of reality.

MAY 26 ★ *be kind to yourself*

An unfriendly square between sweet Venus and sobering Saturn can take the wind out of your emotional sails, leaving you without the resources or motivation to finish your journey. With messenger Mercury and dreamer Neptune turning retrograde today, your fears can create an environment where love and communication are withheld. Don't get discouraged; instead, use this time to reconsider what you truly want.

JUNE

STIRRING THE EMOTIONAL STEW

You may find your life overcomplicated by other people's feelings this month. Still, this offers you a chance to engage in the emotional intensity that you crave with the Sun, Venus, and Mercury in your 8th House of Deep Sharing. Thoughtful Mercury, however, is retrograde until **June 19**, reminding you that this awareness is not just about new experiences; remembering old ones can allow you to reconsider them in a new light. The airy Gemini New Moon on **June 3** also falls in your 8th House, emphasizing the mental twist on your typically more emotional posture. Aside from focusing on intimate relationships, consider making a joint financial investment. Just pay close attention to all the details.

You encounter rougher terrain on **June 18** when innocent Venus stands opposite dark Pluto. This emotional tug-of-war draws you deeper into the passions and turmoil of love. You may have to face all-too-familiar control issues as feelings of possessiveness and jealousy are revealed, for the restless Gemini Full Moon conjuncts Pluto the same day. Although life may feel overly intense as you fight for your survival or something you love, you must also consider what needs to be eliminated to support the process of regeneration. Dissatisfaction deepens as long-lasting effects from expansive Jupiter's sesquisquare to restrictive Saturn culminate on **June 26**. But your obsession to reach your goals will give you the strength to overcome any obstacles that now appear in your path, for your two key planets, Mars and Pluto, form a harmonious trine on **June 30**, ending the month with a self-imposed sprint to the finish line, along with an acknowledgment that you are on the road to success.

> **KEEP IN MIND THIS MONTH**
>
> *The magic of metamorphosis can be completed only once you eliminate the extra weight of outmoded habits or counterproductive emotional patterns.*

KEY DATES

JUNE 7–9 ★ *into the great unknown*
An unusual triple conjunction of the Sun, Mercury, and Venus in thinking Gemini falls in your investigative 8th House. This alignment, spread out over three days, increases your innate curiosity enough that you may spend extra energy researching shadowy areas of reality. You could be even more attracted to studying metaphysics or reading about UFOs, near-death experiences, and spirit communication. Give yourself enough time to explore ideas that can deepen your understanding of life's secrets.

JUNE 12-13 ★ *love hangover*
Even with the best of spiritual intentions, you may not be able to keep your mind off sex when flirty Venus dynamically squares wild and crazy Uranus in your 5th House of Love on **June 12**. A beautiful fantasy can infuse even the most mundane relationship with a rejuvenating sense of magic as Venus then trines Neptune on **June 13**. Keep in mind that you don't have to act on everything you can imagine. As much as you love the thrills, you might find yourself outside your usual comfort zone, which can make you feel a bit anxious. Don't worry; this is just a surreal situation, so you might as well revel in it while it lasts.

SUPER NOVA DAYS
JUNE 18-21 ★ *take no prisoners*
The adventurous Sagittarius Full Moon on **June 18** is conjunct potent Pluto and brings you more than you bargained for as emotions deepen and sweet love can turn into a battlefield of wills. Intimate relationships become the grounds for difficult transformations, yet you may resist the change. But the Sun opposes Pluto on **June 20** and then slides into emotional Cancer the same day—marking the Summer Solstice—so you must bring these issues to a workable conclusion, whatever the cost. If you cannot resolve the problems, you could feel regret on **June 21** as go-getter Mars opposes uncertain Neptune. Although you may be disappointed and less energetic than usual, this can be a signal to slow down and a reminder not to push yourself so hard.

JUNE 30 ★ *relentless progress*
This annual trine between your two key planets—warrior Mars in your 10th House of Career and powerful Pluto—validates your strong commitment to accomplish your goals at work. When these two fighters combine their forces, your passions can become compulsive. You must find ways to express them, or you risk them erupting with great force. By restraining your personal quest for power even mildly, you could greatly increase your odds of getting what you want. Remember that selfish behavior will likely backfire on you, so act only for the greater good.

JULY

SUNNY SIDE OF THE STREET

Opportunities arrive at your doorstep, offering you blue sky and boundless horizons. Paradoxically, however, the month begins on a cautious note, for energetic Mars's range of action is narrowed when it moves into discerning Virgo. Then the nurturing Cancer New Moon on **July 2** falls in your 9th House of Big Ideas and establishes the tone for an over-the-top kind of month. At times, it all looks so good that you're ready to promise anything to make the most of the present moment, yet you must be careful not to let your unbridled passion run roughshod over your common sense.

The theme of overdoing is emphasized as three planets oppose excessive Jupiter, beginning with sweet Venus on **July 3**. Second comes the Sun, on **July 9**, highlighting the positive side of a situation that again can tempt you to be so optimistic that you lose sight of reality. The third opposition to Jupiter in ambitious Capricorn comes from mentally active Mercury on **July 19**. Even the tiniest thought can now grow to grandiose proportions; be watchful for a loss of perspective as you turn molehills into mountains. Fortunately, you will still be feeling the lingering effects of the disciplined Capricorn Full Moon on **July 18**. Balance your overstated intentions with judicious actions and concentrated efforts to bring you closer to your goals. Meanwhile, there is a gradual shift throughout the month that draws all eyes toward you at work with Venus entering proud Leo in your 10th House of Public Status on **July 12**, followed by the Sun on **July 22**, and Mercury on **July 26**. Now is your chance to shine as the leader of the pack.

> **KEEP IN MIND THIS MONTH**
>
> *Confidence is healthy, but when unchecked it can lead to trouble. Exercise a bit of self-restraint, especially when everything appears to be going your way.*

KEY DATES

JULY 2-3 ★ *life is a caberet*

Fun is in the air. You might find yourself entertaining at home with the "family oriented" Cancer New Moon conjunct loving Venus. Additionally, Venus is opposed to joyful Jupiter, stimulating you to jump in and indulge yourself. Unfortunately, you can easily overspend or overeat. Since Venus also symbolizes money, this could be an excellent time to consider a long-term investment—provided that your overconfidence doesn't get in the way of your due diligence.

SUPER NOVA DAYS

JULY 9-10 ★ *metaphysical speed bump*

The Sun's opposition to buoyant Jupiter on **July 9** can inspire you to take on more than you can handle. However, your arrogance is countered by mental Mercury's opposition to dark Pluto on **July 10**, triggering the possibility of a knock down, drag-out fight to the finish. This difference of opinion is emphasized when "go, go" Mars joins with "no, no" Saturn on the same day, heightening frustration and resentment, especially if your inflexible perspective is extreme. Slowing down and yielding to the opinions of others can help you overcome your dissatisfaction.

JULY 18-19 ★ *give and take*

It's challenging for you to find a moderate position right now, with your emotions pulled to extremes by the sensible Capricorn Full Moon opposite the emotional Cancer Sun on **July 18**. Your "all or nothing" approach to relationships may not serve your interests, however; try to find a middle ground. The problem is that bigger isn't necessarily better, though Mercury's tense opposition to giant Jupiter on **July 19** can mislead you to think so. Your best strategy now is to speak your truth and then listen to the response. If you have the courage to talk about your feelings and absorb what is said in return, the path to your future will clear.

JULY 26 ★ *run with it now*

A double planetary whammy fires you up as talkative Mercury enters dramatic Leo, prompting you to put your thoughts on the table for all to see. Additionally, a noticeable boost comes from "action hero" Mars's trine to Jupiter, giving you indefatigable energy and unflappable confidence. The Moon in determined Taurus completes a practical Grand Earth Trine involving both Mars and Jupiter, allowing you to apply your efforts efficiently and helping you realize the current potential in your life.

JULY 31 ★ *in love with love*

Romantic Venus opposes spiritual Neptune on **July 31**, ending the month on a sweet and gentle note. The biggest danger here is that you can set yourself up for future disappointment, for the Venus-Neptune alignment can make your fantasies seem really real. A reality check now can minimize disillusionment later on.

AUGUST

NO HOLDING BACK

You may not have much choice this month as events draw you into unexpected dramas, precipitating personal transformation. The action begins on **August 1** when a powerful New Moon Eclipse in your 10th House of Career and Community puts an end to the previous cycle of significant growth, initiating a phase of hard work and accountability. Trust your thinking on **August 9**, when mental Mercury harmonizes with Pluto, giving you the ability to concentrate on important matters. You continue to be more organized and efficient throughout the month as Mercury enters its home sign of analytical Virgo on **August 10**, followed by the Sun on **August 22**.

You may not fully understand what's unfolding on the home front on **August 16**, when the emotionally detached Aquarius Full Moon Eclipse in your 4th House of Security is conjunct diffusive Neptune. However, once you accept that it may be beyond rational analysis, you'll be able to glean important spiritual lessons from your experience. Your social life can get a bit crazy as Mercury and Venus oppose Uranus on **August 23**. Excitement in romance, coupled with brilliant debate, can make these days memorable, as long as you don't expect everything to go as planned. Mercury and Venus square Pluto on **August 27 and August 29** before moving into gracious Libra. The intensity heats up one more time as you revisit unresolved power struggles from earlier in the month. If you are willing to go the distance, you can wipe the slate clean and move forward with your life. The down-to-earth Virgo New Moon on **August 30** conjuncts stable Saturn, giving finality to the incredible changes that you have had to face this month.

> **KEEP IN MIND THIS MONTH**
>
> *Growth is not painless, and you may be required to give up something dear to move into the next phase of your life. Even the best changes can be difficult at first.*

KEY DATES

AUGUST 5-6 ★ *bet on the truth*

Innocent Venus forms a harmonious trine to tough guy Pluto on **August 5**, thrusting you into an emotionally revealing dance with your shadow that is likely to be played out through an intimate relationship. Mars's opposition to erratic Uranus on **August 6** urges you to take a risk and deal with the consequences as they occur. This is a volatile time when deep tensions can be released. Even if you move through this phase awkwardly, you will ultimately realize that the stress is easier to manage once issues are out in the open.

SUPER NOVA DAYS
AUGUST 13-17 ★ *emotional tug-of-war*
The unpredictable Aquarius Full Moon Eclipse on **August 16** dominates your emotional landscape by reflecting anything you try to avoid. You may feel restrained by the necessity to work with others as Venus and Mercury conjunct restrictive Saturn in your 11th House of Teamwork on **August 13-15**, yet you have something important to learn from the group experience. And although Venus and Mercury both trine Jupiter on **August 16-17**—an uplifting and pleasurable aspect—feisty Mars crosses swords with Pluto on **August 17**. This raises the stakes of any conflict and can pit your will against someone else's. Power struggles may be symptomatic of suppressed anger that needs to find constructive expression. Consider the cost of doing battle before you start a fight that increases tension instead of resolving it.

AUGUST 21-23 ★ *open to surprise*
A surge of passion washes over you as the impetuous Aries Moon activates a Grand Fire Trine with the Sun and potent Pluto on **August 21**. You are ready to do whatever you must to accomplish your goals and woe to anyone who stands in your way. But the Sun's entry into methodical Virgo on **August 22** could soften your drive. Then, when Mercury and Venus oppose independent Uranus on **August 23**, you are again spurred into action as your thoughts and feelings flip-flop at the speed of light. If you're open to the surprising twists and turns, this can be a wonderful time. But if you remain inflexible, an overly tense situation could be shattered by sudden change.

AUGUST 27-29 ★ *let it go*
Logical Mercury squares Pluto on **August 27**, demanding that you journey into the hidden recesses of your mind. Loving Venus repeats this pattern on **August 29**, turning a curious intellectual inquiry into an emotional struggle. The more you try to hold on to an old feeling or perspective, the more resistance you will receive. But bringing buried feelings into the open can positively transform a difficult situation into something promising.

SCORPIO

SEPTEMBER

This month begins with four planets in your 12th House of Soul Consciousness, luring you away from the mundane world as you journey inward to seek peace of mind. You are obsessed with discovering the secrets of the cosmos now and may choose to retreat somewhat from the noise of day-to-day life. Finding a healthy balance between your spiritual quest and your ongoing responsibilities is a challenge as the 12th House planets in open-minded Libra square boundless Jupiter. The surge of conviction from this giant planet on **September 7–11** tempts you to throw caution to the wind as you follow your dreams instead of meeting necessary obligations. Fortunately, expansive Jupiter forms the second of three harmonious trines with contractive Saturn on **September 8**, giving you enough common sense to moderate any personal indulgence. You may need some time alone to process your choices consciously. The alternative is just going along with the flow—only to later discover that you missed an important opportunity.

Your desire for solace and escape into fantasy continues as Mercury, Venus, and Mars harmonize with intuitive Neptune on **September 17–22**. Meanwhile, the Sun squares intense Pluto in a clash of wills on **September 20**, just prior to the Autumn Equinox on **September 22** when the Sun enters peace-loving Libra in your 12th House, again reminding you of the importance of walking your spiritual path. The artistic Libra New Moon on **September 29** is awkwardly sesquisquare Neptune, fueling your creative process with images from your dreams. Fortunately, retrograde Mercury's easy trine to Neptune further opens a direct channel into the hidden recesses of your subconscious mind. Listening to your inner voices will give you the guidance needed for what lies ahead.

> **KEEP IN MIND THIS MONTH**
>
> *Taking care of your responsibilities must be a part of your spiritual practice. It's not just about finding deeper meaning; it's also about making your life work.*

KEY DATES

SEPTEMBER 3-4 ★ *weight of the world*
The Sun's annual conjunction with karmic Saturn on **September 3** is usually a time when you should get what you deserve, but this year its trine to generous Jupiter on **September 4** can counteract some of the potential negativity. You are singularly focused and willing to do whatever's necessary to accomplish your goals. With

Jupiter's influence, you are fully confident that your actions will have the desired outcome. Still, you can feel the weight of responsibility on your shoulders as you assume more than you can handle. Although you want everyone to acknowledge your significant contribution, keep in mind that exhaustion will only defeat your efforts.

SUPER NOVA DAYS
SEPTEMBER 7-11 ★ *selective service*
Work to establish equilibrium between your personal needs and your commitment to others as abundant Jupiter trines taskmaster Saturn on **September 8**. Finding balance may not be easy, for impulsive Mars squares Jupiter on **September 7**, filling you with altruism. You are so eager to help anyone in need that you can say yes before considering your personal sacrifice. Then, when fair-minded Mercury in Libra conjuncts Mars and squares Jupiter on **September 8**, you can push yourself right to the edge. Venus repeats this pattern on **September 9-11**, again suggesting that discipline and restraint are your keys to success, so watch those extravagant purchases and indulgences. Good fortune is indicated as long as you don't go overboard or overlook any significant details.

SEPTEMBER 15-17 ★ *emotional challenge*
The compassionate Pisces New Moon is zapped by a high-frequency conjunction with erratic Uranus on **September 15** in your 5th House of Children and Romance. Sudden shifts in your plans may be prompted by a change in parental responsibilities, or perhaps unexpected romantic yearnings will surface that upset the stability of your life. It may be difficult to know what to do with the crazy emotions arising at this time, leaving you unsettled for days to come, especially as loving Venus and logical Mercury form irritating quincunxes with Uranus on **September 16-17**. If you don't feel it in your heart, then inaction is better than false action.

SEPTEMBER 23-24 ★ *spiritual warrior*
Your words might turn uncharacteristically surly as Mercury the Communicator and Mars the Warrior join on **September 23** for a second time this month—their first conjunction was on **September 8**—as the Winged Messenger slows down to begin its three-week retrograde phase on **September 24**. This prolongs Mercury's visit to your private 12th House of Endings and encourages you to spend enough time in meditation and contemplation to allow you to complete this current cycle of spiritual growth.

OCTOBER

PHOENIX RISING

Your self-imposed solitude carries forward from last month with the willful Sun, thoughtful Mercury, and self-directed Mars all in your 12th House of Odds and Ends. But this emphasis on your inner world comes to completion as your key planet Mars powers its way into fixed Scorpio on **October 4** and fires up your energy in your 1st House of Physicality. Loving Venus is already in your magnetic sign; Mars's presence there now adds heat and a sense of urgency to your personal expression. The trailblazing Aries Full Moon on **October 14** falls in your 6th House of Health and Work, reflecting a need to change old habits that no longer contribute to your well-being. The daily routine of your job can contribute to boredom, stimulating fantasies about shaking up everything. Communicator Mercury turns direct on **October 15**, in your 12th House, giving you a sense of finality before fully emerging from the shadows. The Sun's entry into your sign on **October 22** continues this outgoing trend, lighting up your personality and increasing your self-confidence and charm.

The potent Scorpio New Moon on **October 28** can help you to focus on where you're going and to let go of any recent disappointments that hinder your personal growth. During this lunar cycle, stable Saturn faces off with independent Uranus on **November 4** in the first of five powerful oppositions that could change the direction of your life over the next two years. Meanwhile, Mars's supportive sextile to Saturn and harmonious trine to Uranus on **October 30–31** can surprise you with a very clear idea of how you want to use the power that continues to build in the days ahead.

> **KEEP IN MIND THIS MONTH**
>
> *Become more engaged in every aspect of your life. Although the days may be getting shorter, your light is growing brighter and your actions now have major consequences for your future.*

KEY DATES

OCTOBER 6 ★ *pull back the reins*

Retrograde Mercury passes between the Earth and the Sun on **October 6** as they both square powerhouse Jupiter, gracing you with courage. Your current exuberance can be helpful as long as you temper any tendency to exaggerate or overcommit to a social cause. Being aware of your limitations is a smart practice that will help you moderate excessive behavior.

OCTOBER 10-11 ★ *delightful surprise*

Seductive Venus in Scorpio forms an easy trine with unorthodox Uranus in your 5th House of Love and Creativity on **October 10**. On the one hand, you may be able to successfully persuade someone into joining your exploration of unusual interests and unconventional tastes. On the other, Venus's square to Neptune on **October 11** might have you feeling confused as you try to integrate unrealistic desires with your current reality. Nevertheless, this is a chance to express what you want because your anticipation of breakthrough is greater than your fear of rejection.

OCTOBER 18 ★ *no more drama*

It's time to get outside and take in the wonders of nature's beauty as Venus leaves ruminating Scorpio on **October 18** and steps into the adventurous world of Sagittarius. It is easier now for you to move beyond your comfort zone and be more emotionally available. This phase—lasting until **November 12**—also allows you to connect with others through playful flirting and small talk instead of relying on intensity alone.

OCTOBER 24 ★ *paranoia will destroy you*

This can be a tumultuous day filled with fierce relationship struggles. Your two key planets, direct Mars and obstinate Pluto, are in a tight semisquare aspect, enabling you to see through someone's social niceties and focus on the underlying issues. But your current negativity could turn a well-intended act into a fight with no winner. Understanding the other person's motives can help prevent a needless emotional scuffle.

SUPER NOVA DAYS
OCTOBER 27-31 ★ *don't look back*

The passionate Scorpio New Moon on **October 28** represents a special passage for you if you can get over your past, for elimination and renewal are difficult unless you're ready to let go of jealousy or anger. But if you are willing to move beyond old wounds, then you can experience the power of regeneration. Fortunately, you receive a boost from Mars as it forms supportive sextiles with buoyant Jupiter on **October 28** and constructive Saturn on **October 30**, followed by an energizing trine with electric Uranus on **October 31**. You are truly in your element now and can accomplish amazing things. Think about what you want to do, for there's no better time to get started than now.

NOVEMBER

PRESENT TENSE, FUTURE PERFECT

This feels like the month you've been waiting for all year. Although the stress may be overwhelming at times, you are hopeful about the potential that exists all around you. You might not know the best way to move through the current obstacles, but if you take it one step at a time, you can set a foundation in stone upon which you can build your life for a long time to come. The dilemma, however, is the first of five oppositions between stabilizing Saturn and destabilizing Uranus on **November 4**. This powerful long-term cycle will last until July 2010. If you hang back in fear, rigid structures can buckle under the pressure. The ground may shift beneath your feet, but if you assume a flexible attitude, your life will withstand the shaking and rattling—and be better off for it.

Fortunately, buoyant Jupiter relieves tension as its sextiles Uranus on **November 13** and trines Saturn on **November 21**. Jupiter's supportive sextile to Uranus is the third and last of this series—the first was on **March 28**, the second on **May 21**—continuing to open your mind to new possibilities and exciting opportunities. Good news may arrive out of the blue, offering solutions where none previously existed. Encouraging Jupiter and discouraging Saturn, the cosmic regulators, have been holding your life in balance somewhere between expansion and contraction, so prepare to put your ideas into motion when Jupiter trines Saturn. It's time to review the last few years to see what gains you've made and what lessons you've learned. It's essential now to build on your past efforts rather than hastily acting on something new.

> **KEEP IN MIND THIS MONTH**
>
> *Instead of worrying, keep one eye on the past, one eye on the future, and your feet grounded in the present circumstances.*

KEY DATES

SUPER NOVA DAYS
NOVEMBER 3–4 ★ *no solution in sight*
The long-term opposition between immovable Saturn and irrepressible Uranus on **November 4** can increase stress levels regarding money and love, especially as valuable Venus dynamically squares both planets on **November 3**. You cannot easily hide your displeasure: You want something more than you have, and there may not be a simple path to your heart's desire. Extreme

actions—whether purposefully hiding your true feelings or suddenly demanding that your needs be met now—may not have the desired effects. Don't push for resolution yet; just get the issues out into the open. The stakes increase as communicator Mercury enters probing Scorpio, also on **November 4**, remaining in your sign until **November 23**. Additionally, self-directed Mars squares dreamy Neptune the same day, intensifying the conflict between your current situation and your spiritual inclinations. Gather all the knowledge you can to help you make the big decisions looming on the horizon.

NOVEMBER 12–16 ★ *who do you trust?*
Love becomes a temporary battleground of raw emotions as vulnerable Venus engages in an intense power struggle with your key planet Pluto on **November 12**. But instead of being overwhelmed by someone else's passions, the hopeful Jupiter-Uranus sextile on **November 13** allows you to clear a path to a higher expression of love. A stubborn Taurus Full Moon squares Neptune the same day, signaling that your common sense clashes with your intuition. Fortunately, the confusion dissipates and clarity returns when mental Mercury harmonizes with Uranus, Jupiter, and Saturn on **November 16**. Ultimately, it's best to trust your own thoughts now over the counsel of anyone else.

NOVEMBER 21–23 ★ *into the great wide open*
The easy trine between stable Saturn and visionary Jupiter on **November 21** gives you the ability to organize what you know into a sensible plan of action. It's easier for you to see what's ahead as the Sun and Mercury leave compulsive Scorpio for the more inspirational and philosophical realms of Sagittarius on **November 21 and November 23**, respectively. The change is noticeable, and you must consciously shift your vision from the past to focus with hope on the future in order to best capture the potential of this moment.

NOVEMBER 27–29 ★ *holiday spice*
The high-spirited Sagittarius New Moon on Thanksgiving, **November 27**, joins Mercury and Mars in bringing a fun-loving intensity to your holiday weekend. Your festive mood grows as Venus harmonizes with the Uranus-Saturn opposition on **November 28–29**, calming their conflict between freedom and responsibility. Fortunately, a realistic attitude about money and love during this time can inspire you to make sound investments for your future.

DECEMBER

AFTER THE DELUGE

On **December 1**, a lovely conjunction between pleasant Venus and opulent Jupiter indicates a kinder, gentler month ahead. Your good feelings may not last long, though, for big-talking Mercury, energetic Mars, and the Sun—now all moving through adventurous Sagittarius—square the waning Saturn-Uranus opposition that was exact last month. Mental Mercury squares irrepressible Uranus on **December 5** and restrictive Saturn on **December 6**, signaling that your brilliant ideas could run into an obstacle. The Sun squares Uranus on **December 10** and Saturn on **December 12** as you act impulsively and then reconsider your actions a bit too late. But Mars's square to Uranus on **December 12** overrides common sense, and you rebel against the current restrictions regardless of the consequences. The Gemini Full Moon on the same day increases the hype, heightens the instability, and—with Mercury's conjunction to Pluto—intensifies all forms of communication. Your frustrations may still be running high as feisty Mars squares authoritative Saturn on **December 15**, requiring you to cool your heels, reassess your present circumstances, and then move ahead with caution.

As the holiday spirit picks you up, the dust should settle as three planets exit cavalier Sagittarius and enter conservative Capricorn. Your thinking becomes more pragmatic as Mercury enters Capricorn on **December 12**, followed by the Sun on **December 21** and Mars on **December 27**. The tradition-oriented Capricorn New Moon on **December 27** falls in your 4th House of Roots, enabling you to spend quality time with those you love; this also marks the beginning of an ambitious phase as you work hard to integrate your recent experiences and create your strategy for the year ahead.

> **KEEP IN MIND THIS MONTH**
>
> *Managing your stress through the holidays is crucial. If you take care of each situation as it arises, you will have time to partake in the festivities as well.*

KEY DATES

DECEMBER 5-6 ★ *cruising for trouble*

The Sun's conjunction with "superhero" Mars on **December 5** illuminates your ability to fight for your basic values, but your indefatigable energy runs into a wall, creating a messy situation. You are hot for action, and tempers can flare with communicator Mercury being provoked by a square from rebellious Uranus. But you cannot just walk away from issues once they've been stirred up, for Mercury squares stern Saturn on **December 6**, insisting that you answer to authority—whether it be your boss, your spouse, or your own conscience.

SUPER NOVA DAY

DECEMBER 12 ★ *true confessions*

The restless Gemini Full Moon in your 8th House of Intimacy and Shared Resources can fill your life with stressful changes affecting both money and love. Although Mars squares erratic Uranus, driving you to the edge of frustration, suppression is not the answer. Your ruling planet, Pluto, is joined by the heavenly messenger Mercury, giving wings to your deepest thoughts. They can pack a punch, though, when they erupt into conversation. It won't be easy to overcome your inertia with restrictive Saturn squaring your Sun. But you must express your truth, and it's better to do it gently and preemptively instead of waiting for someone else to provoke it.

DECEMBER 21-22 ★ *point of no return*

The Winter Solstice on **December 21**, marked by the Sun's entry into hardworking Capricorn, can be a significant turning point for you, especially if you set your heart on a goal and commit to achieving it. You cannot go back once the Sun joins transformative Pluto on **December 22** and deepens your resolve. Fortunately, your fierce passion will give you the strength you need. Since the Sun-Pluto conjunction in your 3rd House of Communication shines light on whatever is no longer needed, you may have to give up a belief you once considered important. Don't hold on to a grudge or insecurity that no longer has any purpose. And remember that your current actions may have much greater impact now than you realize.

DECEMBER 28-31 ★ *purposeful and powerful*

Mars's conjunction with intense Pluto on **December 28** reactivates old fears of being forced to do something against your will. You are ready to take a stand, even if it means raining on the holiday parade. You are quite serious and filled with a sense of purpose, so you cannot go along for the ride unless it's heading in your direction. Fortunately, interactive Mercury comes to the rescue just in time for the New Year's celebrations as it joins jolly Jupiter on **December 30**. Release all negativity so you can ring in your future on a happier note.

SAGITTARIUS

NOVEMBER 22–DECEMBER 21

SAGITTARIUS OVERVIEW

There is a definite and noticeable shift in your life this year as both Jupiter and Pluto leave philosophical Sagittarius to enter realistic Capricorn. Jupiter was in your sign throughout most of 2007 and opened your horizons, presented you with new opportunities, and encouraged your growth in many areas of life. Pluto, on the other hand, has been in Sagittarius since 1995. It has gradually yet relentlessly forced you to act on the convictions of your beliefs, confronting you with a need to change. **This is a transitional year**, for Jupiter's entry into your 2nd House of Self-Worth can increase material wealth and your self-esteem. **Instead of starting things anew, it's time to build on what you have already created**. Pluto's entry into Capricorn is at once more subtle and more powerful. Its subtlety derives from the fact that it's so slow in its movement, it tentatively steps into Capricorn on January 25 before retrograding back into Sagittarius on June 14, only to reenter Capricorn on November 26 for a fifteen-year stay. Pluto offers glimpses of a new world—one based less upon your lofty ideals than on a down-to-earth approach to who you are and how you interact with the world.

Saturn and Jupiter were harmoniously trine last year in "action oriented" fire signs, which inspired you to take calculated risks to reach your goals. This year, Jupiter continues its trine with Saturn, but their presence in earth signs limits your vision to that which makes practical sense. This could be a positive change for you, and yet **you may feel as if the fire of enthusiasm has died down and been replaced by the humdrum of daily routine**. The good news, however, is that Jupiter's continuing connection with Saturn—exact on January 21, September 9, and November 21—gives you all the right tools to make last year's dreams come true this year.

When expansive Jupiter moved through adventurous Sagittarius last year, you had many opportunities to open new doors, any of which might have set you on a significant journey. As your key planet, Jupiter, now moves through earthy Capricorn, your perspective shifts and **you see the world through a much more realistic set of lenses**. The thrill of the unknown and your unbridled optimism recede as you assume a more restrained and pragmatic posture. If you're worried that your options are limited, keep in mind that you are on an even greater adventure than you think. **You are ready to make use of every thing you've learned over the past eighteen years** when powerful Pluto moved through your sign. If you have successfully eliminated what you no longer need, the transformation is nearly complete. If there is unfinished business that lingers from your past, take care of it now to free you for the momentous journey that is about to begin.

SLOW START

You're typically able to jump into relationships before you even think about the consequences, because impetuous Mars rules your 5th House of Love. But this year begins with Mars retrograde in your 7th House of Partners, suggesting that you will look twice before you leap. In fact, until Mars turns direct on January 31, you could come up with logical reasons not to move forward in love. Mars enters your 8th House of Intimacy on March 6, intensifying your passions or possibly deepening a current relationship. Logical Mercury enters your 5th House of Romance on April 3, followed by playful Venus on April 7, raising the heat, which may also amplify your stress levels—for your head and your heart may have very different agendas. Relationship activity increases throughout May, but periods of frustration can cool you down around July 10 and from August 12 through August 17 as responsibilities accumulate. Being grounded in your truth strengthens the stability and integrity of a relationship that's meant to last.

NOSE TO THE GRINDSTONE

Taskmaster Saturn in your 10th House of Career indicates that you must work harder than ever to achieve your worldly objectives. Throughout the year, however, you may feel tension building from your responsibilities at work or in the community that can mean regular absence from the home. Additionally, a Lunar Eclipse on February 20 in your 10th House can change the nature of your vocational landscape suddenly—you may need to adjust to a change of business ownership, a new boss, or even a different job. Stay flexible, for what happens may be out of your control.

TURN LEMONS INTO LEMONADE

Abundant Jupiter in your 2nd House of Income this year supports the likelihood of success in financial matters. Karmic Saturn, the ruler of your 2nd House, harmoniously trines Jupiter on January 21, September 8, and November 21, giving you an uncanny common sense when it comes to money. But all is not easy, for Jupiter forms a stressful sesquisquare with Saturn on March 18 and June 25, highlighting areas of concern around professional advancement and how you are compensated for your work. You may feel undervalued, especially if you're working long hours and not receiving enough for what you do. Instead of forcing an issue about money, it's better to channel your frustration into production; you'll reap the financial rewards later.

SAVE YOUR STRENGTH

Your physical well-being improves when you feel good about yourself, because affable Venus rules your 6th House of Health. This year begins with Venus in friendly Sagittarius, so taking special care of your appearance, updating your wardrobe, and paying close attention to your health can be as important as a steady exercise program and a nutritious diet. Focus on activities that build stamina and strengthen your immune system while your key planet, Jupiter, is in conservative Capricorn all year. Introduce new routines or experiment with new therapies when Jupiter receives support from unorthodox Uranus around March 28, May 21, and November 13. But don't expect any quick fixes or sudden cures. Make a plan; your vitality depends upon steady progress and saving your energy for when you need it most.

DELICATE BALANCE

Wild Uranus in your 4th House of Security continues to shake up things at home, as you nostalgically long for a return to quieter times. But on February 20, a Lunar Eclipse that activates your 4th House tells a different story, with the Moon conjuncting serious Saturn in your 10th House of Career. You may be required to assume additional professional responsibilities, at times isolating you from your family. This dilemma may reach a critical point when Saturn opposes Uranus on November 4. Do whatever you can to preemptively address the issues. Instead of thinking you must choose between home and career, juggle family obligations with your work duties as best you can.

DUTY BOUND

The dramatic Leo Solar Eclipse on August 1 falls in your 9th House of Travel, stimulating fantasies of journeying afar this year. Nevertheless, you might need to forget about the extravagant tropical getaway, backpacking up Mount Kilimanjaro, or digging for gold in the high peaks of the Andes. Instead, consider attending a personal development seminar, a business meeting, or a family gathering, because your ruling planet, Jupiter, in hardworking Capricorn requires you to be much more levelheaded now. Still, its sextile to unpredictable Uranus on March 28, May 21, and November 13 can fire up an old familiar wanderlust. Resist the temptation to just go somewhere as a means of escape. You'll be more productive this year if you use your travel budget wisely.

CONCRETE EVIDENCE

Sagittarius is represented by the centaur—half horse, half human—symbolizing your stand between two worlds. This year, your feet are firmly planted on the ground, even while your thoughts of the future carry your imagination away. But it's no longer about blue sky and unlimited possibilities; it's time to bring your high ideals and philosophies down to earth where the real action awaits. Your spiritual path may take you to less exciting places, but you stand to learn some of the most important lessons of your life if you're willing to take care of mundane matters instead of hunting for your next thrill.

RICK & JEFF'S TIP FOR THE YEAR:
Give It Time

Like a caterpillar's metamorphosis into a butterfly, you, too, have become someone you once could not have even imagined. But this year, as Pluto leaves cavalier Sagittarius and enters ambitious Capricorn, you begin to realize how much work it will be to climb the mountain you have placed in front of you. Your challenge now is to concentrate on the new you and do whatever you must to accomplish your goal, even if it takes years to reach the summit. You won't succeed if you think you can just sprint to the top. Keep your eyes on the distance and take your time.

JANUARY

MAINTAIN YOUR BALANCE

"Cautious optimism" is your slogan for the month as your key planet, Jupiter, moves gradually toward an easy trine with taskmaster Saturn, which is exact on **January 21**. Expansive Jupiter and contractive Saturn are considered to be the cosmic regulators, and you can trust your judgment when they are in harmony, especially in matters pertaining to future career goals and your finances. But don't expect to magically solve everything at once, for you are setting up a long-term pattern that impacts your entire year, reaching fruition around **November 21**. Even with this stabilizing effect, you may feel frustrated, because your sense of freedom is curtailed by responsibilities you assume to keep your life moving successfully. Sweet Venus is in friendly Sagittarius through **January 24**, gracing you with extra warmth and charm, yet energetic Mars's retrograde in your 7th House of Partnerships makes you feel as if little progress is being made, especially with lingering relationship issues. Slow down; wait for the others to catch up to avoid disappointment.

The ambitious Capricorn New Moon on **January 8** in your 2nd House of Money is a great time to create a budget for the months ahead. Prudence and self-discipline serve you well now. The proud Leo Full Moon on **January 22** in your 9th House of Travel and Higher Education encourages you to organize a trip or to expand your mind with a new course of study. But your ideas may take a while to manifest, for mental Mercury slows down and turns retrograde on **January 28**, initiating a three-week phase when you must go over your plans one more time before putting them into action.

KEEP IN MIND THIS MONTH

Your naturally positive attitude can smooth over the rough spots, but denial of difficult emotional issues won't help you achieve happiness.

KEY DATES

JANUARY 2 ★ *innovative solution*

Relationships are fraught with complications now as pushy Mars opposes obstinate Pluto, placing you in the middle of a tug-of-war that has no winner. Someone, perhaps even you, is competing for control and won't give up without a fight. Fortunately, positive Jupiter forms a magical quintile with unconventional Uranus, daring you to think outside the box. An original solution can quickly relieve the pressure from the more immediate struggle for survival.

JANUARY 7-8 ★ *choose wisely*
Your confidence swells on **January 7** when the Moon joins Jupiter, preparing you to make a serious commitment at the calculating New Moon on **January 8**. This lunation falls in your 2nd House of Self-Worth, so rely on your core values to help you choose how best to use your resources.

JANUARY 12 ★ *unnecessary thrills*
Anything goes on **January 12** when attractive Venus squares Uranus and you impulsively express your unfulfilled desires. You're even more charismatic and flirtatious when you find yourself drawn to someone different from your normal ideal. Jupiter's tense semisquare to diffusive Neptune, however, suggests that you may inflate a situation, overstate your case, and miss the mark unless you can differentiate between fantasy and reality. Think through the consequences of your actions to avoid landing in trouble.

SUPER NOVA DAYS
JANUARY 21-22 ★ *a picture says a thousand words*
The fortunate trine between Jupiter and Saturn on **January 21** allows you to blend your innate enthusiasm with solid common sense. Career decisions can have long-lasting consequences, so take your time before making a choice. The demonstrative Leo Full Moon on **January 22** falls in your 9th House of Big Ideas, an area of the chart that resonates with your philosophical style. But intellectual Mercury's conjunction with intuitive Neptune in your 3rd House of Communication makes it difficult to put your imaginative concepts into words. Instead of aiming too high, pull back enough to ground your thoughts. Don't strain yourself to describe every detail, but use images and tone of voice to convey what you're feeling, leaving it to others to fill in the blanks.

JANUARY 24-25 ★ *unfulfilled yearnings*
Venus joins intense Pluto on **January 24** just before leaving your sign and moving into cautious Capricorn the same day. Pluto, in your sign since 1995, follows Venus into Capricorn on **January 25**. This can be an uneasy affair, with passions ignited only to fade out. If you are feeling unsatisfied, consider the price you must pay to meet your needs; then decide if it's worth it or time to finally let go.

FEBRUARY

Your world is a friendly place as February begins thanks to the conjunction of lovely Venus and your key planet, Jupiter, on **February 1**. Your senses are deliciously brought to life, and you are ready to enjoy sweet pleasures. Even a difficult situation can be temporarily ameliorated by this cosmic blessing. Assertive Mars, which just turned direct on **January 30**, gives you the feeling that your life is moving forward again, especially with respect to your goals in relationships. But Winged Messenger Mercury remains retrograde in your 3rd House of Immediate Environment until **February 18**, so there is much to do near home as you revise your schedule and recheck all the details before taking the next step.

Two eclipses this month can add instability to the mix and complicate your life. The first, an intelligent Aquarius New Moon Eclipse in your 3rd House of Communication on **February 6**, reiterates the necessity of paying attention to all the information at your disposal and not just what supports your position. The analytical Virgo Full Moon Eclipse on **February 20** has a more serious flavor as it conjuncts stern Saturn in your 10th House of Career. Whether your past efforts are rewarded or punished, you must respond to a critical situation with determination and then diligently apply yourself to fulfill previous responsibilities, along with current commitments. The Sun's annual opposition to Saturn on **February 24** can slow you down by throwing obstacles in your path. This is a chance to make adjustments to your own attitude so you can turn a difficult situation into one that teaches you an important lesson and gives you the strength to keep going.

> **KEEP IN MIND THIS MONTH**
>
> *The resistance you face may appear external, yet taking responsibility for your contribution to a problem can open the door to a viable solution.*

KEY DATES

FEBRUARY 1 ★ *lasting pleasure*

Delightful Venus joins with Jupiter, the planet of bigger, better, and more, making it easy to touch beauty with your heart. Embrace your feelings . . . while being careful not to ask for too much. This wonderful conjunction in stable Capricorn falls in your 2nd House of Self-Worth, gracing you with an extra boost of confidence and even a possible windfall. If money does come your way now, avoid temptations to spend it on the pursuit of pleasure. Be smart and invest in something that has lasting value instead of a lovely experience that will quickly pass.

FEBRUARY 6-7 ★ *high spirits*
Be ready for unexpected news to arrive at your doorstep, for the high-frequency Aquarius New Moon Eclipse on **February 6** is closely conjunct retrograde Mercury the Trickster. Reconnecting with an old friend or making a new one can turn your life upside down. Sexy Venus creates a supportive sextile aspect with unpredictable Uranus, further fueling your desire for excitement. But even with the pleasant distractions, you must focus on the smallest details or everything could fall apart. Take care of business early in the day so you will be free to enjoy the craziness as it unfolds.

FEBRUARY 10-14 ★ *wishing for love*
The Sun's annual conjunction with imaginative Neptune on **February 10** removes the barriers of rationality and encourages you to wander through your fantasies. The spiritual component to this aspect can be felt deeply through rituals such as attending a religious service, practicing meditation, or even going to an inspiring Sunday-afternoon movie. But you may develop pre–Valentine's Day anxiety early in the week as sensual Venus moves toward an irritating quincunx with physical Mars on **February 13**. Fortunately, love can overcome the blues as the Sun's easy trine to Mars on **February 14** gives you the strength to go after what you want.

SUPER NOVA DAYS
FEBRUARY 18-21 ★ *emotional introspection*
This week's highlight is the critical Virgo Full Moon Eclipse on **February 20** that dynamically squares your freedom-loving sign, creating conflicts between your head and your heart. You might be ready to throw in the towel as your moods swing wildly, making you feel like a compass that cannot get its bearings. Mercury turns direct on **February 18**, yet it takes a few days before things start moving forward again. The Sun's entry into compassionate Pisces on **February 19** confronts you with the realization that you cannot overcome your complex feelings with just positive thought. Venus's annoying quincunx to Saturn on **February 21** can further curtail pleasurable activities because of your commitment to your career. Carving out time to enjoy yourself will take strategic planning.

MARCH

STRENGTH FROM CONFLICT

March is full of contradictions as you face new stresses, overcome challenges, and widen your horizons. Physical Mars enters the deep waters of sensitive Cancer on **March 4** in your 8th House of Intimacy, and it's vitally important that you conquer your fears and swim into these deep waters. Mars opposes potent Pluto on **March 7** for the second time this year—the first was on **January 2**—reopening a conflict that you may have thought was put to rest. The intuitive Pisces New Moon, also on **March 7**, is closely aligned with erratic Uranus, so whatever happens may appear to be out of your control, whether it's precipitated by your behavior or something that appears to suddenly happen to you.

The Sun's entry into fellow fire sign Aries on **March 20** signals the Spring Equinox and gives you the ability to start anew. But the tactful Libra Full Moon on **March 21** in your 11th House of Goals runs into stressful squares with tough guys Pluto and Mars, possibly reactivating the difficulties you experienced around the New Moon on **March 7**. Instead of trying to control everything, carefully observe what's happening and learn something about human dynamics and yourself along the way. A thrilling Venus-Uranus conjunction on **March 28** sextiles beneficent Jupiter, urging you to take a risk by expressing your desires in an unconventional manner. Fortunately, this isn't much of a gamble—you will likely receive what you want. If, however, you push too far, the Sun's square to feisty Mars on **March 30** can incite intense reactions, turning the sweetest love into a temporary battleground.

> **KEEP IN MIND THIS MONTH**
>
> *Instead of succumbing to the illusory importance of always being right, find the pearl of wisdom by listening for the real message beneath the conflict.*

KEY DATES

MARCH 7 ★ *something has to give*

You may have nowhere to go but into the center of the storm as angry Mars takes on relentless Pluto in a fight to the finish. Additionally, today's psychic Pisces New Moon is wired by a conjunction with electric Uranus, exacerbating the situation. You can't win by forcing your solution on others. You may honestly think that you're struggling for your life, yet this exaggerated fear will only deepen the stress. It may be hard to just make unpleasant emotions disappear. Instead, get your thoughts and feelings out into the open without having to change them or fix anyone else.

SUPER NOVA DAYS
MARCH 15-18 ★ *temporary freeze*

Warm Venus and talkative Mercury oppose cold Saturn on **March 15-17**, which can throw icy feelings over even the sweetest relationship. You may withdraw your affections when someone acts more like a parent than a lover, friend, or co-worker. Yet Venus and Mercury trine authoritative Saturn on **March 16-18**, helping you rebuild your courage and express what you are withholding. Meanwhile, a deeper note is sounded by confident Jupiter's tense sesquisquare to Saturn on **March 18**, sending you back into a temporary tail-spin as your integrity is questioned, your finances are stretched, or a past decision turns out to be a poor one. Instead of going into denial and pretending that everything is okay, accept your shortcomings and make the necessary adjustments to anything that is salvageable.

MARCH 21 ★ *collision with the present*

It may be overwhelming to keep up with the changes as the indecisive Libra Full Moon in your 11th House of Friends and Associates places peer pressure on you to make up your mind. Your good intentions in business and personal relationships can be stretched to the max, yet financial problems may be at the source of the current stress. You may be tempted to minimize a difficult situation, but others won't buy into your evasive tactics. Instead, manage the obvious problems now or you'll have bigger ones on your hands later.

MARCH 30 ★ *sweat it out*

You may be riding high with an overabundance of physical energy today, yet it can turn nasty if you don't pay close attention to your suppressed feelings. You might withhold your true motives, especially if you are annoyed with someone. But keeping secrets can inadvertently stir up trouble, fueling ego skirmishes with the tinder of subconscious anger. The best you can do is to find healthy ways to express your-self so that your emotions don't get bottled up.

APRIL

SMOOTH SAILING AHEAD

This month brings welcome relief, for life seems bright and enjoyment is easier to find. Spring is in the air and you may be ready to create something special, for the Sun illuminates your 5th House of Romance until **April 19**. Quicksilver Mercury has you thinking about the lighter side of love as it moves through impulsive Aries in the same house **April 2–17**. Meanwhile, Venus joins the fun 5th House party on **April 6**, remaining there until **April 30**. The playful activity continues throughout the month and fills you with joy, allowing you to express your natural spontaneity and appreciate each day for what it has to offer. The rowdy Aries New Moon on **April 5** reminds you to "be here now" and gives you cosmic permission to thoroughly enjoy the present moment.

The good news gets better, for as the planets move from Aries into sensible Taurus, you receive the benefits of a practical Grand Earth Trine, adding longevity to the good times you have created throughout the month. Together, Mercury and the Sun trine constructive Saturn and intense Pluto on **April 18–20**, perhaps taking the excess wind out of your sails while gracefully slowing you down just enough to assure your successful arrival at your destination. Additionally, the magnetic Scorpio Full Moon on **April 20** builds the power to another level, especially since Scorpio's ruling planet, Pluto, is involved in the grand trine. Meanwhile, sensual Venus, opulent Jupiter, and assertive Mars dynamically align on **April 23–24**, filling you with so much confidence that you are likely to successfully leap before you look. Everything begins to settle down, however, by **April 25**, when you move into a more grounded and more practical phase of your life.

> **KEEP IN MIND THIS MONTH**
>
> *This is no time to be complacent. Although you may be riding great waves of optimism, the currents can get tricky at times, so pay close attention to the details.*

KEY DATES

APRIL 5–6 ★ *cool your jets*

The Aries New Moon on **April 5** is one of initiation, confirming your personal passage from winter into spring. Your spirit is refreshed, and you look out to the broad horizons with much anticipation. Flirty Venus is raring to go as she enters feisty Aries on **April 6**, but she immediately squares deep, dark Pluto. Impulsive expressions of unrestrained desire may not be the smartest way to bring up your unresolved feelings. Your perspective may be warped by fear or jealousy, so it's best to underplay your hand for now.

APRIL 10 ★ *fools rush in*
The willful Sun squares giant Jupiter, strongly encouraging you to express yourself in a big way. Unfortunately, you could easily take the energy to extremes and over-state your case or offend others with your strong opinions. Meanwhile, fast-talking Mercury in brash Aries squares "action oriented" Mars, urging you to fire off that e-mail so quickly, you don't even think about the fallout. If you want to be taken seriously now, moderate your comments and temper your arrogance before uncon-sciously swinging into action.

SUPER NOVA DAYS
APRIL 18–21 ★ *discover your dream*
A penetrating Scorpio Full Moon on **April 20** falls in your 12th House of Destiny, putting you in touch with the power of your intentions. You would be wise to take time away from others this weekend to examine your soul for your personal truth. Fortunately, you are being supported by realistic Saturn and transformational Pluto as thoughtful Mercury and the Sun complete a sturdy Grand Earth Trine on **April 18–21**, gracing you with the necessary stamina to reach your career goals. Apply your strength and wisdom with care and you can motivate others—and yourself—to reach even the highest summit.

APRIL 22–24 ★ *to good to be true*
You are flexible enough now to respond to changing circumstances with boldness and originality, for energetic Mars trines brilliant Uranus on **April 22**. But the intensity of the past week continues to build, reaching a crescendo on **April 24** when the unflagging confidence of your key planet, Jupiter, is fueled by an opposition to Mars. Meanwhile, alluring Venus tensely squares both Mars and Jupiter on **April 23**, making everything look so good that you can dive right into an inviting pool before realizing there's no water in it. Although the opportunities may be wonderful, your tendency not to read the fine print can create a real headache. You may find yourself trying to back out of your promises once you realize that you've overcommitted your heart, your money, or your time.

MAY

TO YOUR HEALTH

This month begins on a practical note when lovely Venus—now moving through your 6th House of Work—creates a harmonious Grand Earth Trine with stabilizing Saturn and transformative Pluto on **May 1**. Although this is a very positive aspect, you may be not so much flying high with enthusiasm as simply enjoying a comfortable balance between taking care of business and having fun. This is an opportune time to reevaluate your current exercise routine, enlist the help of a personal trainer, and give serious thought to eating better: Your 6th House of Health and Habits is strongly emphasized for most of May. If last month was one of excessive indulgence, you may need to compensate now by cleaning up your act. The steady Taurus New Moon on **May 5** can help by reinforcing your determination. Although you can use persistence to your advantage by developing a methodical approach to your daily life, it's dangerous to become too fixed about anything at this time.

The Sun's joyful trine to Jupiter on **May 12** can bring acknowledgment and even monetary reward for the hard work you have been doing. The passionate Scorpio Full Moon on **May 19** falls in your 12th House of Endings, and although the Full Moon is often a time of culmination, you might find it uncharacteristically tough to let go of a project so you can move forward. An exciting Jupiter-Uranus sextile on **May 21** is the second of three this year—the first was on **January 21**, and the last is on **November 21**—that can suddenly open a door to prosperity or, at least, improve your life. Meanwhile, expressive Mercury slows down to turn retrograde on **May 26**, signaling snafus and setbacks if you are moving ahead too fast.

> **KEEP IN MIND THIS MONTH**
>
> *Sometimes it's wise to make the best of what you have instead of frustrating yourself by struggling toward an unreachable goal.*

KEY DATES

MAY 1–2 ★ *stay put*
Instead of seeking greener pastures, Venus's smooth grand trine with somber Saturn and evolutionary Pluto on **May 1** can insist that you stay right where you are. Building on what you already have might be the adventure you've been seeking all along. But Mercury's harsh square with Saturn on **May 2** demands that you think seriously about your relationships. If you're forced to make a career decision that complicates your personal life, don't trade happiness for the illusion of success.

MAY 7-9 ★ *over-inflated importance*

Talkative Mercury forms an annoying sesquisquare with Jupiter on **May 7**, inflating you with grandiose ideas like a balloon being filled with helium. Each thought and plan seems better than the last . . . yet you cannot easily bring any of them back down to earth for practical use. Impulsive Mars's entry into dramatic Leo on **May 9** only encourages your bravado. But Jupiter's retrograde phase begins the same day—it will last until **November 8**—reminding you to expand your horizons by developing what you presently have, rather than hunting down the next best thing.

MAY 12 ★ *success in action*

The Sun in easygoing Taurus forms a fantastic trine with your key planet, Jupiter, blessing you with one of astrology's most positive aspects. There is no holding you back now, as long as you are already heading in the right direction. Unfortunately, it's all too easy to waste this beneficial day by being lazy. You have the power to act with confidence, but may feel so comfortable that you procrastinate. Don't wait for a better time to start on a project—this alignment denotes professional success.

SUPER NOVA DAYS
MAY 18-22 ★ *sweet indulgences*

Lovely Venus perfectly harmonizes with Jupiter on **May 18**, casting a sweet glow onto your life. You feel luckier than usual and can see opportunities for wealth and happiness everywhere you turn. Surprising Uranus is between these two beneficent planets, sextiling Venus on **May 18** and Jupiter on **May 21**, adding excitement and uncertainty to any situation. Romance is in the air as spontaneity fuels your feelings. But an intense Scorpio Full Moon on **May 19** can overwhelm you with concern about a potential loss. Expressing your desires will likely bring satisfaction as long as you don't overstep any boundaries. Give yourself permission to dream, even if you must wake up to reality when the Sun squares Saturn on **May 22**, requiring you to leave any unrealistic fantasies behind.

JUNE

RELATIONSHIP DISCOMFORT

Relationships take center stage as June begins, with the willful Sun, communicator Mercury, and beautiful Venus all in your 7th House of Partnerships. A flirty Gemini New Moon on **June 3** is also in your 7th House, closely aligned with Venus, suggesting the likelihood of sweet love in your life at this time. Additionally, between **June 3 and June 8**, each of these planets forms a supportive sextile with energetic Mars in generous Leo, further telling a story of easygoing interactions. But things may appear better than they truly are, for both Venus and the Sun form a crunchy quincunx with your ruling planet, Jupiter, on **June 10–11**, creating differences of opinion that may have no easy resolution. Venus and the Sun square erratic Uranus on **June 13–14**, driving you to the edge of your feelings. This can be thrilling yet stressful as rushes of adrenaline push you to emotional extremes.

The tension eases when Venus and the Sun trine Neptune on **June 13–14**, blowing a bubble of fantasy around any discomfort and giving you the ability to temporarily evade a difficult situation. But escape tactics won't work, and Mars's uncomfortable quincunx to optimistic Jupiter on **June 15** will alert you if you have lost touch with reality. The opinionated Sagittarius Full Moon on **June 18** can add trauma and drama to an already intense situation, but holds within it the promise of resolution if you are willing to engage your heart fully. Although a pair of tension-producing sesquisquares on **June 25–26** can heighten anxiety, you are likely to gain momentum when aggressive Mars harmoniously trines compulsive Pluto on **June 30**, allowing you to draw on deep reserves of energy.

> ### KEEP IN MIND THIS MONTH
>
> *Although business and personal relationships are problematic, adjusting your attitude in negotiation can get you what you truly want.*

KEY DATES

JUNE 6–9 ★ *it's party time*

A lively day is in store for you as the cosmic lovers, Venus and Mars, connect in a sweet sextile on **June 6**, supporting each other with charm and style. Venus forms a triple conjunction with the Sun and Mercury in lighthearted Gemini throughout the weekend in your 7th House of Others, so it may be difficult to resist the enticing offers from friends. You could be lacing up your dancing shoes on **June 7** when the Moon hooks up with active Mars in dramatic Leo. Since Mercury is retrograde, don't assume that everyone else is ready to party until you double-check your plans. The potential for enjoyment is so great that you might still be glowing when Venus makes contact with the Sun on June 9, when you head back to work.

JUNE 12-13 ★ *beautiful illusion*

You are so attracted to someone or something that you act in an impulsive way you may quickly regret. The graceful Libra Moon completes a sociable Grand Air Trine with the Sun and Venus in your 7th House of Partnerships and mystical Neptune in your 3rd House of Communication, making it easy to believe in your dreams. But the Sun and Venus also square "wild and crazy" Uranus on **June 12–13,** giving you an "I don't care what happens" attitude that just adds to the excitement. Still, it's a smart idea to consider what you're doing before it's too late to escape.

SUPER NOVA DAYS
JUNE 18-21 ★ *the impossible dream*

The philosophical Sagittarius Full Moon on **June 18** is conjunct retrograde Pluto and opposed the Sun and Venus, pitting your desires against someone else's beliefs. You may know what you want, even if it's out of reach. Still, you're ready to struggle against all odds to reach satisfaction. You are playing for keeps with Mercury turning direct on **June 19** and the Sun entering tenacious Cancer on **June 20**, marking the Summer Solstice. But when Mars opposes nebulous Neptune on **June 21**, you may temporarily lose direction as your fantasies seep into reality, confusing you and setting the scene for wasted efforts and misunderstandings.

JUNE 26 ★ *slow growth*

It's hard for you to get comfortable when expansive Jupiter is stressing restrictive Saturn. The anxious sesquisquare between these two planetary giants is exact today, causing restlessness and frustration because you cannot accept a great opportunity that's come your way. If previous obligations are preventing your growth, you must fulfill them before moving on. You may be blocked by your boss or some other authority figure, but hard work and a positive attitude can overcome the resistance—though it could take more time.

JULY

THE ROAD OF EXCESS

Financial opportunities may come your way this month, but if you overstep your boundaries, they could slip through your fingers. The Cancer New Moon on **July 2** followed by sweet Venus's opposition to opulent Jupiter on **July 3** tempts you to overindulge your senses and spend money extravagantly. The New Moon falls in your 8th House of Shared Resources, so you might benefit by someone's investment in your work. A series of oppositions to big-thinking Jupiter in your 2nd House of Self-Worth through **July 19**, however, can add stress as emotions get mixed up with financial considerations. The Sun opposes Jupiter on **July 9**, encouraging you to set your goals so high that they may remain out of reach. But Mercury's tense opposition to obsessive Pluto on **July 10**, along with impetuous Mars's conjunction to Pluto the same day, tells a very different story. If you have overextended yourself financially or energetically, you will receive a wake-up call, forcing you to replace blind optimism with cautious realism.

The Moon joins Jupiter in ambitious Capricorn on **July 17**, hyping up your enthusiasm again, but the Capricorn Full Moon on July 18 can mark a turning point, with your inflated confidence gradually diminishing over the next couple of weeks. Although you may miss critical details on **July 22–25**, you adjust willingly because you are fully committed to success. Be cautious, for "action hero" Mars trines Jupiter on **July 26**, making your future look so great that you're signing on the dotted line or saying "I do" before you even realize what you've done.

> **KEEP IN MIND THIS MONTH**
>
> *It's difficult to say no when everything appears wonderful, but sometimes recognizing your own limitations is a better strategy than exhausting yourself by taking on too much.*

KEY DATES

JULY 2–3 ★ *deep dive*
The nurturing Cancer New Moon on **July 2** falls in your 8th House of Deep Sharing, and you fear expressing what's in your heart. Since you often override your feelings with action, being pulled into an emotional drama brings you to the edge of your comfort zone. It gets easier as tender Venus opposes joyous Jupiter on **July 3**. Everything seems more pleasant, but you could end up having little to show for the day as you move from one enjoyable diversion to the next.

JULY 5–6 ★ *out of your hands*

Avoid making impulsive decisions on **July 5** when thinking Mercury squares erratic Uranus. Mars's sesquisquare to Jupiter on **July 6** indicates that your choices will be ill fated if you err on the side of excessive idealism. Other harmonious aspects the same day suggest that it will be difficult for you to restrain yourself. Go ahead and take a risk, but don't fool yourself into thinking that you're in full control of the situation.

SUPER NOVA DAYS
JULY 9–10 ★ *back down to size*

The Sun's annual opposition to giant Jupiter on **July 9** floods you with false confidence and ungrounded positive thinking. Overcommitments or arrogance will be quickly checked by an intense Mercury-Pluto opposition and a frustrating Mars-Saturn conjunction on **July 10**. When reality brings you back to earth, you have no choice but to confront the tangible obstacles before you. Don't just throw in the towel; revise your plan to make it work. Once you face the limits of your finances and your calendar, you'll be able to make a practical itinerary for your next adventure.

JULY 18–19 ★ *ambitious attitude*

The industrious Capricorn Full Moon on **July 18** in your 2nd House of Self-Worth prompts you to reassess your skills so you can increase your income. But if you are asking for more money, make sure to plan your presentation carefully: What with Mercury's opposition to Jupiter on **July 19**, you could easily overlook crucial details. Still, your cheerfulness is contagious as you communicate what's on your mind with vision and emotional sensitivity.

JULY 26 ★ *more than just a good time*

Your anticipation of success grows as messenger Mercury moves into demonstrative Leo and your 9th House of Big Ideas. Additionally, self-directed Mars harmoniously trines joyous Jupiter, adding more enthusiasm to the day. Meanwhile, the sensual Taurus Moon completes a Grand Earth Trine, luring you toward indulgent activities. Instead of using this great potential just to party, apply your positive approach toward achieving practical goals.

AUGUST

LISTEN TO YOUR DREAMS

You dream of grand adventure—perhaps exploring a foreign country—on **August 1**, when the total Solar Eclipse in dramatic Leo falls in your 9th House of Higher Thought and Faraway Places. Whether or not you really travel this month is less important than allowing yourself to visualize life beyond your current horizons, and thereby opening yourself to the possibilities of doing things outside your daily routine. The 9th House also symbolizes higher education, so your desire for additional learning could reawaken. But this doesn't necessarily mean increasing your skill set; it's more about a journey of the mind that can take you to places you've never been.

A second eclipse this month on **August 16**—an intelligent Aquarius Full Moon Eclipse in your 3rd House of Data Collection—represents a very different type of learning than the philosophical 9th House. The 3rd House refers to acquiring information on a day-to-day basis, so the Moon's conjunction to intuitive Neptune during this eclipse suggests that inspiration comes to you through signs and symbols rather than words. Your dreams may be quite active at this time, for instance, telling you much about where you are and what lies ahead. A rare third lunation this month—a hardworking Virgo New Moon on **August 30**—indicates good fortune if you are willing to accept more responsibilities. This New Moon in your 11th House of Friends and Wishes conjuncts taskmaster Saturn and trines joyful Jupiter. It's a sure sign that your involvement with others at work or play can expand your sphere of activities as long as you take your role to heart.

> **KEEP IN MIND THIS MONTH**
>
> *Even when your dreams are unrealistic, they infuse your soul with hope and focus your attention onto your long-term goals.*

KEY DATES

AUGUST 5-6 ★ *baby steps*

Venus harmoniously trines intense Pluto on **August 5** just before slipping into cautious Virgo on **August 6**. Your dreams of an upcoming trip are compelling, but pragmatic concerns could force you to reconsider your plans. Mercury's opposition to whimsical Neptune keeps your fantasies alive, but hot-tempered Mars opposes unpredictable Uranus the same day, galvanizing your hopes and instigating impulsive action. Although you are sorely tempted to do something crazy, it's probably better to move cautiously now.

AUGUST 13 ★ *look on the bright side*

Beautiful Venus meets up with austere Saturn, so you may feel a lack of love, money, or pleasure. You are more likely to do the responsible thing now, possibly passing up an invitation for a good time. You can be quite realistic, even a bit negative, convincing yourself that a wonderful opportunity is not worth pursuing. Don't be overly critical; seeing the potential in a current situation can help you get back on a more positive track.

SUPER NOVA DAYS
AUGUST 15-17 ★ *journey of the soul*

The Sun's opposition to nebulous Neptune on **August 15** opens your heart to fantasy, but your mind can shut it down with Mercury's conjunction to somber Saturn. The eccentric Aquarius Full Moon Eclipse on **August 16** confuses you with its conjunction to Neptune. Fortunately, a harmonious trine between sweet Venus and beneficent Jupiter brings material or emotional rewards that can increase your feelings of joy. A dynamic square between Mars and Pluto on **August 17** may play out as an intense power struggle with someone at work, but open warfare will leave neither party satisfied. Transform any negative feelings into constructive actions through extra-hard work and a process of forgiveness.

AUGUST 23-24 ★ *don't fence me in*

Unexpected events can turn your life upside down this weekend with mentally active Mercury and congenial Venus opposing electric Uranus and quincunx Neptune. It's hard to relax. Still, trying to conform to social norms will only make you more frustrated, and an eagerness to please others can distract you from your personal truth. Do what makes you happy, but be willing to readjust your actions based upon your changing desires.

AUGUST 27-30 ★ *critical disclosure*

An intense couple of days lead up to the stabilizing Virgo New Moon in your public 10th House on **August 30**. You feel pressured to be nice instead of speaking honestly when Mercury and Venus square powerful Pluto on **August 27-28**. Acknowledge your feelings, even if others may not approve of them. It's crucial to bring your emotions out into the open without blaming anyone in order to avoid confusion later on.

SEPTEMBER

INTO THE FUTURE

September begins with four planets in your 11th House of Friends and Wishes, reminding you how much others can help you clarify your aspirations. This month you are challenged to find a healthy balance between your present responsibilities and your hopes for a better future. The planetary currents force you to meet your obligations as the focused Virgo Sun conjuncts authoritative Saturn in your 10th House of Public Responsibility on **September 3**. But the Sun quickly moves on to harmonize with lenient Jupiter on **September 4**, coaxing you to believe that you can slack off and get by on your previous efforts. The long-term effects of Jupiter's trine to Saturn on **September 8**, however, bring your overeager attitude and inflationary thinking down to earth, allowing you to successfully launch a significant project.

The psychic Pisces Full Moon on **September 15** conjuncts unpredictable Uranus. It can all be unsettling, especially if social activities distract you from your own feelings or family issues. A powerful square between the illuminating Sun and domineering Pluto on **September 20** can place obstacles in your career path, especially if your drive to succeed has caused you to overstep the boundaries of a professional association. Your forward progress seems to slow as communicator Mercury readies to turn retrograde on **September 24**, initiating a three-week period of reflection and reevaluation of your relationships with friends and how you operate as part of a group. The rational Libra New Moon on **September 29** in your 11th House of Goals encourages you to look ahead, rather than behind, and to creatively visualize your unrealized dreams.

> **KEEP IN MIND THIS MONTH**
>
> *No matter how eager you are to run up the mountain, you're better off slowing down, talking to others about your mutual goals, and working together for everyone's benefit.*

KEY DATES

SEPTEMBER 4 ★ *mission not impossible*
Although you probably won't lose sight of your responsibilities, today's easy trine from the Sun to optimistic Jupiter paints a very pleasant picture. Your spirit lifts, but you remain practical enough to make a plan that assures success. Still, your overenthusiasm could get the best of you, so if you find yourself convinced that no job is too big and nothing is impossible, then think again. Sustained common sense will all but guarantee a fair return on your investment of time and money.

SUPER NOVA DAYS
SEPTEMBER 7-9 ★ *play it cool*
Your ruling planet, Jupiter, is the king of bigger, better, and more—and he is overactive these days with squares to feisty Mars on **September 7**, chatty Mercury on **September 8**, and friendly Venus on **September 9**. Additionally, Jupiter turns direct on **September 8**, turning up your power another notch. You could easily go overboard, taking on too much work, for instance, or spending too much money. You want it all right now, and it will be challenging to hold yourself back from having another sweet dessert or buying that original piece of artwork you've dreamed of owning. Fortunately, you receive powerful assistance when "boss planet" Saturn trines Jupiter on **September 8**—the second of three such aspects this year. If you don't exercise enough self-restraint, unexpected consequences could make extravagance and self-indulgence more costly. Impulsive or reckless acts are not likely to turn out well.

SEPTEMBER 12 ★ *unpredictable storm*
The Sun's annual opposition to Uranus on **September 12** can suddenly shake things up at home, releasing stored-up tension and unexpressed emotions. The danger comes from your fear of change rather than change itself. Trying to suppress the brewing storm will only feed its intensity. Even if you are tempted to maintain the status quo, remember that opportunities for growth will likely follow once the air is cleared of negativity.

SEPTEMBER 20-22 ★ *spiritual solution*
The careful Virgo Sun in your 10th House of Career squares dark Pluto on **September 20**, shining the light of analysis onto a stressful situation at work. The path through this tough emotional terrain can stir your anger, especially if someone is working against you. Nevertheless, you are driven to find an answer. Mars's trine to Neptune on **September 21** can reduce the pressure, dissolving your ego's need for dominance. The Autumn Equinox is marked by the Sun's entry into diplomatic Libra on **September 22**, illuminating your 11th House of Friends. Remember, it's less important to be right than it is to get along with others.

SAGITTARIUS

OCTOBER

MIRROR, MIRROR, ON THE WALL

Your normally cheerful and outgoing style can soften during October as you become more concerned with your spiritual development and metaphysical growth. This shift begins as dynamic Mars in Libra forms a supportive sextile with obsessive Pluto in Sagittarius, giving you plenty of energy to apply yourself toward whatever you desire. But Mars slips into secretive Scorpio in your 12th House of Privacy on **October 4**, beginning a six-week period when your energy is directed within, instead of onto external circumstances. With gentle Venus already in your 12th House, your desire is for peace rather than just personal accomplishment. This can be somewhat confusing for you if your goals start to seem less meaningful than connecting with your own soul. Mercury, however, is retrograde in your 11th House of Friends until **October 15** and stays in this house throughout the month, reminding you again and again that your connection with your colleagues and close friends should not be sacrificed just because you are seeking solitude.

The impetuous Aries Full Moon on **October 14** in your 5th House of Creativity emphasizes your need for fun and can make you feel more childlike than usual. Enjoying yourself just feels right . . . but don't forget to finish what you've started in preparation for Mercury's direct turn the following day. The passionate Scorpio New Moon on **October 28** in your 12th House can blur the boundaries between your inner and outer worlds while also pushing you to complete your contemplative phase. You must be ready for next month's large-scale changes.

> **KEEP IN MIND THIS MONTH**
>
> *You're standing between two worlds, with one foot comfortably planted on familiar ground and the other ready to step somewhere.*

KEY DATES

OCTOBER 5-6 ★ *talk, talk, talk*
Retrograde Mercury joins the Sun in your 11th House of Friends on **October 6**, possibly bringing an old acquaintance back into your life and filling your calendar with social interactions. Together, the Sun and Mercury square boundless Jupiter in your 2nd House of Self-Worth on **October 5-6**, giving you ample opportunity to ramble on about yourself. A supportive sextile from endearing Venus to Jupiter adds enough sweetness to let you get away with the self-promotional talk as long as you know when to stop. You don't have to try so hard to be part of the team; others are willing to accept the real you.

OCTOBER 10–11 ★ *find stable ground*

Seductive Venus in passionate Scorpio trines "wild and crazy" Uranus on **October 10** and squares diffusive Neptune on **October 11**. You are eager to delve into your fantasies, but with Venus in your 12th House of Secrets, you tend to keep them to yourself. Even without saying a word, romantic potential can spark the air with excitement. But Neptune's involvement can turn your creative imagination into a confusing mix of desire and fear—you might even be attracted to something that exists only within your own mind. Nevertheless, don't relinquish your dreams until you check out their viability in the real world.

OCTOBER 14–18 ★ *fun and games*

The rambunctious Aries Full Moon on **October 14** falls in your 5th House of Children and Romance, expanding your involvement with kids or bringing out your own inner child. With contemplative Neptune trine the Sun and sextile the Moon during this lunation, your imagination is heightened, making it all too easy to slip into fantasy realms without even realizing what's happened. Amorous Venus turns up your love light when it enters your sign on **October 18**, inviting you to indulge your senses. You're likely to overdo—but with your dazzling charm you can get away with it.

SUPER NOVA DAYS
OCTOBER 26–28 ★ *turning point*

Jupiter, the cosmic magnifying lens, turns up the volume in your brain as it squares thoughtful Mercury on **October 26** and sextiles active Mars on **October 27**, making everything seem overly important. Although others may accuse you of a lack of discretion, you are just trying to live life to the fullest. You have the energy to accomplish a lot as long as you don't spread yourself too thin. You are eager for the next intense experience, and the passionate New Moon in Scorpio on **October 28** can help you narrow your scope and gather your forces for what's around the corner.

NOVEMBER

READY TO ROCK AND ROLL

You've had enough time to review your year and realign with your true purpose. Now it's time to make use of everything you've learned along the way and to fully engage in building the future you imagine. Your restlessness may approach an all-time high as dutiful Saturn in your 10th House of Public Status opposes rebellious Uranus in your 4th House of Security on **November 4**. This is the first of five such oppositions that will not be completed until **July 26, 2010**—and it opens the door to an existential dilemma pitting your need for stability against your chronic longing for freedom. Although there may be no simple solution, you now have an opportunity to better understand how these mutually exclusive desires create stress in your life.

The sensible Taurus Full Moon on **November 13** in your practical 6th House of Work squares elusive Neptune, reminding you of the great chasm between your dreams and the task at hand. You are a bit overwhelmed by the potential in your life at this time, yet you might not know how to make the most of it. It's crucial, however, to stay fully attentive to the most pragmatic issues before you in preparation for lucky Jupiter's third and final trine this year to Saturn on **November 21**. The inspirational Sagittarius New Moon on **November 27** is conjunct both cerebral Mercury and courageous Mars, amplifying your vitality and bringing you an abundance of good cheer that should last throughout much of the holiday season.

> **KEEP IN MIND THIS MONTH**
>
> *Make necessary adjustments to lessen your anxiety while developing strategies to live with those circumstances that are currently unchangeable.*

KEY DATES

NOVEMBER 1-4 ★ *close to the edge*

The powerful opposition between stoic Saturn and radical Uranus on **November 4** is activated by the Moon as it moves through Sagittarius on **November 1**, asking you to confront deep dissatisfaction in a very personal manner. Venus then follows the Moon, squaring Saturn and Uranus on **November 3**, increasing your discomfort as irrepressible desires for new adventure conflict directly with your present obligations. Mercury's entry into obsessive Scorpio on **November 4** gives you additional mental acuity with which to get at the real significance of what's happening. You must reinvent your life, but don't push for change too hard and fast or you might lose more than you gain.

SUPER NOVA DAYS

NOVEMBER 10-13 ★ *choices, choices, and more choices*

The Sun trines Uranus the Awakener on **November 10** in a wave of excitement that suddenly ripples through your life, proclaiming the infinite possibilities ahead. But you are brought back to reality by the Sun's sextile to Saturn on **November 11**, reining in your enthusiasm. Venus's conjunction with Pluto and its entry into Capricorn on **November 12** reinforce the seriousness of this shift. Still, the biggest news is Jupiter's third and final supportive sextile to Uranus on **November 12**—the previous ones were **May 28 and April 21**—throwing open the window of opportunity. It is challenging to maintain stability with this much activity; even the stubborn Taurus Full Moon on **November 13** will likely add confusion with its square to illusory Neptune. Consider your options and then pare back your choices before making a final decision about your new direction.

NOVEMBER 16 ★ *free speech*

Energetic Mars enters boisterous Sagittarius, and it remains in your 1st House of Personality until **December 27**, increasing your adrenaline and raising your spirits. Investigator Mercury in intense Scorpio harmonizes with open-minded Jupiter, austere Saturn, and explosive Uranus—pushing your need for intellectual freedom over the edge of social acceptance. You are eager now to initiate discussions about unconventional topics. You may be ready to go places others would rather avoid, so ask before you launch into a controversial subject of your choice.

NOVEMBER 21-23 ★ *window of opportunity*

Make a commitment when hopeful Jupiter trines realistic Saturn on **November 21**, or reactivate a project you started around **January 21 or September 8**—the previous occurrences of this aspect. Don't let this time pass without taking well-considered action toward the goals you now believe to be most important to you. The Sun and Mercury enter adventurous Sagittarius on **November 21 and November 23**, respectively, encouraging you to aim your arrow of intention at distant yet reachable goals.

DECEMBER

METAMORPHOSIS

Your month begins joyfully with messenger Mercury, energetic Mars, and the bright Sun—all in uplifting Sagittarius—infusing you with an early dose of holiday spirit. Throughout the month, however, these planets migrate into the more cautious realms of Capricorn, where they each conjoin Pluto, forcing you into an alchemical process of transmutation. This won't be easy terrain. The changes you are undertaking are not small, incremental steps; they demand total engagement and can result in a complete metamorphosis. Mercury, Mars, and the Sun reactivate the tension of last month's Saturn-Uranus opposition when they each square this opposition on **December 5-6, December 10-12, and December 15**. Your current discomfort with the status quo increases the potential for major change.

Communicator Mercury is the first planet to enter ambitious Capricorn and conjuncts dark Pluto on **December 12**—the same day that a Gemini Full Moon in your 7th House of Partners stimulates relationship activities. Optimistic thinking is not valuable now if you use it to avoid the painful issues you must face. The Sun's entry into Capricorn on **December 21** marks the Winter Solstice—the shortest day of the year and a time for contemplation rather than action. The Sun's conjunction with Pluto on **December 22** once again reminds you of what you are leaving behind to prepare for the unknown journey ahead. Assertive Mars is the last planet to leave your sign, entering strategic Capricorn on **December 27**—the same day as the New Moon. Mars's conjunction with Pluto on **December 28** is the last of the intense Pluto conjunctions, increasing your resolve to change and gracing you with both the willpower and the resources to follow through with your plans.

> **KEEP IN MIND THIS MONTH**
>
> *Your current transitions are profound, although it will take months before you fully appreciate what's happened and completely understand your new direction.*

KEY DATES

DECEMBER 1 ★ *just rewards and sweet desserts*

A lovely conjunction between sensual Venus and opulent Jupiter on **December 1** can put a smile on your face and extra money in your pocket. It's joined by a rather serious Capricorn Moon in your 2nd House of Resources, suggesting that a cautious investment of time or money will be most prudent now. Avoid temptations to overspend your emotional capital or to buy anything you don't really need.

SUPER NOVA DAYS
DECEMBER 10–12 ★ *emotional minefield*

The Sun and Mars dynamically square "anything goes" Uranus on **December 10 and December 12**, triggering a temper tantrum. The scattered Gemini Full Moon on **December 12** may pull your moods all over the map, but you won't be very lighthearted as your thinking intensifies in response to Mercury's conjunction to passionate Pluto. You could minimize upsets through hard physical work or strenuous exercise, yet you won't likely escape the emotional tension. If you withhold your feelings, they can take you by surprise as unexpected events turn your life inside out.

DECEMBER 15 ★ *patience is a virtue*

If you recently went over an emotional edge, circumstances now rein you in—and you won't like having your wings clipped. Although you cannot fly freely, retreat won't solve anything, either. The frustration from assertive Mars's feisty square to repressive Saturn can be quite irksome, especially if you're itching for thrills and adventure. You are wise to postpone your favorite activities until you address the immediate blockages. Be persistent, but don't try to force an issue. Slow down and let the resistance play out.

DECEMBER 24–26 ★ *just in time*

Although you may not be as high-spirited as usual during this normally festive season, a lively Mercury-Uranus sextile on **December 24** can electrify you into action and turn on the holiday lights. You return to reality, however, when Mercury harmonizes with somber Saturn on **December 26**, making you feel as if the party has ended all too quickly. Nevertheless, you are uncharacteristically eager to return to the mundane work of organizing your life and making your plans for next year.

DECEMBER 27–31 ★ *letting go*

The conservative Capricorn New Moon on **December 27** is reinforced by Mars, Pluto, Mercury, and Jupiter in this sign—but Venus's conjunction to idealistic Neptune has you vacillating between your real-world responsibilities and the dreamy illusions you are unwilling to let die. The Mars-Pluto conjunction on **December 28** strengthens your resolve, while Mercury's contact with jovial Jupiter on **December 31** puts you into a celebratory mood at the last moment, making you eager to ring out the old year and enthusiastically bring on the new.

♑

CAPRICORN
DECEMBER 22–JANUARY 19

CAPRICORN OVERVIEW

Optimistic Jupiter is in ambitious Capricorn this year, making it a great time for major expansion and significant personal growth. Traditional astrology's most fortunate planet brings opportunities for increased public recognition, as well as a deeper understanding of yourself. This enables you to recognize your past patterns and see how your successes and failures are connected in meaningful ways. Your ambitions are empowered by these insights, allowing you to plan with foresight and common sense. It's vital, though, to trust yourself; Jupiter in your 1st House of Self represents the power of your innate wisdom. Even if you miscalculate and make a mistake, you can quickly learn from it and adjust your course of action accordingly. **There is no time to settle for less in your life, either personally or professionally.** Aim high and boldly step forward to raise your life to the next level.

Saturn, the planet of hard, cold reality—and the ruler of your sign—is outward bound this year, too, as it occupies your 9th House of Travel and Higher Education. Work-related trips are not as much fun as a week spent on the beach, but can certainly elevate your professional profile. Taking classes or doing independent study is a definite asset for advancing your career. Serious Saturn and optimistic Jupiter form harmonious trines with each other on January 21, September 8, and November 21 that align your current reality with your future hopes. This combination helps you organize plans with a healthy balance of the real and the ideal to ensure your success. On November 4, dutiful Saturn makes the first of five challenging oppositions with independent Uranus that recur through 2009 and 2010. **If the weight of responsibility or drudgery of routine is too great, you may need to force a break to find some breathing room and reassess your situation.** The long-term purpose of this aspect is to reconstruct your life in a way that allows you more freedom of expression and establishes a healthy balance between security and surprise.

Slow-moving Pluto's fifteen-year transit of your sign continues a powerful process of transformation that saw a boost when Jupiter joined this deep, dark planet on December 11, 2007. Visions of major change that were stirred by fear or desire will rumble below the surface throughout this year and can shake your normally stoic view of reality. **You sense that there is so much more to be gained from life; Pluto's message is that letting go is a prerequisite for satisfaction.** Outmoded beliefs about yourself may confront you dramatically to show you how they still shape your thinking. These are golden opportunities to recognize where change is imperative. Many chances to purge old habits will occur this year, but they will be especially potent when mental Mercury, the willful Sun, and active Mars engage Pluto on December 12, 22, and 28.

PURSUIT OF HAPPINESS

The personal growth spurred by expansive Jupiter's passage through your sign is bound to alter your relationships this year. Cautious and caring Cancer in your 7th House of Partnerships tends to make you particularly protective of your spouse. Nurturing others can be such a priority that you unconsciously conceal your needs to maintain the status quo. However, the magnifying power of Jupiter in your 1st House is reflected through its opposite, the 7th House. Just as you expect and need more for yourself now, your requirements for romantic and emotional fulfillment are increasing, too. Pressure on a current relationship will force it to grow or, perhaps, begin to unravel. If you bury your feelings in an attempt to avoid complications, the long-term costs of distrust and disappointment may be greater than whatever price you pay right now. A Solar Eclipse in dramatic Leo on August 1 occurs in your 8th House of Intimacy, where it initiates changes in how you connect on the deepest levels. Open your heart to take more risks by expressing your desires. Don't let pride stop you from taking this significant step toward a more satisfying relationship.

LADDER OF SUCCESS

Professional advancement is quite likely this year if you put in the effort to elevate your profile. It's possible that your ambitions can no longer be contained in someone else's employ, leading you to start your own business. The strategic Jupiter-Saturn trines on January 21, September 8, and November 21 are excellent for charting your career course, whether you're self-employed or seeking a promotion within an organization. Mercury, the communication planet, is retrograde in your 6th House of Work from May 26 until June 19 and your 10th House of Career from September 24 through October 15. Avoid making major moves during these periods, which are better suited for research and review than initiating new projects.

UNEXPECTED SOURCES

You tend to take a very practical and down-to-earth approach to earning money, but this year more cash can come your way if you're experimental. Uranus, the ruler of your 2nd House of Income, picks up favorable sextiles from generous Jupiter on March 28, May 21, and November 12. These supportive aspects could improve your finances in unexpected ways. A sudden windfall or bright new idea might put you on the road to increased prosperity. Thinking outside the box increases your odds of discovering one of these veins of material success, so an open mind could be your greatest resource this year.

WATCH YOUR APPETITE

Expansive Jupiter in your 1st House of Physicality makes this an especially important year to take care of your body. This indulgent planet allows you to put on extra pounds more quickly than usual; fortunately, you are more motivated to exercise as well. This combination could lead to excesses in both directions with swings in diet, appetite, and behavior that might feel fine now but could produce problems in the future. Establish goals and guidelines for consumption and activity, but be flexible enough to allow exceptions from time to time. Jupiter's judgmental side is not an asset to good health, which is better served by forgiveness than guilt.

THINK BEFORE YOU ACT

You may be so occupied with your own activities and ambitions this year that home and family get less attention than usual. However, the Sun's entry in your 4th House of Foundations on March 19 could spark a desire to enhance your living space—or might reveal a budding domestic crisis that requires action. Avoid a tendency to seek a quick fix that instantly resolves the problem; haste will only add fuel to the fire. A slower approach will take more time but also produce a happier outcome. Impatient Mars—the ruler of your 4th House—conjuncts Saturn on July 10, focusing your energy onto family obligations. Think carefully about what commitments you're willing to assume before agreeing to any significant changes in your relationships or daily routine.

TRAVEL FOR A PURPOSE

Saturn, your ruling planet, is transiting your 9th House of Higher Thought and Faraway Places this year, putting you in a serious state of mind. Examining the meaning of your life is not an abstract exercise but rather a helpful step in building a bridge between where you are and where you want to go. Studying philosophy, religion, metaphysics, or foreign cultures enriches you with a wider perspective to support your goals. Don't take travel lightly, however, it could be more arduous than usual right now. Instead of visiting ten cities in two weeks, for example, concentrate on deepening your experience of one or two places. Journeys may be more complicated around February 20 when a Lunar Eclipse falls in your 9th House, and in mid-August when restrictive Saturn joins sociable Venus and mobile Mercury.

 TRUST YOUR INTUITION

The worlds of spirituality, dreams, and imagination become more tangible for you this year. Jupiter, the ruler of your 12th House of Soul Consciousness, in your physical 1st House puts you in direct contact with these sources of inspiration. You may feel guided in your actions, as if you are being carried forward by forces greater than your own. Have faith in what you're doing, even if you can't come up with a rational explanation for every move. This is a time to trust the universe by learning how to ride its energy waves, rather than having to paddle so hard to get where you want to go.

RICK & JEFF'S TIP FOR THE YEAR:
The Power of Positive Thought

In the ongoing struggle between your hope for more and the fear of losing what you already have, go for hope this year. Overcoming a tendency to wrap your ambitions in a blanket of doubt called "reality" is relatively easy now. Whenever you encounter an obstacle, step back from it instead of attacking the problem or simply giving up. Lucky Jupiter is on your side and will provide you with solutions when you take the time to let them develop slowly. This isn't about being passive; just allow your natural wisdom to evolve and give you the answers you need.

JANUARY

CONTROLLED CHAOS

You have a natural ability to turn new ideas into reality, and it's bolstered by the New Moon in methodical Capricorn on **January 8**. The annual conjunction of the creative Sun and nurturing Moon in your sign receives a supportive sextile from inventive Uranus, blending originality with discipline—a perfect combination for putting more spice into your life. Expansive Jupiter may send you on a detour into fantasyland with an impractical semisquare to dreamy Neptune on **January 12**. However, the bubbles of illusion settle back down to earth on **January 21** when Jupiter aligns in a constructive trine with your realistic ruling planet, Saturn. This positive aspect first appeared last spring and will return on **September 8 and November 21** to give you the kind of strategic perspective on your future that's essential for long-range planning.

The Full Moon in generous Leo on **January 22** lands in your 8th House of Deep Sharing to shed light on intimacy and trust issues, altering the nature of your closest relationships. Honesty and high hopes are your allies as you learn that giving more gets you more in return. Potent Pluto enters your sign on **January 25**, where it will stir the roots of your soul; it then retreats to Sagittarius on **June 13** before returning to Capricorn on **November 26**, where it will stay for fifteen years. The immediate effect may not be obvious, but a powerful and long-lasting transformation trend is under way. Informative Mercury begins a three-week retrograde cycle in your 2nd House of Income on **January 28** that is better for reorganizing finances and repairing resources than spending freely. On the other hand, energetic Mars goes direct on **January 30** to jump-start stalled work projects or motivate you to improve your health.

> **KEEP IN MIND THIS MONTH**
>
> *Strong emotional exchanges can leave you feeling unsafe, but if you avoid hasty reactions you'll discover a solid place to stand.*

KEY DATES

JANUARY 6 ★ *tough love*
A slick sextile between the Sun and Uranus sparks creativity and an eagerness for new experiences. However, a tense square between demanding Saturn and sensitive Venus can limit the love or approval you feel from others and possibly make you doubt yourself. Acting independently is a quick and easy solution, but digging in and dealing with relationship issues will have more lasting effects.

JANUARY 13-14 ★ *incomplete message*

Mental Mercury and the Sun both tangle with restrained Saturn on **January 13**, which can make it more difficult to get your message across. If you are frustrated by someone's lack of understanding, don't push the point. Unless detailed information is vital, settle for communication that conveys the general idea. A brilliant and sharp-edged quintile between active Mars and productive Saturn on **January 14** helps you come up with inventive solutions and clever shortcuts to accomplish difficult tasks without breaking a sweat.

JANUARY 20-21 ★ *unorthodox approach*

The Sun enters innovative Aquarius and your 2nd House of Resources on **January 20**, awakening new ideas about making money and maximizing your talents. Socially conscious Aquarius reminds you that being of service to others can also be financially rewarding. The Sun's unsteady semisquare with Uranus, Aquarius's ruling planet, on **January 21** brings out your rebellious side. Turning that unconventional attitude in a creative direction gives you a sense of freedom and a fresh appreciation for your abilities. The harmonious trine between optimistic Jupiter and practical Saturn on the same day provides a well-organized framework for your ambitions.

SUPER NOVA DAYS
JANUARY 24-25 ★ *change of heart*

Romantic Venus dives into a conjunction with dark Pluto early in the morning of **January 24**, pushing relationship issues to the edge. Intense feelings of desire or distaste leave you far from satisfaction. Learning to let go of what's no longer needed now allows you to make room for a deeper love later. Venus then enters Capricorn, a safe, high ground of realism, turning fear into action and desire into determination. Pluto's entry into strategic Capricorn on **January 25** begins a long process of transformation that can ultimately increase your power and sense of purpose.

JANUARY 29-30 ★ *safe landing*

A slippery Venus-Neptune semisquare early on **January 29** serves up romantic fantasies and uncertainty about your self-worth. That evening, however, stabilizing Saturn forms a strengthening trine with Venus to put emotions and relationships on a more solid footing. Active Mars awakens from its retrograde state on **January 30** in your 6th House of Employment, sending a "go" signal for making changes on the job.

FEBRUARY

FINANCIAL FANTASY

Two eclipses are the key astrological events this month. An intelligent Aquarius Solar Eclipse on **February 6** lands in your 2nd House of Money. This special New Moon should stimulate fresh income-producing ideas; however, disorienting Neptune's conjunction to the eclipse may blur your usual good sense and tempt you to spend carelessly. Investing in objects and activities that inspire you will be positive as long as your dreams are balanced with a strong dose of realism. Maintaining a down-to-earth attitude will be easy during the practical Virgo Lunar Eclipse on **February 20**, but it falls in your 9th House of Faraway Places, where it can create travel problems. The 9th House is also associated with philosophy, religion, and higher education, so this eclipse may push you to consider your need for further schooling or to question your beliefs. Serious Saturn is conjunct the eclipse, defining real issues that stop you from hitting the road or presenting obstacles while you're out of town. Fortunately, powerful Pluto harmoniously trines Saturn and the Moon, focusing your intentions and helping you transform a frustrating experience into a deeply fulfilling one.

Attractive Venus enters Aquarius and your resourceful 2nd House on **February 17**, a time to put more pleasure in your experience bank. Creating joy in your life has long-term benefits to your material and emotional well-being. Fun is not a distraction from the serious business of survival; it's vital to your future success. Mercury, the communicator, turns direct on **February 18**, and its forward shift enables a freer flow of information. Data that was lost and details that were overlooked are likely to come back into present focus.

KEEP IN MIND THIS MONTH

Finding the connection between inspiration and making it real takes time. Don't rush the process.

KEY DATES

FEBRUARY 1 ★ *sweet rewards*

Astrology's two most fortunate planets, Venus and Jupiter, join up in your sign to reward you with well-earned delight. Your social and organizational skills mesh perfectly, making you an ideal leader, a trusted friend, and a desirable partner. A refined taste and a strong appreciation of what makes people and things valuable helps you get the best of both. You gain trust, affection, and approval because you've proven your worth over a long period of time.

FEBRUARY 6-7 ★ *play without punishment*

A smooth sextile between well-behaved Venus in Capricorn and inventive Uranus on **February 6** makes it safe to experiment with your style and social life. A new look or unconventional form of fun may be silly, but no one is going to think any less of you for trying. Fortunately, you are able to enjoy this sense of freedom without having to pay a price for it. A talented quintile between active Mars and responsible Saturn on **February 7** suggests original ways to resolve tough problems at work with surprising ease.

FEBRUARY 13-14 ★ *romantic realignment*

An uncomfortable quincunx between Venus and Mars on **February 13** corresponds with a clash of styles that can put stress on your relationships. Try to understand if others don't live up to their commitments; applying pressure may only push them away. A more harmonious mood prevails on Valentine's Day, **February 14**, with a dynamic Sun-Mars trine, energizing you and opening your mind wide enough to overcome yesterday's differences.

SUPER NOVA DAYS
FEBRUARY 20-21 ★ *delayed gratification*

The Virgo Lunar Eclipse on **February 20** is a Sun-Moon opposition in the mental 3rd and 9th Houses of your chart. Stubborn Saturn's conjunction with the Full Moon may unnerve you with doubt or confront you with a critical adversary. Don't fake it if you don't have the facts to fight as an equal. If you lack the information you need to make your case, further education on the subject may be in order. Sensual Venus is sidetracked by duties when it quincunxes Saturn on **February 21**. The most delightful plans can fall by the wayside as responsibility comes calling. Reschedule, if necessary, rather than completely sacrificing the good time you were expecting.

FEBRUARY 24 ★ *limited resources*

A sober Saturn-Sun opposition can put you on the defensive or burden you with obligations that may not be yours to manage. Demonstrating your commitment to help others is one thing; agreeing to provide unlimited service is another. Respecting your own time and energy will allow you to make only those promises that you can keep without wearing yourself out.

MARCH

CONTROLLED INTENSITY

The New and Full Moons this month are power-packed transformational events that can alter your thinking and shift your responsibilities. The psychic Pisces New Moon on **March 7** shocks your mind with strange ideas and surprises due to its close conjunction with electrifying Uranus in your 3rd House of Communication. Your daily routine may be shaken, but what you can gain from a flash of intuition is more valuable than a temporary loss of control. The Full Moon in gracious Libra on **March 21** is closely square potent Pluto and impatient Mars, a combination that can provoke you to take extreme action at home or at work. Pressures on the job or within your family can push your emotional buttons, and you're likely to react strongly. You may be tempted to strike back, but remember that this can be destructive if you're not crystal clear about your intentions. You have the ability to eliminate major obstacles now, opening the way to greater satisfaction and a more effective use of your talents if you apply these intense feelings in a creative and conscious manner.

Extravagant Jupiter in cautious Capricorn forms a tense sesquisquare with Saturn on **March 18**—repeating on **June 26 and January 30, 2009**—that could threaten or slow down a major project. A closer look at details, however, will reveal a more efficient way to advance your interests. The Sun's entry into front-runner Aries on **March 20** marks the Spring Solstice and the beginning of the astrological year. The Aries Sun's spontaneous energy is severely tested by squares from Mars and Pluto that can turn playtime deadly serious. Jupiter brilliantly sextiles Uranus on **March 28**, bringing sudden inspiration now and repeating on **May 21 and November 13**.

> **KEEP IN MIND THIS MONTH**
>
> *Focus on one task at a time. A major breakthrough is possible now, but only if you apply your total attention.*

KEY DATES

MARCH 4 ★ *make your move*
Passionate Mars slips into your 7th House of Partnerships to bring a new level of dynamism to your relationships. This is an excellent time for you to deepen your current connection or begin a new one. This transit is also beneficial for going public with a project. You might encounter more aggressive individuals who try to force their agendas on you. Compromise is a much better response than combat.

SUPER NOVA DAYS
MARCH 7-8 ★ *when push comes to shove*

The explosive New Moon conjunct Uranus on **March 7** occurs in the midst of an exact opposition between Mars and Pluto, a potent pair that tends to push issues to the edge. There's no easy retreat now: You may have little choice but to make a major change or just give up on the relationship. The Sun's union with unpredictable Uranus on **March 8** while the Moon is in impulsive Aries is a volatile combination that could make you lose your cool. Yet this can be productive if it forces you to address a problem you've been previously unwilling to face.

MARCH 14-15 ★ *just out of reach*

A sturdy Mars-Saturn sextile on **March 14** helps you work efficiently, even with irrational partners. Mental Mercury's entry into sensitive Pisces feeds your imagination, but also demands a gentler tone in your communication. A tough opposition between demanding Saturn and sweet Venus on **March 15** makes every reward hard-earned. If you feel underappreciated, remember that recognizing the source of your dissatisfaction can be a strong first step toward rectifying it.

MARCH 21-23 ★ *no regrets*

The accommodating Libra Full Moon on **March 21** lands in your 10th House of Career and Public Responsibility, which normally implies a need to negotiate and compromise. Yet an "all or nothing" Sun-Pluto square makes it hard to find a common point of agreement. You may have to burn a bridge now—just make sure that you're willing to pay the price before striking a match. A Sun-Saturn quincunx on **March 23** continues the theme of potential conflict with authority figures. This time, though, you have more room to maneuver and can make smart adjustments to save the situation.

MARCH 27-28 ★ *taste test*

Fast thinking prevails as intellectual Mercury joins inventive Uranus and sextiles philosophical Jupiter on **March 27**. Delicious Venus also aspects these stimulating planets on **March 28** when they form their exact sextile, attracting you to eccentric people and unorthodox pleasures. Breaking your own rules about spending or loving is worth the risk right now if it expands your palette of delight.

APRIL

DOWNSHIFTING

You start the month at full speed, but will likely mellow out before it ends. The fiery Aries New Moon on **April 5** in your 4th House of Roots is supercharged by tense squares from impatient Mars and excessive Jupiter—lifting your ambition to a higher level. While this may be the catalyst you need to advance your career, transform your home, or even relocate, it's very possible that you may take on too much, too soon. It's not your habit to allow impulsiveness to lead you astray, and slowing down a bit will help you maintain control of these turbulent times. Mental Mercury and romantic Venus entering speedy Aries on **April 2 and April 6**, respectively, excite your head and heart. This can be thrilling, but you may rush past important details that skew your normally sound judgment.

The pace starts to slow on **April 17** when Mercury enters patient Taurus in your 5th House of Romance, Children, and Creativity, followed by the Sun on **April 19**. Take the time to savor life's pleasures during this playful and sensual period. The Full Moon in passionate Scorpio on **April 20** can increase emotional intensity, especially with friends and groups. Yet serious Saturn and powerful Pluto form stabilizing trines to the Full Moon to turn these deep feelings in a productive direction. Additionally, garnering support from others for a personal project will accelerate its development. Sweet Venus enters easygoing Taurus on **April 30** to increase your potential for pleasure. Its four-week stay in the most playful part of your chart rewards you with delicious experiences as a lover, parent, or performer when you stop working and allow yourself to enjoy these well-deserved treats.

> **KEEP IN MIND THIS MONTH**
>
> *Push hard when the opportunities to advance your interests arrive, but avoid forcing issues that are not yet ripe for action.*

KEY DATES

APRIL 6 ★ *timely intervention*
This may be a less-than-lazy Sunday, with Venus's entry into rowdy Aries followed by its tense square to unyielding Pluto. You may see unresolved relationship issues rise to the surface, which is better than burying them in resentment. Even if hurt feelings and disappointment seem too hard to face, a mature Sun-Saturn sesquisquare requires you to be an adult. Addressing uncomfortable concerns now earns you respect and keeps a situation from becoming even messier.

APRIL 10-11 ★ *managed growth*

An expansive Sun-Jupiter square on **April 10** encourages you to promise too much or express your opinions too bluntly. Another tense square, this one between chatty Mercury and feisty Mars, intensifies the day with anger, irritability, or impatience. A small disagreement could blow up into a major battle, so it's wise to temper your intemperate comments. Strong convictions and grand ambitions are allies for growth, but a demanding Mercury-Saturn sesquisquare on **April 11** reveals any flaws in your plan—a reminder to stick closely to the facts.

APRIL 14 ★ *don't take it personally*

Active Mars is mashed by an unyielding semisquare from strict Saturn that permits no deviation from the rules. If your efforts are thwarted by another person, providing clear and calm direction will go over better than making demands. Pride can impede progress if either one of you puts personal issues before the task at hand. Progress may be slow, but concentrated effort can finish off a difficult job and leave you tired yet content.

APRIL 18-19 ★ *hurry up and wait*

Mercury forms a grand trine with Saturn and Pluto on **April 18**, making you a more powerful communicator. Your ability to add urgency and clarity to any conversation commands attention. But the joy of the Sun in Taurus entering your 5th House of Fun and Games on **April 19** may be delayed by a less-than-generous sesquisquare between tough Saturn and soft Venus. Your hard work might not be matched by the recognition you receive, so put in the effort to satisfy yourself now. Hopefully others will come to appreciate it later.

SUPER NOVA DAYS
APRIL 21-24 ★ *shake, rattle, and roll*

A stable Sun-Saturn trine on **April 21** builds self-trust and puts you on a solid foundation to handle the upcoming high-powered aspects. Dynamic Mars trines revolutionary Uranus on **April 22**, a sure sign of inventiveness and originality, breaking you free from limiting patterns in partnership. Emotions run high, though, on **April 24**: Venus in stubborn Taurus is stressed by a square from pushy Mars and an opposition to ravenous Jupiter. You may feel blindsided by increased demands in relationships, excessive expenses, or extreme anger. Take healthy risks instead of futilely trying to hold back the tide.

MAY

Four planets change directions this month. The action starts with pragmatic Saturn's forward turn on **May 2**, enabling you to transform blue-sky ideas into down-to-earth reality. This direct shift of your ruling planet may reveal practical limitations that can dampen your dreams, but this is only to reshape them into a workable form. Expansive Jupiter, on the other hand, begins its retrograde cycle on **May 9**, reminding you to consolidate gains, restrain growth, and manage your physical resources more carefully. Idealistic Neptune and rational Mercury both go retrograde on **May 26**. Neptune's reverse turn, a subtle influence that will last for months, brings inspiration from within, signaling a growing faith in yourself and your untapped potential. Mercury retrograde in your 6th House of Work and Service requires greater attention to detail on the job, where petty errors and miscommunication could cause problems. A change of mind about your tasks and duties is possible during the next three weeks, so avoid locking yourself into any long-term commitments at this time.

The New Moon in indulgent Taurus on **May 5** plants seeds of romance and creativity in your playful 5th House. You can feel young and innocent, opening yourself to simple pleasures and sensual delight. Generous Jupiter's supportive trine to this Sun-Moon conjunction shows you ways to make these feelings last, transforming them into enduring sources of joy that remind you to have fun in your overly serious moments. The intense Scorpio Full Moon on **May 19** in your 11th House of Groups squares nebulous Neptune, which can wear you out when you're part of a team. While altruistic activities with others are rewarding, limit your responsibilities to keep them from becoming a burden.

> **KEEP IN MIND THIS MONTH**
>
> *Small but solid steps will take you far, while giant leaps forward are more likely to leave you out on a limb.*

KEY DATES

MAY 1–3 ★ *down to business*

Loving Venus forms supportive trines with tough guys Saturn and Pluto on **May 1** that help you cut to the chase in relationships. You can dig deeply to find value while also reducing waste in your financial and personal life. Saturn goes direct on **May 2**, adding a serious tone to the day as chatty Mercury enters clever Gemini. The communication planet is usually curious and flexible in the sign of the Twins, but its challenging quincunx with Pluto and square to Saturn on **May 3** intensify conversations with control issues and can darken your thoughts with doubt.

MAY 9–12 ★ *creative enterprise*
Macho Mars storms into dramatic Leo on **May 9**, setting off sparks of passion in your 8th House of Deep Sharing. Your emotions are stirred by powerful people— some who attract you strongly and others you want to avoid. It's not easy aligning yourself with innovative partners, but it might be worth the effort. The Sun trines Jupiter and sextiles Uranus on **May 12**, bringing enormous powers to life with bright ideas and bold action.

MAY 18 ★ *boundless joy*
Vivacious Venus creates a delightful trine to Jupiter as well as a sextile to Uranus, and both open you up to unconventional forms of fun. A feeling of confidence and generosity allows you to shine in any group. This is a great time to express your feelings openly and share the joy that's in your heart with your family, a lover, or friends old and new.

SUPER NOVA DAYS
MAY 20–22 ★ *the call of duty*
The Sun's entry into jumpy Gemini on **May 20** could make you nervous about having too much to do. But a clever Mercury-Saturn quintile the same day and a purging Sun-Pluto quincunx the next show you how to cut through clutter and set priorities. The Jupiter-Uranus sextile on **May 21** is another source of inventiveness that can get you out of a sticky situation. Yet complex conditions on **May 22** pull you in two directions. You have a naturally strong sense of duty, but there's a part of you that yearns for freedom now as well. Following the rules can be too restricting, so you may need to create new ones to meet your obligations in a more interesting way.

MAY 26 ★ *self-assessment*
The information planet, Mercury, turns retrograde in your 6th House of Work, while a stressful Venus-Saturn square can leave you feeling unappreciated. The upside of this tense aspect, though, is a clear recognition of your worth, which could even lead to a change of employment. Whether you're ready for such a drastic move or not, greater awareness of your assets will eventually lead to greater rewards.

JUNE

INNER TRANSFORMATION

This month's New and Full Moons illuminate the service sectors of your chart, but there's also plenty of social activity on the way—two planets are now entering your 7th House of Partnerships. The jaunty Gemini New Moon on **June 3** is joined by artistic Venus and cerebral Mercury, and supported by a smart sextile from energetic Mars that sparks bright ideas in 6th House of Work and Hobbies. The plethora of possibilities may overwhelm your usual good sense of order and time management. Try to limit your distractions, especially now that Mercury retrograde challenges your ability to handle details. Pluto backs out of Capricorn on **June 13** for one last visit to philosophical Sagittarius, and your 12th House of Secrets, until **November 26**. This gives you more time to look within and complete unfinished business before the intense work to come later this year. The extravagant Sagittarius Full Moon on **June 18** conjuncts transformative Pluto and squares rebellious Uranus, a surefire sign of explosive moods, unexpected crises, and radical shifts of perspective. Since it's in your private 12th House, all this action may be so internal that others don't even notice your turmoil. The profound changes may have more to do with your spirituality and connection to nonmaterial worlds than with the external one.

KEEP IN MIND THIS MONTH

Exploring unfamiliar ideas and emotions can be enlightening—and it's completely safe if you just observe and don't take action on all of them.

More visible activity occurs in relationships, both personal and professional, when Venus enters your 7th House on **June 18**, followed by the Sun on **June 20**. These are favorable times to reach out to others: You're likely to find sympathetic support and warm companionship more easily than you might expect. Communicative Mercury turns direct on **June 19**, underscoring how critical it is to extend yourself to enrich a current relationship or initiate a new one.

KEY DATES

JUNE 6-9 ★ *time for play*

An intense Mars-Pluto sesquisquare on **June 6** applies pressure that could provoke anger. Fortunately, gracious Venus forms a charming sextile with Mars, giving you the skills to avoid conflict or settle it amicably. These are passionate connections that can also express themselves through creative partnership or erotic attraction. Sweet talk and playful conversations make for a highly entertaining weekend as Mercury joins the party with a triple conjunction involving the Sun and Venus on **June 7–9**. Share this time with friendly folks who allow you to let your guard down and relax.

JUNE 13-14 ★ *escape reality*
The Sun's square with electric Uranus on **June 13** may put you on edge with last-minute changes and interruptions in your routine. A bright idea could help you find a way to stay loose, but so could a break from your responsibilities. A lazy Venus-Neptune trine is ideal for escaping reality with some frivolous shopping or by means of a romantic fantasy. However, don't jump into a new relationship on **June 14**, when Mars's conjunction with the karmic South Node of the Moon is likely to bring more fighting than fun. Still, a Sun-Neptune trine on the same day helps you to forgive, forget, and renew faith in yourself.

SUPER NOVA DAYS
JUNE 18-20 ★ *safe landing*
Venus opposes Pluto for a last-minute emotional purge before slipping into caring Cancer and your 7th House of Relationships on **June 18**, opening you to the gentle support of a loved one who provides emotional nourishment to warm your life after the storm. A crispy Mars-Uranus quincunx very early on **June 19**, however, may temporarily interrupt the mellow mood with a fast-moving crisis. The drama may be greater than necessary, so avoid impulsive reactions that only add fuel to the fire. Mercury's direct turn permits everything that's been on hold to finally start flowing again. The Sun opposes threatening Pluto on **June 20** before entering protective Cancer—the turning point of the Summer Solstice. You may feel as if you're struggling against a dangerous riptide before you finally land safely on the beach.

JUNE 25-26 ★ *strategic review*
The Sun's smooth sextile with practical Saturn on **June 25** earns you respect, yet an idealistic Venus-Neptune sesquisquare can blind your judgment about others. Be kind, but don't give away more than you can afford. A Jupiter-Saturn sesquisquare on **June 26** may put a kink in your plans. This is a perfect time to review what you've done since this pair's first aspect on **March 18**, and to adjust your efforts before the last in the series on **January 30, 2009**.

JULY

A LITTLE HELP FROM YOUR FRIENDS

Deepening emotional connections with others remain a major theme in your life this month. Paradoxically, active Mars opens up new territory by moving into your 9th House of Faraway Places on **July 1** as the nurturing Cancer New Moon on **July 2** puts close relationships back into the spotlight. This Sun-Moon conjunction in your 7th House of Partnerships is joined by attractive Venus and opposed by expansive Jupiter, improving the quality and increasing the quantity of people in your life. A tendency to overestimate others is possible, but it's important to take the risk of putting your personal feelings and professional ideas out there, where they are likely to be well received. Talkative Mercury enters your 7th House on **July 10**, opening even more lines of communication and encouraging you with validating information. A heavy-duty Mars-Saturn conjunction the same day, however, can present you with some very clear restrictions or duties that slow you down. Patience and practicality are essential under these demanding circumstances.

Your normally reserved emotions may spill over during the Full Moon in your sign on **July 18**. If insecurities surface, it's not an indication that all is lost, but simply a chance to highlight personal issues that need extra attention. Health and vitality may be at the top of the list, so make sure you get proper nutrition and exercise to deal with your daily stress. The Sun's entry into Leo in your 8th House of Intimacy on **July 22**, followed by Mercury on **July 26**, raises the stakes in relationships. If you're willing to give more of yourself, the rewards could be priceless. It's time to open up your heart and make your pitch for the emotional or material support necessary to bring you more happiness.

KEEP IN MIND THIS MONTH

Instead of stoically driving yourself forward without complaint, asking for assistance invites others in and makes your life much easier.

KEY DATES

JULY 2-4 ★ *great expectations*
The super-sweet Cancer New Moon on **July 2** is ideal for sharing joy with others. But an opposition between indulgent Venus and excessive Jupiter on **July 3** can stretch hopes beyond reason. Avoid overspending or putting your faith in promises that cannot be kept. You don't need to be cynical; just temper optimism with a dash of reality to keep your feet on the ground. In any case, serious Saturn's testing

semisquare with Venus on **July 4** will put the brakes on runaway expectations by confronting you with the practical limits of the here and now.

SUPER NOVA DAYS
JULY 9-10 ★ *save your strength*
You may be ready for a big move personally or professionally on **July 9,** when the Sun opposes Jupiter in ambitious Capricorn. But if it puts more responsibility on your shoulders, make sure you have a solid support system in place. This expansive impulse encounters some very down-to-earth demands with a no-nonsense Mars-Saturn conjunction and a sharp-eyed Mercury-Pluto opposition on **July 10.** Both help you narrow your focus and concentrate on one task at a time. Don't waste these precious resources on protracted struggles when you can do your own groundbreaking work right now.

JULY 14-15 ★ *intuitive powers*
An intelligent Mercury-Saturn sextile and an inventive Sun-Uranus trine on **July 14** show you angles that others can't see. Share your insights discreetly, since announcing them publicly could be embarrassing to a person in authority. Mercury hooks up smartly with active Mars on **July 15** and then slips on a sesquisquare with Neptune while the Sun clashes with the warrior planet and quincunxes illusory Neptune. Your mind may shift in and out of focus, and actions could be uncertain. Still, if you're receptive to feedback, you can make subtle adjustments that maintain your dignity and keep your efforts on track.

JULY 22 ★ *back to the basics*
The Sun's entry into proud Leo could bring an arrogant person into your life. Display your confidence, but don't get into a showdown: A sticky Mercury-Saturn semisquare can bog you down in petty details that distract from the big picture. Stick to the facts and keep conversations simple to make your point without making waves.

JULY 26 ★ *passion play*
Mercury enters showy Leo and forms a testy semisquare with fiery Mars as it trines enthusiastic Jupiter. The first aspect spurs fast thinking, while the second increases your sense of adventure. This is excellent for play, passion, and romance, but the sheer force of your personality can overpower the meek. There is no need to suppress your excitement; try redirecting it, instead.

AUGUST

SETTLING ACCOUNTS

This amazing month has two New Moons and two eclipses that indicate significant shifts in your life. The Leo New Moon Eclipse on **August 1** is in your 8th House of Shared Resources, altering the dynamics of a financial partnership or possibly an intimate relationship. You may suddenly discover that previous promises are not as solid as you thought, and you may wish to withdraw from a commitment. Either way, it's vital to discuss these issues openly. Show the courage to express your needs and be honest about what you are willing to give in return. This straightforward approach is your best guarantee for reinforcing a connection you want to keep or setting yourself on a path to establishing more fulfilling ones. The intelligent Aquarius Full Moon Eclipse on **August 16** is in your 2nd House of Income, generating changes in your revenue stream. Dreamy Neptune conjunct the eclipse tempts you to pursue financial fantasies . . . or extracts a price if you've already done so. At its best, this event can inspire you to develop your talent in creative new ways, but monetary restraint is recommended no matter what.

The meticulous Virgo New Moon on **August 30** joins businesslike Saturn in your 9th House of Higher Thought and Faraway Places. Traveling with a purpose is smart, but you could find a leisure trip complicated by delays or cancellations. This lunation also reveals the need for specialized training to advance your career or for personal growth. You typically learn more within a clearly defined, hands-on education than by studying abstract ideas or theories. Mastering new material can be slow at first, but the skills you develop are well worth the time invested.

> **KEEP IN MIND THIS MONTH**
>
> *You can't control the course of a relationship all by yourself—not even with compromise and communication. It takes two to make a partnership work.*

KEY DATES

AUGUST 6 ★ *permission to wander*

Venus moves into fussy Virgo where she likes everything neat and orderly, but none of the other planets want to fall in line. A voracious Sun-Jupiter quincunx leads to overdoing and overpromising, and a Mars-Uranus opposition is too impulsive and independent to follow any rules. Your mind won't cooperate, either, with a muddy Mercury-Neptune opposition that fuzzes facts with vague feelings. So relax now and enjoy this creative, imaginative, and unconventional environment.

SUPER NOVA DAYS
AUGUST 13-16 ★ *flexibility works*

You may be very sensitive to criticism as evaluative Venus joins with rigid Saturn on **August 13**. If you aren't getting the approval you desire, or others disappoint you, don't take it hard—it's all too easy right now to see things in a negative light. The Sun's unsettling quincunx with eccentric Uranus on **August 14** can shake up your routine, and your confidence. Stay light on your feet and adapt to changes rather than getting caught up in a battle over authority. This easygoing attitude will also serve you well on **August 15**, since the Sun's opposition to squishy Neptune may have other people bailing out on their responsibilities. A mentally tough Mercury-Saturn conjunction has you looking for solid answers, but if you try to pin people down, they will probably come up with sob stories or weak excuses. The tension breaks on **August 16** with a generous Venus-Jupiter trine that encourages you to spend your money and time on pleasure.

AUGUST 22-23 ★ *change of tune*

The Sun's entry into fellow earth sign Virgo on **August 22** helps put you at your practical and strategic best. Your ability to handle details without losing sight of the big picture makes you an effective leader and planner. The tone is very different, though, on **August 23** when Mercury and Venus oppose volatile Uranus. This is a day of surprises that's best taken with a sense of humor and a willingness to change direction at a moment's notice.

AUGUST 27-30 ★ *the naked truth*

Mercury forms a hard-edged square with secretive Pluto on **August 27** that is likely to intensify all communications. The mental planet's shift into fair-minded Libra on **August 28** would normally lift the dark mood, but Venus squares Pluto on **August 29**, keeping suspicion and mistrust in the air. Finally, on **August 30**, gracious Venus enters her peaceful home sign of Libra. Now you can let go of recent wounds and begin the process of reconciliation.

SEPTEMBER

ON-THE-JOB DIPLOMACY

This month is a key time of transition as visionary Jupiter turns direct in ambitious Capricorn on **September 8**. The forward movement of the planet of opportunity advances plans that have been brewing under the surface for the past few months. This Jupiter station is exceptionally powerful, because the giant planet forms a constructive trine with solid Saturn as it changes direction. The cooperative alignment of these two worldly planets cultivates solid ground that should bear fruit when their long series of aspects ends on **November 21**. The Full Moon in imaginative Pisces on **September 15** can bring surprises to your daily life and send your thinking in a new direction. Its conjunction with eccentric Uranus in your 3rd House of Information sparks your intuition and interest in unusual subjects, but can also lead to strange conversations or sudden breakdowns in communication.

The Sun enters diplomatic Libra and your 10th House of Career on **September 22**, emphasizing your professional life—especially how you connect with your colleagues. You'll gain insights, but it may take time to implement them, because Mercury turns retrograde on **September 24**. This three-week reversal of the messenger planet in your 10th House requires greater care in how you share information on the job. Miscommunication can cause conflict, so speak clearly and directly to head off potential trouble. Bright ideas work best when you think through all of their ramifications before revealing them to others. The New Moon in Libra on **September 29** is square Jupiter in your sign, convincing you to seek more responsibility in your current position or consider looking for greener pastures. Who you know now is as important as what you know, so shore up your alliances before making a major move.

> **KEEP IN MIND THIS MONTH**
>
> *Responding to the needs and desires of other people will help you enlist their cooperation—as well as promoting your own ambitions.*

KEY DATES

SEPTEMBER 3-4 ★ *your future is calling*

The Sun joins your ruling planet, Saturn, on **September 3**, which is often a time for slowing down and taking stock of your life. The potential for frustration is limited, though, since the creative Sun is on its way to a generous trine with boundless Jupiter on **September 4**. This might feel like a trip from a tiny closet to the great outdoors, but it's actually a preview of the life-shaping trine between Jupiter and

Saturn on **September 8**. Here's your chance to glimpse the future and to give it a nudge in the direction you want it to go.

SUPER NOVA DAYS
SEPTEMBER 7-8 ★ *strategic commitment*

Energetic Mars squares overenthusiastic Jupiter on **September 7**, which might stretch your resources too thin. You could see a small dispute grow into a major battle, or a little task into a giant chore. Narrow your focus to harness the power you're feeling now and channel it more judiciously in the days ahead. Jupiter's direct turn and positive trine with Saturn on **September 8** give you a perfect balance between high hopes and down-to-earth common sense. You can apply your force effectively to bring about long-term changes. Intense Pluto is also shifting into forward gear, showing that you are ready to express your deepest desires in a constructive manner.

SEPTEMBER 14-15 ★ *skillful adaption*

A socially skillful Mercury-Venus conjunction on **September 14** makes you a delightful communicator; creative ideas flow in a friendly manner. This peaceful mood may pass on **September 15**, however, when the Full Moon's emotional high tides are intensified by the presence of wild Uranus. Stay alert to catch unexpected waves of inspiration and avoid being blindsided by unexpected news.

SEPTEMBER 20-22 ★ *tough and tender*

A stressful Sun-Pluto square on **September 20** spawns power struggles, but at least it finally brings deeper issues out into the open. Fortunately, a sweet Mars-Neptune trine on **September 21** softens conflict and turns a potential tug-of-war into a playful pillow fight. The Sun enters harmonious Libra on **September 22**, the Autumn Equinox, for a last-minute evaluation of relationships two days before Mercury goes retrograde when serious negotiations should be shelved.

SEPTEMBER 28 ★ *quick-change artist*

A jumpy Venus-Uranus sesquisquare may upset your social plans. Even your most reliable friends could fail to follow through on commitments, but the possibility of meeting someone new could make up for it. Besides, you're ready for fresh ways to play, and an easygoing Mercury-Neptune trine allows you to be more relaxed and less concerned about the rules.

OCTOBER

BUILDING A TEAM

The month starts with a highly focused Mars-Pluto sextile on **October 1**, pushing you toward greater efficiency when working as part of a team. When active Mars enters your 11th House of Groups on **October 4**, your innate drive for productivity increases. This could trigger your competitive streak or a battle of wills, even with your closest friends. Balancing your desire to get work done quickly with a gentle touch ensures that peace and harmony are maintained during these intense times. The relationship between independent action and compromise is highlighted by the rowdy Aries Full Moon on **October 14**. This fiery lunar event occurs in your 4th House of Roots, perhaps stimulating an impulse to go it alone. Stress at home can cause impatient reactions that you might regret. Rapidly rising feelings reveal where you feel constrained by compromise, yet their purpose is to stimulate further contemplation rather than immediate action.

Mercury the Messenger turns direct on **October 15** in your 10th House of Career, enabling you to move on ideas stirred during the previous three weeks. Yet the impatience of the Aries Full Moon still burns inside you, so think carefully before making provocative statements. The Sun's entry into the water sign Scorpio on **October 22** forces you to deeply examine your surroundings before making a move. The relentless Scorpio New Moon on **October 28** in your social 11th House quietly feeds your ambition as you recognize the untapped resources around you. Combining your efforts with others makes it possible to transform organizations, resurrect discarded projects, or produce events that powerfully impact your community.

> **KEEP IN MIND THIS MONTH**
>
> *Even if your efforts have failed in the past, you can do things differently this time and enjoy a rousing success.*

KEY DATES

A semisquare from immovable Saturn on **October 5** slows down assertive Mars, reminding you not to work so hard. Resist the pressure of a pushy pal, especially with a Venus-Pluto semisquare that may make you feel indebted to this person. If you want to give, do it voluntarily; coercion will only elicit resentment. Fortunately, a hopeful Venus-Jupiter sextile can bring a happy ending to even the most contentious interaction. Retrograde Mercury joins the Sun on **October 6** as both form excessive squares with Jupiter. This could produce an "eureka" moment when a long-standing mystery is solved. Just give yourself time to think it through—Jupiter loves jumping to conclusions. A stabilizing Venus-Saturn sextile on **October 7** restores reason and restraint, contributing to sound judgment and more solid relationships.

OCTOBER 11 ★ *let go*
Venus in emotionally powerful Scorpio squares diffusive Neptune in Aquarius, which can leave you confusing a dream with reality. Your fantasies invest people or objects with more value than they may possess, so spend your love and money cautiously. Your compassion and inspiration empower you to heal even the harshest of wounds.

OCTOBER 17–18 ★ *inner quest*
Relationship repairs are in order on **October 17** when a brilliant Venus-Saturn quintile helps you create joy even under difficult circumstances. You can earn respect from someone who has been unable to appreciate your talent in the past. When Venus fires into adventurous Sagittarius and semisquares extravagant Jupiter on **October 18**, you leave caution behind as you pursue love and pleasure in an uncharacteristically reckless manner. Remember, fulfilling your quest may be about looking within, not chasing someone or something outside yourself.

OCTOBER 25 ★ *out in the open*
Competition may create friction as a tense Sun-Saturn semisquare encourages a struggle for control. Aggressive Mars squares the karmic Lunar Nodes, sharpening edges that make compromise more difficult. While you may feel uncomfortable with an honest difference of opinion expressed openly, the tension will pass more quickly than if you deny your personal truth.

OCTOBER 27–30 ★ *beyond smoke and mirrors*
A friction-free sextile between mobile Mars and buoyant Jupiter enriches you with energy on **October 28**. A spirited partner is there to back you up, but Mercury caroms off crazy Uranus with a quincunx that complicates conversations. Fortunately, the communication planet's healing trine with understanding Neptune on **October 30** can fill in the gaps with feelings when the words aren't clear. A strong Mars-Saturn sextile brings you reliable help to get your work done more efficiently.

CAPRICORN

NOVEMBER

IRREPRESSIBLE CHANGE

The month begins with a powerful Saturn-Uranus opposition on **November 8** that will return four more times during the next two years. This face-off between orderly Saturn in Virgo and revolutionary Uranus in Pisces across your educational 3rd and 9th Houses can leave you restructuring your entire worldview. Saturn in your 9th House of Higher Truth corresponds with a need to prove your beliefs in concrete terms, but intuitive Uranus in the 3rd House of Immediate Environment opens your mind with inexplicable ideas and exceptions to your intellectual rules. You're likely to question authority—even the very nature of reality—but there's no need to resolve these issues right now. This long-term aspect gives you plenty of time to explore the many contradictions you may experience first.

All-embracing Jupiter helps you make room for living both in the familiar world of reality and in a new and exciting world of wonder by forming harmonious aspects to Uranus and Saturn this month. Jupiter forms its third and final sextile to Uranus on **November 13** to advance bright ideas and breakthroughs that originated in late March and May. Jupiter makes its last trine with Saturn on **November 21** in a series that began on **March 16, 2007**. This creative balance between optimism and practicality gives you a solid foundation for professional and spiritual growth. The planet that can tie all these pieces together is penetrating, pressurized Pluto, which reenters Capricorn on **November 26** for a fifteen-year stay after its brief retrograde retreat into Sagittarius. Pluto has the power to squeeze out what you no longer need to direct your life in a more purposeful way. You have already made some significant changes, but these may just be preparation for bigger ones yet to come.

KEEP IN MIND THIS MONTH

It is reasonable to feel secure in some ways and uncertain in others. You don't need to be a superhero to achieve your goals.

KEY DATES

NOVEMBER 3-4 ★ *wait out the storm*
Venus squares Saturn and Uranus on **November 3**—one day before their exact opposition—creating confusion in relationships and personal values. Feelings can bounce from excitement to fear and back again, making commitment or clarity difficult. With pushy Mars squaring mushy Neptune on **November 4**, it's common to waste energy and fight the wrong battles; doing less is the wise choice. Mental

Mercury's move into perceptive Scorpio the same day is bound to reveal a secret or two, you will soon have more information upon which to make a decision.

SUPER NOVA DAYS
NOVEMBER 10-13 ★ *head over heart*
The Sun's positive aspects with Jupiter and Uranus on **November 10** bring you hope and originality, perhaps with the aid of a friend or colleague. The Sun's sextile with Saturn on **November 11** supports you with competence and quiet confidence. However, an intense Venus-Pluto conjunction in your 12th House of Secrets on **November 12** can rouse distrust with others that undermines relationships. Venus then enters your sign, giving you clarity to address this issue and reestablish a healthy bond. The sensual Taurus Full Moon on **November 13** falls in your romantic 5th House in opposition to passionate Mars but square, unrealistic Neptune. Powerful feelings of desire may provoke foolish action. Let your head lead the way, and your heart can follow safely.

NOVEMBER 16 ★ *journey within*
Intellectual Mercury gets even smarter with harmonious aspects to Jupiter, Saturn, and Uranus. This brilliant trio of vision, logic, and originality empowers your ideas and makes you an engaging conversationalist. Yet with active Mars entering adventurous Sagittarius in your 12th House of Privacy, you might be more interested in taking a long walk by yourself than chatting the day away.

NOVEMBER 21 ★ *guiding light*
The Sun slingshots into Sagittarius as its ruling planet, Jupiter, trines Saturn, allowing you to peer far into the future. You may feel guided by a higher power, but it's really your own awareness that's expanding to show you a clear connection between where you are now and where you're going next.

NOVEMBER 27-29 ★ *practice self-restraint*
The New Moon in extroverted Sagittarius on **November 27** occurs as brilliant Uranus turns direct, giving you a double dose of intuition and inspiration. You may be excited by your discoveries and anxious to share the news, but it's not for everyone's ears. Following a gossipy Mercury-Mars conjunction on **November 28** that urges you to spill the beans, a discreet Venus-Saturn trine on **November 29** brings maturity and tact to help you gain control over your impulses.

DECEMBER

SEASON OF RENEWAL

Vivacious Venus enters unconventional Aquarius and your 2nd House of Resources on **December 7**, putting you in a spending mood just in time for the holidays. Your taste could be a little unusual this year, which is fine for you, but it also might tempt you to buy some strange gifts. The airy Gemini Full Moon on **December 12** is especially intense with militant Mars in opposition while strict Saturn and rebellious Uranus make challenging squares. This jittery event occurs in your 6th House of Employment, which could produce a crisis on the job. The additional pressure of unpleasant colleagues or an unexpected shift of duties could trigger your desire to seek greener pastures. Yet even if another opportunity opens up, conditions are so volatile now that it's better to carefully consider all the angles than to suddenly make a change.

The Sun's entry into traditional Capricorn on **December 21** marks the Winter Solstice and a return to longer days in the Northern Hemisphere. The uplifting potential of this event is temporarily delayed as the Sun passes over mysterious Pluto on **December 22**. This conjunction may plunge you into complete self-examination that focuses on your deepest desires. If they seem achievable to you, this transit can empower and propel you toward them. Yet if what you want most seems impossible to reach, you could feel desperate. Happily, industrious Mars enters Capricorn on **December 27** to invigorate you hours before the New Moon in your sign, giving you hope for a better tomorrow. Mars's passage over Pluto on **December 28** reveals hidden reserves of energy and willpower, motivating you to take on any challenge and giving you the strength to come out on top.

> **KEEP IN MIND THIS MONTH**
>
> *Instead of just working hard out of habit, stop and consolidate your resources for a climb to heights you've never reached before.*

KEY DATES

DECEMBER 5–6 ★ *rapid response*

An early-morning Mercury-Uranus square on **December 5** speeds up your thinking and speech. This is great if you have a creative way to apply your ideas—a Sun-Mars conjunction the same day tends to incite fast and furious reactions. In addition, a testing Mercury-Saturn square on **December 6** is a sobering reminder of responsibility. Thoughtful strategic actions will earn you respect, but careless ones can bring regret.

SUPER NOVA DAY

DECEMBER 12 ★ *many directions at once*

The supercharged Full Moon in multifaceted Gemini combines active and impatient Mars and Uranus with serious Saturn, making this an "emotional earthquake" day. If you're feeling dazed and confused, don't struggle to control the situation. It's best to be as flexible as you can when buffeted by wildly fluctuating feelings inside and suddenly changing events outside. The good news is that all this activity can wake up new insights, shake out bad habits, and inspire you to try an unorthodox approach to your work.

DECEMBER 15 ★ *the right stuff*

Speedy Mars and slowpoke Saturn hook up in a tense square, demanding that you follow the letter of the law. A reckless friend or colleague might encourage you to cut corners or make a questionable claim, but even if they get away with it, you have a good chance of getting caught. Integrity is essential since your willingness to face facts and do things the right way—even if it's the hard way—will not only keep you out of trouble but actually save you time and effort in the long run.

DECEMBER 21-22 ★ *all or nothing*

You deserve recognition for your ongoing efforts with the Sun's entry into your sign on **December 21**. However, a jealous Venus-Pluto semisquare may reduce the appreciation others show you now. A fearful or controlling person could make relationships less satisfying—or perhaps one of you expresses needs the other just won't meet. The Sun's conjunction with Pluto on **December 22** could bring things to a head with a threat to sever your connection. The real issue is whether you value this relationship enough to dig in, face your own doubts, and do what you must to make it work.

DECEMBER 27 ★ *the dance of love*

The New Moon in dedicated Capricorn arrives as Warrior Mars enters your sign, which should toughen your resolve, but lovable Venus joining sensitive Neptune matches strength with vulnerability. Knowing when to lead and when to follow ideally creates a delicious combination of physical desire and romantic openness.

AQUARIUS

JANUARY 20–FEBRUARY 18

AQUARIUS OVERVIEW

This is a year filled with paradox and mystery, for you know that **many new experiences are just around the corner, even if you aren't quite ready to meet them.** Saturn, the planet of hard work and responsibility, was opposite your sun sign from July 16, 2005, until September 2, 2007. No matter how hard you applied yourself during that time, you probably struggled just to keep up with the many responsibilities you were facing. Now, with Saturn in efficient Virgo moving through your 8th House of Deep Sharing, you must **apply yourself diligently to strengthen your ties with others, both in business and personally.** This work will not be easy, because Saturn reveals where you meet resistance in your life. As one of your key planets, reality-based Saturn symbolizes your ongoing quest for knowledge and your need to be right. Armed with technical information and skills, you have an innate ability to understand complex systems and know how to handle nearly any situation. You can run into trouble, however, when you think you have all the answers and are unwilling to change your mind. Therefore, it's crucial to **remain open to what you still need to learn as you delve into the less-than-logical emotional realms.**

Radical Uranus, your other key planet, describes your need to break the rules of Saturn when they no longer serve any purpose. Uranus the Awakener continues to move through temperamental Pisces and your 2nd House of Self-Worth this year, preventing you from becoming too complacent with your financial situation and your relationship to your possessions. Your two ruling planets—traditional Saturn and unconventional Uranus—gradually move toward an opposition that is exact on November 4, agitating suppressed tensions and motivating you to make drastic changes that free you from restraints that were once tolerable. This marks the beginning of a dramatic, long-term transition that can change the direction of your life, but will take until July 26, 2010, to complete. **This key theme emphasizes your desire for total and immediate change, balanced by your need for ongoing stability.** Without any simple solutions, the stresses will likely increase until something gives—so it's best to process any discord as it arises, rather than waiting for the lightning to strike.

Jupiter, the planet of prosperity, is in ambitious Capricorn and your 12th House of Spirituality this year, indicating that **the most extraordinary growth may come to you in ways that are not necessarily apparent to others.** Meanwhile, transformative Pluto—the slowest moving of all the planets—enters Capricorn and your 12th House on January 25, reinforcing Jupiter's effect. You are being offered an unparalleled chance to travel beyond the logical and analytical world and into an alternative universe of myths and symbols. If you have the courage to alter your relationship with the real world, you will be ready to take the extraordinary opportunities that come your way next year when Jupiter moves into your sign.

EXPLORING DEEP WATERS

Solemn Saturn's visit to your 8th House of Intimacy and Transformation indicates that relationship work won't be easy, even if it is quite rewarding. On a lighter note, active Mars is in your 5th House of Romance until March 4 and charming Venus is in your sign from February 18 until March 12. These transits can attract love and give you more energy to go after your heart's desire. When Messenger Mercury enters your playful 5th House on May 3 and Venus joins it there on May 25, you receive another boost of heartfelt adrenaline. Mars's visit to your 7th House of Partnerships on May 11–July 2 can really heat up the action. You may, however, experience natural cooling-off periods around July 10 and August 13–16 when Mars, Venus, and Mercury each meet up with stern Saturn. Although you may be more comfortable in the realm of intellect, you have many lessons to learn this year by delving into your feelings.

PRACTICAL PERSISTENCE

Transformative Pluto and combative Mars, the rulers of your 10th House of Career, begin and end the year engaged in a struggle for power. Their opposition on January 2 and conjunction on December 28 suggest that you will need to stand up for your rights, possibly against a formidable opponent. Pluto's transition into strategic Capricorn adds powerful inspiration to your drive for success. Saturn means business, and fortunately it receives encouragement this year from beneficent Jupiter on January 21, September 8, and November 21, helping you turn your dreams into practical realities. Meanwhile, Jupiter forms supportive sextiles with inventive Uranus on March 28, May 21, and November 12, signaling sudden breakthroughs in your own self-esteem thanks to bright ideas that can advance your career.

DO IT DIFFERENTLY

Your key planet Saturn paves the way for joint business ventures as it visits your 8th House of Shared Resources. But the going can be fraught with difficulty unless you have a solid business plan that carefully delineates each person's responsibilities. Saturn indicates arduous effort, so immediate profits are unlikely. Instead, hedge your investments by working to bring them to fruition. It may take another couple of years for your finances to fully stabilize with erratic Uranus in your 2nd House of Money.

BODY, MIND, AND SPIRIT

A high-strung Aquarius New Moon Eclipse on February 6 is conjunct intellectual Mercury and dreamy Neptune, emphasizing the mystical connection between your beliefs and your health. The dramatic Leo New Moon Eclipse on August 1 falls in your 7th House of Partnerships, establishing a link between your relationship health and your physical well-being. Imaginative Neptune is strongly activated in both of these Solar Eclipses, reaffirming the power of your positive thoughts. Use your dreams to create your reality rather than to escape from it. Of course diet and exercise are always important, but this year your mind plays the most important role in your overall health.

DOWN TO EARTH

You may be more emotionally attached to your family than you appear, yet common sense is more reliable than your feelings. When Mercury and the Sun enter your 4th House of Roots in mid-April, you begin a communication process at home to create stability and a sense of togetherness that can last through the rest of the year. Contentment with your kin increases when loving Venus enters your 4th House on May 1, and you may temporarily forget about your need for outside social activity. Venus, the ruler of your 4th House, visits nurturing Cancer on June 19–July 13, enticing you to cool your heels and spend quality time at home, but your energy begins to disperse by late July. Disagreements over money could create stress that boils over around November 4, but dealing with issues as they surface can make your household a more pleasant environment for everyone.

DETAILS, DETAILS, DETAILS

You're more likely to travel this year for business than for pleasure—though a friend may talk you into a quick getaway sometime between March 21 and April 30. When friendly Venus, the ruler of your 9th House of Travel, enters flighty Gemini on May 25, you may again find yourself taking a short trip; just watch out for Mercury's retrograde from May 27 to June 19, which can create delays unless you pay extra-close attention to details before and during your journey. Look for a more extended trip from August 20 to November 4, yet once again beware of Mercury's retrograde in your travel house from September 24 until October 15. Extra planning can minimize the bothersome effects of trickster Mercury when it's moving backward.

 SPIRITUAL QUEST

You have much to gain this year by exploring nonphysical dimensions, for expansive Jupiter is now visiting your 12th House of Soul Consciousness—widening your metaphysical horizons, increasing your intuition, and opening your mind to mystical traditions. Studying with a special teacher can be enlightening as long as you apply what you learn by undertaking some sort of spiritual practice in order to give your ideas fertile ground in which to root. What you experience on this inner journey can infuse your spirit with an original perspective that offers new direction and meaning to your life.

RICK & JEFF'S TIP FOR THE YEAR:
Be Open to Change

Just when you think you know what you're doing and why you're doing it, something will change and you won't be as certain anymore. It's crucial to be flexible at times like these, for your natural tendency is to hold on to the status quo. Still, one of your greatest strengths is your ability to take quantum leaps when necessary. The changes ahead are monumental. Instead of reacting with fear and rigidity, step into your future with confidence so you can make the most of the dynamic year ahead of you.

JANUARY

SLOW MOTION

Forward progress is elusive this month with active Mars retrograde until **January 30**; no matter how hard you try to advance yourself, you feel as if you're revisiting familiar territory. Additionally, communicator Mercury enters your intelligent sign on **January 7**, slows down throughout the month, and turns retrograde on **January 28**. You're capable of brilliant planning now, but it might not impact your life until Mercury turns direct on **February 18**. Although January seems to unfold in slow motion, it begins with a bang as pushy Mars in your 5th House of Love tensely opposes passionate Pluto on **January 2**, forcing you to hold your ground in a struggle for power. The stand-off between these two planetary tough guys can transform even the sweetest romance into an emotional battleground. The calculating Capricorn New Moon on **January 8** in your 12th House of Destiny reminds you of your higher purpose as you map out a strategy for the year ahead.

Your plans take shape when the Sun moves into futuristic Aquarius on **January 20**. This is followed by a constructive trine between expansive Jupiter and contractive Saturn—the first of three such aspects throughout the year—creating a useful equilibrium as you balance your dreams with other people's expectations. The dramatic Leo Full Moon on **January 22** in your 7th House of Partnerships encourages you to ask for what you need. You may be less excited about the present than the future, but if you attempt to fast-forward your life, you'll only bring frustration. Slow down and sink into a more relaxed pace; you'll be happier and better prepared for what's to come.

> **KEEP IN MIND THIS MONTH**
>
> *You don't need to execute your plan right away. Moving ahead in thought while exercising patience in action may be your best strategy.*

KEY DATES

JANUARY 2 ★ *take the high road*

Retrograde Mars engages obstinate Pluto in a tug-of-war to see if you're strong enough to fight for your convictions. Tensions can erupt, reactivating a dramatic rivalry or firing up a new one. You can, however, transform heated conflict into mutual respect by seeking common ground instead of fighting for victory. Focus on the greater good and a magical quintile between buoyant Jupiter and unpredictable Uranus can catapult you out of the fearful shadows and into the brilliance of enlightenment.

JANUARY 6 ★ *can't always get what you want*

Sweet Venus dynamically squares restrictive Saturn today, reminding you of what you lack in your life. You may feel lonely, even if you're married or in an intimate relationship; you might not have enough money to take a pleasurable trip you deserve. Don't be too discouraged by the shortcomings of your life. Instead, use this time to clarify what you really need and what you're willing to pay, emotionally and fiscally, in exchange.

JANUARY 12 ★ *reckless abandon*

You're galvanized on **January 12** as sassy Venus squares your ruling planet, outrageous Uranus—making it very difficult to hold back your feelings. You are likely to forget whatever reservations you have when Venus squares somber Saturn on **January 6**. You may not even care what happens tomorrow as you express your unconventional needs today. A Saturday-night party could throw a romantic surprise your way that is fueled by your maverick attitude. Go ahead and enjoy yourself, but keep in mind that you might have some damage control to do over the days ahead if you go to extremes.

SUPER NOVA DAYS
JANUARY 21–24 ★ *distant horizon*

The stabilizing Jupiter-Saturn trine on **January 21** has long-lasting effects, so it's a smart idea to set aside time to develop your strategy for business or to discuss the future of a relationship with your significant other. Emotional and financial investments are favored now, as long as you don't expect immediate rewards. The showy Leo Full Moon on **January 22** encourages you to reveal more than is prudent, but mental Mercury's conjunction with nebulous Neptune makes it difficult to describe your feelings clearly. Try using music, poetry, or photography instead. Magnetic Venus's conjunction with Pluto on **January 24** can show a darker side of love, giving you a chance to express desires you'd normally keep to yourself. Reserve some of your thinking for the long-term planning you should be doing, even while you're dealing with intense day-to-day circumstances.

AQUARIUS

FEBRUARY

ON THE LAUNCH PAD

This is an incredibly dynamic month for you, with up to five planets at a time clustered in progressive Aquarius, invigorated by energetic Mars now moving direct in fellow air sign Gemini. The month begins with a sweet conjunction between crafty Venus and opulent Jupiter in your 12th House of Imagination. Since this falls in solid Capricorn, it emphasizes your ability to dream with the intent of turning your fantasies into something concrete. But Mercury the Messenger is retrograde until **February 18**, making the first part of the month a time for completion. Review your old files, reconnect with friends who've dropped out of sight, and reconsider your current situation. Get ready to put your master plan into action, but don't rush in; Mercury will stay in your sign until **March 14**, which means you have plenty of time to get it right.

An electrifying Aquarius New Moon Eclipse on **February 6** can shake your world, yet also surprise you with brilliant insights. Beautiful Venus enters Aquarius on **February 17**, gracing you with unconventional style and charm until **March 12**, but you may be less energetic when the Sun leaves your sign on **February 19**, moving on to compassionate Pisces. The efficient Virgo Full Moon Eclipse on **February 20** tells a different story, for it conjuncts austere Saturn and it helps you narrow your focus and take care of business in a disciplined manner. In some ways, this month is one of final preparation: You can make progress toward your goals, but nothing happens quickly. By the end of the month, however, you're ready to launch yourself into your future.

> **KEEP IN MIND THIS MONTH**
>
> *You tend to take day-to-day problems too personally now, which can distract you from the more important issues ahead.*

KEY DATES

FEBRUARY 1-2 ★ *instinctive wisdom*
A delightful day is indicated when gentle Venus meets up with joyful Jupiter on **February 1** in your sequestered 12th House, rewarding you with spiritual rather than material blessings. Retrograde Mercury aligns with intuitive Neptune on **February 2**, drawing your thoughts away from the real world. Your dreams will tell you what you need to know—but trust your intuition, or you can miss a significant message.

SUPER NOVA DAYS
FEBRUARY 5-7 ★ *lend a helping hand*
The Sun's annual conjunction with Chiron the Wounded Healer on **February 5** can bring up painful childhood memories, but it's important not to confuse what happened in the past with what's going on now. The New Moon Eclipse in your sign on **February 6** overloads you with flashes of inspiration and overwhelms you with feelings of compassion. A charismatic Mars-Saturn quintile on **February 7** increases your motivation to channel your energy into constructive action.

FEBRUARY 13-14 ★ *dust yourself off and try again*
An annoying quincunx between impulsive Mars and charming Venus on **February 13** can accentuate your discomfort when you don't get the response you expect from others. Even endless adjustments don't seem to bring you any closer to satisfaction. Nevertheless, keep at it, for your efforts will be rewarded when the Sun harmoniously trines Mars on **February 14**. Yesterday's irritations fade, and your innate ability to influence others returns.

FEBRUARY 17-20 ★ *take a chance*
Venus brings her sweetness to your sign on **February 17**, Mercury turns direct on **February 18**, and the Sun reawakens your emotional world as it enters watery Pisces on **February 19**. Additionally, romantic Venus semisquares eclectic Uranus the same day, encouraging you to make a risky investment or to gamble with your heart. The energy reaches a crescendo at the analytical Virgo Full Moon Eclipse on **February 20**, as you attempt to balance your need for freedom with the promises you've made to others. Hard work will get you through the storm. Soon you'll be looking back at these wild few days with a calm perspective.

FEBRUARY 24 ★ *karmic payback*
The Sun's annual opposition to frugal Saturn on **February 24** activates your money houses and brings up financial concerns, possibly involving a joint investment or budget disagreements with your partner. If you've been applying yourself diligently over the past weeks, this can be the culmination of your work, but things can fall apart if you slacked off. Either way, you are receiving a clear message from the universe. Take it to heart.

MARCH

NO TIME LIKE THE PRESENT

This month is a study in contrasts as you bump up against obstacles and responsibilities—but are so excited by the possibilities ahead that you can't wait to make
your move. You are pressured to tighten up your schedule and take care of the
details that can make the difference between failure and success. Your emotions
are more challenging than usual, as the imaginative Pisces New Moon on **March 7**
activates anxious fantasies that can suddenly deflate your self-confidence.
Although the stakes seem high and you may be overwhelmed by the littlest
things, you must face your fears now; don't project them onto anyone else.
Own your feelings, express them as compassionately as possible, and handle
the circumstances as they unfold.

Sweet Venus leaves your sign and enters compassionate Pisces on **March 12**,
followed by Mercury on **March 14**, encouraging you to trust your intuition and act
on your feelings rather than so-called facts. The Sun's entry into pioneering Aries
on **March 20** marks the Spring Equinox, an optimal time to launch a venture, for
the natural energies support the creation of anything new. Even as you surf the
creative spring tides, the Sun's dynamic square
to Pluto on **March 21**, along with an uncharacteristically stressful Libra Full Moon the same
day, can test your will to see if you have the
stamina to follow through on your great ideas.
Fortunately, a lucky Jupiter-Uranus sextile on
March 28—recurring on **May 21 and November
12**—is a blast of positive energy that makes you
feel better about yourself while also strengthening your chances for financial success.

> **KEEP IN MIND THIS MONTH**
>
> *Whatever you start now is
> influenced by a long-term cycle
> that will take months to
> culminate. Instead of making
> too many sudden changes,
> keep your eyes on the future.*

KEY DATES

MARCH 4–8 ★ *inside out*

Energetic Mars leaves your fun-loving 5th House and moves into protective Cancer
and your 6th House of Work on **March 4**. Although you realize that you have to be
more serious about your job, you may not be prepared for the intensity on **March 7**,
when Mars runs into an opposition from potent Pluto. This powerful standoff could
reactivate a similar struggle from **January 2**, when Mars last opposed Pluto. The
confused Pisces New Moon on **March 7** is conjunct erratic Uranus, heightening your

emotions and provoking you to express yourself without considering someone else's perspective. The turbulence continues as the Sun conjuncts unpredictable Uranus on **March 8**. Before unconsciously slipping into a defensive mode, first consider if it's important enough to turn your life around.

SUPER NOVA DAYS
MARCH 15–18 ★ *overcoming the odds*
You aren't necessarily comfortable when you have to interact without knowing what's real. Brainy Mercury and alluring Venus in dreamy Pisces test your confidence as they oppose authoritative Saturn on **March 15–17**. Mercury and Venus are now in your 2nd House of Money, along with the Sun and Uranus, so you may find yourself short of cash or thinking about refinancing to stabilize your finances. But even if circumstances don't force an issue, trines to Mars on **March 16–18** make it a smart idea to prepare in advance. Some projects are progressing well, but Jupiter's tense sesquisquare with restrictive Saturn on **March 18** can push you to realize the shortcomings of your strategy. Make the necessary changes to your plan before promising what you cannot deliver.

MARCH 27–28 ★ *open road*
Brilliant Uranus is joined by talkative Mercury on **March 27** and sexy Venus on **March 28**, revitalizing your spirit and encouraging you to take a quantum leap to further your money-making ambitions. You're feeling good about yourself and are ready to risk your comfort for a shot at something better. A supportive sextile from powerful Jupiter to Mercury, Venus, and Uranus can clear the way suddenly, allowing you to easily move toward your goals, even if you were previously struggling along this very same path.

MARCH 30 ★ *stay on point*
An action-packed square between impatient Mars in watery Cancer and the Sun in feisty Aries on **March 30** can stir up an emotional tempest that distracts you from the work at hand. Expressing your anger can clear the air of any lingering negativity, but it's also crucial to stay focused on the real issues. Otherwise you can get swept up in an irrelevant ego skirmish that wastes your valuable time and energy.

APRIL

SPICE OF LIFE

Life is anything but boring this month. The overall pace speeds up, and the increased variety of interactions overstimulates your mind. There can be so much happening that you waste precious time running in circles. The Aries Sun brightens your 3rd House of Data Collection until **April 19**, making it difficult to stay focused on any one thing. When Mercury blasts its way into excitable Aries on **April 2**, followed by sexy Venus on **April 6**—both joining the Sun in your 3rd House—new information comes at you through all your senses so fast, it may be difficult to integrate everything until later in the month. The spontaneous Aries New Moon on **April 5** can urge you to start one project after another without necessarily finishing any of them. It could be difficult to establish a healthy balance between your penchant for distractions and meeting obligations as a string of disruptive aspects encourage you toward self-indulgence and avoiding obligations on **April 10-14**.

But the Moon's conjunction with responsible Saturn on **April 15**, along with Mercury's entry into practical Taurus on **April 17**, shifts the prevailing winds and steers you into a more practical phase. Intelligent Mercury creates a stabilizing Grand Earth Trine with heavyweights Saturn and Pluto on **April 18**, followed by the Sun on **April 20-21**. The resourceful Scorpio Full Moon in your 10th House of Career on **April 20** has you thinking about what you can do during the following week to consolidate recent gains and increase your effectiveness at work. If, however, you push too hard or risk too much—especially on **April 22-24**—you will have to make adjustments sooner than anticipated.

> **KEEP IN MIND THIS MONTH**
>
> *Being busy doesn't guarantee that you'll reach your goals. Working smarter is a much better tactic than working harder.*

KEY DATES

APRIL 3-6 ★ *don't look back*

You're bounced around by intense crosscurrents on **April 3** when talkative Mercury in your 3rd House of Communication dynamically squares dark Pluto. Your adrenaline surges as the volatile Aries New Moon on **April 5** dares you to wing it. The New Moon's tense aspect to taskmaster Saturn demands that you focus on the real issues instead of wasting energy with endless distractions. Additionally, amorous Venus squares Pluto on **April 6**, stimulating both romantic desires and your fear of losing independence. Although you're tempted to bury your feelings, it's time to leave your comfortable intellectual world behind to discover the richness that waits in the vulnerable realms of intimacy.

APRIL 10 ★ *stay calm*
The Sun's powerful square with giant Jupiter prompts you to act with confidence—even if the situation doesn't warrant it. You need to be somewhat cautious now, for you can quickly find yourself in way over your head. Additionally, quicksilver Mercury squares bossy Mars, tempting you to replace logic with anger. Impulsive rants will only instigate further conflict. Remember, it's not *what* you say that's argumentative; it's *how* you say it.

SUPER NOVA DAYS
APRIL 17-21 ★ *true ambition*
The impulsive Aries energy recedes as Mercury and the Sun enter the practical sign of Taurus on **April 17 and April 19**. The magnetic Scorpio Full Moon on **April 20** falls in your 10th House of Career, reemphasizing your need to get ahead professionally. Karmic Saturn and potent Pluto are already cooperating, offering you prosperity in return for hard work. Mercury harmoniously trines these tough guys on **April 18**, followed by the Sun on **April 20-21**, increasing your power base and allowing you to take care of business without resistance.

APRIL 22-24 ★ *shot of adrenaline*
The emotional winds quickly shift as an exhilarating trine between feisty Mars and erratic Uranus on **April 22** stirs excitement. You're ready to rock and roll as Mars's opposition to boundless Jupiter on **April 24** infuses you with unrealistic enthusiasm. Even if everything looks great, don't let down your guard. Proceed with caution or you will quickly pay the price for overcommitting.

APRIL 28-29 ★ *irrational solution*
Although you're often attracted to mental puzzles, they aren't as enjoyable when weird emotional complications arise. Nebulous Neptune, now stressed by Mars and Mercury on **April 28-29**, makes it hard to know what to do because you don't have the complete picture. A supportive Mercury-Jupiter aspect on **April 28** helps you stay positive during the confusion. Ultimately, your generosity of spirit will solve your current dilemma.

MAY

THE CHALLENGE OF SIMPLIFICATION

Your work bears the richest fruit when you keep your goals down to earth and within reach. Venus forms a stabilizing Grand Earth Trine with authoritative Saturn and obsessive Pluto on **May 1**, demanding that you simplify your life, earn your living by doing what you love, and establish integrity in relationships rather than only seeking instant gratification. But Mercury's entry into curious Gemini on **May 2**, along with Saturn turning direct, reactivates your restlessness and tempts you to trade in your very real gains for a pie in the sky. Mercury's restrictive square to austere Saturn on **May 3**, however, quickly puts a damper on your wanderlust while the sensual Taurus New Moon on **May 5** brings it all back home. Seek pleasure by tending your emotional garden and cultivating current relationships, even if you must wrestle with your old fears about giving up freedom to maintain stability. Mars pushes his way into boisterous Leo and your 7th House of Partnerships on **May 9**, the same day giant Jupiter begins its retrograde phase. Although you are likely to express yourself boldly, it may feel as if the opportunities that seemed so close last month are now slipping away.

The intense Scorpio Full Moon on **May 19** can be an end—or at least a fork—in the road as it squares resolute Saturn. Meanwhile, sweet Venus squares Neptune on **May 20**, stimulating your imagination and clouding your intellect with unfulfilled dreams on the same day that the Sun moves into interactive Gemini in your 5th House of Fun and Games. Previous commitments may not be enough to prevent you from opening the door to a new romance or giving a second chance to one you already passed by.

KEEP IN MIND THIS MONTH

Don't get discouraged if it feels like you've missed your target; you just need more time before being able to proceed according to your plan.

KEY DATES

MAY 1-3 ★ *roll with it*
Life is looking good when sensual Venus forms easygoing trines with serious old Saturn and shadowy Pluto. This down-to-earth reality check is likely to show that you're on track—but if you are overextended, this Grand Earth Trine can gently yet firmly pull you back to center. You might feel somewhat constrained, but your safety and comfort can more than justify the self-restraint that's required of you now.

Remember, the emotional currents are stronger than they seem. Remain flexible; if you stiffen up with fear, you could hit the rocks.

MAY 12 ★ *your future beckons*

You could regain lost enthusiasm when the Sun sextiles electric Uranus and trines confident Jupiter on **May 12**. You may be more willing to take a financial or emotional risk to revitalize your life. This is a feel-good day and can even ease your fear of the unknown. Powerful dreams are being activated with Jupiter in your 12th House of Destiny, and they contain very practical messages for you. You would do well to listen to the advice welling up from your subconscious. Remember, however, that everything looks a little better than it truly is. Don't be in a hurry. If an opportunity is real, then it will last.

SUPER NOVA DAYS
MAY 18-22 ★ *change will do you good*

Tender Venus harmonizes with surprising Uranus and generous Jupiter on **May 18**, soothing a challenging emotional situation with assurances of unconditional love. But the emotionally complex Scorpio Full Moon on **May 19** in your 10th House of Public Status opposes the stubborn Taurus Sun in your 4th House of Home and Family, bringing you to a turning point in your ongoing struggle to balance your personal and professional lives. A quantum leap of consciousness is possible when visionary Jupiter forms a supportive sextile with erratic Uranus on **May 21**—the second of three this year—convincing you that there's no time like the present to make something happen. Expect delays as the Sun squares inflexible Saturn on **May 22**, but remember that your persistence will bring success.

MAY 26 ★ *the crying game*

You may be hesitant to ask for what you want as caring Venus squares sobering Saturn today. It's as if you know that you will be denied satisfaction if your needs aren't simple. Even a great relationship can buckle under the stress of this restrictive aspect. Money and love are withheld for a variety of reasons, and you must temporarily get along with less. Additionally, both Mercury and Neptune turn retrograde today—another indicator that you'll have to wait for the goodies you seek.

JUNE

TIME TO SMELL THE FLOWERS

You may finally have some time to kick back and enjoy yourself this month as the Sun, Mercury, and Venus all move through your 5th House of Romance, Children, and Creativity—until Venus begins the planetary exodus and slips into cozy Cancer on **June 18**. If, however, you're in a hurry to make something happen now, expect retrograde Mercury to slow you down even more until it turns direct on **June 19**. Scheduled activities may be delayed, important meetings may be missed, or party invitations may be misplaced unless you pay extra attention to all the details.

The communication-oriented Gemini New Moon on **June 3** instills a lighthearted tone for the weeks ahead. Make the most of this time by filling your calendar with entertaining activities. Life can get pleasantly chaotic on **June 9–14** when the Sun and flirty Venus illuminate indulgent Jupiter, unconventional Uranus, and dreamy Neptune in a series of aspects that can present exciting distractions and even turn your head around. Children can be a source of great pleasure, or they can drive you crazy with their changing demands on your schedule. Instead of frustrating yourself by setting unrealizable production goals, relax and enjoy the ride. Suppressed feelings can stand between you and a good time as innocent Venus opposes dark Pluto on **June 18**, the same day that the adventurous Sagittarius Full Moon conjoins Pluto, intensifying all emotional exchanges. But your actions lose focus as self-directed Mars opposes fuzzy Neptune on **June 21**. Fortunately, you can regain your clarity as Mars pushes toward a powerful trine with Pluto on **June 30** that increases your energy and your endurance.

KEEP IN MIND THIS MONTH

Make time for lively conversations, playful activities with children, and pleasurable romantic pursuits. But schedule in advance, or opportunities for fun can pass you by.

KEY DATES

JUNE 1–3 ★ *just the way you are*

An intelligent quintile between trickster Mercury and somber Saturn on **June 1** can have you tap dancing to impress an authority figure with your work ethic. But it's a tough act to pull off if you can't keep from laughing. You don't mean to be disrespectful; you're just so amused at your own cleverness, you can't play it straight. Ultimately, you'll get your message across, for the versatile Gemini New Moon on **June 3** receives additional charm from its conjunction with gracious Venus.

JUNE 7–9 ★ *no strings attached*

A triple conjunction among the Sun, Mercury, and Venus in flighty Gemini falls in your playful 5th House this weekend, distracting you from your regular routine. Be wary when a fast-talking friend breezes into your life with a money-making scheme or a last-minute invitation to a party. Whatever you do now won't have lasting importance, so just enjoy the distractions without any expectations.

JUNE 12–13 ★ *surprising consequences*

Watch your checkbook and your heart on **June 12–13**, when unpredictable Uranus in your 2nd House of Self-Worth is squared by the Sun and Venus. Reckless behavior isn't your best path to happiness. What begins as an exciting thought could turn into a clash over freedom of expression. Fortunately, Venus's soothing trine to diffusive Neptune on **June 13** can save the day by sprinkling magic fairy dust over a tense situation to put everyone in a mellower frame of mind.

SUPER NOVA DAYS
JUNE 18–21 ★ *back to your center*

The bold Sagittarius Full Moon on **June 18** is activated by passionate Pluto and sexy Venus, luring you into the emotional shadows and forcing you to con- front any dissatisfaction. When Mercury turns direct on **June 19**, intellectual dams give way to the pressure of forward thinking. The Sun enters nurturing Cancer on **June 20**, marking the Summer Solstice—a great time to reconnect with your roots. Mars's opposition to nebulous Neptune on **June 21** brings in the clouds of illusion, making it difficult to know exactly what's going on. Don't push your agenda now; instead, retreat, take time to share your dreams, and worry less about the future.

JUNE 30 ★ *for the common good*

The end of the month may also feel like the end of a road as brash Mars—spending his last day in dramatic Leo—is strengthened by a trine from relentless Pluto. You can be quite obsessive, believing that this is your final chance. Riding roughshod over others, however, won't work. You must strive for the betterment of all. Selfish behavior will meet more resistance than you can imagine.

JULY

SCARCITY AND PLENTY

July is a month of extremes: One day you're running into insurmountable obstacles, and the next you're sailing toward happiness. The month begins with active Mars entering analytical Virgo in your 8th House of Deep Sharing on **July 1**, suggesting an underlying theme of avoiding uncomfortable emotional situations where intellect is less useful than intuition. The quiet Cancer New Moon on **July 2** falls in your 6th House of Daily Routines, focusing your energies onto seemingly mundane details. But attractive Venus's opposition to overbearing Jupiter on **July 3** can quickly draw you out of your shell, luring you into a sensual feast that's less about what others think than how good you feel. Trickster Mercury squares unruly Uranus on **July 5**, adding uncertainty to the weekend; your best-laid plans could fall apart. Paradoxically, you may be relieved, even thrilled, with the change, for you gain your independence in the process.

The reliable Capricorn Full Moon on **July 18** is a reminder that you must honor your commitments before indulging your fantasies. This Full Moon falls in your 12th House of Secrets and can put you in touch with a practical side of your spirituality that you may have set aside. By honoring your forgotten dreams, you can hold on to a vision of a better future while still fulfilling your promises. The Sun enters lively Leo and your 7th House of Partnerships on **July 22**, followed by Mercury on **July 26**—shifting the emphasis toward working and playing with others, rather than by yourself.

> **KEEP IN MIND THIS MONTH**
>
> *Worry less about the day-to-day fluctuations of your good fortune than about keeping your life on course. Decide what's most important and don't let yourself be distracted.*

KEY DATES

JULY 2-5 ★ *pace yourself*

Protecting yourself in an emotionally vulnerable situation seems like a good idea when the sensitive Cancer New Moon on **July 2** stirs insecurities about your competence. Still, you aren't likely to have much self-restraint with alluring Venus opposing indulgent Jupiter on **July 3**. Don't squander your resources chasing after sensual pleasure. It's a better idea to save some energy for the electric buzz of Mercury's square to exciting Uranus on **July 5**. You could exhaust yourself unless you're well rested beforehand.

SUPER NOVA DAYS
JULY 9-10 ★ *taking care of business*
The Sun reaches an opposition to elastic Jupiter on **July 9**, stretching the limits of your common sense. You could be unrealistically optimistic, but you cannot ignore the cold truth when communicator Mercury delves into Pluto's shadow on **July 10**, the same day that red-hot Mars crashes into severe Saturn. This reality check can be crucial to your success, especially if you're overextended. Don't get too discouraged, even if you must struggle to work through the current conflict. This is a wake-up call, reminding you that you must slow down and meet your obligations rather than going back to sleep.

JULY 18-19 ★ *restore the balance*
A sentimental Cancer Sun opposes a calculating Capricorn Full Moon on **July 18**, deepening your feelings, which makes you even more uncomfortable about sharing them. Insecurity flip-flops with certainty as thoughtful Mercury moves toward an opposition with buoyant Jupiter on **July 19**. If you're overwhelmed, take a deep breath: The mountains will revert to molehills soon enough.

JULY 22-26 ★ *valiant effort*
Mental Mercury's superconductive trine to brilliant Uranus on **July 22** can bring you one amazing thought after another, but putting your ideas into action won't be simple. A series of crunchy quincunxes on **July 23-25** indicate that whatever you try to do could be sidetracked by problems, even if you're quick to adjust your plan. Fortunately, Mars trines lucky Jupiter on **July 26**, gracing you with a positive attitude and sufficient energy to overcome whatever minor obstacles you face.

JULY 31 ★ *is it real?*
Beautiful Venus opposes illusory Neptune, creating a heightened sense of fantasy. With Venus currently in your 7th House of Relationships, you want to experience ideal love and won't be satisfied with physical pleasure unless the elusive spiritual component is also present. It may be challenging to distinguish between your dreams and reality, so be careful about believing that all is well if it isn't.

AUGUST

FREE BIRD

This month highlights an ongoing dilemma that resurfaces from time to time during your life. Yours is a social sign, and your attraction to groups of like-minded people, political involvement, and community participation is legendary. Yet you remain a loner at times, reserving your right to be separate from the same groups you join. Two eclipses reactivate this struggle between wanting to be part of something greater than yourself and your need to maintain autonomy. The first, a dramatic Leo New Moon Eclipse on **August 1**, can suddenly change the nature of a relationship and force you to reevaluate your commitment to it. But Venus's opposition to spiritual Neptune tempts you to avoid the real issue, especially if you depersonalize what's happening and turn it into a more existential and spiritual question.

The second eclipse, a dreamy Full Moon Eclipse on **August 16** in your eccentric sign, is conjunct Neptune, again offering you an escape route. But Mercury's conjunction with strict Saturn will not let you off the hook so easily this time. You must seriously reevaluate your position and learn a hard lesson from the situation. Luckily, a Venus-Jupiter trine makes even the most difficult medicine go down as if it's been sweetened with a spoonful of sugar. Both Mercury and Venus oppose shocking Uranus on **August 23**, rattling your windows and perhaps shaking up your bank account with unexpected expenditures. A rare second New Moon this month on **August 30** is in efficient Virgo, focusing your attention on the details. Its conjunction with practical Saturn shifts your thinking away from the recent turmoil, enabling you to balance your life and restore lost equilibrium.

> **KEEP IN MIND THIS MONTH**
>
> *Don't avoid your feelings just because you're more comfortable living in your head. Your life will be more meaningful when you also express what's in your heart.*

KEY DATES

AUGUST 5-9 ★ *humble pie*
Sexy Venus and fast-talking Mercury form trines with passionate Pluto on **August 5 and August 9**, respectively, intensifying your desires and empowering you to talk about them. Still, be cautious when impulsive Mars tensely opposes erratic Uranus on **August 6** to push you right to the edge. Mars's annoying quincunx with murky Neptune on **August 8** makes it difficult to know how far you can go. Accepting that you aren't in control can be a humbling experience, yet it can also alleviate your anxiety.

AUGUST 13 ★ *alone again, naturally*

Affectionate Venus and reserved Saturn conjoin in your 8th House of Intimacy, dampening your emotions and isolating you from those you love. You may believe that your feelings have changed, but don't be too harsh. This is an opportunity to reevaluate the give-and-take within a partnership and put things back in order or, if needed, move on.

SUPER NOVA DAYS
AUGUST 15–17 ★ *no free lunch*

You're flooded with mixed messages as the high-strung Aquarius Full Moon Eclipse on **August 16** turns your life upside down. Everything looks great one moment then seems unreachable the next. The eclipsed Moon is conjunct spiritual Neptune, allowing you to look at a difficult situation through rose-colored glasses. But analytical Mercury joins austere Saturn on **August 15**, narrowing your vision and increasing your mental acuity. These few days can be transformative, but the powerful Mars-Pluto square on **August 17** demands that you work hard rather than taking the easy way out even if it's an available option.

AUGUST 21–23 ★ *pandora's box*

The Sun trines formidable Pluto on **August 21**, permitting you to tap into deep energy reserves the same day as a Mercury-Venus conjunction in picky Virgo focuses your thoughts on what you want. You can give voice to your desires, but you are likely to think twice about your needs before saying anything. Your careful analysis probably won't prevent you from impulsively telling all as Mercury and Venus oppose surprising Uranus on **August 23**. Be brilliant and speak your mind, but don't expect others to be comfortable with your sudden disclosures.

AUGUST 27–30 ★ *emotional discord*

Mercury and Venus square Pluto on **August 27–29**, provoking a conflict that can test your willingness to be open. Yet it's much more dangerous to bury your feelings than to express them. Still, you have your doubts as Mercury and Venus enter even-keeled Libra on **August 28 and August 30**, followed by a pragmatic Virgo New Moon the same day. You are on solid ground now; have courage and talk your way through any fears.

SEPTEMBER

SUSTAINING GROWTH

This month presents you with an interesting dilemma: You must dig in your heels and meet your current obligations, but your anticipation of better days ahead tells you to throw caution to the wind. To see this in action, just compare the serious Sun-Saturn alignment on **September 3** with the explosive Sun-Uranus opposition on **September 12**. It's an irresolvable contrast likely to be emphasized throughout the remainder of the year, culminating on **November 4**, when Saturn exactly opposes Uranus for the first time in four decades. Fortunately, the stress will be temporarily alleviated by the harmonious interplay between expansive Jupiter and contractive Saturn when these planetary regulators form an exact trine on **September 8**. It's the second of three such aspects this year—the first was on **January 21** and the last will be on **November 21**—making this a perfect time to weigh your gains and defeats, reevaluate your current direction, and enact strategic changes to stabilize your continued growth.

The intuitive Pisces Full Moon on **September 15** falls in your 2nd House of Money. This Full Moon is conjunct unpredictable Uranus and can mean a financial surprise—either an unexpected expense or a sudden windfall. The Sun's entry into Libra the Scales on **September 22** marks the Autumnal Equinox. With four planets now in airy Libra, you could be preoccupied with theory to the exclusion of more practical considerations. The creative Libra New Moon on **September 29** can offer you enough time to reflect on your current circumstances, dream of what's around the next corner, and balance the differences between what you have and what you want.

> **KEEP IN MIND THIS MONTH**
>
> *Even if you can see amazing possibilities everywhere you look, you must first take care of your current obligations if you want more measurable results.*

KEY DATES

SEPTEMBER 3-4 ★ *opposites attract*

The Sun's annual conjunction with oppressive Saturn on **September 3** is like a cosmic restraining order that prevents you from pursuing your vision of the future. But the Sun's trine to adventurous Jupiter on **September 4** encourages you to let loose, jump up on your horse, and gallop into the sunset. Although these might feel like very different situations, you can now blend the two quite well. Take full responsibility for your actions; this will free you to pursue your dreams.

SUPER NOVA DAYS
SEPTEMBER 7-12 ★ *be the change you seek*
The stabilizing trine between optimistic Jupiter and realistic Saturn on
September 8 can steady your emotions and place your feet on the ground.
But staying practical is tough when opportunities for travel, education, or
plain old fun arrive at your doorstep. Diplomatic Mercury, charming Venus,
and tactful Mars—all in fair-minded Libra and your 9th House of Big Ideas—
take turns squaring Jupiter from **September 7 until September 11**, tempting
you to forget about your obligations. Overconfidence can be a trap now, for
you may actually believe that your success is assured. Unfortunately, you
could overlook important details and end up discouraged when the outcome
doesn't meet your expectations. The Sun's annual opposition to your key
planet Uranus on **September 12** can wreak havoc on an intimate or business
relationship, shining bright light on a difficult situation. If you've been considering your options, it may be time to trust your intuition and act decisively.

SEPTEMBER 16-21 ★ *complications abound*
The inner planets—Mercury, Venus, and Mars—form irritating quincunxes with
Uranus on **September 16-19**, along with trines to Neptune on **September 17-21**.
Although your powers of deduction continue to be strong, it can be challenging
to stay in the moment when you're already thinking about what's next. But the
Sun's dynamic square with paranoid Pluto on **September 20** can create emotional
stress. Find a way to compromise instead of building up your defenses against a
nonexistent attack.

SEPTEMBER 24 ★ *back to the drawing board*
Your date with destiny may be postponed as trickster Mercury turns retrograde in
your 9th House of Faraway Places on **September 24**. This initiates a three-week
period when you must go back over your current plans and ideas before bringing
them to fruition when Mercury resumes direct motion on **October 15**. If you're
planning a trip during this time, pay extra attention to the details to avoid snafus.

OCTOBER

JUST AROUND THE BEND

Whatever tensions you have successfully suppressed over the past few years may now slowly work their way back into your awareness as your two key planets—dutiful Saturn and rebellious Uranus—move toward an exact opposition on **November 4**. This is the first of five such oppositions through **July 26, 2010**, that will have profound impact on your relationships—both business and personal—and on the long-term trajectory of your life. And although this opposition peaks next month, its long-lasting influence sets the tone now as your irrepressible feelings conflict with others who are unresponsive to your needs. You may not make much progress through **October 15** as retrograde Mercury forces you to revisit previously covered ground and rework your plans to make them more relevant.

The free-spirited Aries Full Moon on **October 14** in your 3rd House of Data Collection harmonizes with otherworldly Neptune, increasing your intuition and your ability to inspire others. Instead of endless analysis, this is a time to walk your talk without worrying about strategy. It's your integrity and not your plan that is your strength now. The Sun's entry into Scorpio and your professional 10th House on **October 22** is a sign that it's time for you to think less about your personal needs and more about your professional life. The powerful Saturn-Uranus opposition is stressed by the Sun and the Moon on **October 25–27** in the days leading up to the intense Scorpio New Moon on **October 28**. You may have to battle with internal demons to maintain a healthy perspective about an oppressive situation at work. You might be tempted to turn everything upside down, but working toward stability is a better strategy for now.

> **KEEP IN MIND THIS MONTH**
>
> *Dig in your heels and concentrate on long-term change, not immediate gratification.*

KEY DATES

OCTOBER 4-6 ★ *healthy expression*

Mars's entry into passionate Scorpio on **October 4** can make you uncomfortable, for you prefer cool logic to the intense emotions that now surface. Meanwhile, retrograde Mercury conjuncts the Sun on **October 6** while they both square opulent Jupiter—pumping you up with extra enthusiasm. You're energized by waves of change that are greater than personal interests, but it can be hard to harness this power. Go for the ride, knowing that these currents can carry you beyond your original destination.

OCTOBER 10-11 ★ *gambling on a dream*

Alluring Venus, in your 10th House of Public Status, harmoniously trines surprising Uranus on **October 10**. You may be overcome with desire, risking what you've gained simply for the exhilarating freedom of expression. This can be dangerous, for you are motivated more by emotions and adrenaline now than common sense and intelligence. Your fantasies come into play, too, further distracting you from your responsibilities. Venus stressfully squares fuzzy Neptune on **October 11**, blurring the boundaries between imagination and reality. If your career expectations are too unrealistic, you will need to rein in your dreams before you go too far.

OCTOBER 18 ★ *life of the party*

Beautiful Venus enters charismatic Sagittarius and your 11th House of Friends on **October 18**—and remains there until **November 12**—drawing you into social situations where you can have fun instead of furthering your career goals. Be ready to receive appreciation and admiration from your peers. It's okay to seek companionship rather than intimacy, for it's time to enjoy life without worrying about emotional complications.

OCTOBER 24-27 ★ *back to the present*

Mars in magnetic Scorpio can drive you through emotionally difficult territory as it harshly aspects fierce Pluto, the soulful Moon's Nodes, and wounded Chiron on **October 24-26**. Instead of contracting with fear, acknowledge your previous failures and shift your focus from the past to the future. An enthusiastic Mars-Jupiter sextile comes to your rescue on **October 27**, allowing you to reclaim lost confidence and turn this difficult passage into a positive experience.

SUPER NOVA DAYS
OCTOBER 30-31 ★ *comic relief*

On **October 30**, Mercury's easy trine with intuitive Neptune, combined with Mars's supportive sextile with hardworking Saturn, offers the best of both worlds. You draw inspiration from your dreams and are fully capable of turning them into reality. Mars also trines unorthodox Uranus on **October 31**, allowing you to get away with daring solutions to your problems. In general, the increasing tension from the approaching Saturn-Uranus opposition on **November 4** is temporarily relieved by Mars's flowing aspects to both planets, empowering you to express yourself in a bold yet nonthreatening manner.

AQUARIUS

NOVEMBER

THE ROAD AHEAD

You are standing at a fork in the road, and the decisions you make this month can reverberate for years to come as three separate yet interrelated long-term cycles are activated. The first of a series of five oppositions between stable Saturn and disruptive Uranus is exact on **November 4**, bringing a sense of uncertainty into a month that is otherwise steadied by more harmonious aspects. While you want to be responsible, Uranus's presence can have you wondering whether your current plans will limit your freedom and prevent you from accomplishing your goals. Second, a supportive sextile between opportunistic Jupiter and surprising Uranus on **November 12** revisits familiar avenues of growth that you traveled during previous alignments on **March 28 and May 21**. Third, a superconductive trine between Jupiter and realistic Saturn on **November 21** suggests recognition and reward for your hard work with a karmic balance that has already shaped much of your year—going back to their previous contacts on **January 21 and September 8**. Although this stabilizing influence will wane over the weeks and months ahead, extra effort now can strengthen your position and assure success.

The earthy Taurus Full Moon on **November 13** is a call to common sense. You are being pushed and pulled in many directions, so your best course of action is to simplify your life as much as you can. Although this Full Moon reflects the great potential of the moment, its square to nebulous Neptune can also be the source of confusion—overwhelming you with too many emotions. The uplifting Sagittarius New Moon on **November 27** can clear the air of residual tensions and help you set the Thanksgiving table with hope for the future, rather than attachment to the past.

> **KEEP IN MIND THIS MONTH**
>
> *Although certain aspects of your life may not meet your expectations, the changes you seek are big enough that they could take years to unfold.*

KEY DATES

SUPER NOVA DAYS
NOVEMBER 3-4 ★ *no sudden moves*
The first few days of the month can be quite unsettling as friendly Venus squares Saturn and Uranus on **November 3**, intensifying frustrations that surface around the Saturn-Uranus opposition on **November 4**. It's hard to remain

optimistic when you wonder if the payoff is even worth your effort. Venus's square to Saturn can be discouraging, even depressing, and it gives you good reason to withhold your affections. But Venus's square to "wild and crazy" Uranus tells a different tale—one of impulsive expression and risk taking to shake up the status quo. Self-directed Mars squares mystical Neptune on the same day, confusing you with strong feelings that may be difficult to integrate. It could be all too easy to do the wrong thing and actually make matters worse.

NOVEMBER 10-12 ★ *time to regroup*
The Sun forms harmonious aspects with Jupiter, Uranus, and Saturn on **November 10-11**, reassuring you that self-restraint still is a sensible course of action. Even if you're deeply absorbed in reconsidering something as important as a primary relationship or your overall life direction, it's apparent now that rash actions won't bring you any closer to happiness. Temporarily accepting that which cannot be easily changed is not the same as defeat—it just buys you time. Venus's conjunction with volatile Pluto on **November 12**, however, brings suppressed feelings to the surface. An emotional discussion could turn intense, especially if you're struggling to keep a relationship alive or defend your reputation.

NOVEMBER 16-17 ★ *crazy genius*
Perceptive Mercury in your public 10th House forms a harmonious trine to quirky Uranus on **November 16**, throwing your innermost thoughts out into the open. Don't hold any ideas back, no matter how outrageous they seem. One stroke of genius will guarantee that everyone forgets about the rest. But you grow less logical when Mercury squares whimsical Neptune on **November 17**. You can mislead others as you unconsciously bend the truth with your strong feelings. If possible, delay important decisions for a few days.

NOVEMBER 27-30 ★ *happy days are here again*
On **November 27**, gregarious Mercury and eager Mars join the optimistic Sagittarius New Moon in your 11th House of Friends and Wishes, reminding you how much you enjoy this time of year. Although you may have a lot on your plate, take time to revel in the camaraderie of your family and friends. The positive energy continues as Venus harmonizes with the Saturn-Uranus opposition on **November 28-29**, revealing a creative connection between obligation and freedom.

DECEMBER

ROMANCE AND REBELLION

Romance is in the air now, but not without its complications. Venus, the love planet, enters Aquarius on **December 7**, increasing your sense of self-worth and casting you in a more attractive light. Yet getting close without losing the emotional breathing space you need is a challenge. The contrast between intimacy and independence is stimulated by the Full Moon in flirtatious Gemini on **December 12**, which occurs in your 5th House of Romance. The lighthearted delight of this event is touched by tension as aggressive Mars opposes the Moon while erratic Uranus and strict Saturn form tense squares to it. Feelings can flip from passion to flight, discovery to duty, and everywhere else on your emotional compass. Even the mildest restriction or briefest delay can seem like an unbearable obstacle that you must handle immediately. This intense atmosphere can lead to breakthroughs in relationships, but a sense of humor will reduce the chances of triggering destructive behavior.

The tone is quite different beginning on **December 21**, the Winter Solstice, when the Sun enters responsible Capricorn. The inherent self-restraint of this earth sign is reinforced by its presence in your 12th House of Privacy. You're unlikely to make any scenes as your thoughts turn introspective and in a more spiritual direction. The conflicts and stresses of relationships will not disappear entirely, but they're now balanced with a compassionate recognition that crises are best met with patience and planning. The New Moon in conservative Capricorn on **December 27** normally plants seeds of ambition deeply into your unconscious to ripen slowly over time. However, impatient Mars enters Capricorn on the same day, pushing you to advance your interests more quickly.

> **KEEP IN MIND THIS MONTH**
>
> *Thoughts moving at the speed of light do not require immediate expression. Digest this mental fast food before taking action.*

KEY DATES

DECEMBER 5-6 ★ *thinking outside the box*

Mental Mercury fires off innovative ideas with a square to Uranus on **December 5**, but you may let inappropriate comments fly as well. The willful Sun's conjunction with feisty Mars could instigate a fight with a friend or colleague caused by a careless remark. All this force can be employed positively by launching a new project or engaging in playful competition. Accountability arrives on **December 6** as Mercury squares Saturn, when every word will be weighed and measured. Communication can be cumbersome, so keep it simple and stick to the facts.

SUPER NOVA DAYS

DECEMBER 10-12 ★ *enough is enough*

A seismic Sun-Uranus square on **December 10** stirs your originality and reduces your inclination to cooperate. You're tempted to rebel against authority figures, but discovering something new about yourself is more rewarding. More tense aspects to Uranus from Venus on **December 11** and Mars on **December 12** churn up restlessness and spawn surprises leading up to the explosive Full Moon in Gemini on the latter day. Your feelings can run hot and cold, then hotter still as pressure mounts to a breaking point. There is some logic available, though, with brainy Mercury entering practical Capricorn and the Sun squaring serious Saturn. Meanwhile, a sulfurous Mercury-Pluto square can turn your mind in a negative direction. Consider your audience carefully before expressing strong opinions.

DECEMBER 15-16 ★ *stress fades*

Active Mars slams into a square with resistant Saturn on **December 15**, which can leave you overburdened with responsibilities or frustrated with friends and colleagues. Avoid a showdown, though, since Mars slips into a forgiving sextile with spiritual Neptune on **December 16** to wash away resentment and reestablish peace.

DECEMBER 21-22 ★ *hidden reserve*

On **December 21**, the Sun enters pragmatic Capricorn while sensitive Venus semi-squares dark Pluto, engendering mistrust in relationships that forces you to examine your desires more carefully. The Sun then conjuncts Pluto on **December 22**, an aspect that often produces power struggles. If you can find some quiet time alone, however, this is a chance to tap into an unused source of passion and potency.

DECEMBER 27-28 ★ *constructing dreams*

Sweet delight can be found in the midst of struggle on **December 27**. Macho Mars enters industrious Capricorn while loving Venus hits new heights of sensitivity with a conjunction to Neptune. Serious work and imaginative play create an unusual combination that just might help make a dream come true. Mars joins Pluto on **December 28**, revealing what you must jettison and where you must amplify your effort if you want to turn fantasy into reality.

PISCES

FEBRUARY 19–MARCH 20

PISCES OVERVIEW

You can reach new levels of fulfillment this year when you participate as part of a team, because optimistic Jupiter, your co-ruling planet, is in your 11th House of Groups. Opportunities to advance professionally depend on the support of colleagues and your ability to network professionally. **You're ready for more responsibility and higher achievement, but ultimately your success depends on the quality of relationships you create with others.** Serious Saturn is in your 7th House of Partnerships now, making your closest alliances the most challenging area of your life. Your tender heart hates to reject or criticize people, yet it's vital to associate yourself with those who are dedicated, competent, and willing to work as hard as you do. **Carrying the load of a less-than-capable partner can wear you down in your personal life or hold you back in your career.** Fortunately, Jupiter and Saturn form three harmonious trines this year that help you discover a balance between being compassionate and setting limits. These giant planets align on January 21, September 8, and November 21 in the practical earth signs of Capricorn and Virgo to connect your lofty ambitions with reality. Establishing well-defined goals and creating a strategy to achieve them is well within your reach.

Your other key planet is Neptune, and this year it will underscore your innate spiritual inclination as it continues the long journey through your 12th House of Soul Consciousness that began in 1999. **Two eclipses in the 12th House, though, turn this into a critical year of letting go of old metaphysical concepts and religious beliefs, preparing you for new dimensions of awareness.** The Solar Eclipse on February 6 is conjunct diffusive Neptune, carrying waves of feeling that are overwhelming even to you. Yet if you can just let go and ride them with faith, they will bring you to a place of deep wisdom and inspiration. The Lunar Eclipse on August 16 is as powerful as an inner tsunami that pulls you far from familiar territory. You could easily feel lost and anxious to return your feet to solid ground. But when you are willing to release the past and fully embrace the present, old wounds and doubts are washed away and the world becomes fresh and new again.

Visionary Neptune can supply another magical moment when it conjuncts the karmic North Node of the Moon on May 2, with rippling effects throughout the year. **This rare meeting is one more reminder of the spiritual freedom that can be yours now.** You may attract a teacher or companion who touches your soul and helps you overcome any sense of separation you have with others and the world around you. If you're already advanced on a path of personal awakening, you might become a source of inspiration for those seeking enlightenment. Take time out from your worldly ambitions and responsibilities to fill yourself with the spirit that can be found in nature, music, yoga, or meditation. The benefits may not appear on your résumé or bank statement, but they are precious nonetheless.

TAKE CHARGE

Authoritative Saturn's transit through your 7th House of Partnerships signals a need to take a stronger stance in relationships. Know what you want from others, be willing to state it, and then back it up with action. If you don't follow these critical steps, you won't experience the quality of companionship you deserve. You may not be comfortable playing such a demanding role, yet it's more loving to be honest about what you expect than hiding your feelings or expressing them indirectly. A Lunar Eclipse on February 20 in your 7th House could mark a significant turning point in relationships. A near opposition between aggressive Mars and passionate Pluto can precipitate a showdown—a point of no return where a situation must change or end. Happily, Pluto forms a supportive trine to the Moon that can direct difficult emotions toward a productive discussion, possibly transforming a painful partnership into a fulfilling one. If you're single, don't be afraid of your feelings. Even if they lead you to a place of hopelessness, don't give up. When you stay open to your heart, the intensity of your emotions can lead to a breakthrough—removing the barriers blocking you from the intimacy you desire.

CREATIVE OPPORTUNITIES

The supportive trine between hopeful Jupiter, the ruler of your 10th House of Career, and realistic Saturn provides a stable base for your advancement this year. You will be able to separate professional issues from personal ones with this highly practical pair working on your behalf. However, the Solar Eclipse in your 6th House of Employment on August 1 has long-lasting effects that could spur you to take creative risks on the job. Ideally, it encourages you to be bolder, express yourself more fully, and put more of your heart into daily life. Rather than simply accepting a humdrum routine, you may take chances by seeking new employment, starting your own business, or demonstrating more leadership in your present position. This could ruffle the feathers of an insecure boss or colleague, so consider his or her feelings before taking action.

 ## STEADY AS SHE GOES

Your financial picture is relatively solid this year . . . with two exceptions. The New Moon in impetuous Aries on April 5 lights up your 2nd House of Resources to encourage spending. Spontaneous Mars, the ruler of this house, forms a tense square to the New Moon, as does expansive Jupiter. While you may long to spend your money on short-term fun, you'd be better off investing in training or equipment that increases your potential for long-term income. Also, be especially careful about borrowing or lending money September 24–October 15, when logical Mercury loses its bearings while moving retrograde through your 8th House of Shared Resources.

 ## ALTERNATIVE HEALTH

Inventive Uranus transiting your 1st House of Physicality picks up dynamic sextiles from adventurous Jupiter on March 28, May 21, and November 13 that can generate sudden changes of habit. New forms of exercise or an unconventional diet could reshape your body and boost your energy levels. Use your intuitive understanding of what's naturally healthy to make positive choices based on your own instincts rather than relying so much on the judgment of others.

 ## SETTING LIMITS

Additional responsibilities for relatives or close friends can cramp your style at home this year. If you do have to bear a heavier burden of care for others, try to set clear boundaries about what you will or won't do to avoid being drained by endless demands. This is especially important May 26–June 19, when communicative Mercury marches backward through your 4th House of Home and Family and the chances for misunderstanding increase. Avoid any major changes to your residence during these weeks, too, unless they're for emergency repairs.

MIX PLEASURE WITH BUSINESS

Short trips for practical purposes can be very productive for you this year. Keep your agenda well defined so you can take care of business without sacrificing time off for fun. Group travel can be rewarding, but it's almost certain to entail complications. Work out all the details in advance to reduce the number of snags you're likely to encounter. Educational pursuits work best when you have a specific goal in mind. Gaining certification or a degree to advance your career makes good sense, but aiming for a master's degree in art history because you love art probably isn't a wise investment.

 ## SIXTH SENSE

Pisces has a closer connection to the spiritual dimension and dream world than any other sign, and this is an excellent year to put your awareness into practice. You are no longer a novice, but can act as a direct channel for soul-centered information. Your planet Neptune nurtures your intuition, so trust it every chance you get. Even if your interpretations are off from time to time, continue to use your psychic powers—your accuracy will improve. If there are moments when your faith flags, see what you can do to help someone in need. When you give to others, your compassion lifts you above your own doubts and fears and quickly returns you to your center.

RICK & JEFF'S TIP FOR THE YEAR:
Find Your Center

Your idealism makes it all too easy to experience extreme ups and downs. The search for the divine, for the perfect romance, for the most sublime experiences takes you to places few people ever go—which is why the fall can be so hard when these journeys end. This is a year to temper those highs and lows by finding beauty in the little things and delight in your daily life. This is not meant to limit your emotional range, but to widen your center so that satisfaction is never beyond your reach. The greatest joys of the universe exist as much within you as anywhere else.

JANUARY

LIGHTEN YOUR LOAD

The year starts with energetic Mars moving retrograde in your 10th House of Career, leaving you backpedaling professionally or feeling overloaded with unfinished chores. This isn't the best time to take on additional responsibilities, even if you enjoy juggling several tasks at a time. An intense opposition between Mars and penetrating Pluto on **January 2** requires all the concentration you can muster to deal with demanding issues at home or on the job. The New Moon in orderly Capricorn on **January 8**, though, falls in your 11th House of Groups and could bring much-appreciated assistance from friends or colleagues. It's a signal for you to act as a leader and organize team efforts instead of carrying the ball by yourself. On **January 21**, your traditional ruling planet Jupiter forms the first of three constructive trines with responsible Saturn, a pattern that will repeat on **September 8 and November 21**. This cooperative alignment between the planets of hope and reality helps you establish strategic plans for reaching your long-term goals.

The Full Moon in dramatic Leo on **January 22** sparks creativity that can be applied to your job or a hobby. Pluto enters ambitious Capricorn and your 11th House on **January 25**, beginning a lengthy process of transition in your role within groups or in community work. Thoughtful Mercury turns retrograde on **January 28** to kick off a three-week review of spiritual values and personal dreams. Take extra care in communication to avoid misunderstandings during this detail-challenged period. You may feel the urge to initiate a project when dynamic Mars turns direct on **January 30**. Its forward movement greases the wheels of activity, but it's best to avoid major moves until Mercury also goes direct on **February 18**.

> **KEEP IN MIND THIS MONTH**
>
> *It's flattering to be offered a leadership position, but carefully consider the additional demands on your time and energy before accepting.*

KEY DATES

JANUARY 6-8 ★ *foot in mouth*

A clever quintile between loving Venus and whimsical Neptune on **January 6** can turn an ordinary day into one inspired by new forms of pleasure, romance, and delight. Mercury enters intelligent Aquarius and your 12th House of Soul Consciousness on **January 7**, strengthening your natural intuition. A taut semi-square between Mercury and eccentric Uranus on **January 8** may have surprising ideas popping into your head and out of your mouth. Yet with the New Moon in strict Capricorn, you could be held accountable for every word you say. If you do stumble verbally, correct yourself quickly, apologize, and move on.

JANUARY 12 ★ *keep the faith*
Your two ruling planets, visionary Jupiter and spiritual Neptune, cross paths in a semisquare that can blur your judgment with boundless hope. Overlooking details is to be expected, but this planetary pair might infuse you with faith in something larger than yourself, lifting your spirits and reducing the stress of daily life.

JANUARY 16 ★ *compassionate heart*
An awkward quincunx between the willful Sun and impatient Mars can waste your energy or cause an inadvertent clash with a family member or colleague. But any wounded feelings will quickly heal, because you can respond graciously with a lovely sextile between diplomatic Venus and forgiving Neptune. Your natural instinct to see the best in others makes it easy to dismiss their faults and appreciate their talents. A touch of artistry adds beauty, even in the midst of a challenging task.

SUPER NOVA DAYS
JANUARY 20–22 ★ *secret support*
The Sun's entry into unconventional Aquarius on **January 20** shines light in your 12th House of Divinity, where it warms your soul and heightens your psychic powers. Help can come your way from unexpected sources, while the energy you have to offer those in need continues to grow. On **January 21**, a trine between Jupiter and Saturn, the cosmic regulators, rocks you in a big cradle of security. You know that you can take your time getting where you want to go in life because you're already on the right track. Retrograde Mercury conjuncts nebulous Neptune on **January 22**, turning ordinary reality into a magical world where imagination flourishes but facts and details may get fuzzy.

JANUARY 28–30 ★ *dazed and confused*
Like ships passing in the night, talkative Mercury turns retrograde on **January 28** and assertive Mars goes direct on **January 30**. In between, a vulnerable Venus-Neptune semisquare on **January 29** can leave you feeling lost. Seeking escape via careless spending or romantic fantasies is a short-term fix with the potential for long-term problems, so keep your diversions simple.

FEBRUARY

RELATIONSHIP REALITY

This is a dynamic month highlighted by two eclipses, Mercury turning direct, and the Sun entering imaginative Pisces. The Solar Eclipse on **February 6** in unorthodox Aquarius falls in your 12th House of Destiny and can have a profound impact on your most cherished spiritual beliefs. Its conjunction with your ruling planet Neptune makes you feel as if a curtain has opened, allowing you to peer into a magical new world. The vision you see has the potential to touch your soul and inspire you for years to come. Unfortunately, it might be difficult to describe this experience to others. In fact, quietly nurturing the flame you feel inside is the best way to ensure its continuation. Too much conversation can dissipate its intuitive power. Mercury stops dead in its tracks on **February 18** and slowly begins moving direct again after its three-week retrograde cycle. This forward shift of the communication planet frees up data that's been lost in translation and reveals messages hidden in the bottom of your e-mail box. Mercury's turnaround in your 12th House of Spirituality continues this month's trend of opening your awareness to other levels of consciousness.

The Sun's entry into your inspirational sign on **February 19** feeds your creativity and boosts your self-confidence. You know how to push ahead with sensitivity to advance your interests while avoiding friction. A Lunar Eclipse in critical Virgo on **February 20** is likely to result in a thorough reevaluation of relationships. Its conjunction with limit-setting Saturn in your 7th House of Partnerships shows that the time has come to clarify where you stand with others. Commit to those who are willing to work with you and kindly cut loose those who aren't.

> **KEEP IN MIND THIS MONTH**
>
> *Shifting your mind from the boundless world of spirit to the limits of relationship requires a flexible attitude and a strong sense of realism.*

KEY DATES

FEBRUARY 1–2 ★ *sweet distraction*

A juicy conjunction between sociable Venus and jovial Jupiter on **February 1** almost guarantees you pleasant company. The planets' union in your 11th House of Groups shows off your ability to organize and entertain for a perfect mix of business and pleasure. Retrograde Mercury backs over fanciful Neptune on **February 2**, which is wonderful for intimate conversations and spiritual connections, but facts get fuzzy and messages are easily misplaced or misunderstood. Double-check details to avoid mix-ups.

FEBRUARY 6 ★ *save yourself*

Mental Mercury joins the Sun during today's electric Aquarius Solar Eclipse, and offers an unexpected chance for introspection—reawakening memories long-buried. Pay attention to your dreams; they are a rich source of information that can help you make sense out of your past and put you on a clear path to the future. Someone you idealize may take a fall in your eyes. The message is that you don't need a hero to show you the way; you have all the inspiration and power you need within.

FEBRUARY 10 ★ *lost in wonderland*

The annual conjunction between the Sun and Neptune carries you beyond the bounds of ordinary reality. This could be a trip to fantasyland that winds up distracting you from the practical issues facing you. Yet you could also experience a sense of connection that erases barriers, washes away criticism, and reminds you of the divinity in all things. Nevertheless, you're going to have to live with the choices you make when you come off this cloud, so avoid making promises you can't keep.

SUPER NOVA DAYS
FEBRUARY 17–20 ★ *narrow your focus*

An overly optimistic semisquare between the Sun and excessive Jupiter can prove overwhelming if you make too many social commitments on **February 17**. Intellectual Mercury's direct turn on **February 18**, though, can get you back on track mentally as your thinking and communication sharpen. The Sun's entry into sweet and sensitive Pisces on **February 19** is buttressed by a supportive sextile with Pluto. Your sign's faith is channeled by deep perceptions that show you where to focus and where to let go. The Lunar Eclipse on **February 20** in practical Virgo, joined with "no nonsense" Saturn, demands complete concentration and shuts down your efforts where there's nothing to be gained.

FEBRUARY 24 ★ *relationship tests*

The Sun's opposition with Saturn is a reality check for your relationships. You may reach the end of the road with one person, recognizing that you may never get what you desire. But it can also solidify partnerships when you share the same goals and are willing to put in an equal amount of work to reach them.

MARCH

STORMY WEATHER

Impulsive Mars enters watery Cancer and your 5th House of Romance and Self-Expression on **March 4**, making this a time to act on your feelings. It's your turn to take the initiative in matters of the heart and to demonstrate your creativity. You often wear your emotions on your sleeve, yet you're now able to direct them with a sense of purpose, making you more attractive to others. Staying calm, however, can be tough this month with the sensitive Pisces New Moon closely conjunct to shocking Uranus on **March 7**. The presence of astrology's most rebellious planet at the annual union of the Sun and Moon in your sign indicates that you're in a very dynamic period of change—one that might generate dramatic events and strong reactions without warning. You can apply this revolutionary force productively by letting go of outmoded habits and actively engaging in new and unconventional experiences.

Creative Venus and intellectual Mercury enter spiritual Pisces on **March 12 and March 14**, respectively. The presence of these fast-moving personal planets in your sign adds magic, imagination, and idealism to your life. Yet the high hopes they engender may loosen your grip on reality enough to lead you to some careless decisions. There's no limit to how far your mind or heart can travel, but keeping one foot solidly on the ground will keep you from floating off into dreamland. You may encounter a bump in the road when restricting Saturn forms a tense sesquisquare with encouraging Jupiter on **March 18**. Adjusting long-range plans now will help you solidify your future when this aspect returns on **June 26 and January 30, 2009**.

KEEP IN MIND THIS MONTH

Stay loose in your thinking and fast on your feet to keep up with the rapid pace of change in your life.

KEY DATES

SUPER NOVA DAYS
MARCH 6-9 ★ *lightning strikes*
A smart sextile between the Sun and wise Jupiter brings an optimistic perspective on **March 6**. A romantic Venus-Neptune conjunction only enhances this upbeat mood, painting the world in heartwarming colors . . . yet also blurring your judgment. The mood shifts radically on **March 7**, when a contentious opposition between aggressive Mars and unyielding Pluto brings

emotions to a peak. The day's New Moon in Pisces joined with Uranus shakes your world with unexpected events, but can also excite you with the prospect of new discoveries and more freedom. The Sun's exact conjunction with electric Uranus on **March 8** keeps the buzz going, yet might also foster rebellion against an authority figure. Mental Mercury joins Neptune on **March 9**, allowing for more sensitive conversations but also enabling fantasy to carry your thinking far from reality.

MARCH 12-15 ★ *waking from a dream*
Sweet Venus enters gentle Pisces on **March 12**, making you more alluring as you tune in to your own special gifts. Then, on **March 13**, a strengthening Venus-Pluto sextile tempers this delicate and idealistic transit, giving you clarity about your deep desires. A practical Mars-Saturn sextile on **March 14** helps you work productively with others and solidify ideas spawned by Mercury's entry into visionary Pisces. Relationships and self-worth may fluctuate considerably on **March 15**, when romantic Venus goes too far with a semisquare to Jupiter and is then deflated by a corrective opposition from serious Saturn.

MARCH 20-21 ★ *let go to grow*
The Sun enters go-getter Aries and your 2nd House of Resources on **March 20** to mark the Vernal Equinox. The fiery force of the spring season can prompt money-making ideas and energize the process of increasing your income. The creative Sun's square to purging Pluto on **March 21**, however, shows a need to cut back or reallocate expenses of cash or energy. If you face doubt or get caught up in a power struggle, letting go will work better than settling in for a long fight.

MARCH 26-28 ★ *high-frequency buzz*
A mushy Mars-Neptune sesquisquare on **March 26** may push your efforts off target and waste your time unless you concentrate on what you're doing. Mental activity is running high on **March 27**, when Mercury conjuncts Uranus and sextiles Jupiter one day before these outer planets sextile each other. Brilliant ideas pop into your head so quickly, it may be difficult to describe them. Your nervous system could be overstimulated, so take time to relax and breathe if you get too wound up. Sexy Venus sextiles Jupiter and conjuncts Uranus on **March 28**, adding chills and thrills to your social life.

APRIL

MONEY ON YOUR MIND

A fresh look at finances is the key issue this month as the Sun continues to move through your 2nd House of Resources until **April 19**, picking up the company of brainy Mercury and charming Venus on **April 2 and April 6**. The presence of these planets in the pioneering sign of Aries reminds you how innovative you can be when it comes to money matters. The New Moon in spontaneous Aries on **April 5** can trigger a daring move, especially when dynamic squares from pushy Mars and enterprising Jupiter add their ambitious energies. A serious investment in a new venture can be the right choice if it has the potential to change how you earn your income. Boldly creating a business or expanding an existing one makes more sense than spending recklessly for your own pleasure.

The tone shifts on **April 17** when Mercury enters stable Taurus in your 3rd House of Information, followed by the Sun on **April 19**. If you slow down to clear your thinking and simplify your communication, you'll increase your credibility and earn more trust from others. Your imaginative mind is ready to come down to earth and absorb practical data, which makes you a more receptive student. The Full Moon in passionate Scorpio on **April 20** illuminates your 9th House of Philosophy and Religion, stimulating feelings of political or religious fervor. Powerful emotions provoke you to share your opinions with greater force than usual. Still, you'll likely have all the facts you need to back up these statements thanks to responsible Saturn in detail-oriented Virgo's supportive sextile to the Full Moon. You can apply what you now know to successfully build on any recent investments.

> **KEEP IN MIND THIS MONTH**
>
> *Spend more time and energy on yourself: Focusing on your own needs now will pay dividends in the long run.*

KEY DATES

APRIL 5-7 ★ *calculate the risks*

The rowdy Aries New Moon on **April 5** can lead to leaping without looking, especially with pleasure-seeking Venus entering this fast-moving fire on **April 6**. However, Venus then forms a demanding square with exacting Pluto that will drive up the cost of careless spending. A forgiving semisquare between Mercury and Neptune on **April 7** can produce soft words, but there is no room for sloppy thinking as constricting Saturn makes a tough quincunx with Venus that can keep a relationship on edge.

APRIL 10 ★ *with a grain of salt*

Beware of an overly expansive square between boundless Jupiter and the motivating Sun that encourages you to make promises too big to be kept. Confidence is warranted, but show some restraint to avoid overindulging or saying more than you should. Even a reliable friend or colleague can stretch the truth, so take what you hear with a dash of skepticism.

SUPER NOVA DAYS
APRIL 13-14 ★ *hope floats*

Idealism rises on **April 13** with a Sun-Neptune sextile, yet you could definitely go overboard. A Venus-Neptune semisquare tends to overlook reality for a more romantic view of life, while a tense square from opinionated Jupiter to Mercury is prone to exaggeration. Filter through all the ideas around you to focus on the few that have immediate value. Serious Saturn hooks up with active Mars in a semisquare on **April 14**, narrowing your choices and requiring a more concentrated effort. A sensitive Mercury-Neptune sextile instigates inspiring conversations, but you need to take care of business before letting your mind wander.

APRIL 23-24 ★ *more, more, more*

A sassy Venus-Mars square on **April 23** makes you extra creative in your pursuit of pleasure. This talented but teasing pair's saucy planetary dance is dramatized by an indulgent Venus-Jupiter square on **April 23** and a super-energized Mars-Jupiter opposition on **April 24**. It's hard to avoid spending or socializing to the nth degree. Ideally, you can explore new flavors of delight without taking in more than you can digest.

APRIL 28-29 ★ *altered states*

A careless Mars-Neptune quincunx on **April 28** makes it easy to drift off course. Fortunately, a highly perceptive trine between sharp-eyed Mercury and visionary Jupiter quickly realigns your thinking and places you back on track. Your communication skills are on point as you master details without losing sight of the big picture. The story is very different on **April 29** when Mercury's square to cloudy Neptune fogs your vision and skews your judgment. Don't rush into making important decisions until you've had a chance to gather more data and study the issues carefully.

MAY

CROSSCURRENTS

Four planets shift direction this month to swirl the waters of change. Structuring Saturn turns forward on **May 2** after traveling backward all year. This stabilizing influence is especially helpful for strengthening your position in relationships. If you've been thinking about altering a current partnership or seeking a new one, this is a smart time to put those wheels in motion. But don't act too quickly, for lucky Jupiter turns retrograde on **May 9.** You can continue to accrue gains during its four-month backward cycle, but digest experiences in small bites rather than gulping them down so hungrily that you can't assimilate all their benefits. Visionary Jupiter's reversal is also a reminder that the truth you seek exists within you, so rely on your inner guidance more than external authorities. Both Neptune and Mercury go retrograde on **May 26.** Your key planets, Jupiter and Neptune, urge you to reexamine your faith and invite you to deepen your spiritual journey during their retrograde phases. Mercury's three-week reversal in your 10th House of Career calls for greater caution in all of your communications and handling details related to your professional or public responsibilities.

The determined Taurus New Moon **May 5** sows seeds of curiosity in your 3rd House of Information. A supportive trine from wise Jupiter in practical Capricorn focuses your attention on utilitarian subjects that will give your words more credibility. Your actions may turn more dramatic when Mars enters theatrical Leo in your 6th House of Work and Service on **May 9.** Yet just as this creative force gets rolling, Mars forms an awkward quincunx with dominating Pluto on **May 11.** This demands the elimination of unnecessary activities prior to the intense Scorpio Full Moon in your expansive 9th House of Big Ideas.

> ### KEEP IN MIND THIS MONTH
>
> *Slow and steady will get you much farther than fast and erratic, so manage your time and energy wisely to find a pace you can sustain.*

KEY DATES

MAY 2-3 ★ *only the facts*
Chatty Mercury enters its airy home sign of Gemini on **May 2**, which normally sets your mind spinning with a bouquet of stimulating ideas. Unfortunately, the communication planet slams into a square with limiting Saturn and a quincunx with obstinate Pluto on **May 3** that can complicate a conversation. If you want to

make a point while avoiding an argument, keep it simple, stick to the facts, and be prepared to back them up with proof.

MAY 7 ★ *mind stretch*
Mercury, the planet of details, clashes with Jupiter, the planet of big ideas, in a stressful sesquisquare. Under this aspect, exaggeration and overstatement can turn minor issues into major ones. Yet this can also be an opportunity to stretch yourself by processing complicated concepts or discussions—as long as you can distinguish the difference between facts and opinions.

MAY 12-14 ★ *be true to your heart*
Your creative powers blossom on **May 12** when the Sun connects favorably to inventive Uranus and abundant Jupiter. Even if you've been knocked down recently, these energetic aspects give you the originality to find a fresh perspective and the confidence to express yourself. A square between the self-conscious Sun and sensitive Neptune on **May 14**, however, is more vulnerable, and may leave you feeling unrecognized for your efforts. It's tempting to let these emotions fade, but if they involve an ongoing pattern in an important relationship, it's best to speak up now.

SUPER NOVA DAYS
MAY 18-22 ★ *a brilliant way out*
A vivacious Venus-Jupiter trine on **May 18** brings you delightful help from your friends. But the passionate Scorpio Full Moon on **May 19** in your 9th House of Faraway Places increases your hunger for something more. A tense square from illusory Neptune stimulates visions of escape from the routine of your daily life. Within these fantasies, though, is a core idea worth your attention: Let go of the impossible dream and you'll find one that you can make real. The Sun's entry into fickle Gemini on **May 20** usually brings distractions, but its stressful quincunx with Pluto on **May 21** demands that you deal with a persistent question of control. At the same time, a genius Jupiter-Uranus sextile enlightens you with flashes of insight that arouse an itch for change. The Sun's tough square with stern Saturn on **May 22**, though, still holds you in check with inescapable responsibilities. Tension can build as these restraints contrast with an explosive Mars-Uranus sesquisquare. You might feel your only choices are fight or flight, but right now you're inventive enough to find a much more creative solution.

JUNE

EYE-OPENING EXPERIENCES

The New Moon in inquisitive Gemini on **June 3** falls in your 4th House of Home and Family, where it stimulates a desire to add more variety to your life. Flirty Venus and friendly Mercury join this lunation, along with a supportive sextile from outgoing Mars in Leo—offering creativity and connections that could make your personal life much more interesting. Bright ideas and encouragement from others push you forward, yet it's best to make changes slowly. Gemini's ruling planet, Mercury, is still retrograde, so promises are only possibilities and not commitments until the Messenger shifts into forward gear on **June 19**.

Transformative Pluto retrogrades back into truthful Sagittarius on **June 13** for one last visit before returning to Capricorn on **November 26**. This is likely to stir issues on the job front as it touches your 10th House of Career. The Full Moon in strident Sagittarius on **June 18** also occurs in this house; differences of opinion on the job may upset your equilibrium. The Archer's penchant for frankness takes on added punch with the Moon's conjunction to potent Pluto. Excitable Uranus's square to this Full Moon increases the intensity, possibly inciting extreme reactions. You may be ready to quit without notice—or even have the rug pulled out from under you. But this is also your chance to break unhealthy habits, clean up unfinished business, and allow yourself enough time to take a long look into the future. Sagittarius is a visionary sign that opens your eyes to a more magnanimous view of life. Simply coping with the crises of the moment may only delay the inevitable. It's wiser to start considering major professional changes now.

> **KEEP IN MIND THIS MONTH**
>
> *Instead of immediately reacting to a shock and dissipating your emotional energy, keep stirring your feelings to fuel an even greater leap forward.*

KEY DATES

JUNE 3-4 ★ *delightful diversions*

The curious Gemini New Moon on **June 3** is filled with delightful distractions. Communications from close friends or family members who have been out of touch bring laughter and joy to the day. All this stimulation, though, can make it hard to focus, so tune out the extraneous noise if you have serious work to do. Fortunately, a sextile between the Sun and active Mars on **June 4** could make you clever enough to take care of business no matter how much fun you're having.

JUNE 13-15 ★ *forgive and forget*

A skittish Sun-Uranus square kicks **June 13** off to a restless start, but uncertainty is calmed with a healing trine between Venus and Neptune. This compassionate planetary pair doesn't let weirdness get in the way of love. If you're feeling strange, look around and you'll find beauty that gives life meaning and reestablishes your connection with the earth. A Sun-Neptune trine on **June 14** continues the theme of forgiveness, which is crucial right now due to a contentious conjunction between Mars and the Moon's South Node that awakens conflict. The battle is probably over an old issue that's better forgotten than fought over. Still, feisty Mars's quincunx with overdoing Jupiter on **June 15** inhibits compromise. If you have extra energy, use it on a healthy outdoor adventure rather than in anger or spite.

SUPER NOVA DAYS
JUNE 18-20 ★ *tumultuous waters*

Emotions escalate on **June 18** as sweet Venus opposes dark Pluto and then enters watery Cancer. If a partner is unresponsive, pushing harder may not help. It's clear that you need more satisfaction in love, but creating joy for yourself is the best way to attract what you want. An edgy Mars-Uranus quincunx brings impatience on **June 19** that may rush you to seek a quick solution. Yet impetuous acts are more likely to carry you off track than lead you where you want to go. Mercury turning direct can open new channels of communication, but then the prideful Sun follows Venus's path from Pluto to Cancer on **June 20**, intensifying feelings on the Summer Solstice. Cancer may be cuddly, but Pluto's presence suggests that something's got to go before you can feel safe again.

JUNE 25-26 ★ *foolish illusions*

A fuzzy sesquisquare between Venus and Neptune on **June 25** puts fantasy ahead of reality when you're evaluating people or making purchases. The cost of excess becomes clear when strict Saturn sesquisquares lenient Jupiter on **June 26**—use prudence to temper runaway enthusiasm. Additionally, revolutionary Uranus turns retrograde, signaling that personal freedom primarily comes from within during the next five months.

JULY

TAKE THE LEAD

Relationships and interactions of all kinds heat up this month as assertive Mars enters your 7th House of Partnerships on **July 1**. This dynamic planet's presence in detail-oriented Virgo can attract as much criticism as passion, but don't allow yourself to be bullied by aggressive people. Stating your needs clearly reduces confusion and increases your chances for gaining cooperation in a peaceful fashion. Hope for love springs from the cozy Cancer New Moon in your 5th House of Romance on **July 2**. Tender feelings can make you shy, yet your sensitivity is an asset that makes you more appealing when you're willing to show it. Communicative Mercury's entry into your expressive 5th House on **July 10** opens the door to intimate conversations where the quality of connection is more important than the words themselves. Loving Venus enters outgoing Leo on **July 12**, bringing more joy to your work and daily routine as you find fun in the most ordinary activities.

The businesslike Capricorn Full Moon on **July 18** occurs in your 11th House of Groups and Friends, making it eminently clear how much is expected of you as a member of a team. A supportive sextile from ingenious Uranus to the Full Moon shows you ways to meet these responsibilities with more freedom and less stress. Perhaps most important is holding colleagues and pals accountable for their actions so that you don't have to carry more than your fair share of the load. The Sun and Mercury enter proud Leo and your 6th House of Work and Service on **July 22 and July 26**, increasing your confidence and creativity on the job and empowering you to be a more effective leader.

> **KEEP IN MIND THIS MONTH**
>
> *Act on your own initiative instead of trying to figure out what others want and adapting your behavior to their needs.*

KEY DATES

on time and performing at your peak potential build trust in relationships. You don't need to be perfect, but you do need to be vigilant. A more playful mood prevails with an extravagant Venus-Jupiter opposition on **July 3** that promises pleasure and delight. The cost in cash, calories, or concentration may be high—but it's probably worth it.

JULY 9-10 ★ *back to earth*
An opposition between the expressive Sun and benevolent Jupiter on **July 9** opens your heart and raises your hopes. However, you must follow up on big promises from friends or co-workers to keep them from fading away unfulfilled. A hard-core conjunction between Mars and stern Saturn on **July 10** imposes limits that separate fantasy from reality. Relationships can be tested by a lack of trust or by mounting stress. If you value the connection, stay calm, be practical, and focus on fixing the situation rather than adding more emotional fuel to the fire.

JULY 15 ★ *lost in space*
Favorable aspects from the Sun and Mercury to energetic Mars make for some zippy thinking, but moving too quickly can lead you astray. Foggy Neptune's disorienting aspects to the Sun and Mercury may cloud your judgment with idealism that's not grounded in reality. Apply your imagination in spiritual or creative ways where strict adherence to the rules isn't necessary.

JULY 18-19 ★ *relationship accounting*
The rational Capricorn Full Moon on **July 18** can open your eyes to see where you truly stand with your friends. Make a point of acknowledging those who support you with some appreciative words. Notice those who take more than they give and start changing the equation to make it more balanced. Talkative Mercury has plenty to say with an opposition to wide-open Jupiter on **July 19**. Exaggeration is possible, and you could easily blow little details out of proportion. If you feel anxious, take a breath and reassess before letting emotions go too far.

JULY 26 ★ *bold steps*
You can speak with confidence as Mercury enters brash Leo on **July 26**. A high-energy Mars-Jupiter trine provides integrity and enthusiasm, giving you the power to successfully sell your ideas. This physical planetary pair also encourages vigorous activity, making this a fantastic time to explore the great outdoors.

AUGUST

PARTNERSHIP POTENTIAL

A pair of eclipses and two New Moons make this an unusually transformative month. The Solar Eclipse in fixed Leo on **August 1** in your 6th House of Work and Service could produce a tiring battle of wills on the job. Yet if you let go of your expectations, you can discover a creative solution in which everyone comes out ahead. A Lunar Eclipse in unorthodox Aquarius on **August 16** sends your imagination off into fantasyland. Psychic Neptune's conjunction to the Full Moon floods your 12th House of Spirituality with images and feelings of worlds beyond this one. Don't act impulsively on these impressions or try to make sense of them now. Allow yourself time to absorb this nonlinear information before making any major changes. The New Moon in analytical Virgo on **August 30** brings relationship issues into focus with a crystalline clarity that signals exactly where you stand and helps you make a logical decision.

Three planets enter virtuous Virgo and your 7th House of Relationships this month, bringing new opportunities to connect with others. Sociable Venus starts the process on **August 6**, drawing appreciative individuals into your life. Thoughtful Mercury follows on **August 10**, opening the door to more reasonable dialogue that helps you work through complicated issues in a calm and rational manner. The life-giving Sun moves into Virgo on **August 22** to increase your confidence, gain the support of creative allies, and encourage you to express yourself more boldly within one-to-one relationships and in dealing with the general public. Verbal Mercury enters your 8th House of Intimacy on **August 28**, followed by creative Venus on **August 30**, taking personal and professional partnerships to a deeper and more powerful place.

> **KEEP IN MIND THIS MONTH**
>
> *Thoughtless and unkind remarks tend to undermine trust, but constructive criticism can be a major asset for building stronger relationships.*

KEY DATES

AUGUST 1–2 ★ *round and round*

Drama at work triggered by the showy Leo Solar Eclipse in your 6th House of Employment on **August 1** can blow a small issue into a major event. Humor and generosity are the keys to turning what could be a tragedy into an outright comedy. On **August 2**, communicative Mercury skids off a quincunx with Jupiter, the multiplier, which can drag discussions off track by mixing up facts with opinions. If a conversation starts going around in circles, or change the subject to avoid wasting time or wearing yourself out.

AUGUST 6 ★ *no rules*

Romantic Venus's entry into cautious Virgo and your 7th House of Partnerships normally indicates a careful step forward in relationships. But the situation is far from stable: Mental Mercury is firing up your nervous system in a quincunx to electric Uranus while Mars opposes it, instigating impulsiveness and possible outbursts of anger. Tense aspects to boundless Jupiter and imprecise Neptune lure emotional communications far from reality, yet this can be a highly creative time.

SUPER NOVA DAYS
AUGUST 13–16 ★ *relationship dilemma*

A hard, cold Venus-Saturn conjunction on **August 13** can put a chill on relationships, but don't give up on love. If you aren't receiving the appreciation you desire, state exactly what you want. Be prepared to invest in a partnership for the long term—or start thinking about a way to escape. Your imagination is wide open with a Sun-Neptune opposition on **August 15**, but a rigid Mercury-Saturn conjunction can confront you with an individual who only wants to deal with facts. The gulf between you may feel enormous, yet a generous trine between lovely Venus and jovial Jupiter on **August 16** can drive away despair by revealing an unlimited source of joy.

AUGUST 21–23 ★ *social surprise*

A sweet Mercury-Venus conjunction on **August 21** draws you into pleasant conversations, while the Sun's entry into discerning Virgo on **August 22** may attract a powerful ally. Meanwhile, oppositions from Mercury and Venus to "wild and crazy" Uranus on **August 23** can evoke irrational behavior. Unusual individuals or your own unexpected impulses can be exciting but destabilizing. Stay open-minded and light on your feet to adjust to the sudden changes.

AUGUST 28–29 ★ *transforming love*

Mercury's entry into diplomatic Libra on **August 28** opens the way to meaningful negotiations, yet an intense square between sensual Venus and disruptive Pluto on **August 29** stirs deep emotional waters. A sense of loss or betrayal might undermine trust; however, sharing these feelings without shame or blame can heal a significant relationship and restore your sense of self-worth.

SEPTEMBER

RIDER ON THE STORM

Just as long-range plans seem to be lining up logically, an unexpected event or change of heart can lead to a major course shift this month. Jupiter and Saturn align in an organizationally gifted trine on **September 8** for the second time this year, bringing a healthy balance of optimism and realism to your life. This stabilizing aspect occurs for the third time on **November 21** to complete a building process that started last year. Your newly earned security, however, is interrupted by an explosive Full Moon in your sign on **September 15**. Full Moons always raise emotional tides, yet this one is especially volatile: Uranus, the planet of shock, rebellion, and breakthrough, is closely conjunct, releasing unexpected circumstances and unpredictable responses. You may be bored with routine, restless for change, and ready to turn your life upside down. It's also possible that you're comfortable where you are—but the world around you suddenly seems to start spinning in the opposite direction. Regardless of how fast things turn, your intuition can respond quickly enough to keep up.

Ordinary thinking just isn't good enough with cerebral Mercury slowing down as it heads toward its retrograde period, which starts on **September 24**. The Sun's entry into accommodating Libra and your 8th House of Intimacy on **September 22** brings you assistance from objective individuals who can offer you wise counsel. Seductive Venus plunges into the emotional depths of Scorpio on **September 23**, where she helps restore a sense of purpose to your life. The Libra New Moon on **September 29** in your 9th House of Higher Truth lifts your spirits and invites you on a philosophical quest.

> **KEEP IN MIND THIS MONTH**
>
> *If you keep a light hand on the wheel, the road will tell you which way you need to turn to avoid accidents and safely reach your destination.*

KEY DATES

SEPTEMBER 3-8 ★ *set the stage*

The creative Sun's passage over strategic Saturn on **September 3** and trine with fortunate Jupiter on **September 4** provide you with insights and allies to manifest your grand ambitions. Still, a sloppy Venus-Neptune sesquisquare on **September 5** puts hope before reason and can obscure your judgment. Wearing rose-colored glasses can distract you from your objective, but then a highly energized square between aggressive Mars and Jupiter on **September 7** propels you forward with great force. Tense aspects to your key planet Jupiter on **September 8** fire you up with strong opinions that can provoke clashes. This is also the day of the Jupiter-Saturn trine, as Jupiter turns direct—a pivotal point when the decisions you make can have lasting effects.

SUPER NOVA DAYS
SEPTEMBER 12-15 ★ *chaos and change*
A jumpy Sun-Uranus opposition on **September 12** can surprise you as a reliable person fails to perform as expected, a shy friend turns bold, or even you take uncharacteristic risks in sharing your true feelings. **September 14** looks like a slippery Sunday with a Sun-Neptune quincunx better suited for escapism than practical pursuits. The powerful Pisces Full Moon on **September 15** is electrified by its conjunction to Uranus, while a tense square to the Sun and Moon from extreme Pluto makes this an even more transformational time. There's too much happening for you to comprehend at once; keep things simple rather than adding fuel to the raging fire. Small moves have major effects, so temper your responses to maintain some semblance of control.

SEPTEMBER 17 ★ *love heals*
A sweet Venus-Neptune trine brings pleasure to soothe the rawness of your emotions. This can be an island of calm in the midst of the swirling waters of change. Indulge in a healthy escape—go shopping, or lose yourself in a feel-good movie—to take your mind off life's larger challenges. Moments of delight with an easygoing person remind you of the healing power of love.

SEPTEMBER 20-22 ★ *pros and cons*
A compelling square between the Sun and Pluto on **September 20** brings buried issues to the surface. Power struggles and feelings of resentment aren't your idea of fun, but they can show you what's really important so you can clear out what you don't need and concentrate your efforts where they count. A creative trine between assertive Mars and idealistic Neptune on **September 21** demonstrates that self-interest and spirituality can be compatible. Sharing the day with supportive friends makes the differences between work and play disappear. The Sun enters fair-minded Libra on the Autumnal Equinox, **September 22**, showing you that it is possible to see both sides of a situation without losing your center.

OCTOBER

HUNGER TO LEARN

Your personal life heats up this month with Venus and Mars, the cosmic lovers, changing signs. Physical Mars turns more passionate on **October 4** when it enters Scorpio, a fellow water sign bound to warm up your emotions. Its passage through your 9th House of Faraway Places urges you to expand your horizons and, perhaps, express discontent with your current situation. Sensual Venus moves into freedom-loving Sagittarius and your 10th House of Public Status on **October 18**, which tends to put you in the spotlight. Your artistic abilities and people skills garner respect that increases your sense of self-worth, making you even more popular. The spontaneous Aries Full Moon on **October 14** in your 2nd House of Resources could send you on an impromptu shopping spree, but a spark of originality that generates new sources of income is a more useful expression of this energizing event.

Rational Mercury turns direct on **October 15** to get discussions moving forward with a new line of thinking. Negotiations in your personal or professional life open up with fresh perspectives that help overcome barriers to communication. The unyielding Sun enters Scorpio and your 9th House on **October 22**, adding conviction to your beliefs and passion to your presentations. You may appear to be less flexible when it comes to matters of principle if others pressure you. Fortunately, when you're allowed to explore on your own, an obsessive curiosity can motivate you to examine religion, philosophy, or politics through study and travel. The New Moon in penetrating Scorpio on **October 28** deepens your desire to understand your life and enrich it with meaning. Although a charismatic teacher may influence your thinking, put more trust in your own innate instincts to find the truth.

KEEP IN MIND THIS MONTH

Tune in carefully to what others are saying and you'll discover the best way to satisfy their needs while also fulfilling your own desires.

KEY DATES

SUPER NOVA DAYS
OCTOBER 4–6 ★ *stop and go*
Mars's passionate push into intense Scorpio on **October 4** can lead directly to an obstacle when it makes a tense semisquare to restricting Saturn on **October 5**. If you aren't getting the support you need, be very clear about what

you want instead of silently bearing the burden alone. Venus's semisquare with extreme Pluto can undermine trust and leave you scrambling for resources. Fortunately, the tide starts to turn as a positive sextile between Venus and Jupiter encourages you with a helping hand. Extravagant squares from the Sun and Mercury to Jupiter on **October 6** may find you susceptible to exaggeration, unrealistic promises, or an information overload. The Sun's conjunction with retrograde Mercury can tie you up with someone who's stuck on an old idea. If reason doesn't work, postpone further discussion for now.

OCTOBER 11 ★ *the curse of pollyanna*
A fuzzy square between attractive Venus and nebulous Neptune turns up the volume on your fantasies. Acquaintances appear more alluring, and worthless objects glitter like gold. Seeing the best in everyone and everything is one of your greatest talents, but your judgment may be especially unreliable now. Avoid a tendency to sacrifice your needs to make others happy, no matter how much you care.

OCTOBER 14–15 ★ *limited resources*
The fiery Aries Full Moon on **October 14** is superheated by a square to overdoing Jupiter and supported by Neptune and the Sun. If you volunteer in a group situation or offer to help a friend, set some realistic limits rather than making an open-ended commitment. Mercury's direct turn on **October 15** is a perfect time to stop and take a fresh look at a relationship before getting in over your head.

OCTOBER 21–22 ★ *quiet strengths*
You have the ability to ask for more from others as a savvy Sun-Pluto sextile on **October 21** clarifies your desires. Your strong convictions send a message that doesn't require shouting to make your point. The Sun's entry into fellow water sign Scorpio on **October 22** imbues your actions with a deeper sense of purpose.

OCTOBER 26–28 ★ *true believer*
Direct Mercury square gregarious Jupiter on **October 26** can make you very chatty, or possibly indiscreet. Be careful talking about friends or colleagues—even an innocent remark may be perceived as gossip. Active Mars's friction-free sextile with outgoing Jupiter on **October 27** increases your enthusiasm, enabling you to be a strong motivator, skillful team leader, and effective spokesperson for your ideas. The New Moon in magnetic Scorpio on **October 28** charges your beliefs with heartfelt intensity, sending you on a quest to spread the word wide and far.

NOVEMBER

ENDINGS AND BEGINNINGS

There's a cosmic changing of the guard this month: Two long-term planetary patterns end, and a new one begins. Rigid Saturn opposes revolutionary Uranus on **November 4**, starting a series of aspects that will continue through **July 26, 2010**. This tense angle between the principles of order and chaos has a major impact on how you connect with others. The urge to break free from the constraints of judgment and guilt may upset or even dissolve a partnership. If you don't act impulsively, however, this can be a manageable step toward overcoming the limits you experience within a current relationship or your beliefs about creating a new one. Jupiter makes the last in a series of smart sextiles with Uranus on **November 13** and its final trine with Saturn on **November 21** to inspire an exciting vision for the future and to provide you with a strategic, organized plan to turn it into reality.

Two planets turning direct add waves of forward movement. Dreamy Neptune leads off on **November 1** to externalize your spiritual aspirations; then inventive Uranus releases lightning bolts of originality on **November 28**. Additionally, five planets change signs this month, shifting the colors of your personal landscape. Perceptive Mercury's entry into Scorpio on **November 4** deepens your thinking to reveal underlying motives. Stylish Venus turns formal in Capricorn on **November 12**, requiring clarity about what you want from friends and within groups. Adventurous Mars shoots into Sagittarius and your 10th House of Career on **November 16**, encouraging risk taking in your professional life. When the Sun follows Mars's path on **November 21**, you can express your intentions openly and act more confidently in public. Powerful Pluto reenters ambitious Capricorn on **November 26**, where it will powerfully redefine and reshape your position in groups for years to come.

> **KEEP IN MIND THIS MONTH**
>
> *No matter how irritated you are by an obstinate person, gentle persuasion will be more effective than an emotional eruption.*

KEY DATES

NOVEMBER 3–5 ★ *relationship breakthrough*

Relationships are rattled when affectionate Venus bounces off squares from Saturn to Uranus on **November 3**. Feelings of rejection incite strong emotions to break free of restrictive patterns in partnership and release some of the building tension of the Saturn-Uranus opposition due **November 4**. A misguided Mars-Neptune square can stir up misplaced anger or an attempt to escape reality. However, your exquisite sensitivity can provide the tender touch needed to diffuse a volatile situation. A gentle Venus-Neptune sextile on **November 5** reveals common ground.

SUPER NOVA DAYS
NOVEMBER 10-13 ★ *practical genius*
Use your willpower and creativity wisely when the Sun harmonizes with Jupiter, Uranus, and Saturn on **November 10-11**, connecting unconventional concepts with logical thinking to turn brilliant ideas into reality. Your trust in someone is shaken on **November 12** when Venus conjuncts Pluto. Go ahead, express your dissatisfaction—without going to extremes. Venus then enters responsible Capricorn, where relationships and self-worth improve with discipline and diligence. The Full Moon in sensual Taurus on **November 13** opens your eyes to everyday delights. A Sun-Neptune square, though, can lead to self-sacrifice, illusions about your capabilities, or promises that will be hard to fulfill.

NOVEMBER 16-17 ★ *strategic thinking*
Mars motivates you to try harder at work when it enters gung-ho Sagittarius on **November 16**. This urge to advance is supported by sextiles from Mercury to successful Jupiter and pragmatic Saturn. Your sense of strategy is excellent, as is your ability to share your thoughts with authority without sounding aggressive. Ideas may become less clear on **November 17** when Mercury squares misty Neptune. Double-check your facts to ensure their accuracy.

NOVEMBER 21 ★ *change for the better*
The final Jupiter-Saturn trine occurs as the Sun enters long-distance Sagittarius to set your sights on a brighter future. You can see far and can support that vision with your feet solidly planted on the ground. Trust yourself: You now have the right balance of hope and realism to reinforce long-term constructive changes to your life.

NOVEMBER 27-28 ★ *information indigestion*
The outspoken Sagittarius New Moon on **November 27** in your 10th House of Public Status marks a time to express your opinions more openly. However, holiday conversations can slide off point with destabilizing semisquares between detailed Mercury and "big picture" Jupiter on **November 27** and the Sun and Jupiter on **November 28**. Making outrageous statements can reduce your credibility.

DECEMBER

SERIOUS ABOUT GETTING AHEAD

A combative Sun-Mars conjunction on **December 5** in your 10th House of Career can stir up conflict on the job. Regardless, this may be an excellent time to launch a new project if you nail down the necessary details in advance. Vivacious Venus enters Aquarius and your 12th House of Privacy on **December 7**, which can pull you away from your usual social circle. You might appreciate more time alone or with spiritual groups, where you feel less judged and are free to be yourself. Mental Mercury enters constructive Capricorn on **December 12**, helping you turn inspiring ideas into concrete events, yet the chatty Gemini Full Moon may resist the Capricorn call for order. The natural mobility of the Sun in Sagittarius opposing the Moon in Gemini is heightened by a tense square with electric Uranus. An impulse to change your job, drop an obligation, and seek greener pastures is understandable. Meanwhile, responsible Saturn's square to the Full Moon reminds you that tossing aside one obstacle may present you with another one, so create a workable plan before making a sudden move.

The Sun enters traditional Capricorn and your social 11th House on **December 21**, marking the Winter Solstice and bringing your attention to group activities just in time for the holidays. A harsh square between the Sun and compulsive Pluto on **December 22**, however, can produce power struggles, but is more creatively expressed by eliminating superfluous activities that distract you from your heart's desire. Resentment of others may seem justified, but it's not an effective way to spend your resources. The New Moon in ambitious Capricorn on **December 27** is conjunct a potent Mars-Pluto conjunction that can bring you the support of powerful allies . . . if you just ask for their help.

> **KEEP IN MIND THIS MONTH**
>
> *You can achieve great things if you focus on yourself and let your ambition fuel the fire in your belly.*

KEY DATES

DECEMBER 5-6 ★ *tempestuous thoughts*

A brilliant but erratic Mercury-Uranus square on **December 5** spawns unusual ideas and odd conversations that make the day's forceful Sun-Mars conjunction even hotter. Tempers can flare, so choose your words carefully. A strict square from Saturn to Mercury on **December 6** stops wild speculation and demands down-to-earth communication. A kind Mercury-Neptune sextile follows to soften hearts and open minds.

SUPER NOVA DAYS
DECEMBER 10–13 ★ *boiling over*
The brilliant yet explosive power of Uranus enters the foreground with harsh aspects to the Sun, amicable Venus, and excitable Mars on **December 10–12.** These high-frequency alignments of rebellion and restlessness are likely to upset your equilibrium. The positive potential for intuitive breakthroughs, new pleasures, and innovative problem solving requires a cool head to keep your nervous system from overheating. The Full Moon in versatile Gemini on **December 12** adds tension, especially if restrictive Saturn's square to the Moon is totally resistant to change. You are unlikely to be in a compromising mood, so unless you want a crisis to escalate, it's wise to back off. A sweet sextile between the Sun and Neptune on **December 13** adds tolerance and awareness to help you find mutual common ground.

DECEMBER 15–16 ★ *sigh of relief*
A two-day two-step of planetary pressure and release occurs with a hard square between Mars and stern Saturn on **December 15** and a relaxed sextile between Mars and pliable Neptune on **December 16.** The action planet passes from a tight squeeze where there is no margin for error, especially at work, to an easygoing attitude that values peace and imagination more than productivity.

DECEMBER 21–22 ★ *stay in charge*
Group responsibilities weigh heavily when the Sun enters your 11th House of Teamwork on **December 21.** Take command and control the process as much as you can rather than trying to make everyone happy. The Sun's square with unrelenting Pluto on **December 22** reveals that if you aren't totally on top of a situation, you may wind up buried by it. Concentrate on business now and you can play later.

DECEMBER 27–28 ★ *total commitment*
Mars enters industrious Capricorn just before the New Moon in this earthy sign on **December 27.** These indicators of seriousness and hard work can serve your highest ideals in the company of an inspired Venus-Neptune conjunction. If you're going to exert maximum effort, make sure it's for something you truly value. Mars joins Pluto on **December 28,** which can also focus intense power in a narrow beam. If you dedicate yourself fully right now, you can make lasting changes.